CHALL

DEF

The Great Tradition of Tibetan Buddhist Monastic Debate

Nancy A. Scherl

CHALLENGER DEFENDER

ENGENDER

Preface by His Holiness the 14th Dalai Lama

Foreword by Tashi Tsering

Essays by Nicholas Vreeland, Dadul Namgyal, Carol M. Worthman, Richard K. Raker, Paul García, and Arri Eisen

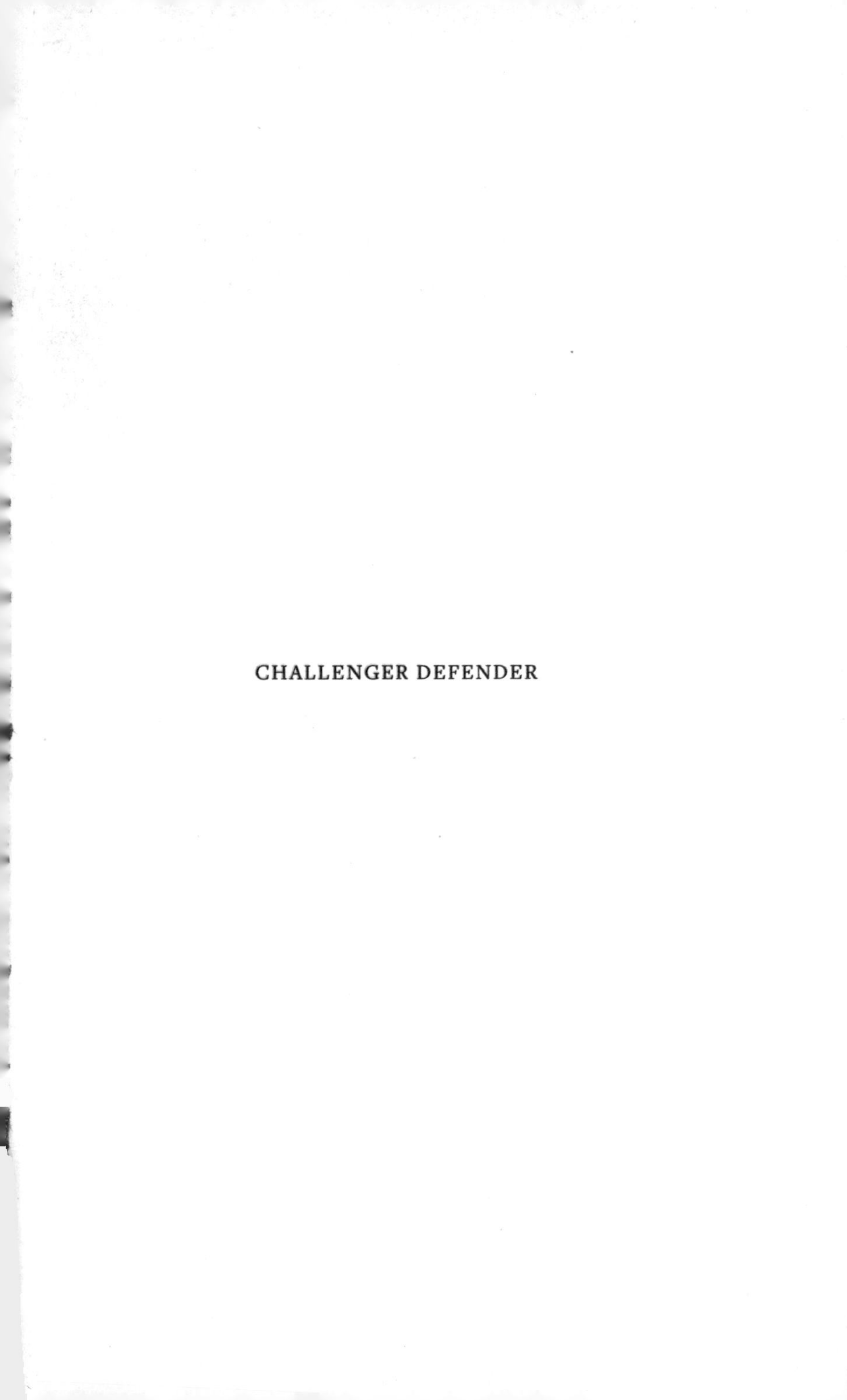

Texts by Thupten Khetsun, Jampa Gyaltsen, Kalden Gyatso, Dadul Namgyal, Rigzin Nurbu, Lobsang Dhondup, Ngawang Norbu, and Tenzin Topden

I dedicate this book to the Tibetan Buddhist monks at Sera Mey, Sera Jey, and Tashi Lhunpo Monastic Universities and to all the Tibetan Buddhist monks and nuns who dedicate their lives in training and meditation toward enlightenment in service of humanity. Your generous spirit and selfless giving remain as the most memorable aspect of my visit to the monasteries in 2019. Your kindness, compassion, graciousness, and welcoming manner will forever reside in my heart.

Contents

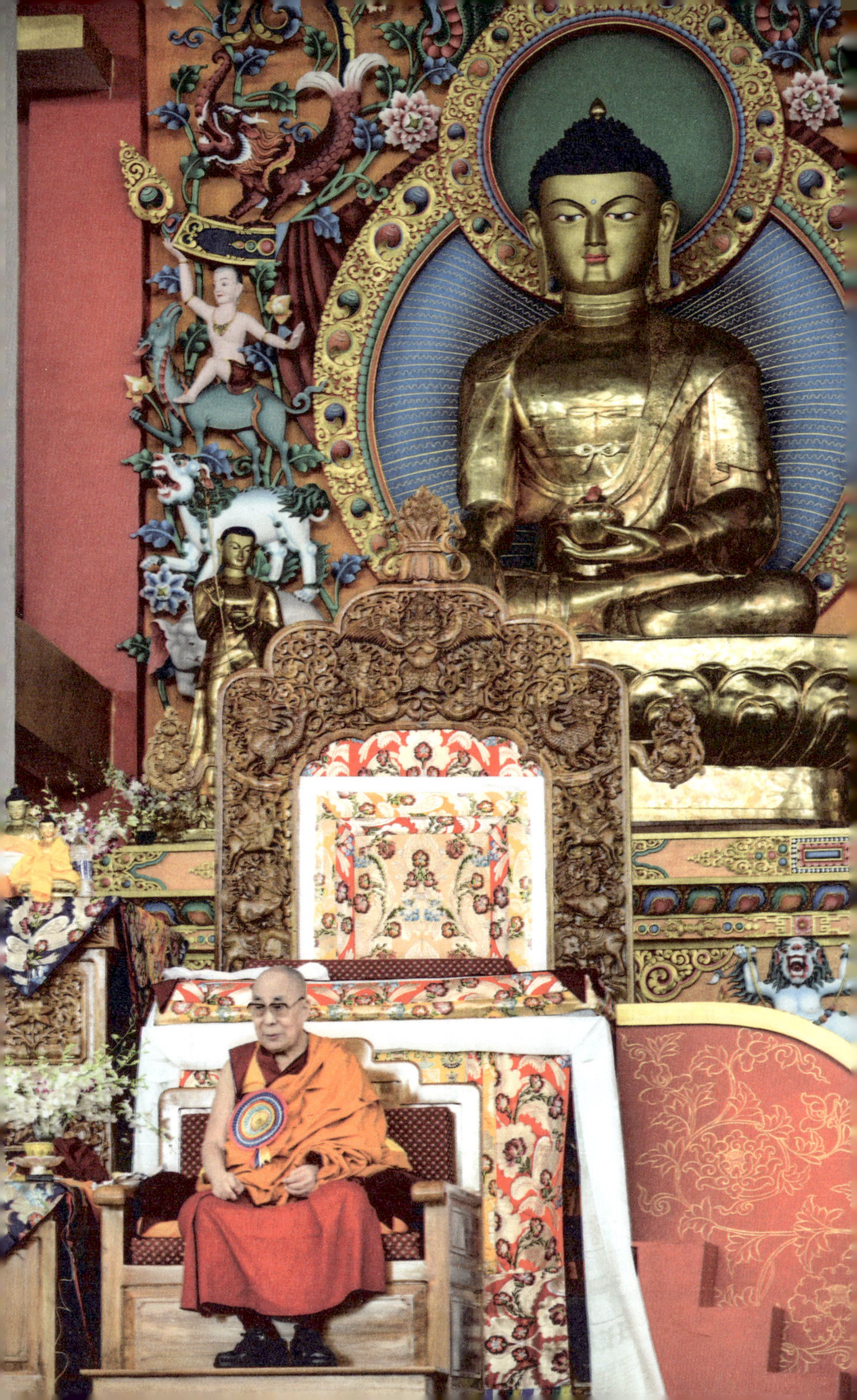

THE DALAI LAMA

Preface

I am pleased by the publication of *Challenger Defender: The Great Tradition of Tibetan Buddhist Monastic Debate* by Nancy Scherl. Having emerged from the ancient Indian Nalanda tradition, debate became an essential tool for critical inquiry in Tibetan monastic education. This book highlights and explains the techniques of monastic debate, which has been practiced for centuries.

In my own experience, debate has had a profound effect on sharpening my thought process and developing understanding of the complex topics found in Buddhist philosophy and epistemology. I find that this process of logical scrutiny has been of great benefit in my day-to-day life as well.

Today, debate is no longer confined to monastic education. It has been incorporated into the techniques employed in Tibetan schools in exile, and I have noticed that some trans-Himalayan people of the Indian subcontinent use it in their critical study of other disciplines such as science.

I very much hope that modern educators will appreciate the value of debate that Nancy Scherl so eloquently presents in *Challenger Defender*.

4 March 2021

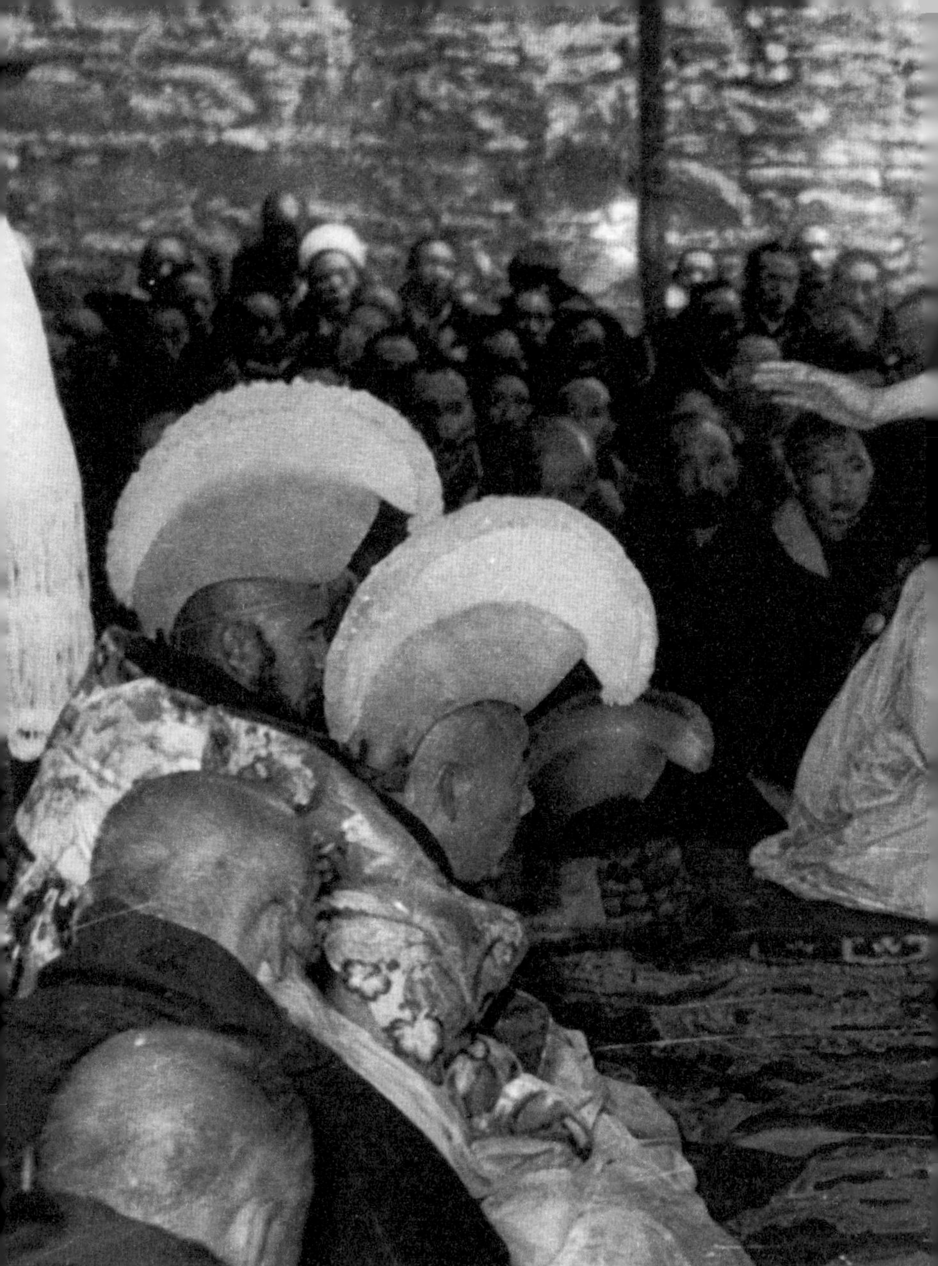

In 1959, when he was twenty-four years old, His Holiness the 14th Dalai Lama sat for his final examination at Jokhang Temple in Lhasa, Tibet, during the annual Great Prayer Festival (Monlam Chenmo). He passed with honors and was awarded the Geshe Lharampa degree, equivalent to the highest doctorate in Buddhist philosophy.

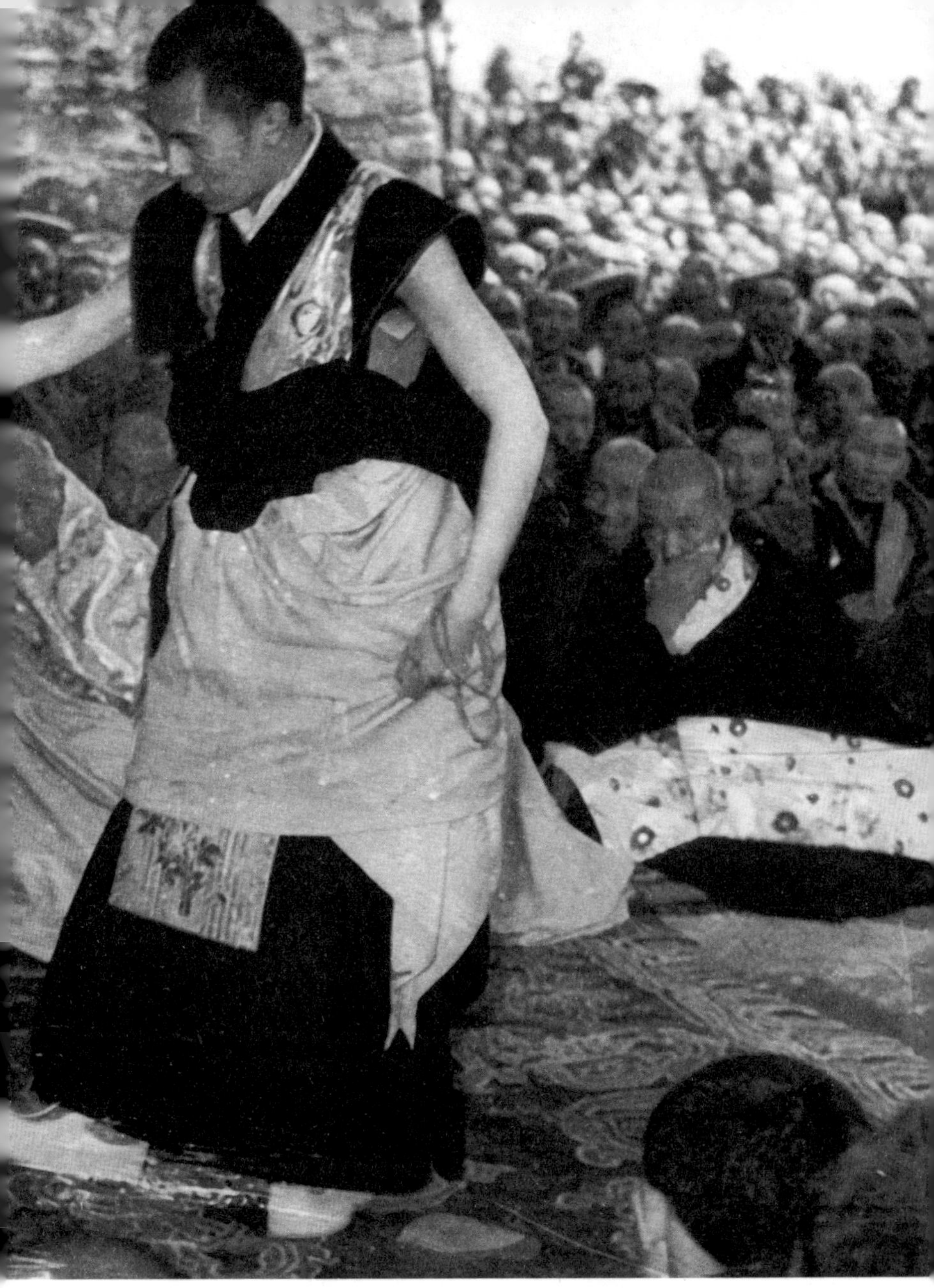

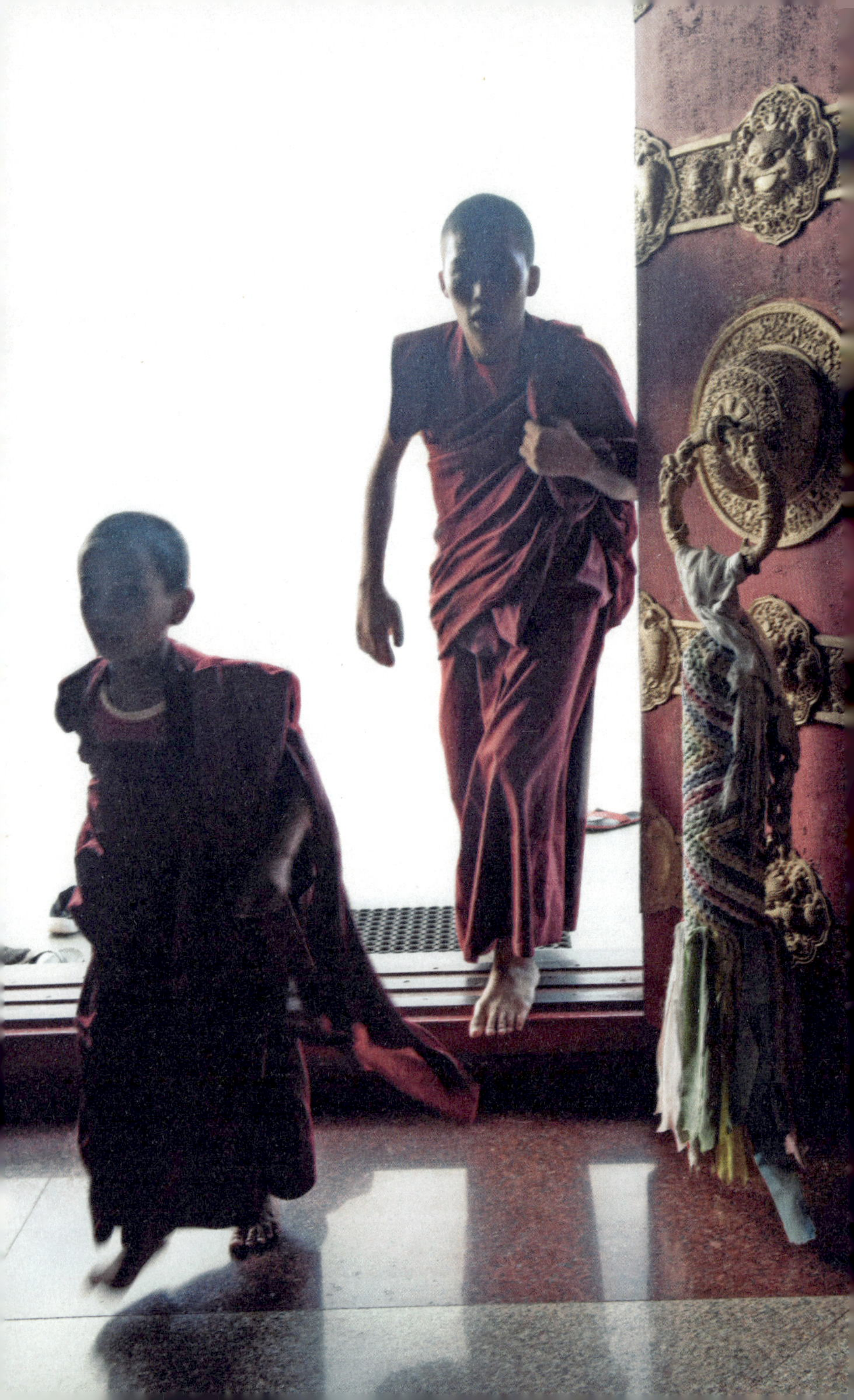

Foreword

Tashi Tsering

It is my great joy and honor to contribute to the American fine art photographer Nancy Scherl's account of the debate practice unique to Tibetan Buddhist monks. This beautiful book illustrates the dramatic debate methodology associated with the Tibetan study of the ancient Buddhist texts. Through these photographs, one gets a sense of this vibrant practice by which students absorb the teachings.

In the second century CE, the great philosopher Nāgārjuna and his disciple Āryadeva initiated a rich Indian tradition of deep philosophical analysis based on the historical Buddha's teachings. Buddha taught that cultivating an analytical understanding of the nature of our own minds and emotions can transform our lives, and a succession of Indian masters developed a culture of philosophical inquiry that investigated the nature of the human mind, leading to disciplines such as Buddhist philosophy, Buddhist psychology, and Buddhist epistemology. This tradition also gave rise to practices enabling us to cultivate loving kindness, compassion, equanimity, mental quiescence, and intense concentration, with the ultimate goal of gaining wisdom.

These teachings and the accompanying commentaries were studied over centuries by Buddhist teachers and followers, particularly in the Nalanda tradition, which emphasizes seeking to transform the life of the mind not through simple faith but through critical analysis and examination of arguments alongside devotional practices performed to accompany the transformation.

This tradition traveled from India to Tibet in the late seventh and early eighth centuries, and by the eleventh century it had been fully embraced by the Tibetan masters, who transformed the dynamics of study by developing structures for demonstrating these analytical skills through debate. They devised techniques for using the physical body as the vehicle for displaying the argument by means of dramatic movements, hand clapping, and facial expressions. These gestures were developed to forcefully buttress the oral presentation of a thesis, to pose questions opposing a thesis in the most probing manner possible, and to display conclusions so that the evolution of the argument may be seen in action. The pedagogical aim is that those engaged in this study not merely acquire a deep understanding of the underlying philosophy but also absorb and indeed come to embody the process and rhythm of argument and counter-argument through bodily projection. Nancy's photographs beautifully capture those techniques.

In making these images, Nancy also visited some of the monks in their private quarters to better understand how the monks live and thrive in their communities. She documented students interacting with their teachers, younger monks learning and making connections with older monks, and the discipline of debating, which enriches community relationships through these teaching-learning structures. Through her photographs, readers get a vivid sense of how these unique Tibetan traditions live on in the monasteries. Although the Tibetan monastic community lives in a state of exile, it is nevertheless flourishing and even adapting to twenty-first century lifestyles.

I extend my sincere gratitude to Nancy, who has put tremendous effort and time into presenting these photographs as a gift for the outside world and in particular for those who are not able to visit these places of learning and practice in India.

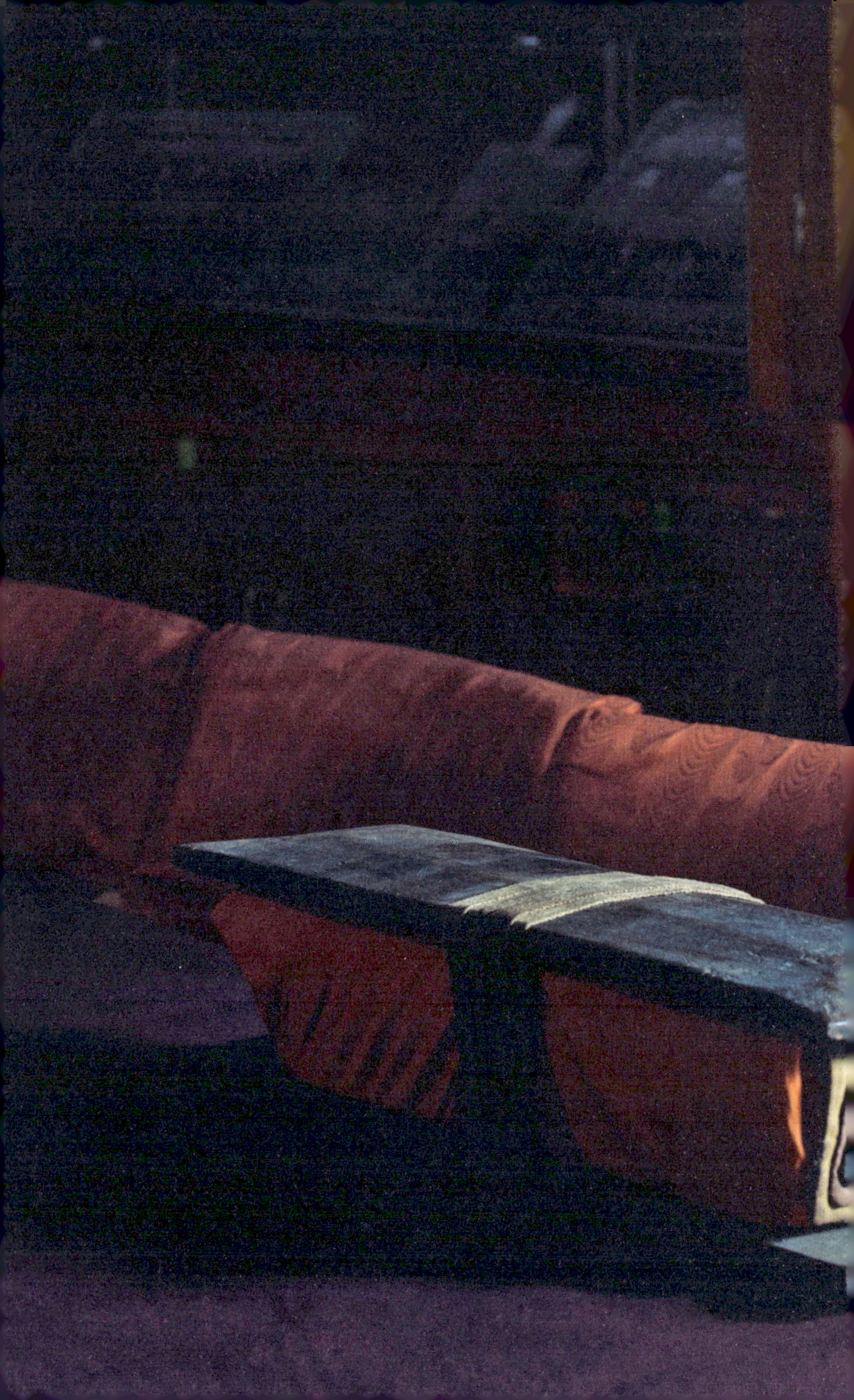

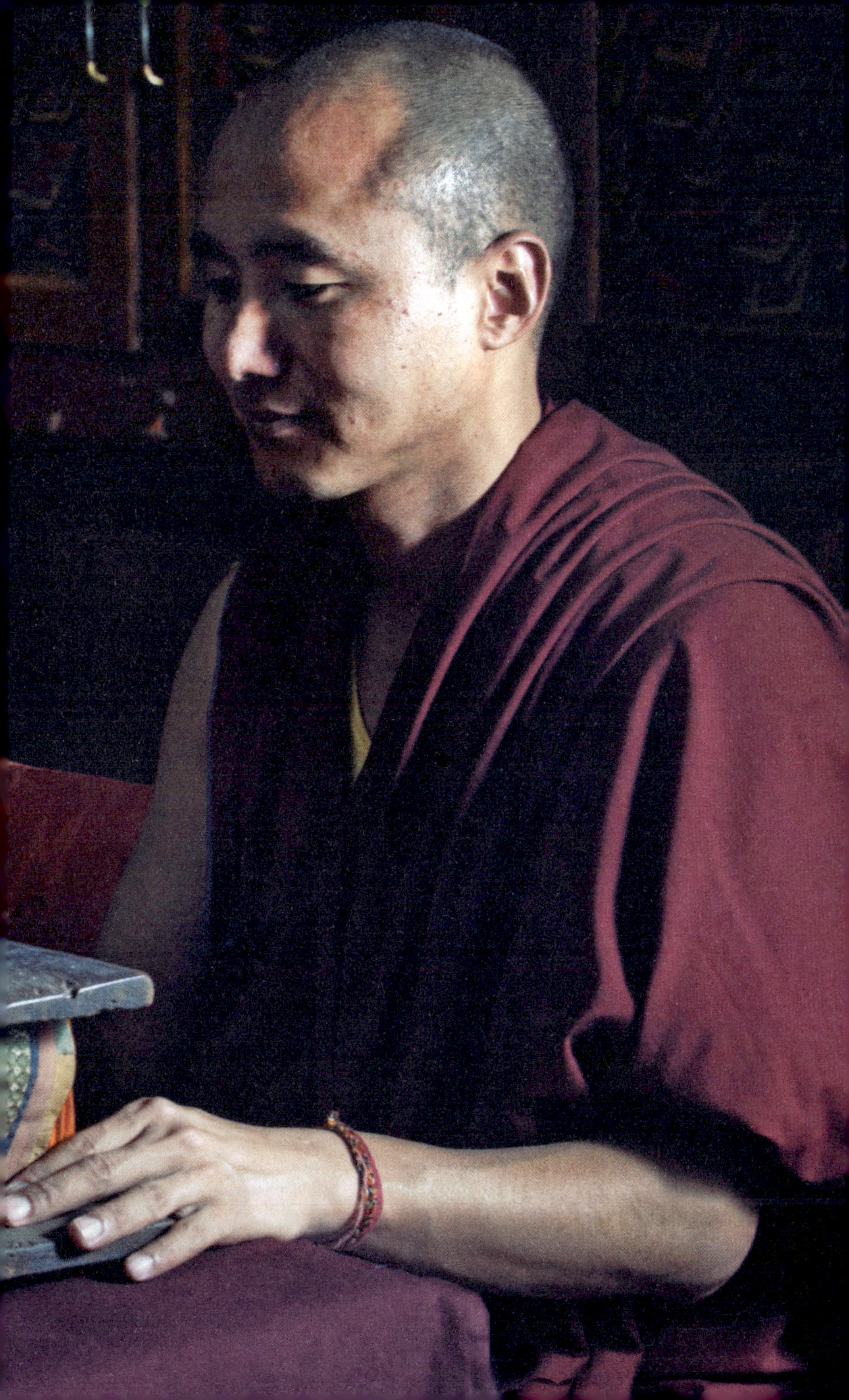

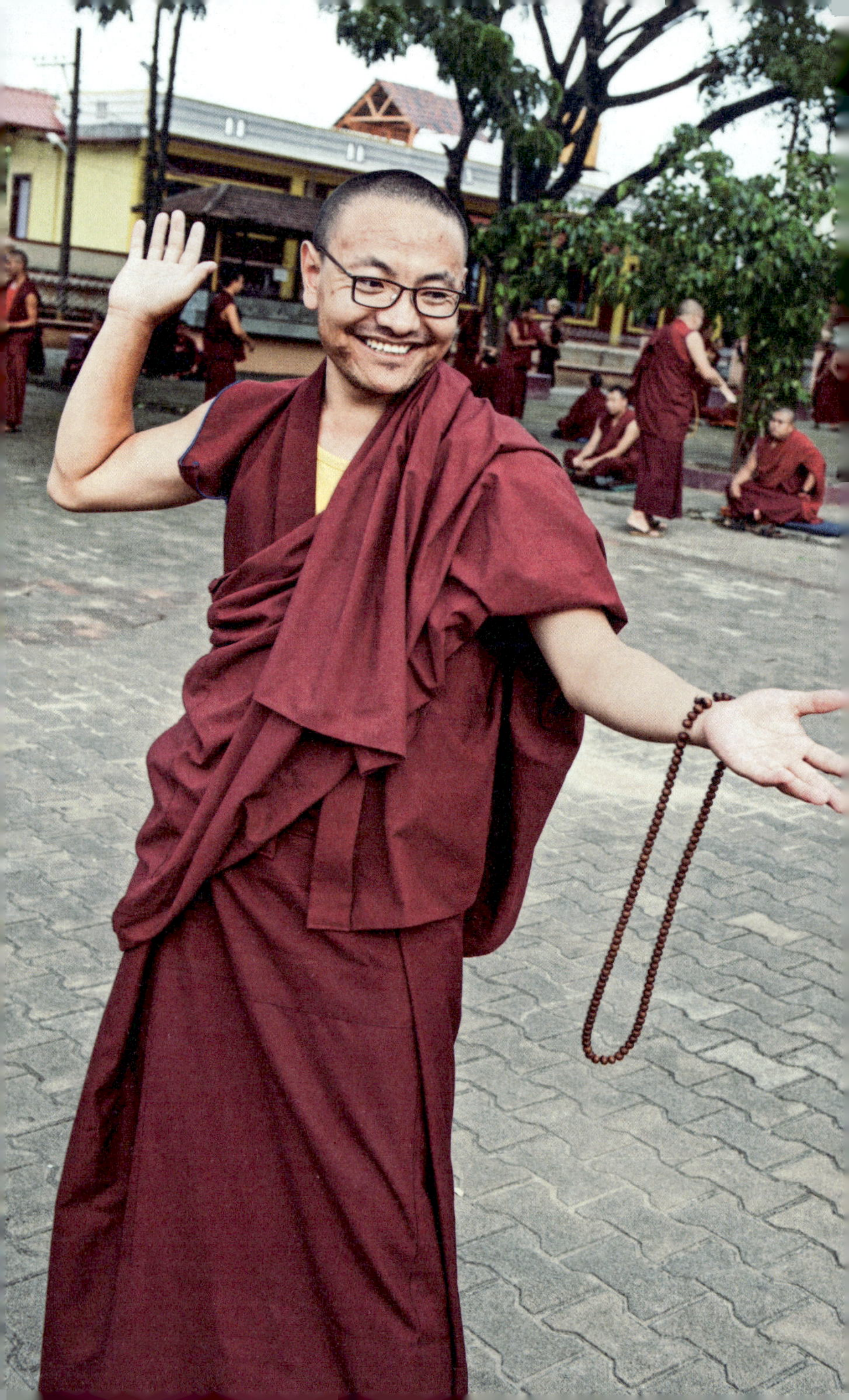

Establishing Truth Through Reasoning

Nicholas Vreeland

Just as the Buddha instructed his disciples to examine his teaching carefully before accepting it, we must analyze what we are taught to determine if it is true. Debate is the method by which we Buddhist monks do this. In the company of fellow students, we explore the ramifications of our understanding in the light of logic and reason to determine whether it is sound. Sometimes we challenge and sometimes we respond, and as we whittle away our misconceptions through this method of inquiry, we develop a more solid and profound comprehension. With effort and over time, this will grow subtler, and faith will develop in the knowledge we have acquired. This is no longer blind faith, but rather faith evolved from scrutiny and grounded in understanding. It is a faith on which we can depend.

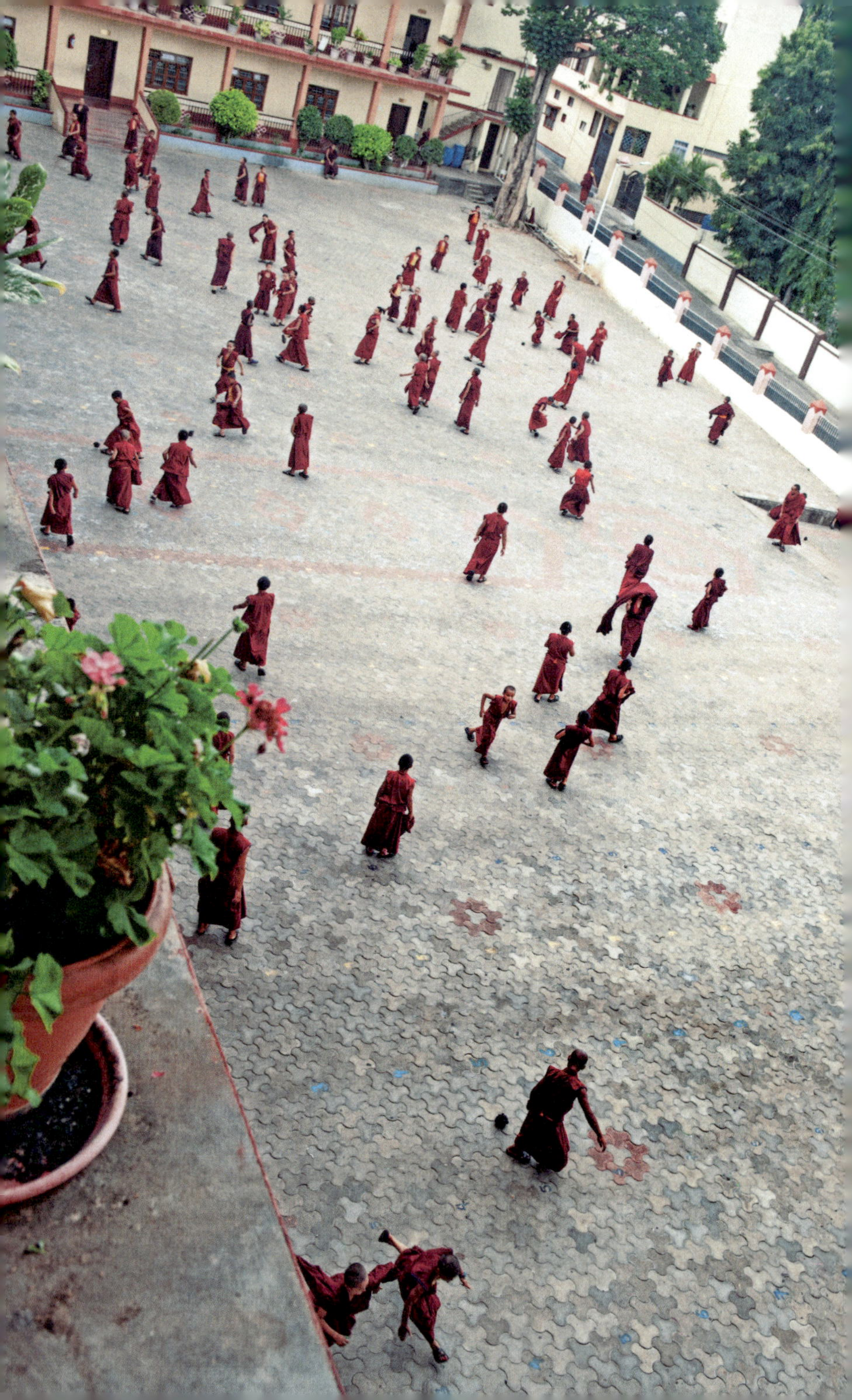

Introduction

Nancy A. Scherl

Respect, dignity, and compassion pervade the scholarly atmosphere at Sera Mey and Sera Jey Monastic Universities in Bylakuppe, southwest India. I had the opportunity to visit the monasteries in 2019, as part of the Emory-Tibet Science Initiative (ETSI), which operates under the auspices of Emory University in Atlanta. ETSI began in 2006, when His Holiness the 14th Dalai Lama invited Emory to collaborate with the Library of Tibetan Works and Archives to create a curriculum for monastics. The goal was to develop an ongoing relationship between Western science and ancient Tibetan Buddhist wisdom for the benefit of humanity.

In 1959, after the People's Liberation Army of China occupied Tibet, His Holiness and many other Buddhist monks emigrated to India, where they established a government in exile in Dharamsala. Tibetan refugees also founded settlements and monasteries in Bylakuppe and other locations throughout India, and these monasteries were rebuilt to replicate those in the monks' homeland.

The silence and calm of dawn and dusk at the monasteries are punctuated by crickets clicking, birds chirping, and dogs barking as the resident monks begin and complete their daily routines. Daily activities and rituals take place within the vibrant palette of maroon, brilliant orange, red, salmon, watermelon, pink, green, and blue, with accents of yellow and gold. Sonorous Buddhist ritual chants and spoken lessons flow through the living quarters, school corridors, debate courtyards, and temples during the long waking hours.

The day begins before the sun rises. Mentors and their disciples meet for prayers and meditation, followed by a simple breakfast, then studies and routine tasks continue the daily cycle. The mentor acts as friend, spiritual guide, and educator to his younger disciple. When a monk becomes too old to care completely for himself, his disciple usually takes on the role of a caregiver, similar to families in which once a parent ages, the child often reverses roles and looks after the daily needs of that parent.

Young monks attend secondary school, where they study subjects including math, reading, language, calligraphy, and drawing. The names of the classes are handwritten above the doors of each classroom. "Dialectic" was my favorite—this is where debate is taught. Scripture, the foundation of each monk's education, is reinforced by memorization and debate throughout a monk's life. Debate is a practice that allows each monk to exercise his unique ability to challenge the positions and points of view of other monks on scholastic topics and to defend his own beliefs.

I was enthralled by the monks' detachment from worldly ambitions, their cooperation, and their simple lifestyles. Daily activities are scheduled and orderly, and there are specific times for debate during the day and evening. No matter how vehement and even chaotic the monks appear in debate practice, once the debate is over, so is the argument. The vigor that is often displayed during what can appear to be a theatrical performance is instead an impassioned expression of the challenger's or defender's point of view as they break down the logic of the topics they are investigating. Following the debate, the monks move on with their daily routines, eat, pray, study, and walk side-by-side, in visible harmony. The debate may change what they understand about life, but this does not change their respect or care for one another.

In my photography, I use social commentary and social documentary to make humanistic portraiture that highlights psychological and cultural issues. I often blur the boundaries between these two similar but very different genres. In my social commentary work, I emulate *cinéma vérité* and often use formal lighting in a specific location to stage my portraits. My social documentary work is more spontaneous, and I draw from Cartier-Bresson's idea of "the decisive moment." Though I might use a predetermined background, or sometimes, controlled lighting, I am more often waiting for my subjects to appear within my camera frame without any direction.

The monastery turned out to be an ideal venue for my photographic vision and style. As darkness rolls over the evening debate courtyards, which are lit with floodlights, monks in the debate groups—one on one, two on one, and large groups—are in shadow but their animated discussions are still visible. As the light from the sky changes from day to dusk to darkness, the monks appear to be enacting a theatrical performance carrying the history of Tibetan Buddhist culture. As I witnessed in the debates at twilight, I felt as though the scenes had been magically staged, lit, and choreographed for me. I was mesmerized by the visual collage and distinctive sounds of the event.

The Tibetan Buddhist community is thriving yet fragile in diaspora. My hope is that both Easterners and Westerners alike may embrace the value of Tibetan Buddhist debate, learn from the practice, and gain the understanding that how we think and formulate our own points of view are key to learning and practicing compassion while engaging different opinions and experiences. This is a gift that each of us can draw upon to increase our own and others' well-being.

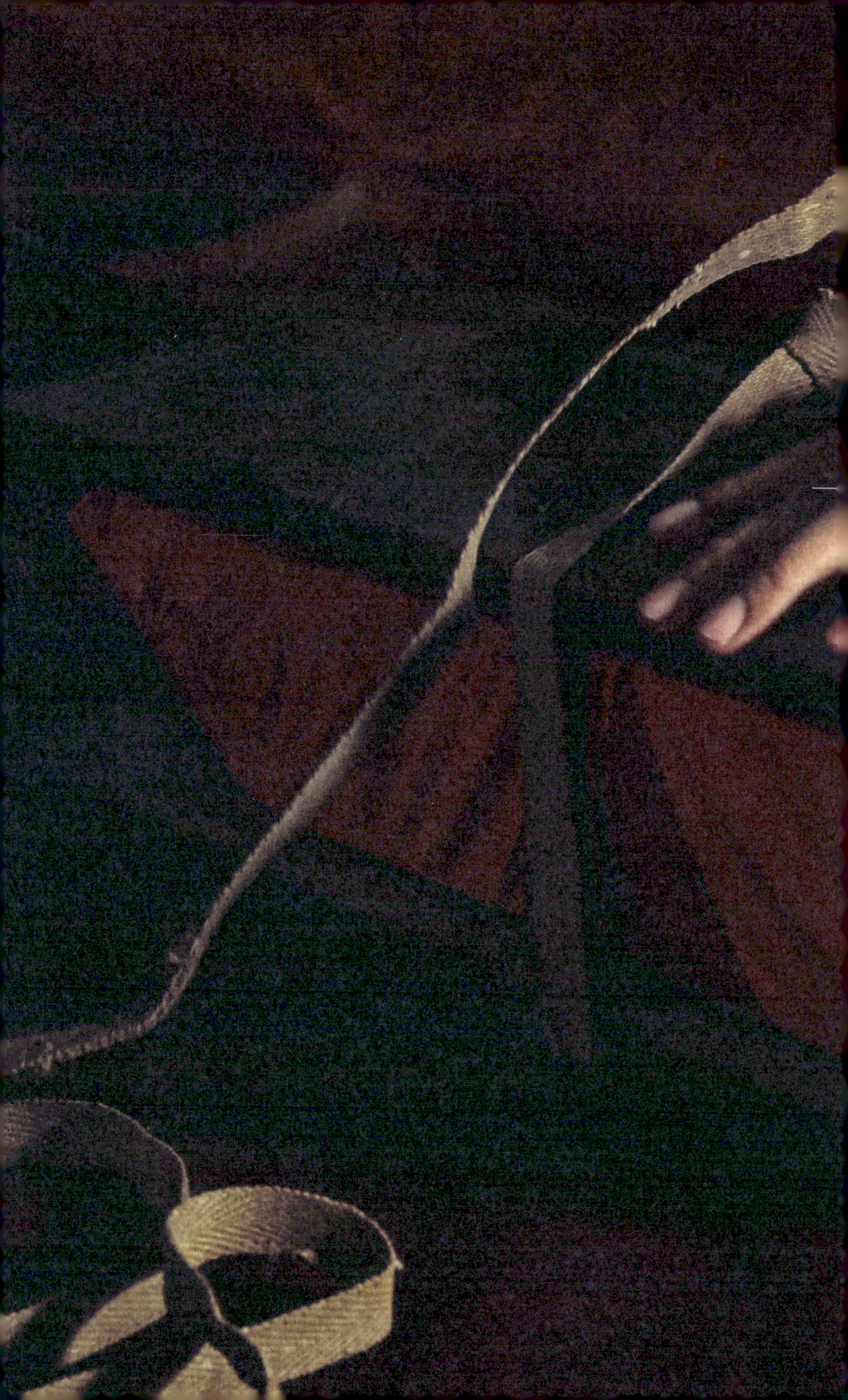

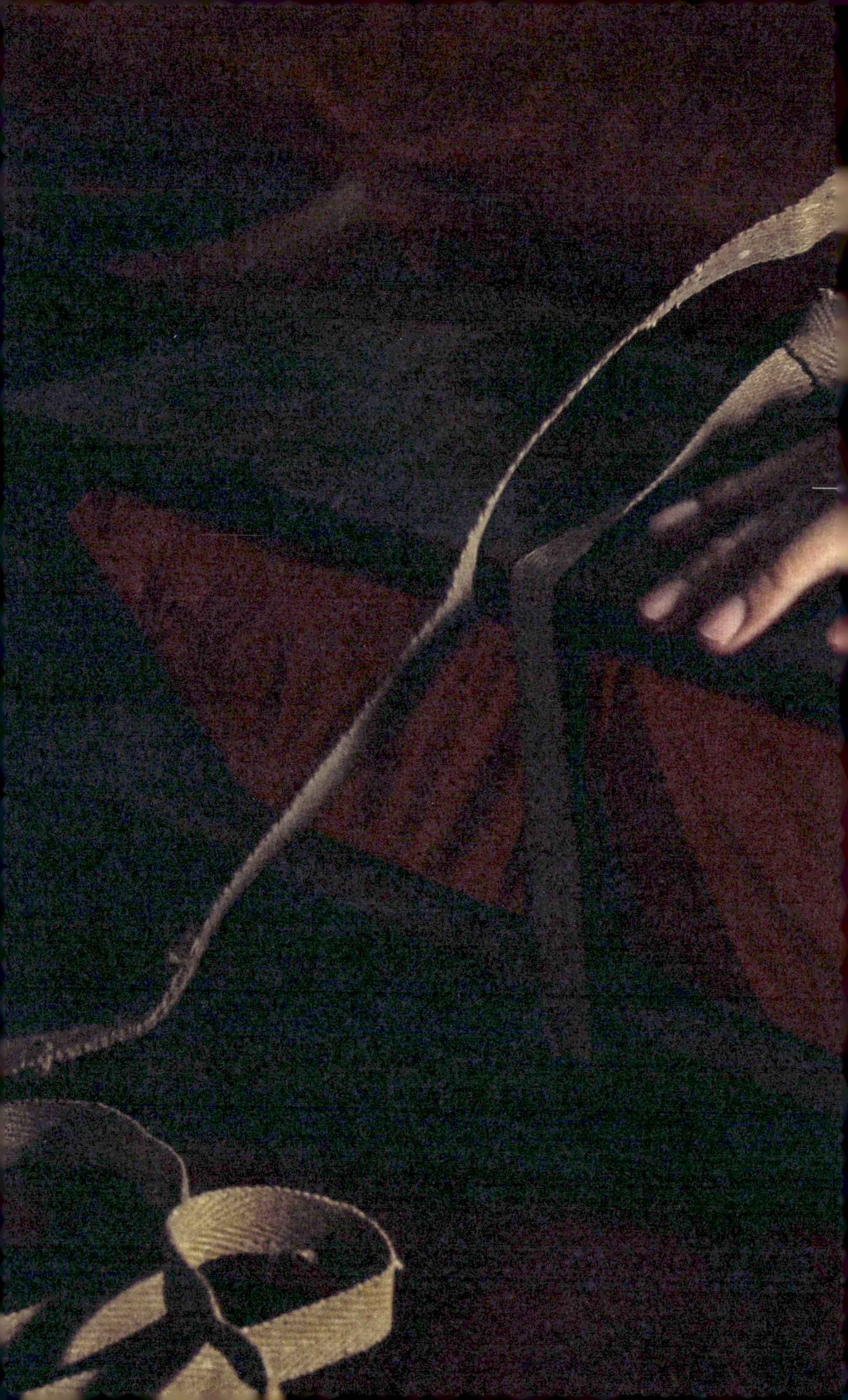

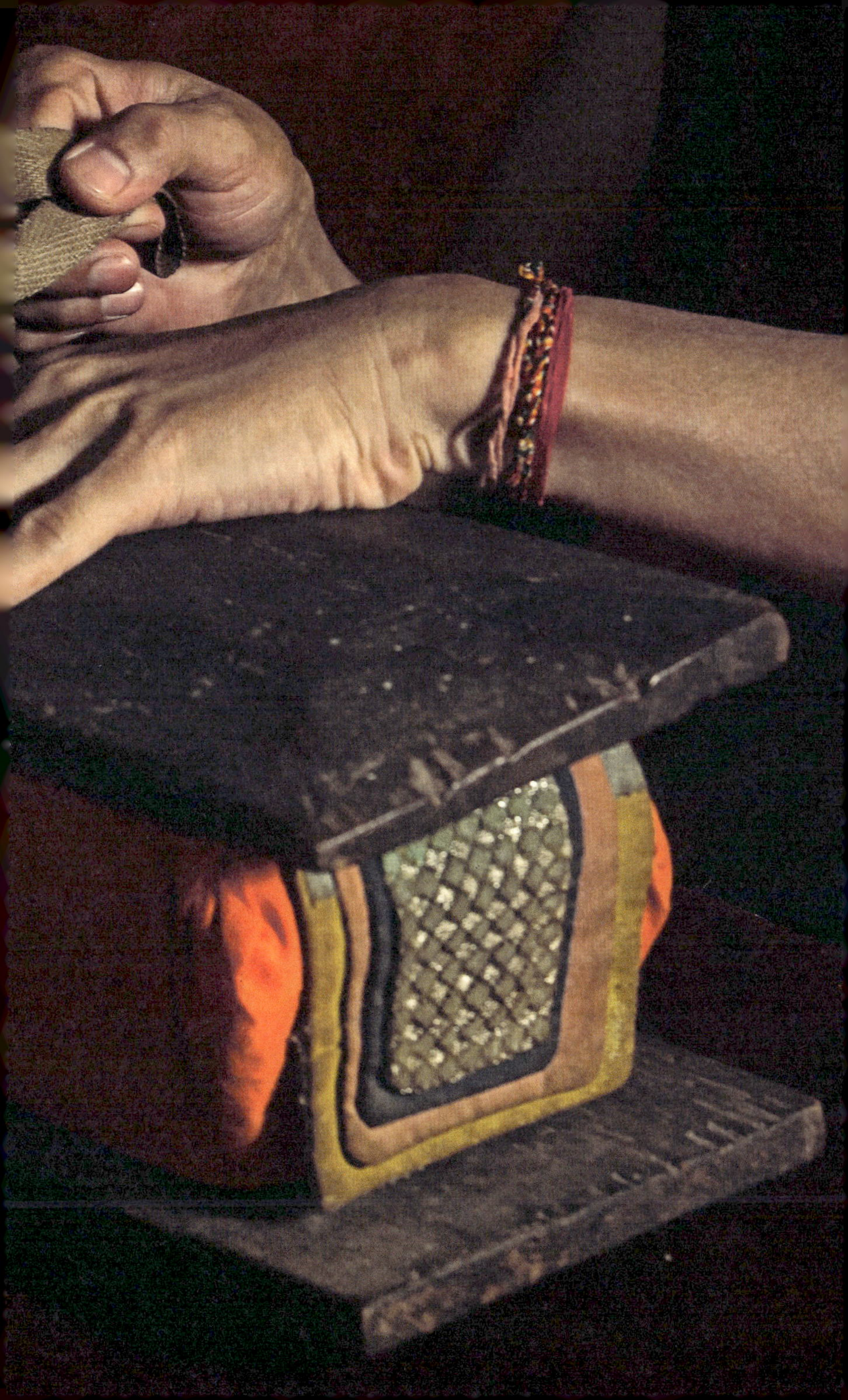

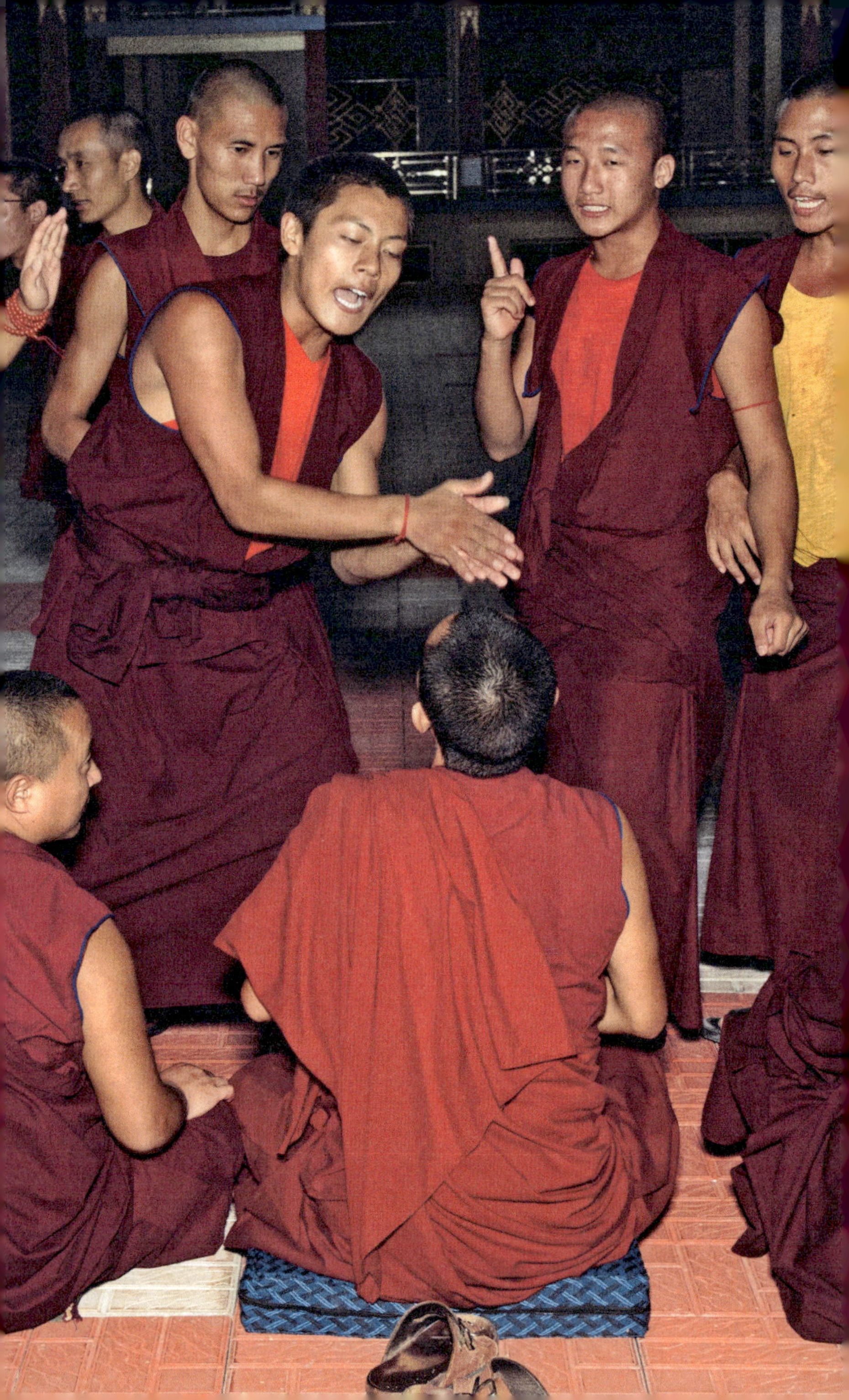

Tibetan Buddhist Debate at Monastic Universities

Dadul Namgyal and
Carol M. Worthman

Challenger Defender draws readers into the world of Buddhist education at Sera Mey Monastic University, one of the great Tibetan monastic universities in southern India. The images in this book offer glimpses of students' lives and training in Tibetan Buddhism, including its striking debate practices, which feature dynamic performative qualities and the intense engagement of debate participants. Yet beneath such surface characteristics lies a deep bedrock of learning and purpose. For the monks, debate is highly structured and plays an integral role in their education and scholarship.

Why debate? Its purpose in Tibetan Buddhism is unlike that of Western traditions. In the latter, the aim is to win, while in the former, the aim is to learn. The distinctive goals of Buddhist monastic education—building the knowledge and skills for pursuing a project of self-transformation toward enlightenment—demand a rigorous process that seeks to eliminate misguided perceptions (ignorance) and related actions that cause suffering. Doing so involves identifying obstacles such as deep-seated destructive habits of mind or behavior, then counteracting them to attain clear understanding and, ideally, to eliminate ignorance and achieve enlightenment, commonly over many lifetimes. Debate, whether conducted internally or with others, is a way both to identify and clear away mistaken views and undermine negative impulses and to hone the mental tools to do so. As such, it is a valuable skill for the central Buddhist project of training the mind.

The contemporary debate practices depicted in this book can be traced back through a long arc of history in south Asia that predates Buddha, when debate was common among sincere seekers of spiritual growth. Formative periods for Buddhist theories of perception, inquiry, and knowledge benefited from challenges from outside as well as within the tradition. The stakes of a debate's outcome could be profound, such that a master and his entire following might convert if a challenger's views triumphed, meaning the debate had established that the challenger held a more valid or unassailable view of an existential subject. Indeed, Buddha himself engaged in such debates before attaining enlightenment and beginning his own role as teacher. Thereafter, debates with non-Buddhists were common and propelled the development and codification of Buddhist logic, first by the sixth-century master logician Dignāga, with further elaboration in the seventh century by the philosopher Dharmakīrti. These foundational concepts were organized, systematized, and improved through successive encounters with non-Buddhists also in search of *pramana*, Sanskrit for "valid cognition" or "right view." The foundation for the Tibetan scholastic tradition was strengthened by Ngok Loden Sherab (1059–1109), the Tibetan translator of major Indian Buddhist classics on logic and epistemology, and the Tibetan logician Chapa Chökyi Senge (1109–1169), who formulated the Tibetan system of dialectical debate that has survived and thrives today. Debate in search of clarification rather than victory has endured as a powerful medium for cultivating both knowledge and wisdom with their inevitable transformative effects.

Given its integral role in the learning process, debate training begins early in monastic studies. Students begin by learning the basic framework and technical rules of debate using rigorous logic and everyday topics such as color and shape, universals and particulars, affirmation and negation, or double and multiple negation. They move on to tackle slightly more challenging intellectual puzzles such as causes and conditions, dichotomies and relationships, forward and backward entailments, concepts and percepts, language and agents, inference and *reductio ad absurdum*, along with some fundamentals of Buddhist psychology. It takes at least a couple of years before students are ready to delve into the classical texts. In this initial training period, they learn to read quickly but carefully, and they spend several hours each day memorizing the root texts on the five major Buddhist disciplines—logic and epistemology, perfection of wisdom studies, Middle Way philosophy, ethics and monastic discipline, and psychology and metaphysics—to prepare them for advanced study of those disciplines through their root texts and commentaries, including the individual monastic texts for each. These texts present Buddha's own words along with commentaries that interpret and expand on his teaching. Students also may study secular subjects such as grammar, medicine, poetry, or arts and crafts, but these do not constitute the main topics of debate.

Daily debate practice requires that students recall, apply, and delve deeper into the material they are learning. Topics may be quotations, words, or phenomena to be systematically explored using scrupulous Buddhist deductive logic and formal debate techniques. At the early stage of training, these topics are drawn from sources that serve as debate primers. Students apply their knowledge of logic and debate techniques to clarify the significance of the texts and consolidate understanding to build a strong foundation in Buddhist thought. Using formal debate techniques and Buddhist logic, monks systematically explore debate topics, identify and elucidate key points, interrogate them logically, and integrate them across sources and perspectives, thereby converting knowledge into understanding. The back-and-forth dialectic of debate also reveals and resolves misunderstandings, ambiguities, and discrepancies.

Once they have established a good grounding in debate skills, critical inquiry, and logical reasoning, the students then embark on their formal study of the Buddhist classics in the five disciplines, one by one, until they are completed. Learning the core curricula based on Buddhist texts builds a common basis for cooperative student learning, providing a pathway to attain a deep and comprehensive grasp of Buddhist wisdom and practice. During this phase of advanced study, for each progressive theme within a discipline, students start by working through the monastic texts and other mandatory commentaries. They apply their training in logic and debate techniques to examine their contents, clarify their significance, and consolidate their growing knowledge of the vast Buddhist cannon. Those who are so inclined may widen their readings to scholarly texts of other monasteries, relevant texts of other Tibetan Buddhist orders, additional reference texts, then full sutras and beyond to become scholars in their own right who have the learning and skills to take on any topic (including disciplines in western science) during their monastic career.

Debate takes several forms. Most common are one-on-one debates between students at the same stage of their studies. These are conducted en masse during plenary debate periods held daily in large courts or halls. During such sessions, the monastery grounds fill with the animated rumble of hundreds of debating monks. Another format involves teams and audiences. For example, the daily session commonly concludes with an intra-class debate among selected students, while the rest of the students are spectators. An annual cycle of competitions is also held between classes or monasteries, and debates include both one-on-one and team formats, at times conducted before very large audiences.

Debates are dialectics between challengers and defenders, who respectively question and uphold a thesis. Procedures are codified in Buddhist texts and employ technical terms in questions and responses. A challenger, usually standing before a seated defender, assertively explores lines of weakness or logical implications of the topic chosen from a Buddhist text. The defender listens carefully and agrees or disagrees with the challenger's statements. The challenger deploys logical reasoning and scriptural citations to maneuver the defender into contradicting himself or committing a logical fallacy. When an audience or monastic group is watching the debate proceedings, they gather in a U-shaped seating arrangement on either side of the debate participants. When abbots and senior officials are present, they sit on raised seats behind the defender.

Each element of the debate has meaning. First, the challenger utters the sound "*dhii*" and claps his hands. *Dhii* is the seed syllable of Manjushri, the Buddha of wisdom; voicing it invokes him and the transcendent wisdom he embodies. The formal hand clap both begins the debate and is used throughout it. The right hand strikes downward onto the upward-facing palm of the left hand, pressing it down as though blocking the left from rising. This gesture recalls the fundamental purpose of monastic debates, which is to benefit sentient beings by warding off realms of suffering generated by ignorance. The left hand represents wisdom and the right represents method, which comprises qualities such as compassion, patience, diligence, and forgiveness. Joining the two by clapping signifies the synergistic relationship between wisdom and method in the struggle to overcome ignorance in pursuit of enlightenment.

Next, the challenger poses a question that sets the theme for the debate, using a word, phrase, or quotation, and rubs a *mala* between his hands. Worn or carried on the left arm, the *mala* (Tibetan: *threng wa*) is a string of 108 beads which, according to one interpretation, represents all phenomena as classified into 108 units or themes (described and elaborated in the full-length Perfection of Wisdom sutras), and signifies the comprehensive nature of debate topics, which address all classes of phenomena.

The defender's response to the opening question states his position. The challenger's initial queries serve to assess the defender's knowledge by asking "Who said it?" or "What textual source is it from?" Questions such as, "What is the context or outline of that section?" will deepen the challenger's assessment of the defender's position. The defender must respond swiftly, or else the questioner may challenge with "*chir, chir, chir*" ("quick, quick, quick").

Proving a thesis and establishing valid knowledge during debate involves a process of inference based on logical reasoning that identifies the subject of the inference and its relationship to the property in question via causality or identity. One example questions seeing smoke on a mountain and concluding that there is fire on it although the fire cannot be seen. "Smoke" is the logical reason for inferring fire if the observer can establish that there really is smoke on the mountain rather than dust, fog, or anything else, and that, where there is smoke there always is fire.

Once a common starting point for debate has been established, the challenger may elaborate on the theme by posing further contextualizing statements concerning the theme's meaning—such as the relationship of smoke and fire—and its implications—such as for establishing valid perception. Most of the challenger's remarks come in the form of statements or questions that apply logic to investigate points and their ramifications. Ideally, the defender's answers should be as brief and concise as possible, sticking to one of four responses permitted by the rules of debate—agree, disagree, irrelevant, does not follow. The defender must be definitive about his stance on the point under discussion because of the constraints placed on him. The challenger's task is to find fault with those responses. He aims to identify gaps of knowledge or logic in the answers, push him to think about things he may not have considered, and thereby clarify and expand the theme as well as position it within the larger frame of Buddhist thought.

Gestures and terms play specific roles in the choreography of debate. Whenever the challenger makes a substantive point, he advances toward the defender and claps, palms together, alerting the respondent to the need for a reply. As he claps, he stamps his left foot to indicate blocking the door to a lower rebirth. He then extends his left arm (wisdom), pulling the *mala* up that arm with his right arm (method). This move underscores the interlocking role of wisdom and method in escaping from ignorance with the consequent relief from suffering.

At times, the challenger claps by hitting the left palm with the right hand facing up and exclaims "*tsha*," either once or thrice, signaling a claim to have refuted the defender's position and requesting that the defender withdraw his previous position. If the defender does not agree, then he continues his defense. If he does agree to recant, he has a chance to pose a fresh answer to the same question. This process may be repeated several times during a debate and allows for course correction along the way. In another gesture, the challenger holds his *mala* in the right hand, swirls it over the respondent's head three times, and calls out "*korsoom*!" With this move, he indicates that what the defender said was way off the mark. Then, the challenger must go on to prove why and how the defender was so mistaken.

A debate concludes when one side or the other concedes the point, once the defender is either maneuvered into contradicting his thesis or successfully maintains it. The challenger may also hit a dead end, or a stalemate may be reached. The debaters may then switch roles and continue to debate on the same topic and see how the new defender maneuvers through the complication they had encountered. Alternatively, they may open a new topic, or they may go to a nearby debate, decide to take sides there, and join the discussion. This goes on until the stipulated time for debate is over.

In this tradition, debate is a means, not an end. Debate practice rests on the Buddhist dictum that spiritual growth can only begin with systematic study, critical inquiry, and cultivation of understanding which, when integrated through meditation, advance the process of self-transformation. Yet in its physicality and fervor, it resembles an intellectual sport. Given the intellectual demands, dynamic strategizing, and dialectics, it also resembles a game of strategy such as chess.

After hours of study, students are unleashed to mobilize their learning and engage in deep play. Debate motivates study and the desire to build proficiency and avoid the shame of poor performance. Yet simply memorizing texts is not enough. Students must strategically use what they know. This requires real-time analysis and marshalling relevant points, which demand mental simulations of alternative viewpoints and directions that an argument might take. In this process, students let imagination and scholarship take flight. There is the fun of exhibiting mastery, achieving new insights, and seeing aspects of oneself or reality in a different light.

As the photographs in *Challenger Defender* vividly demonstrate, participation in debate inspires a range of emotions: excitement, confusion, elation, dismay, reflection, and much more. These images also illustrate how social this activity is and how effectively it mobilizes the power of student learning as they engage in it together. The more others work, the more a student benefits. This inspires each student to work hard as well. Thus, the many hours of shared intellectual effort nurture collaborative learning and build community. Students develop deep appreciation and gratitude toward each other as both peers and teachers.

Although debate may appear to be academic sport, it sparks intellectual development and insight while building powerful mental skills to tackle ever deeper topics such as the meaning of life, the nature of reality, and how best to make use of one's limited lifetime. Debates provide mentally and socially salient "teachable moments" where concepts, from the apparently simple to the most complex, can be explored and enduring lessons learned. Monks have contributed insights to this book, some of which recall the most memorable debates they have experienced. A successful debate happens when both parties emerge with new insights, those indelible "aha!" moments that truly change the mind. Kalden Gyatso (p. 109) recalls that he became a vegetarian after debates about *bodhicitta* (awakening mind, rooted in profound compassion), and Tenzin Topden says that debates have deepened his understanding of the importance of experiential knowledge (p. 166).

What ingredients combine to produce such outcomes? The ideal challenger is widely read and can see the bigger picture framing the topic at hand. With that, he can place the defender's answers in different contexts so that together they can strengthen the applicability of each answer to various scenarios. Contextualization within a wider set of ideas permits debaters to recognize logical contradictions and discern how they do or do not fit within layers of understanding. Likewise, a good defender is someone who also has wide knowledge and has worked through the complexities and contradictions, so that the challenger discovers things he has not previously considered.

Debate practices advance the daring, tremendous Buddhist project to which monastics have dedicated themselves, training the mind and subduing ignorance in pursuit of enlightenment.

A final thought to carry with you as you peruse this book: What can we learn from Tibetan Buddhist debate that would capture the spirit of joyful inquiry, cooperative learning, and unflinching commitment to critical analysis for enriching and strengthening the practices of formal education today?

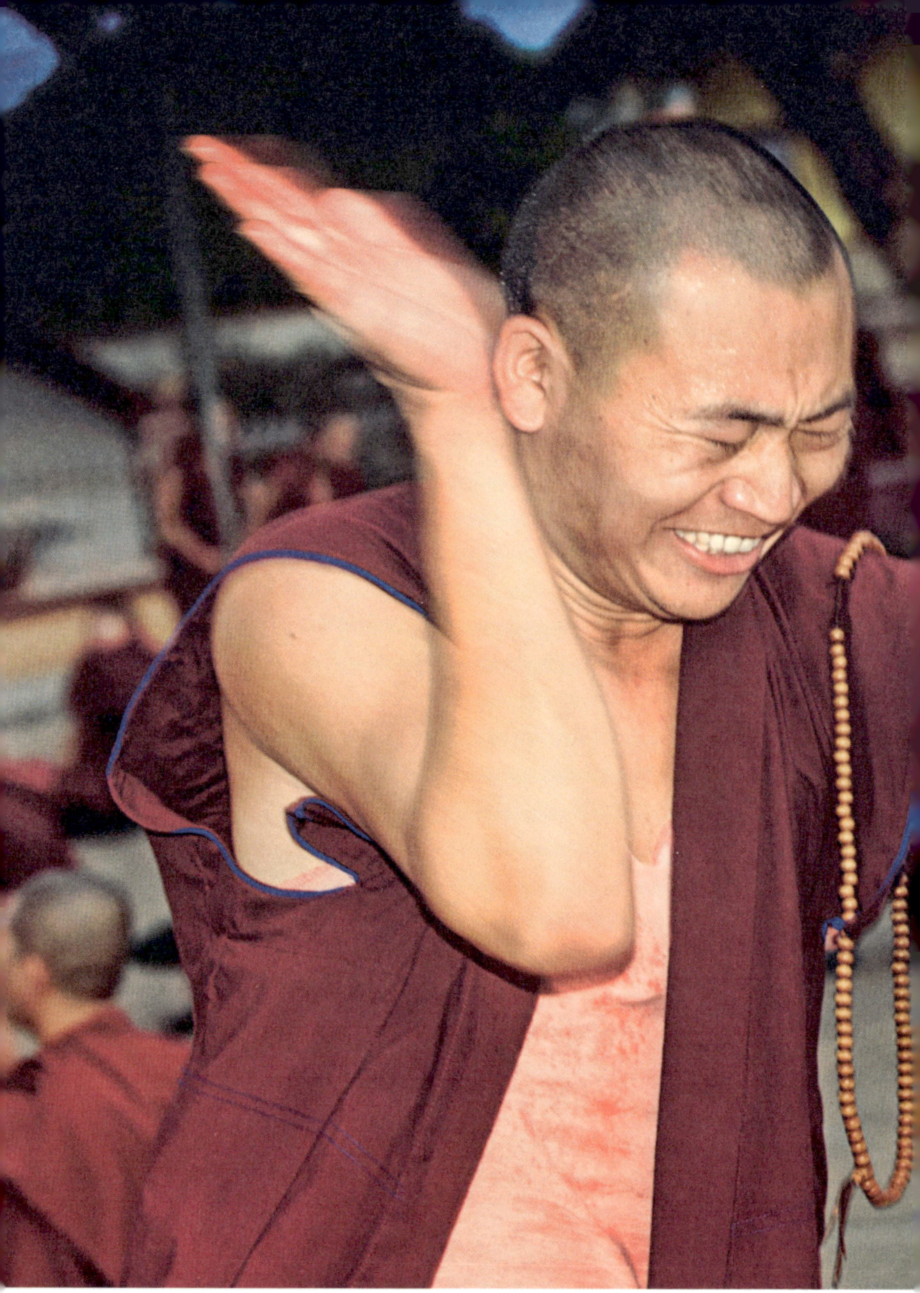

Evening debate begins at dusk and continues with vigor until well after dark, when the monks gather in the courtyard for an end-of-day debate before returning to their respective home quarters.

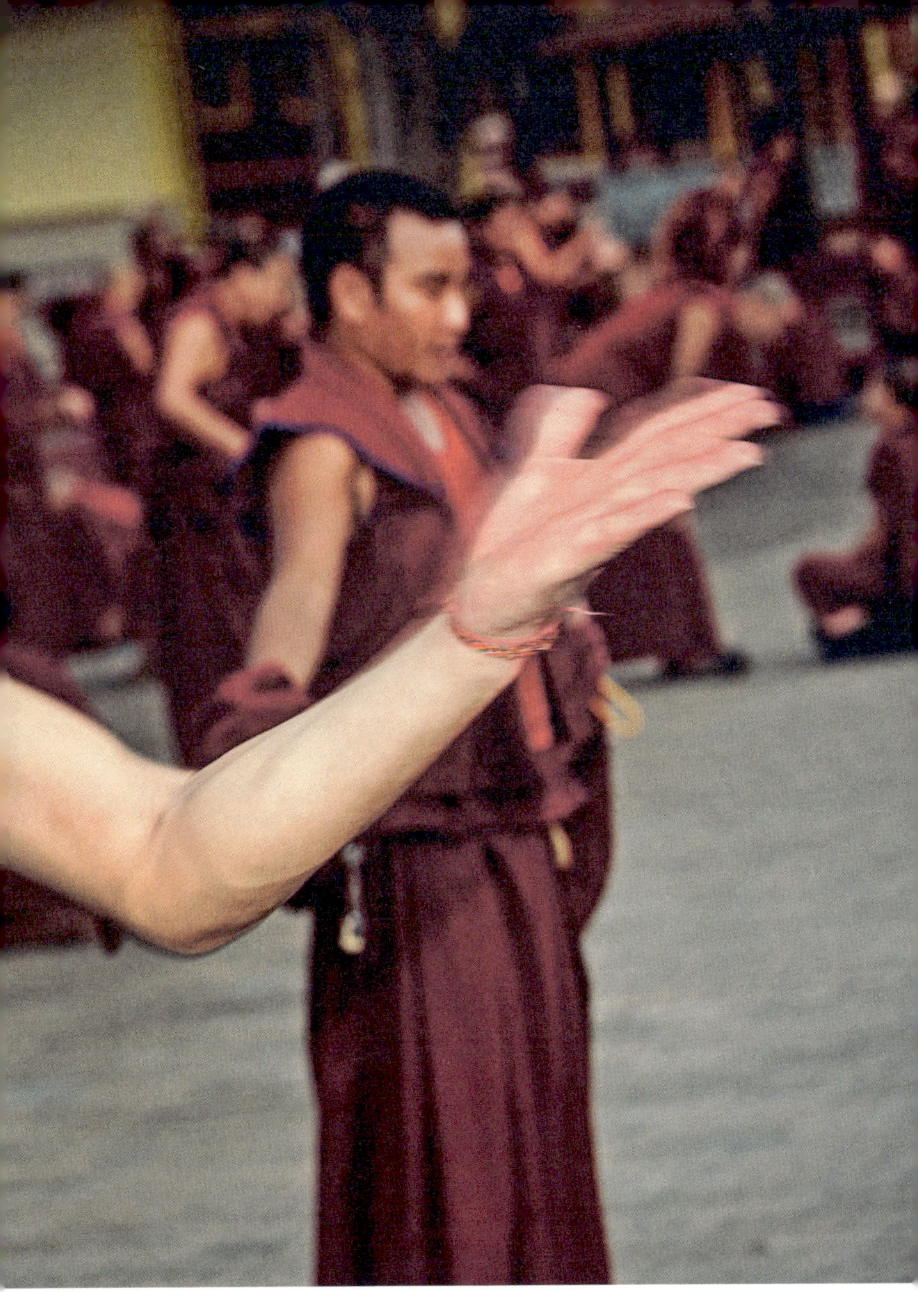

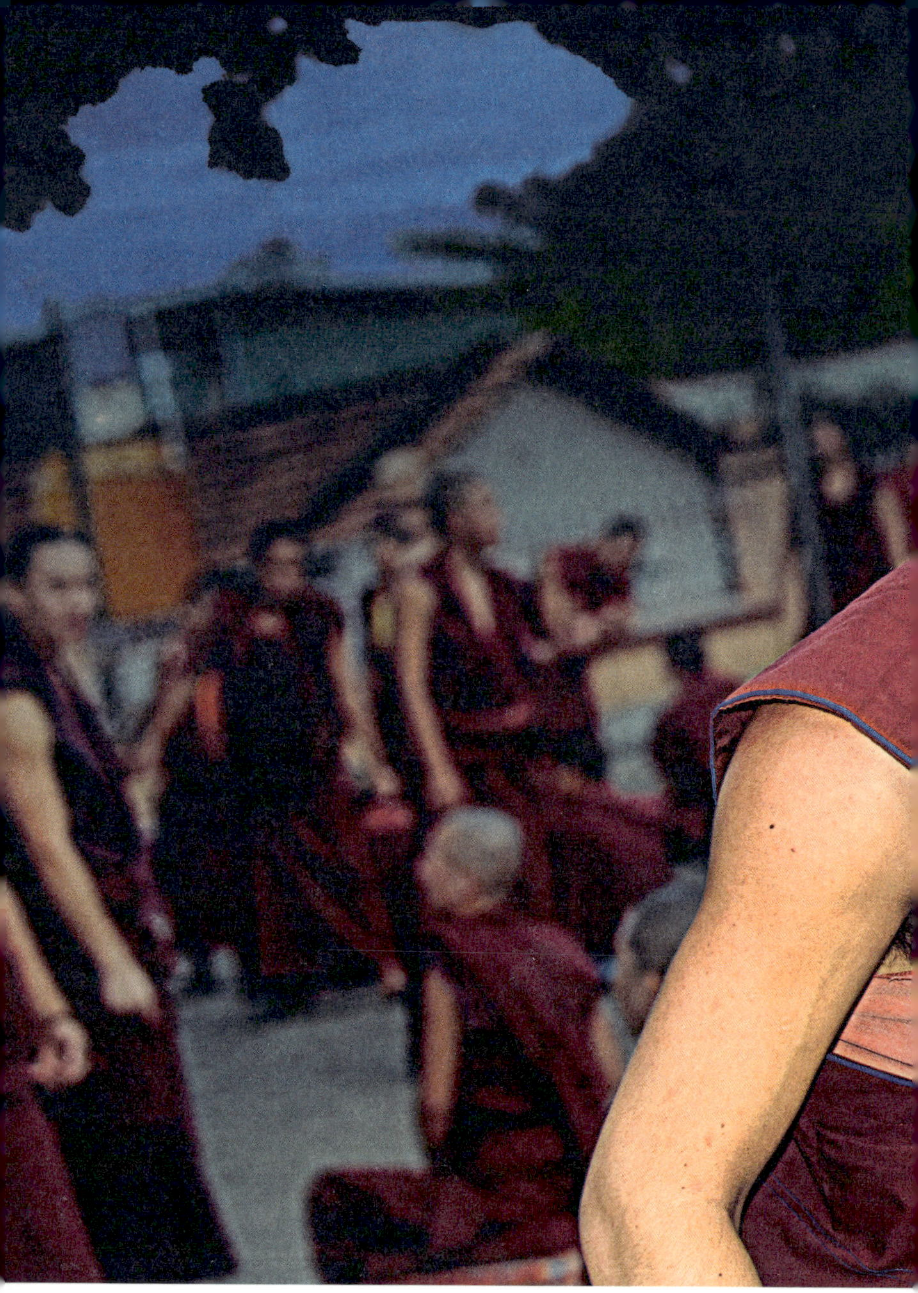

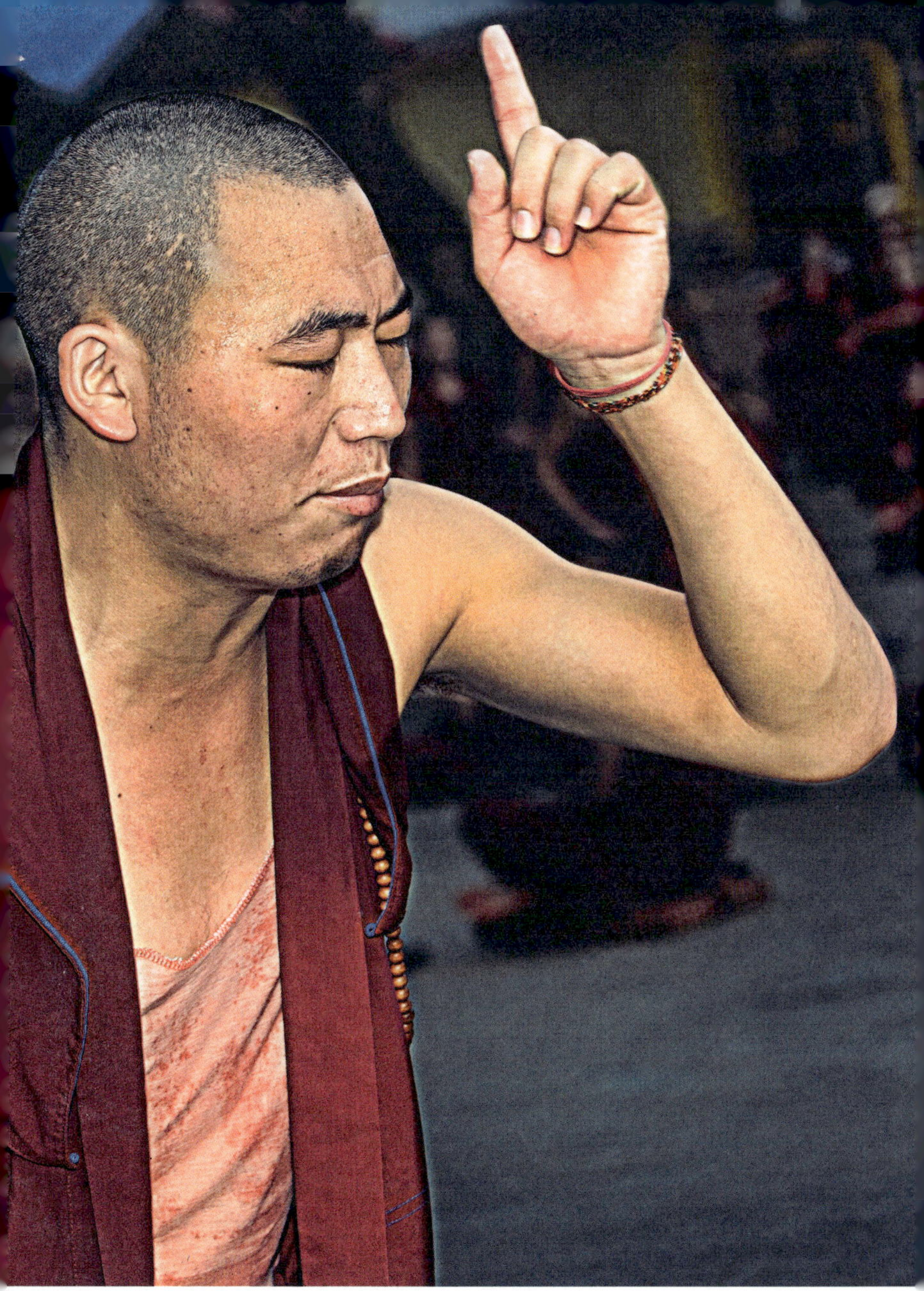

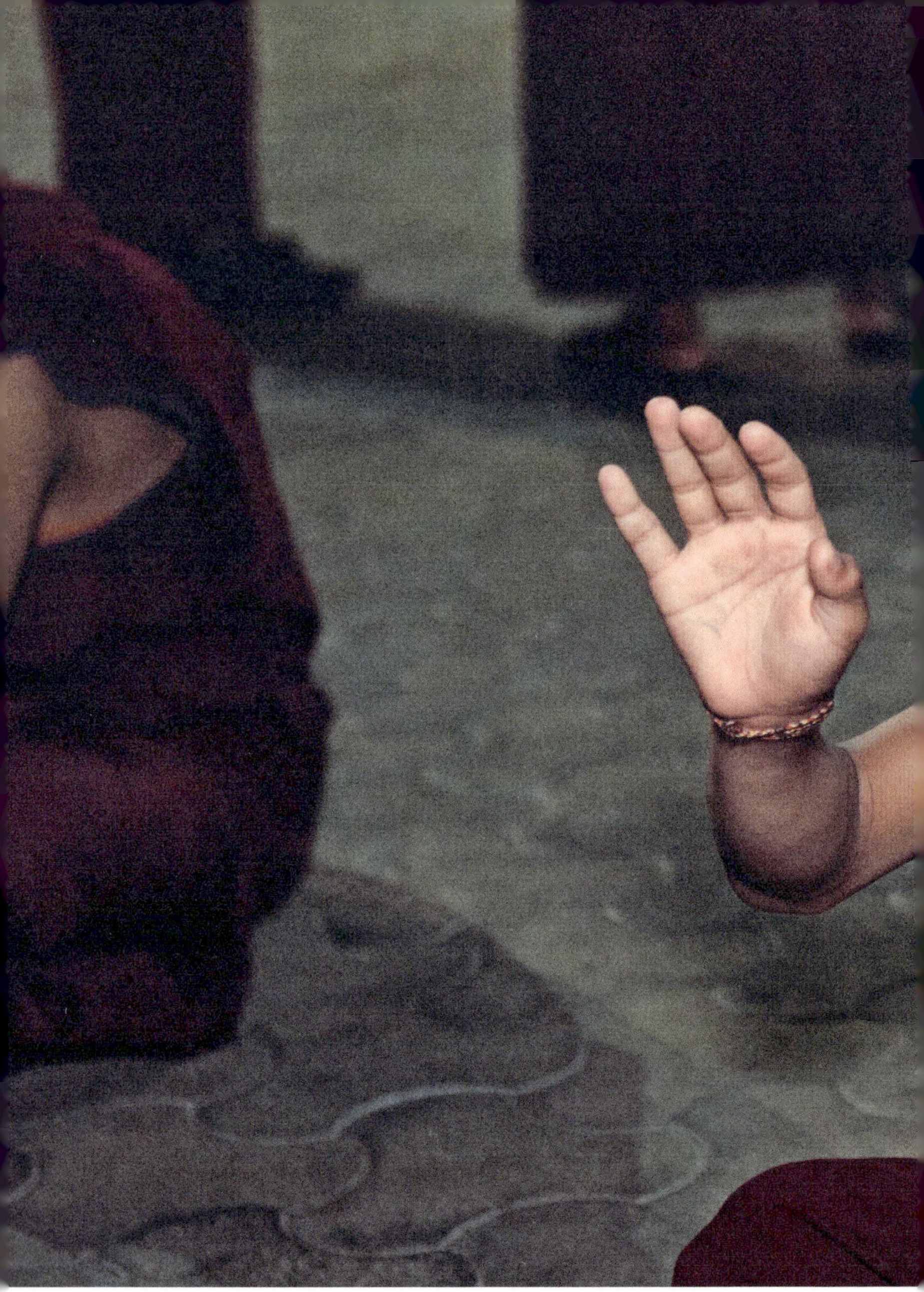

Young monks practice the gestures and movements of the verbal give-and-take distinct to Tibetan Buddhist debate.

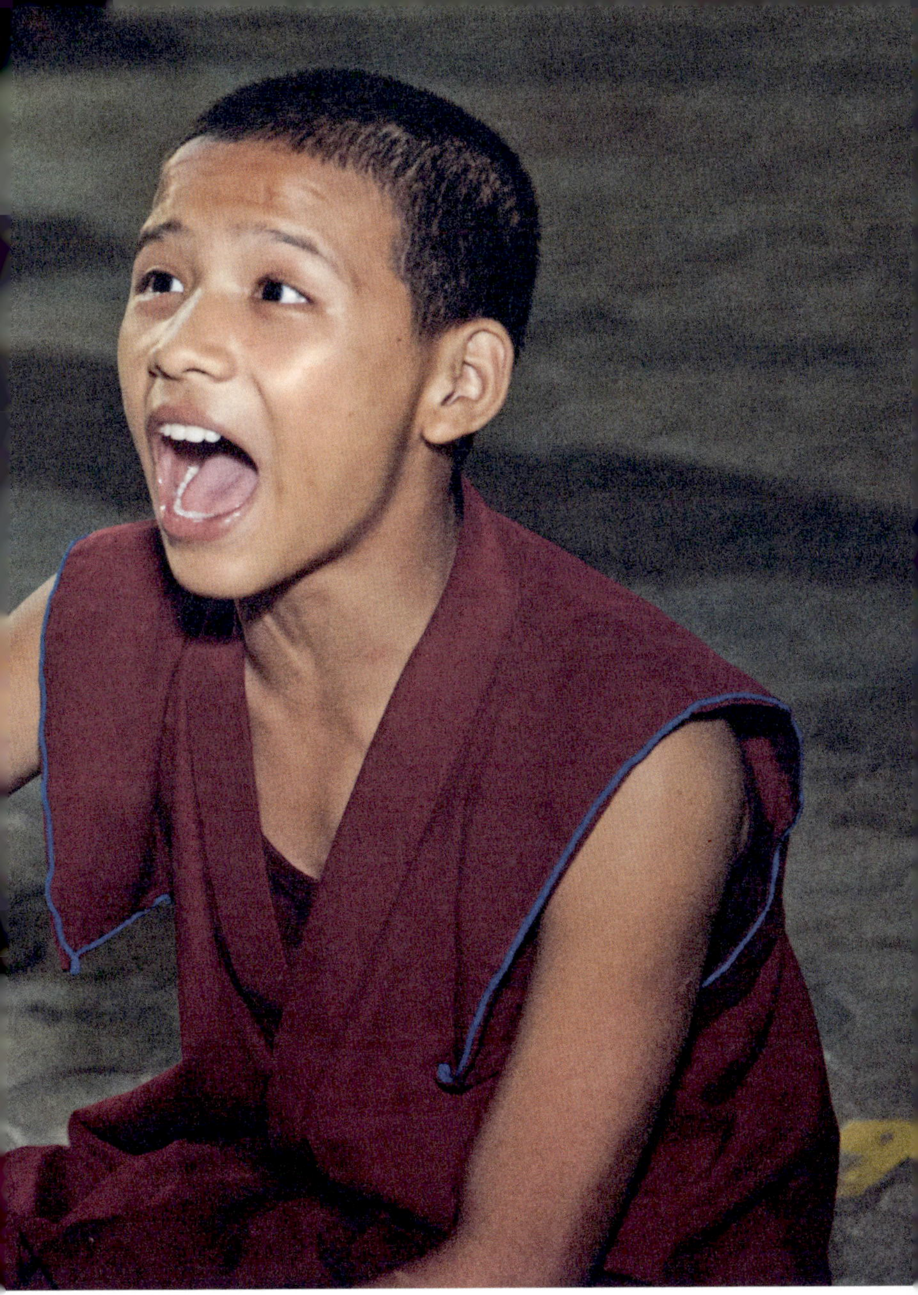

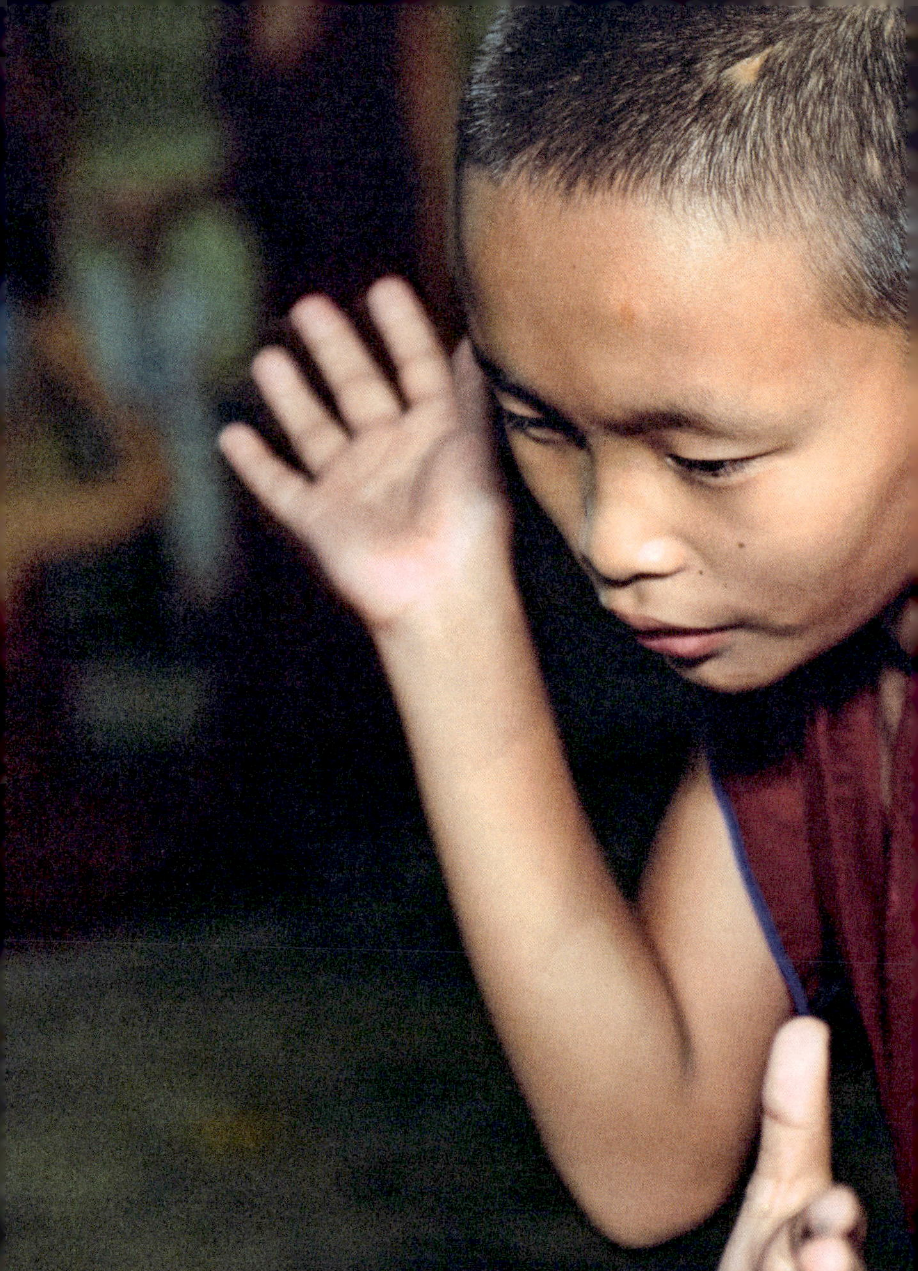

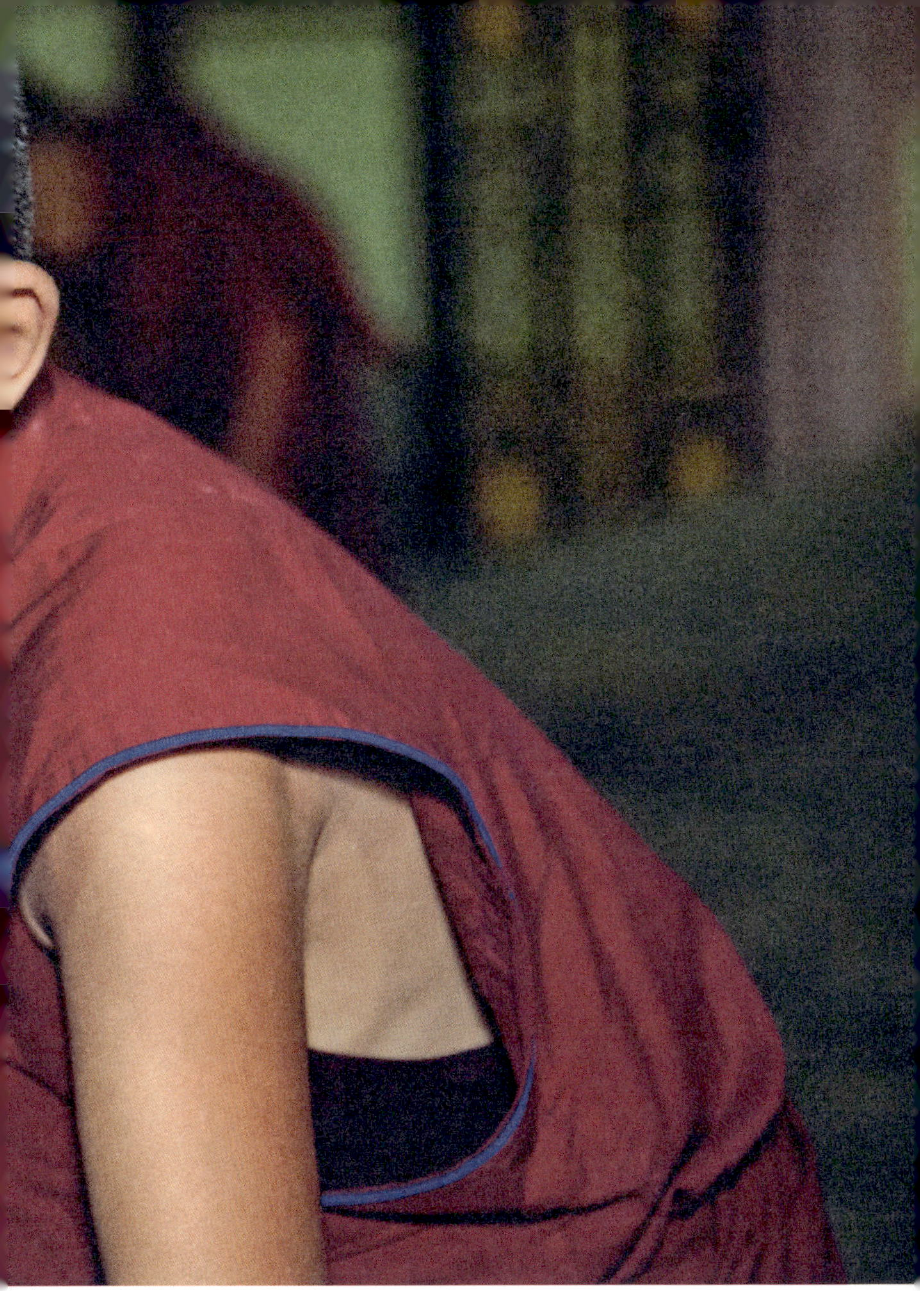

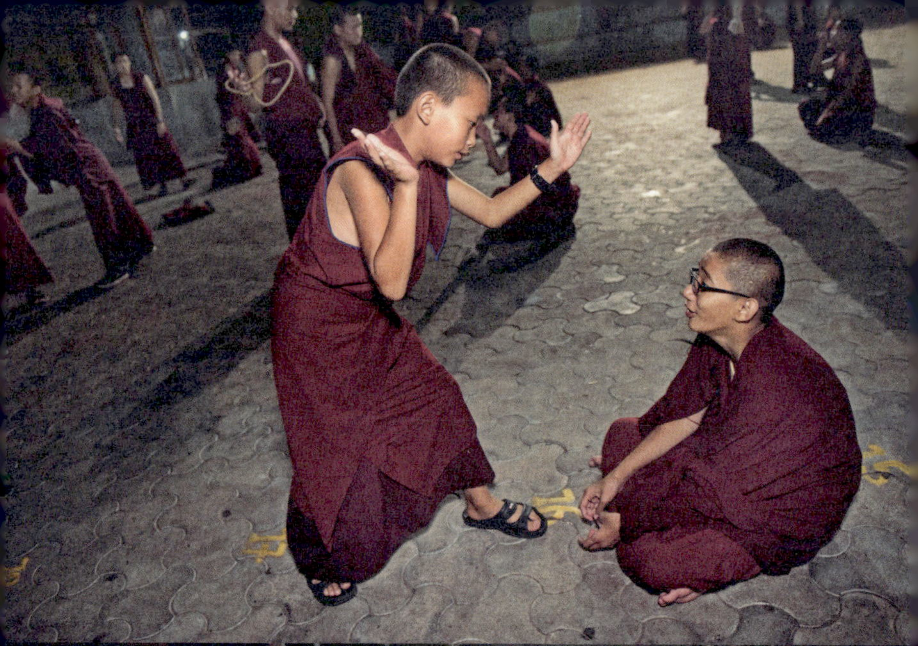

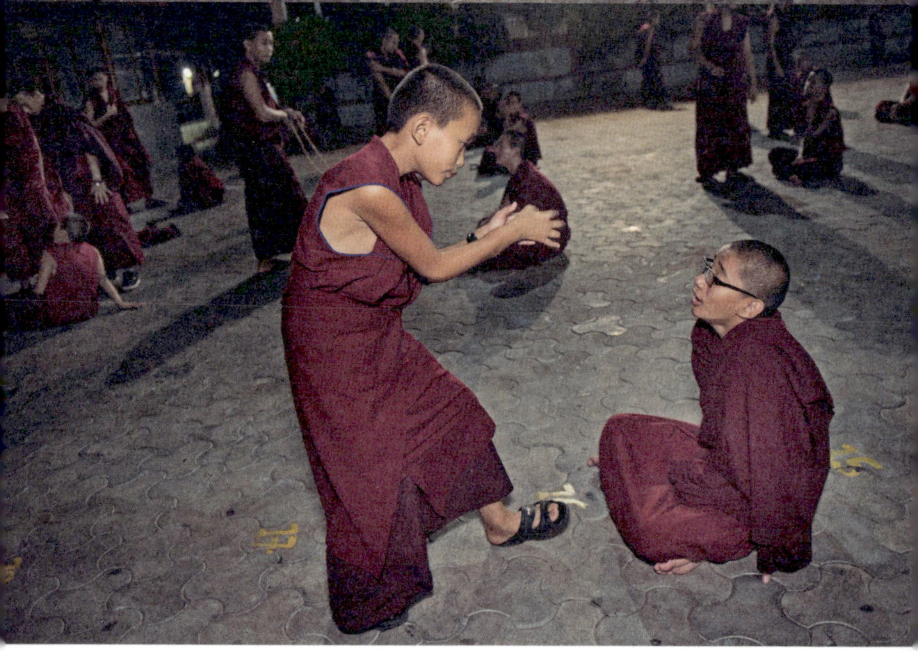

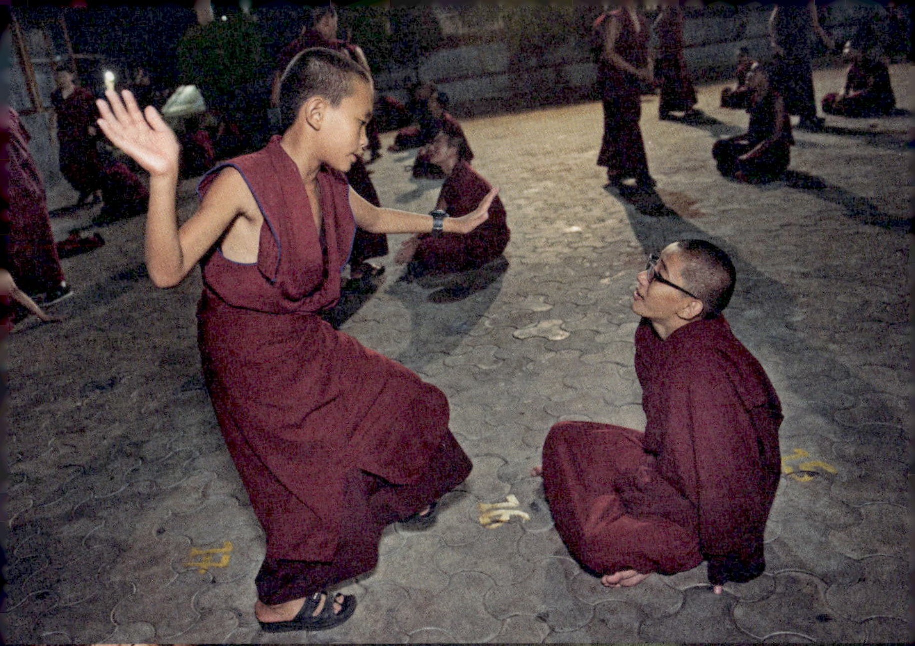

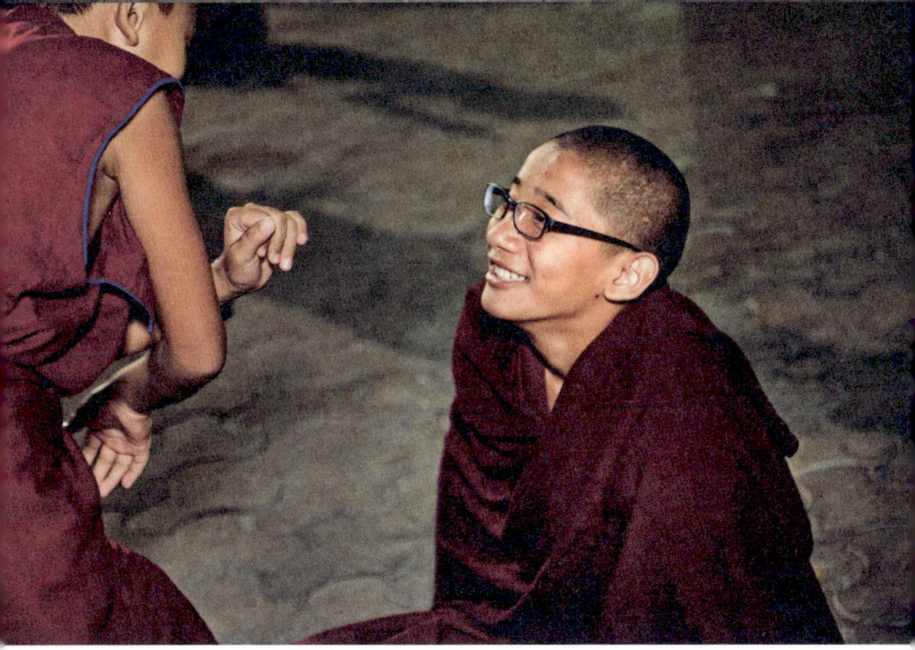

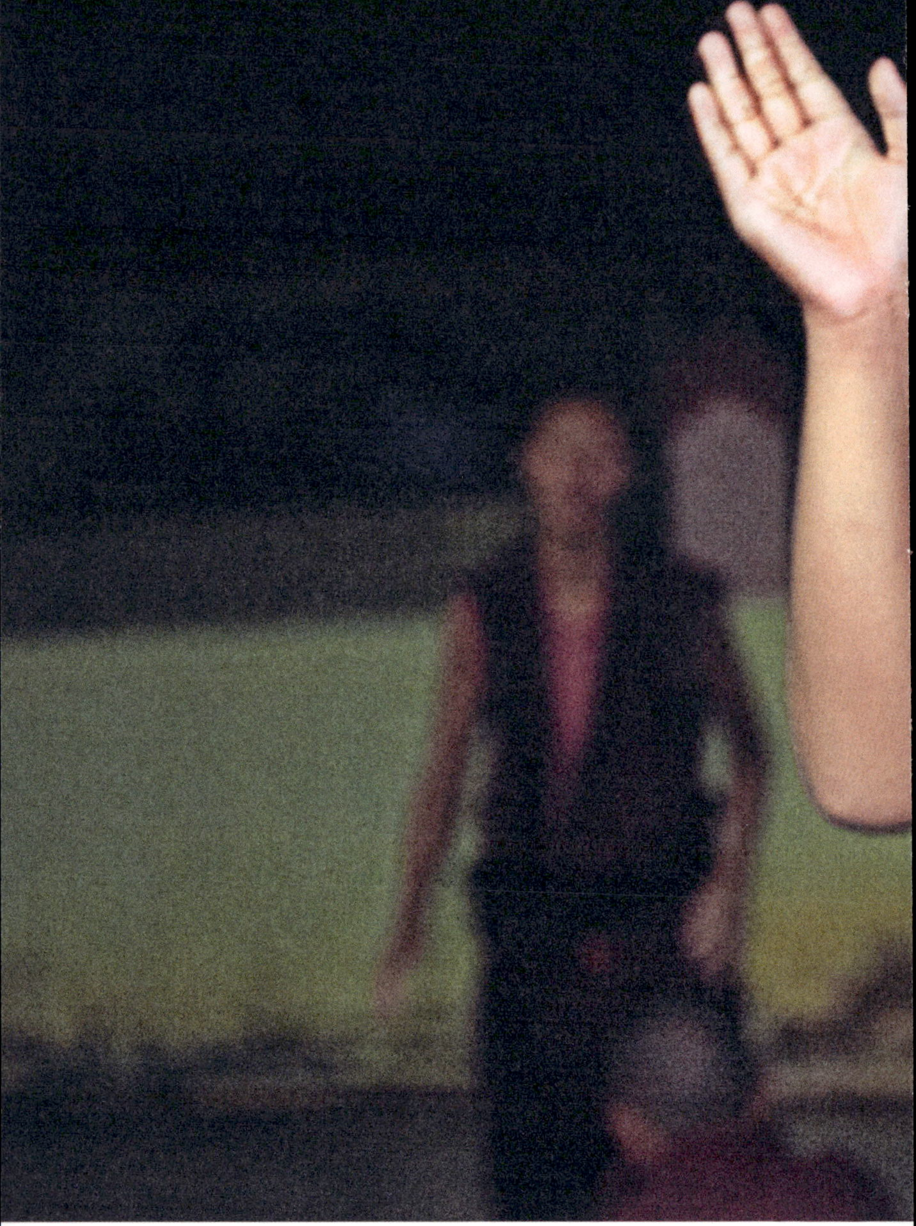

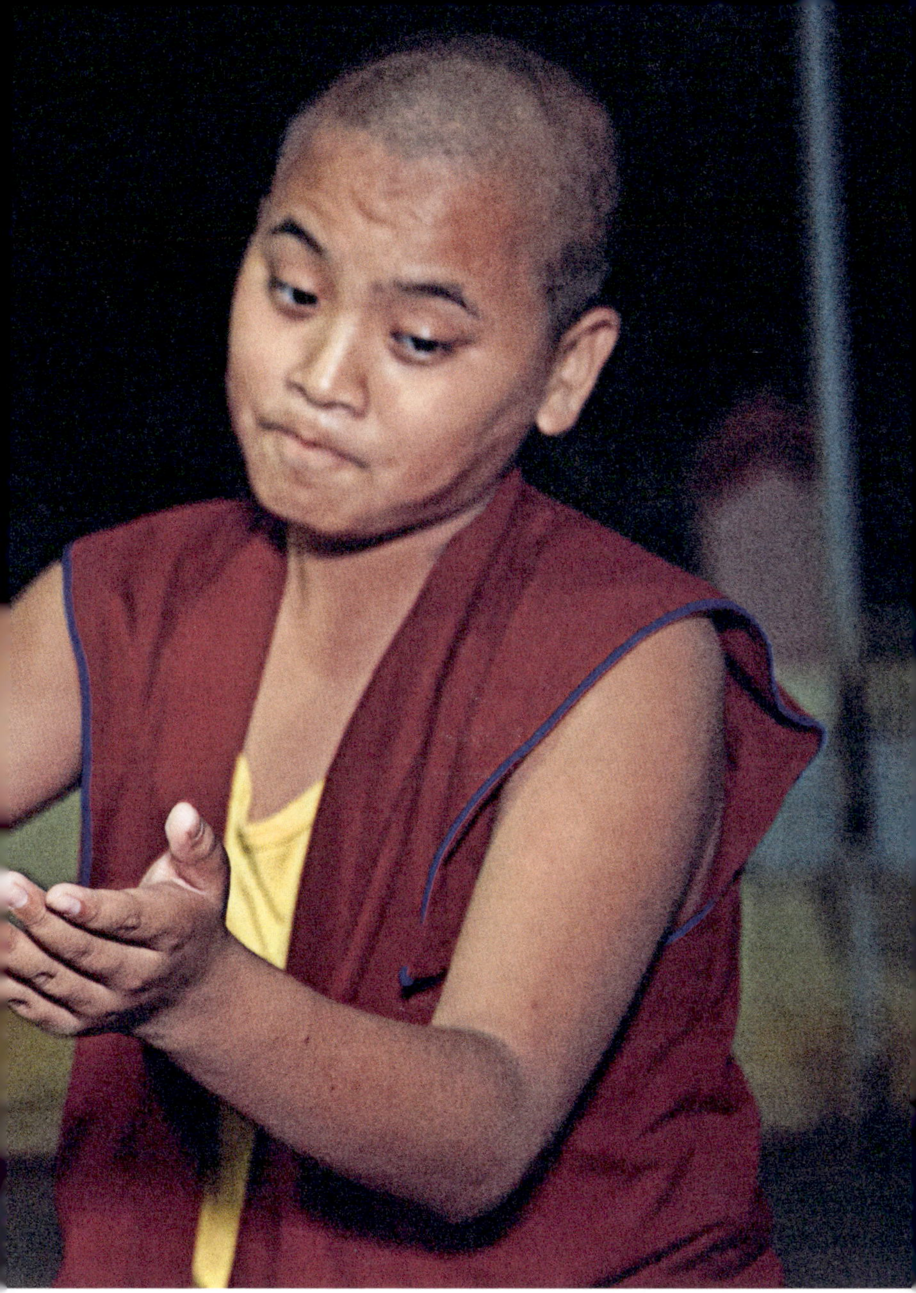

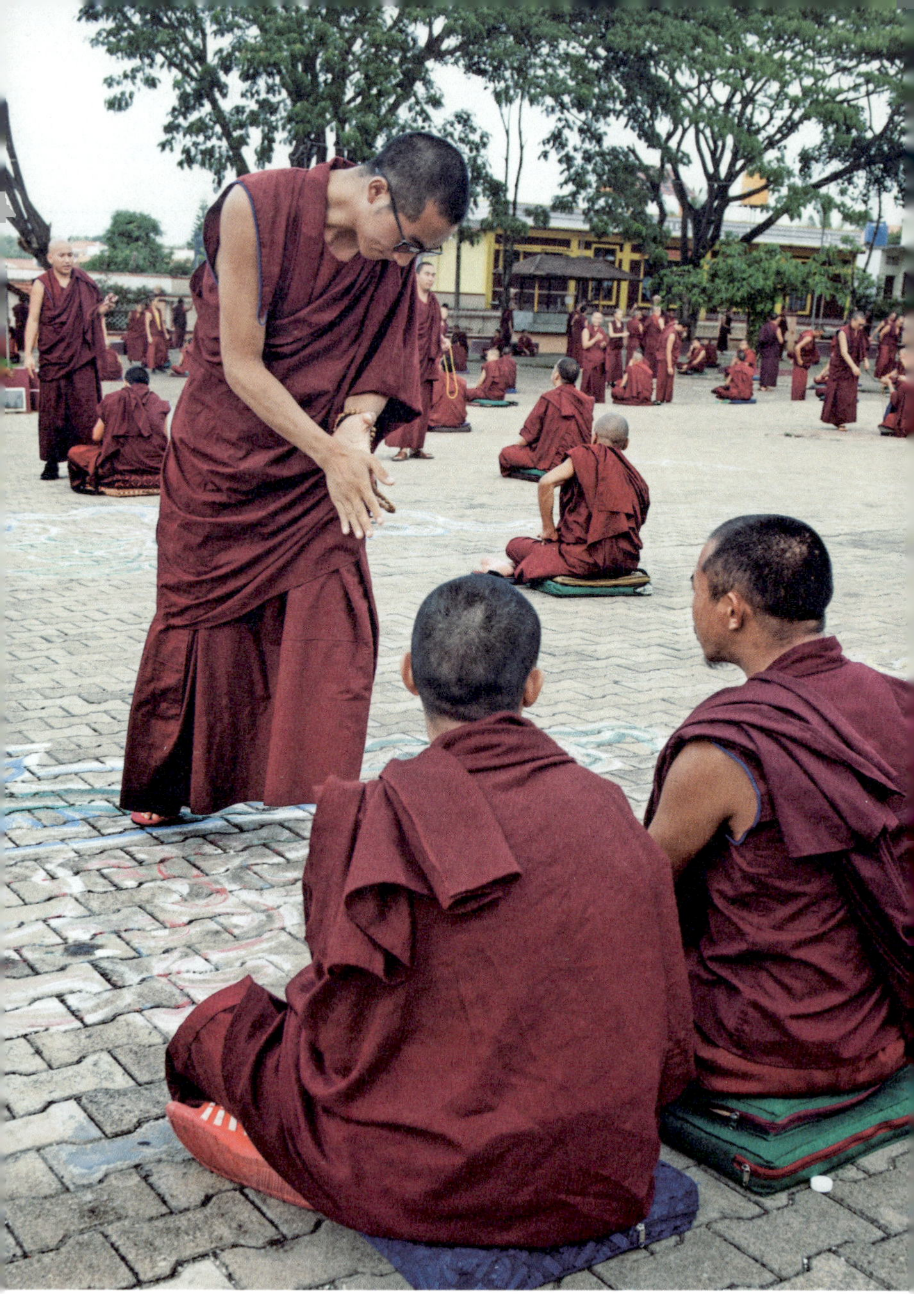

When monks engage in debate training, challengers and defenders arrange themselves in a variety of groupings, creating dynamic situations that allow them to practice maintaining composure, focus, and quick thinking.

In one debate I remember well, I tried to grapple with the meaning of the "correct non-observation of sign," which relates to the principle that without having a full picture of a situation with as much information as possible, you shouldn't rush to pass judgment. As one sutra states, "I and those who like me can perceive others, but not by others. If they judge others, they will degenerate."

Studying "Signs and Reasoning," a foundational text we use for epistemology and logic, along with engaging in preliminary debate topics have had the biggest impact on me, increasing my enthusiasm to study debate. But I also use debate outside of scripture study. When I interact with people, my training allows me to understand others' questions and respond with appropriate answers. I do not blindly accept others' opinions, but instead I examine their reasoning.

— Thupten Khetsun

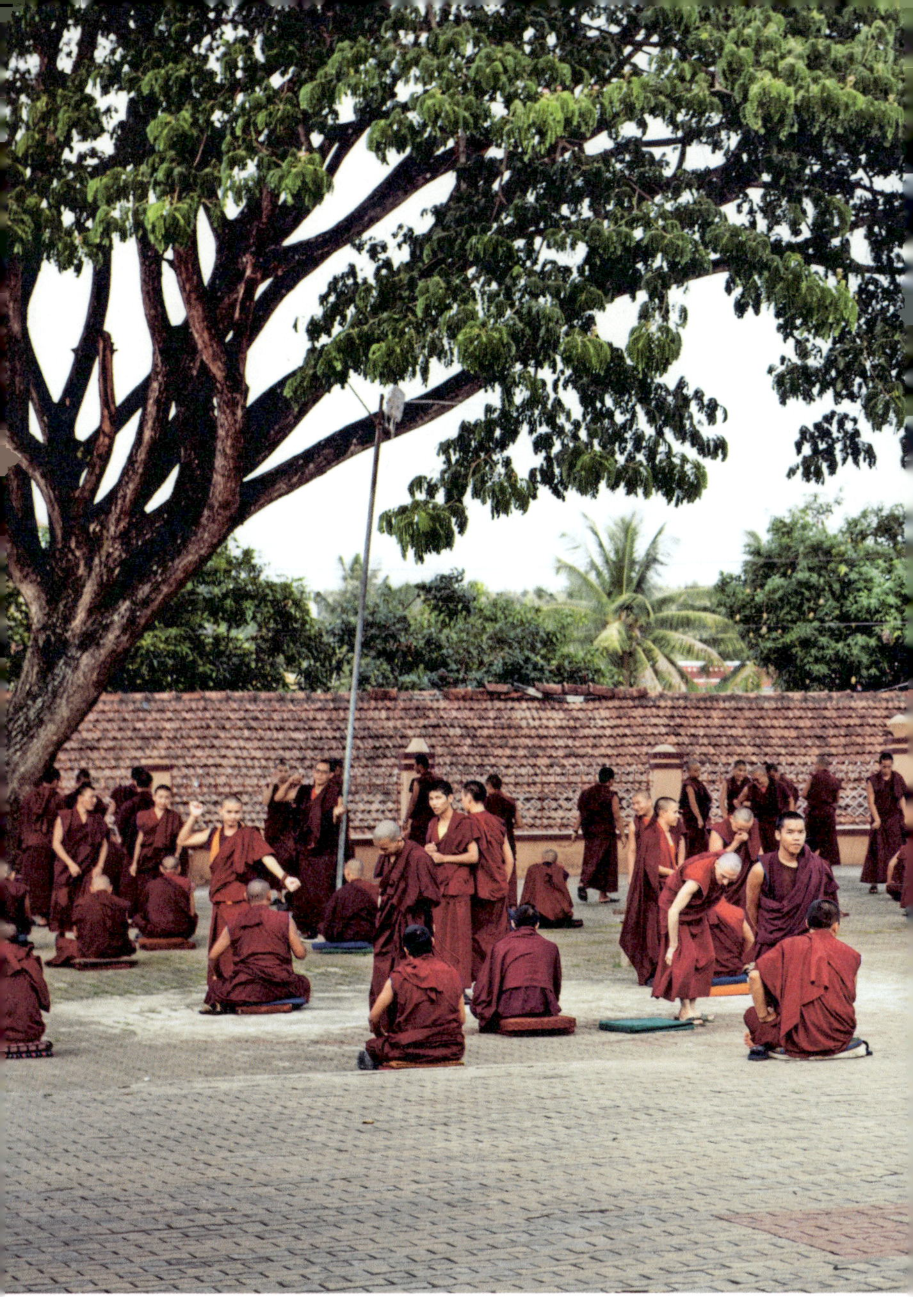

The debate courtyard fills with challengers and defenders taking their positions in large and small groups, and the chatter is already lively.

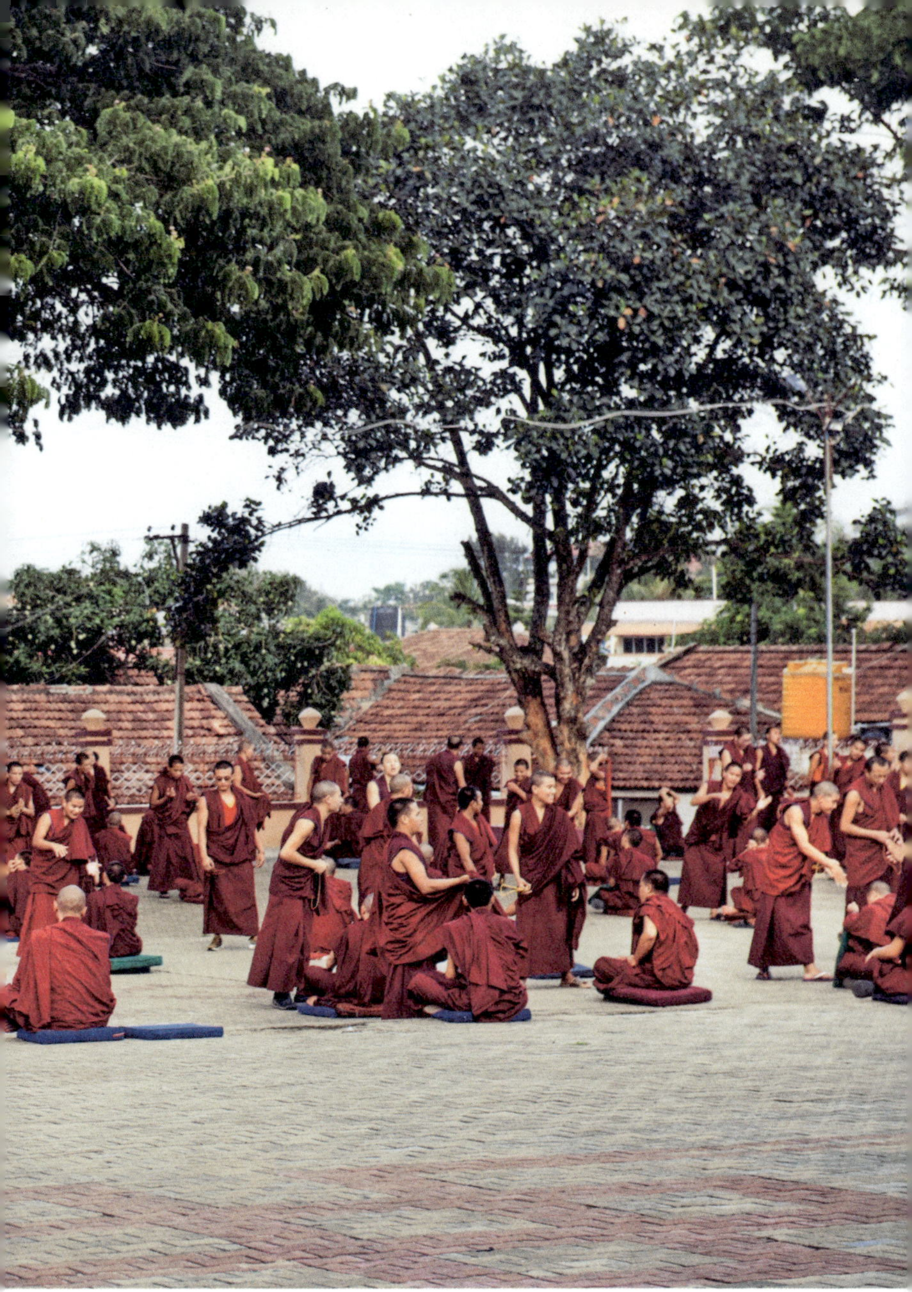

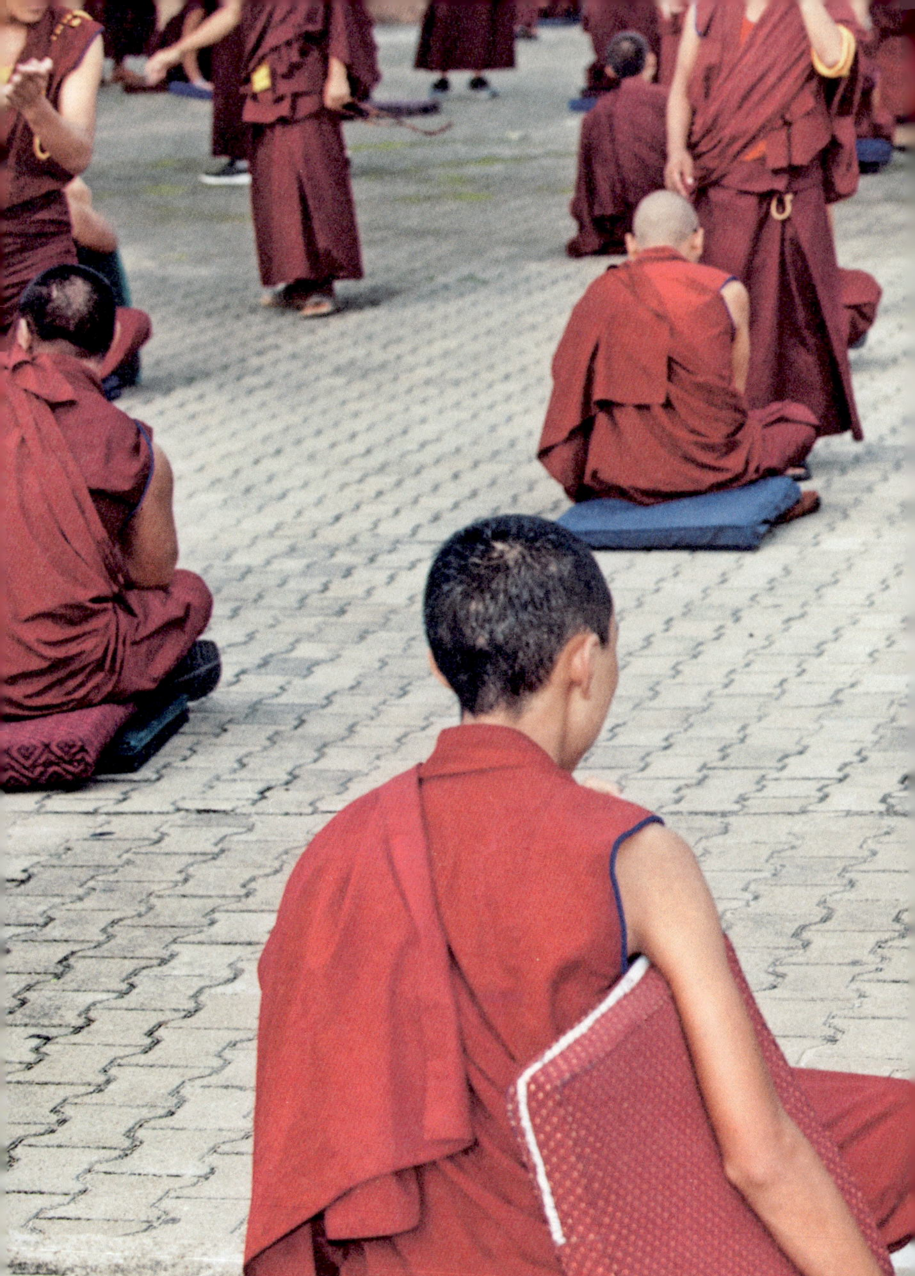

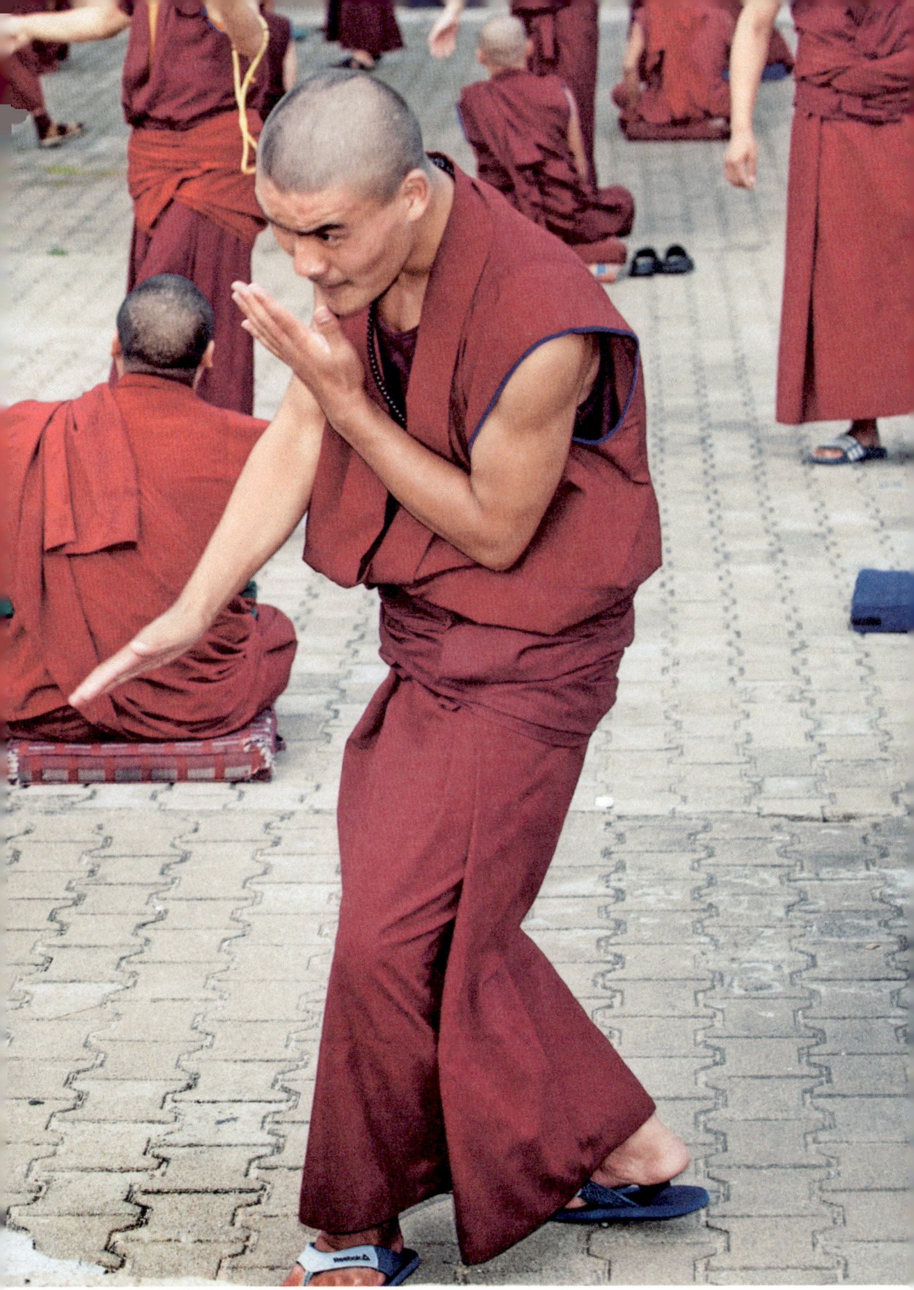

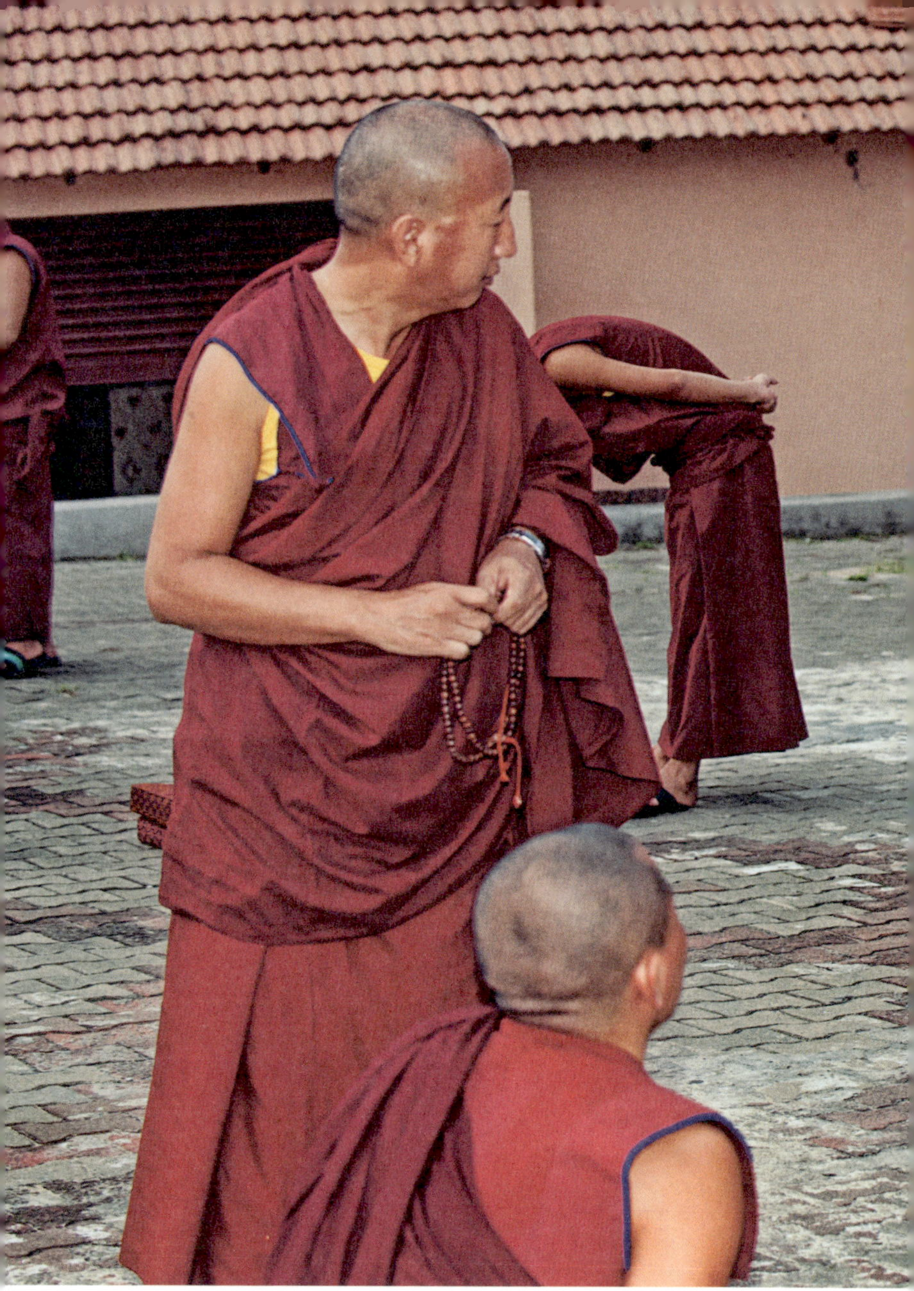

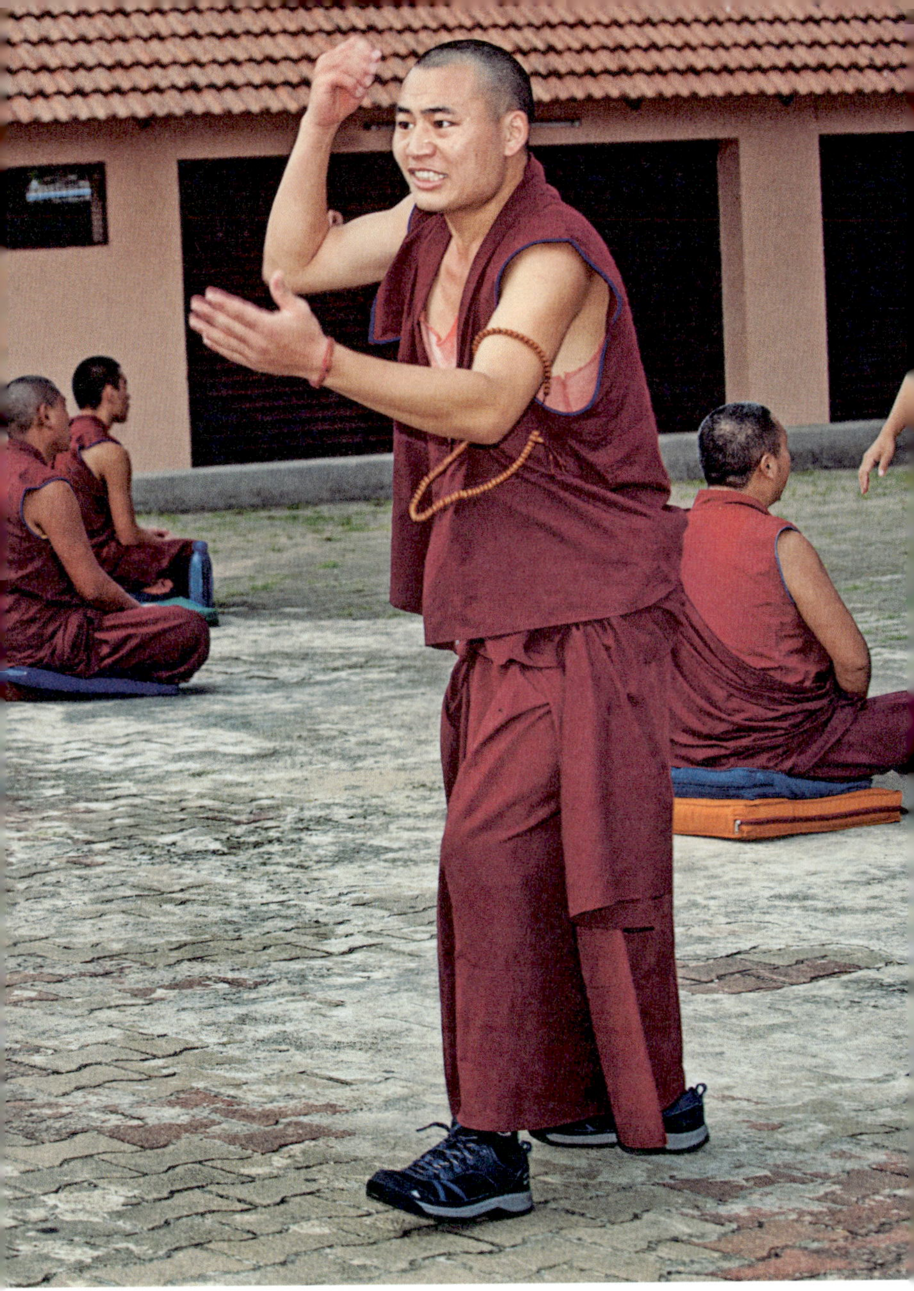

> *"The kind spiritual master is the foundation of all good qualities. And following him appropriately is the root of the spiritual path. Having clearly seen that, with continuous effort, may I be blessed to rely on him with great respect."* — Lama Tsongkhapa

The relationship of the mentor and disciple in the Tibetan monastic community is akin to that of a father and son, because the mentor takes care of both the spiritual and social development of his disciple with genuine compassion. Their guidance extends beyond teaching scriptures, encompassing essential life lessons to cultivate strong moral character. Teachers take full responsibility for the well-being of their novice students, some of whom join the monastery as young as six or seven years old, and they attend to much more than just pedagogical matters—washing their clothes, sewing for them, and providing support for their medical care and daily needs. When I was a young monk in Nepal, my teacher took me and the other novices to the nearby river to do laundry about twice a month. While he patiently scrubbed our clothes by hand, my friends and I swam and played freely in the water. Once he finished washing, he called each of us over for a proper bath, using his strong hands to scrub away every trace of dirt.

As teachers grow older, the roles often reverse. Disciples assume the responsibility of cooking meals for their teachers and assisting them with daily tasks. The bond between teachers and novice monks is profound and deeply rooted in respect and devotion. When a teacher falls seriously ill, the disciples selflessly dedicate themselves to his care by cleaning his bedding, clothing, and personal belongings and demonstrating their gratitude and reverence through tireless acts of service. In this way, the mentor-disciple relationship comes full circle.

— Jampa Gyaltsen

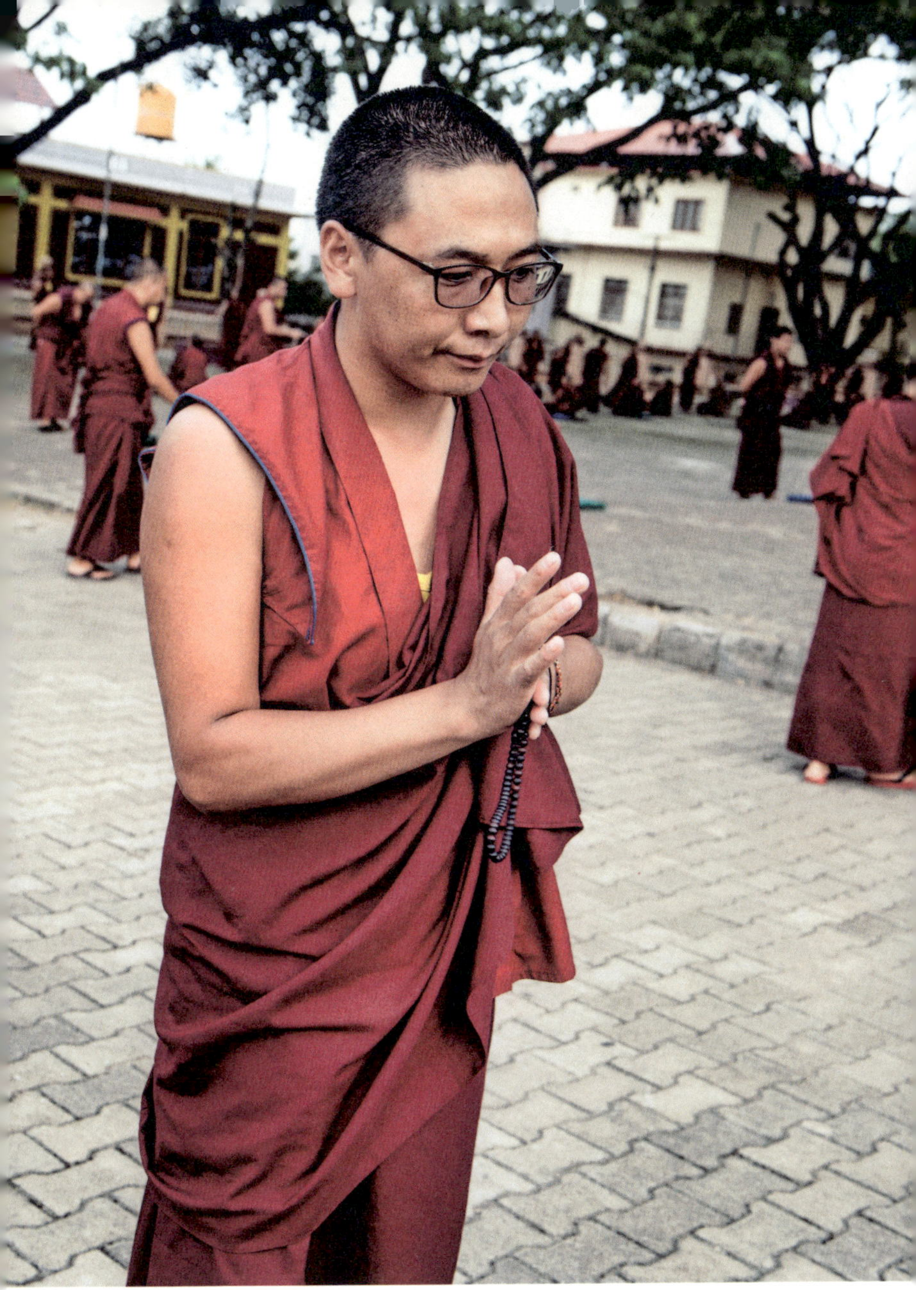

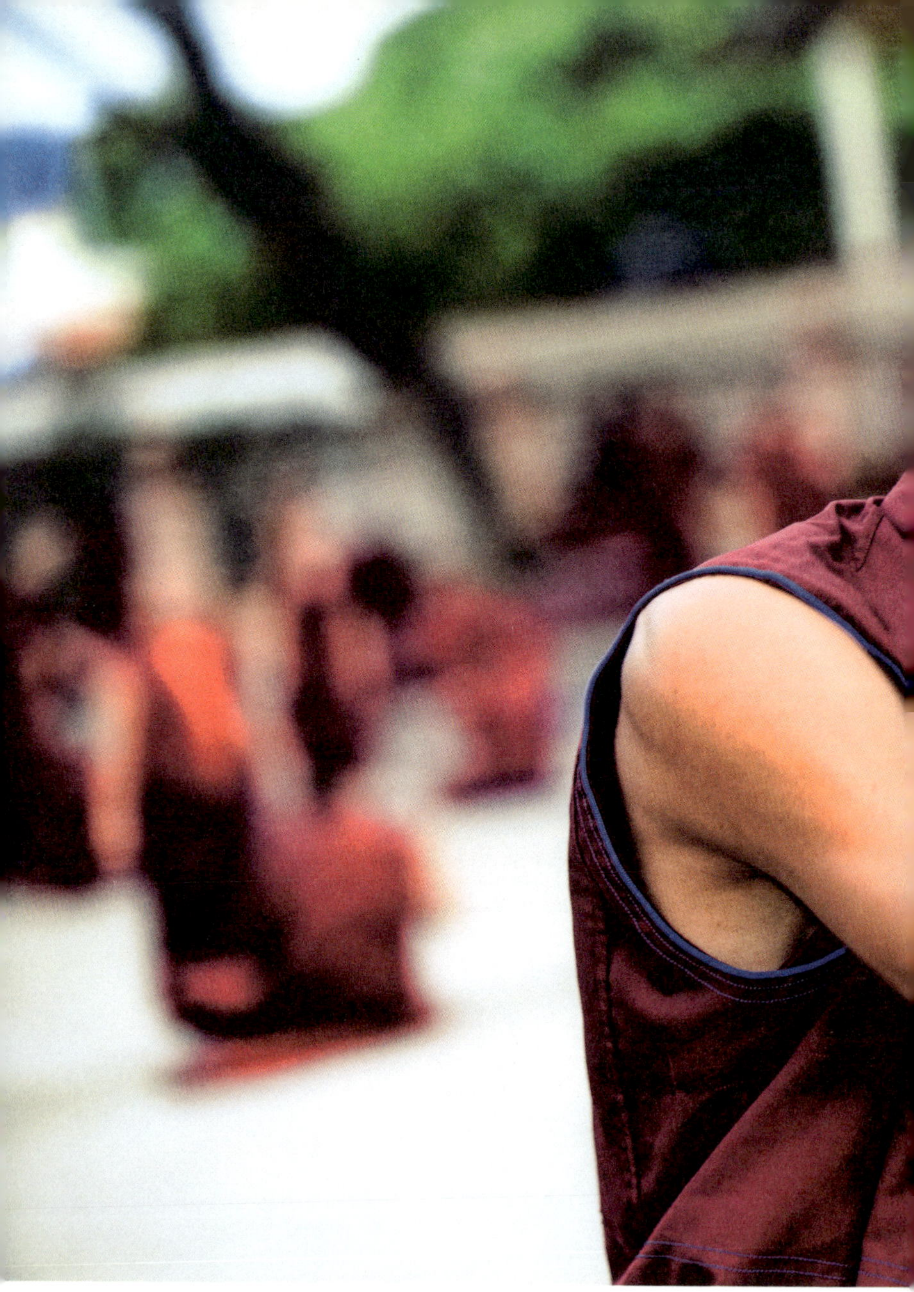

Challengers vigorously and passionately question a defender's point of view.

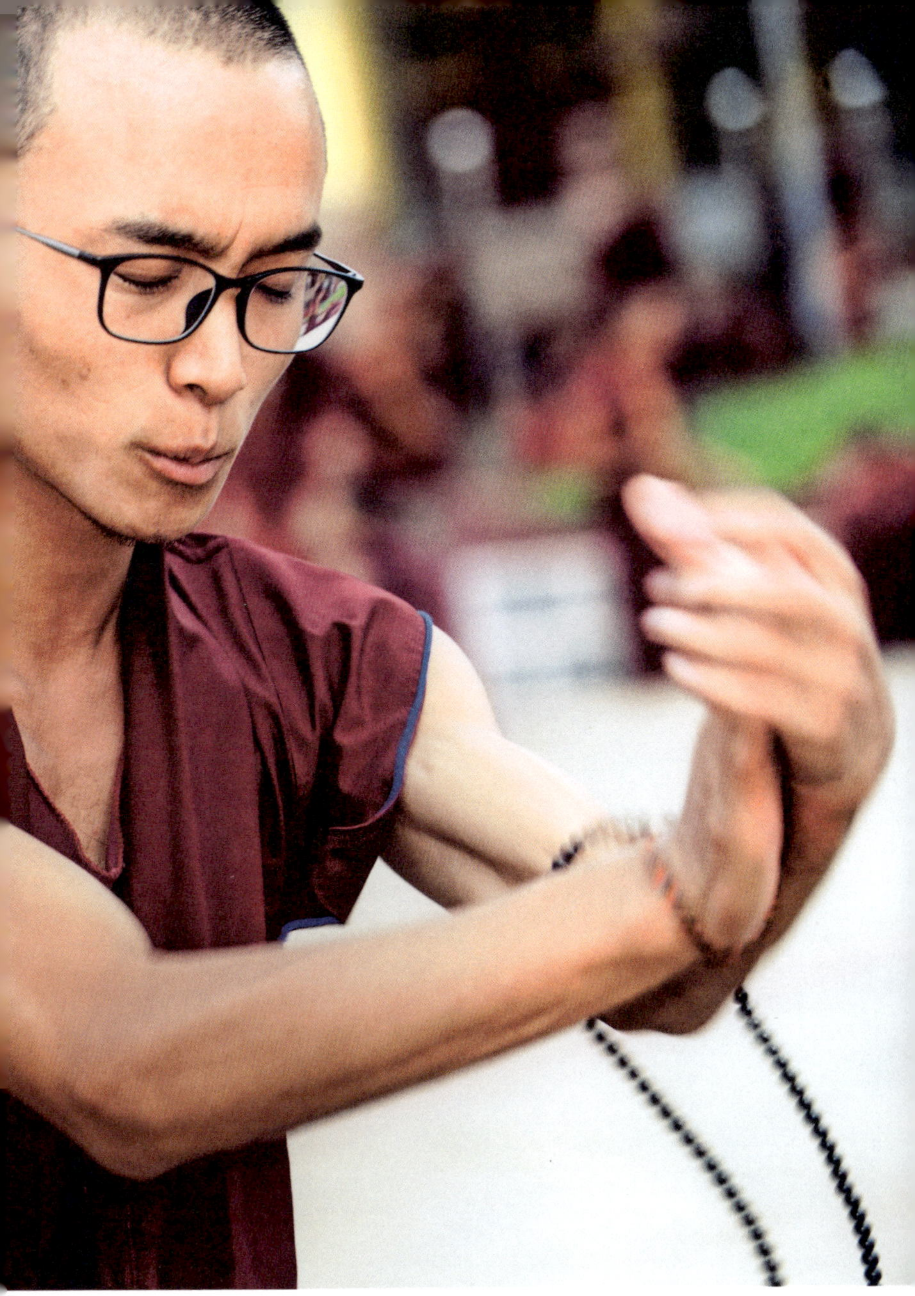

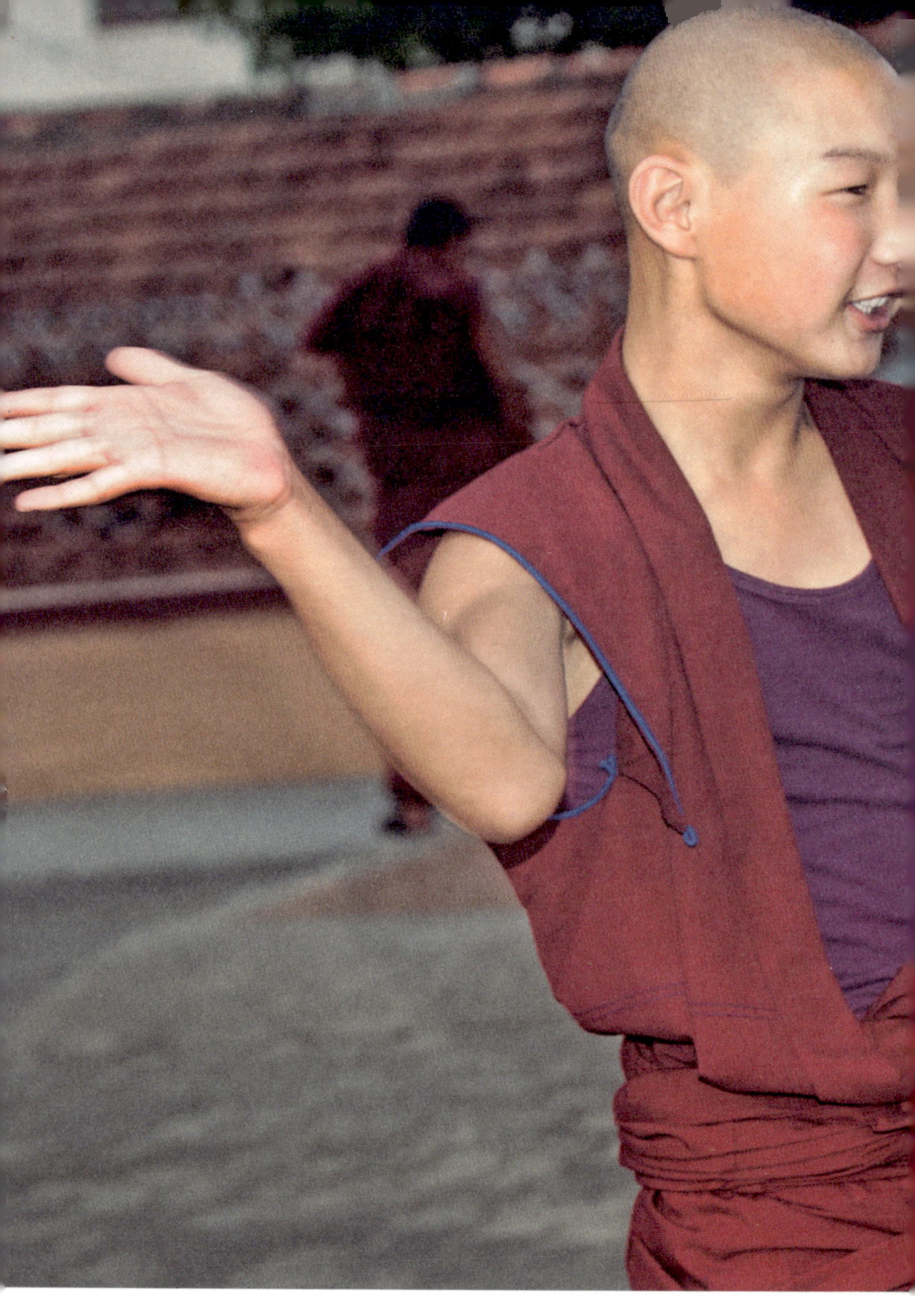

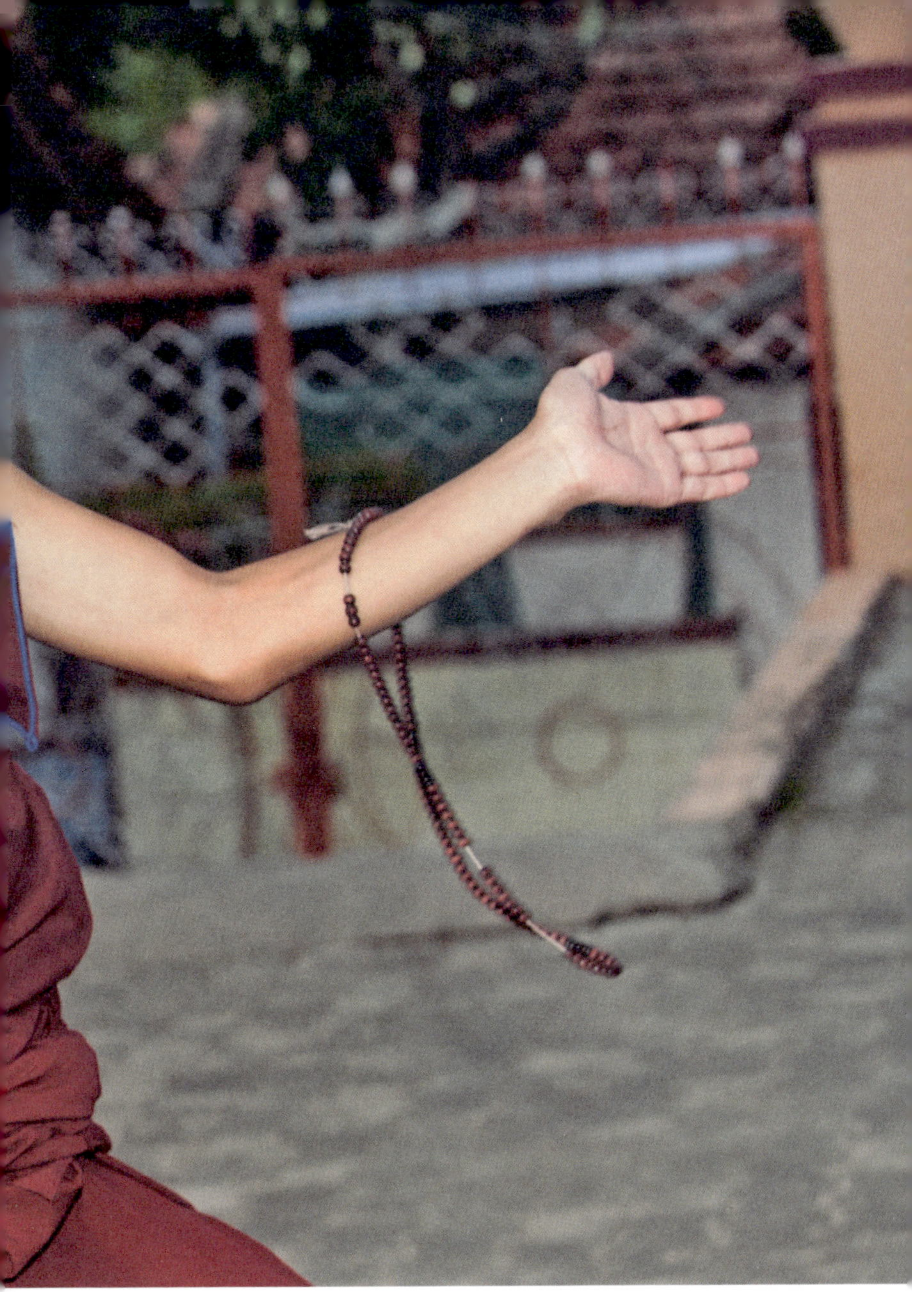

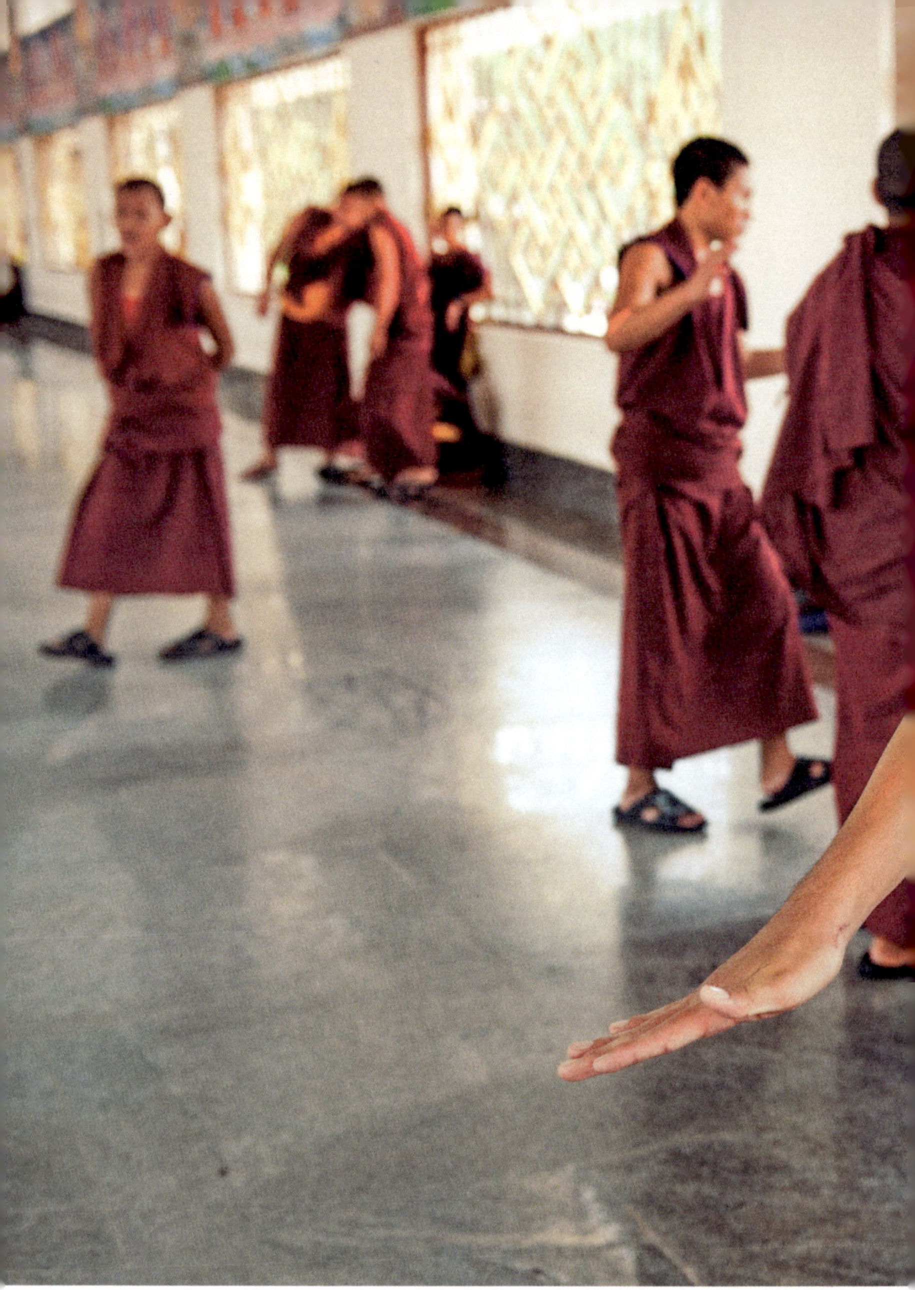

This challenger has just finished making his point with the characteristic sudden clap, after which he withdraws his hand, moving it upward along his arm, which signals the defender to respond.

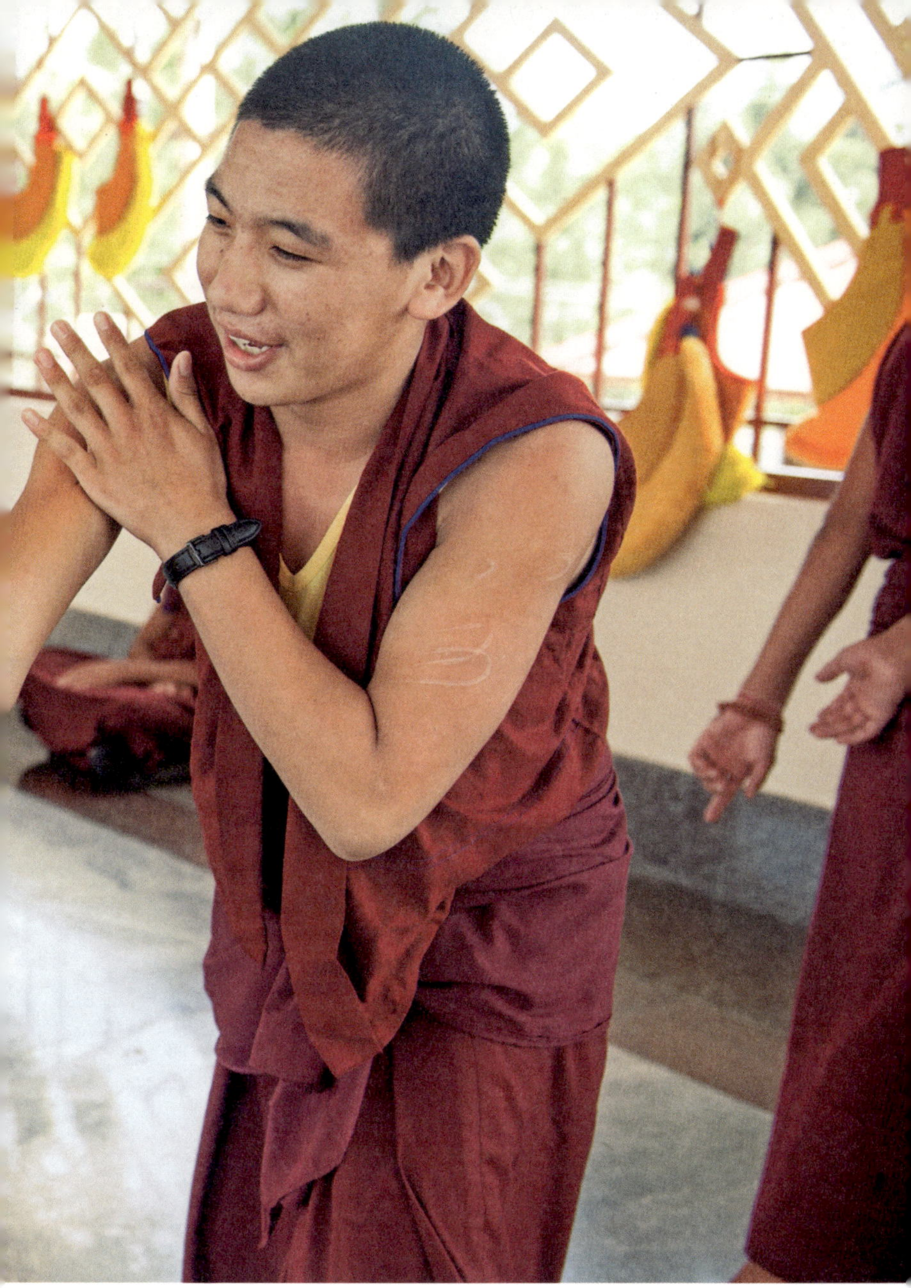

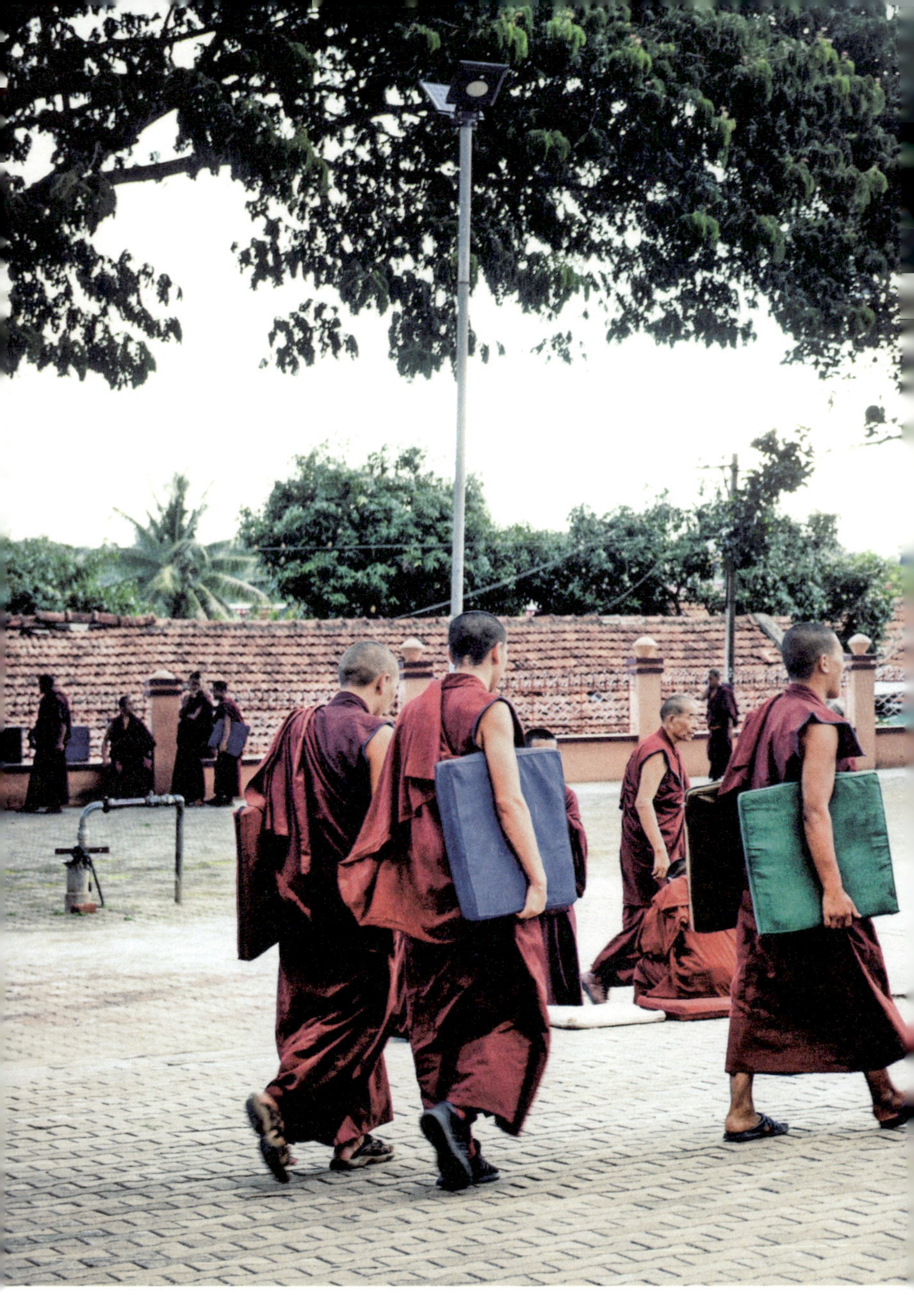

Monks carrying their sitting cushions walk through the courtyard to meet up with fellow debaters for the evening session.

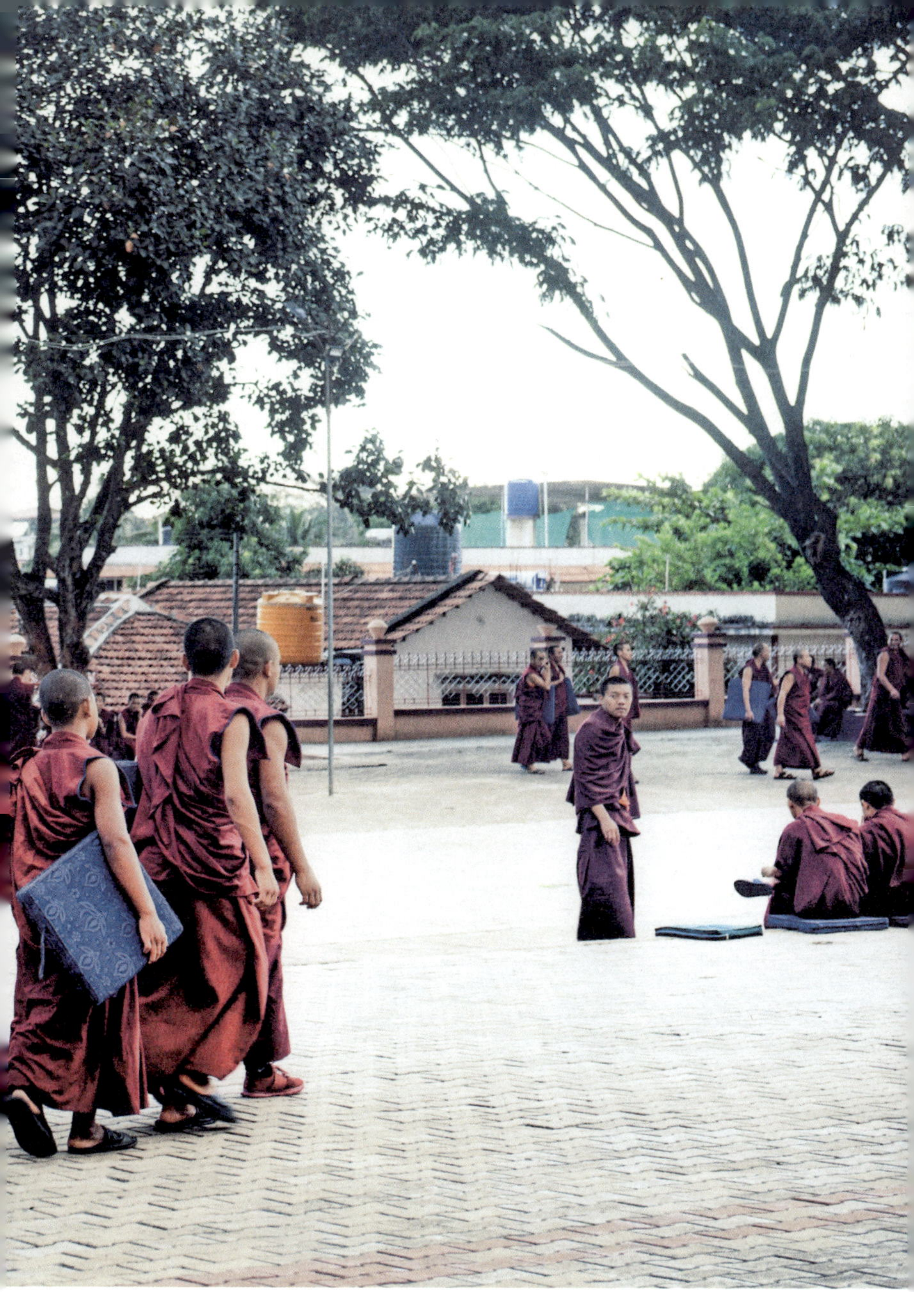

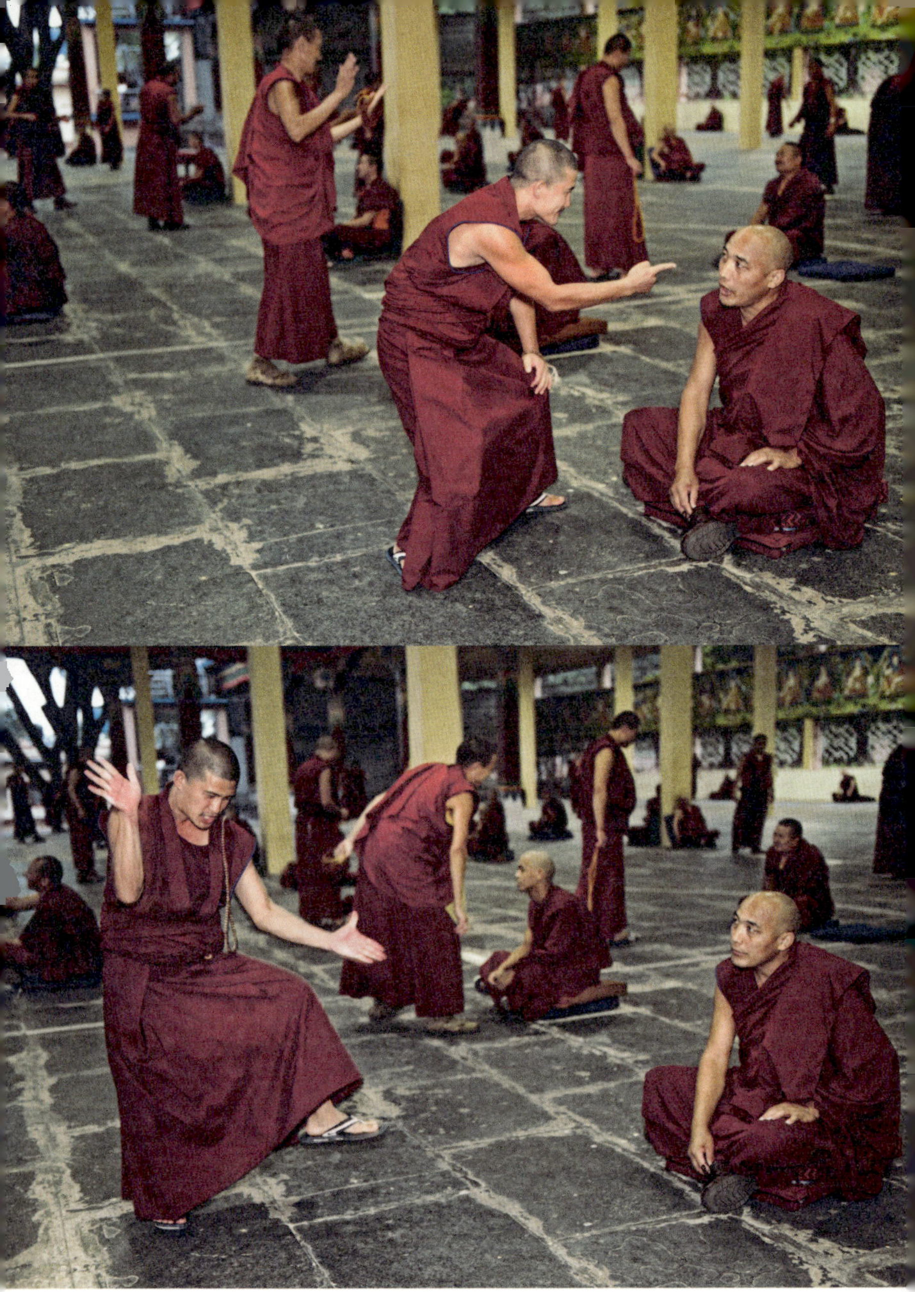

The sequence of hand movements during debate, whether one-on-one or in groups, includes a clap after the challenger's point is made, a pause while listening closely to the defender, followed by a more vehement hand clap as the challenger delves deeper into making the challenge.

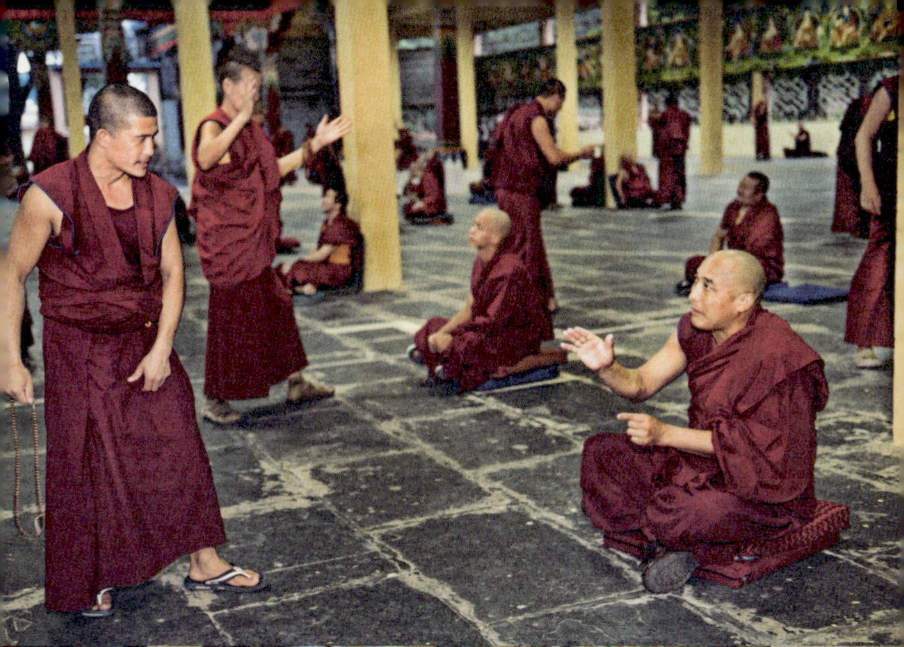

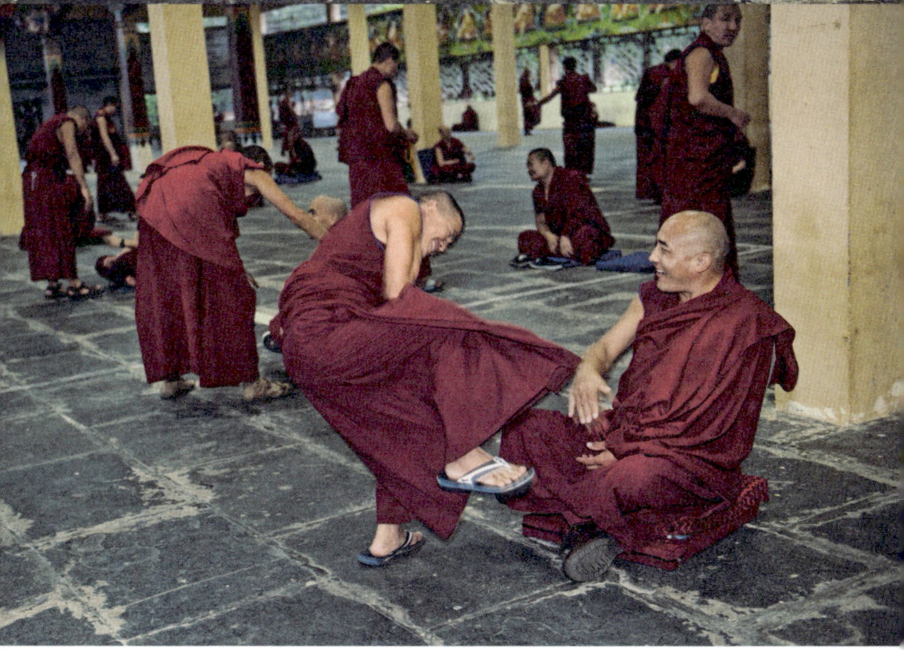

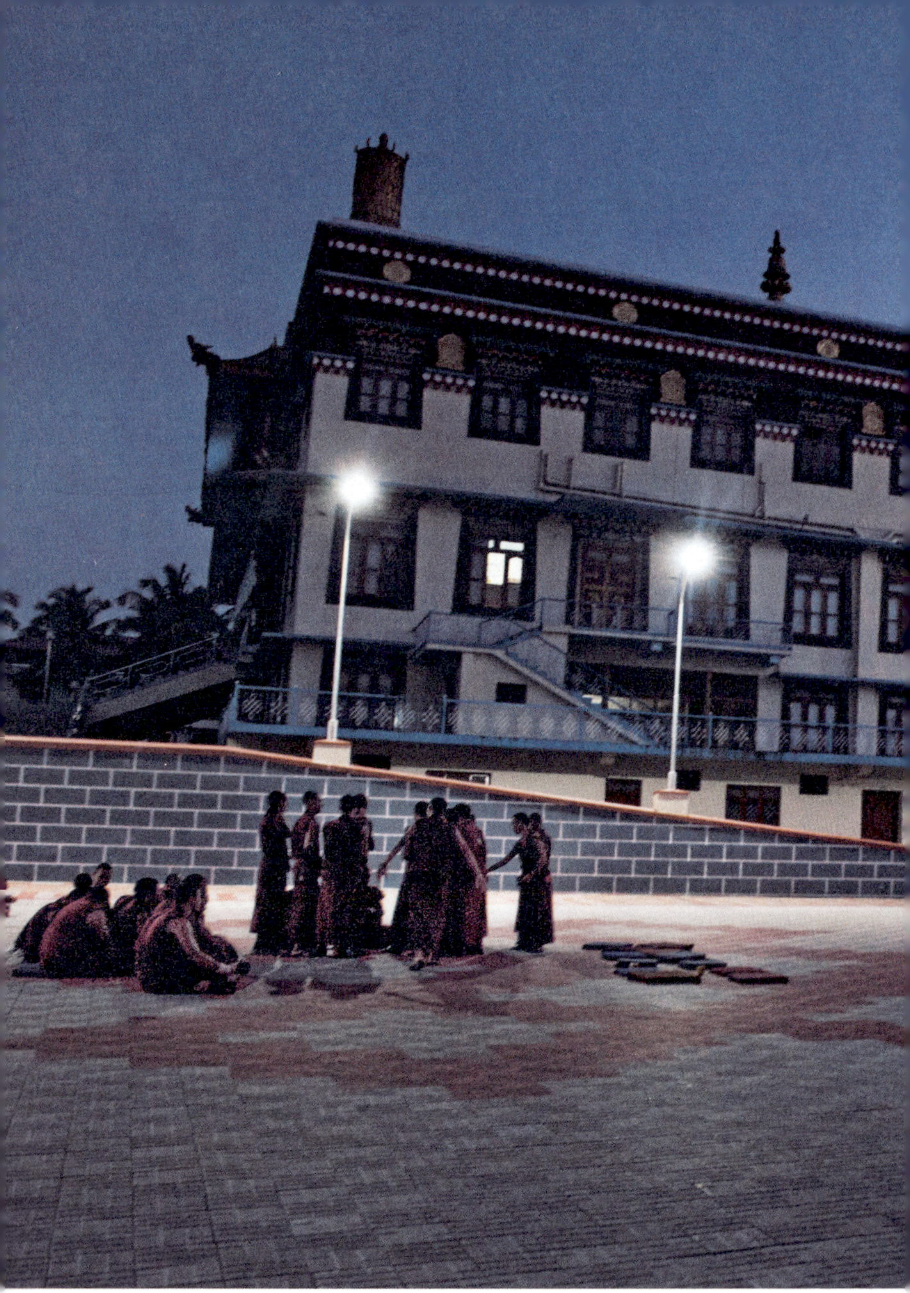

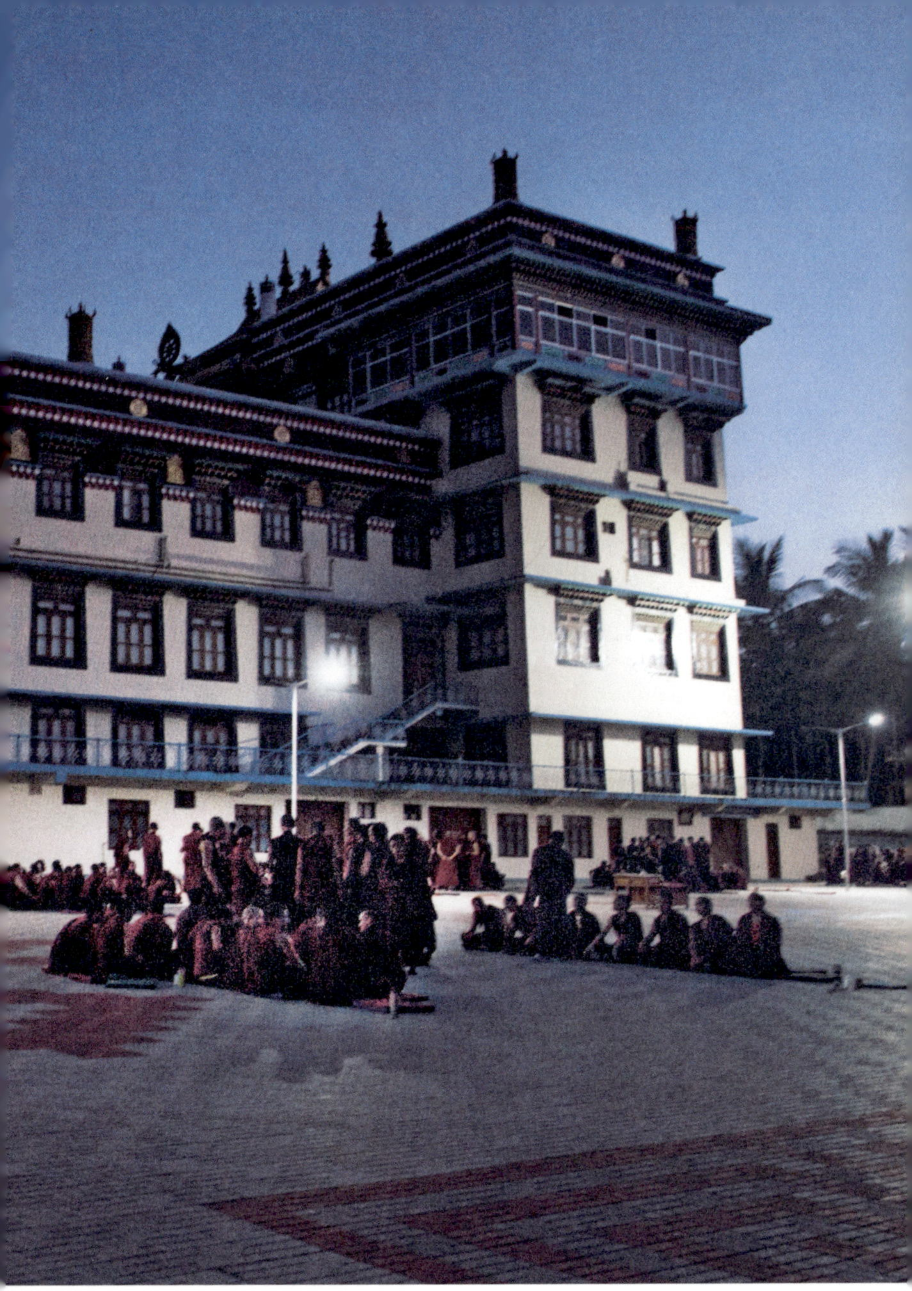

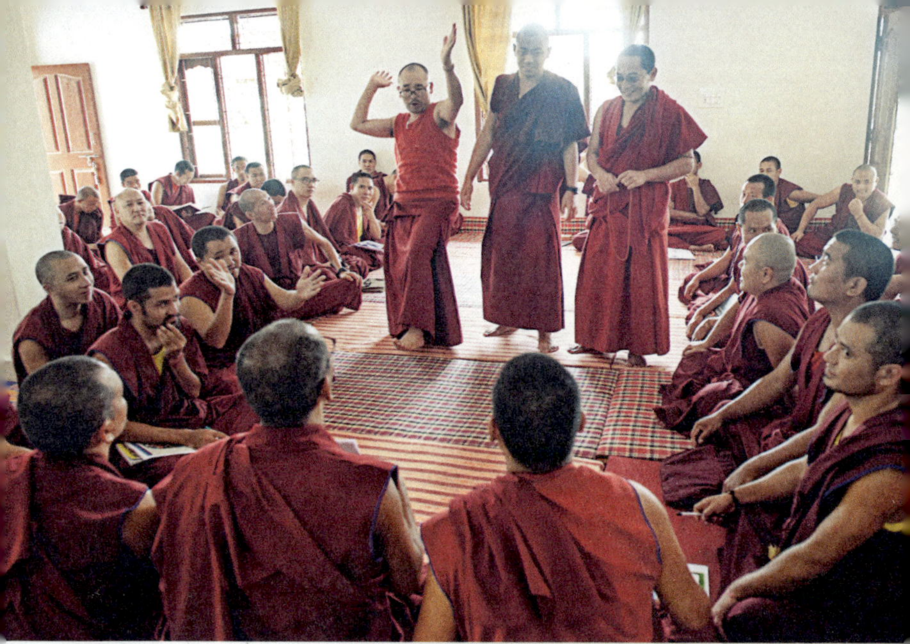

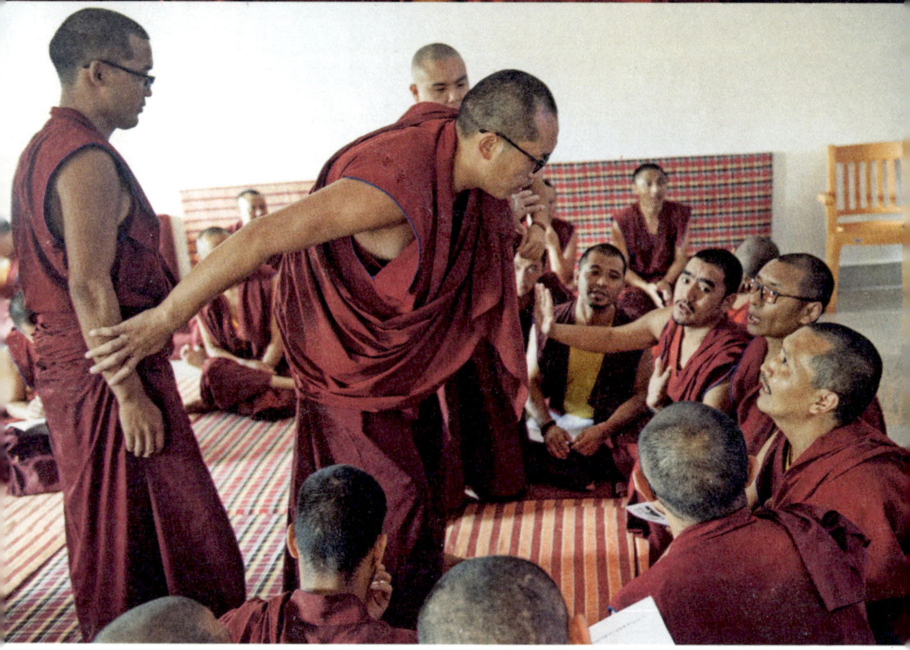

During a first-year neuroscience class, monks intensely debate scientific principles.

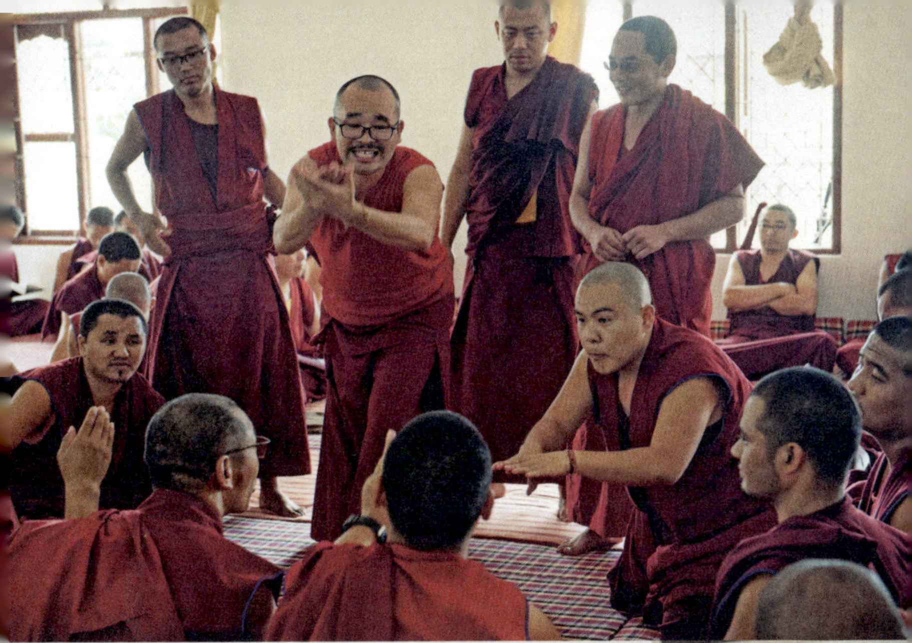

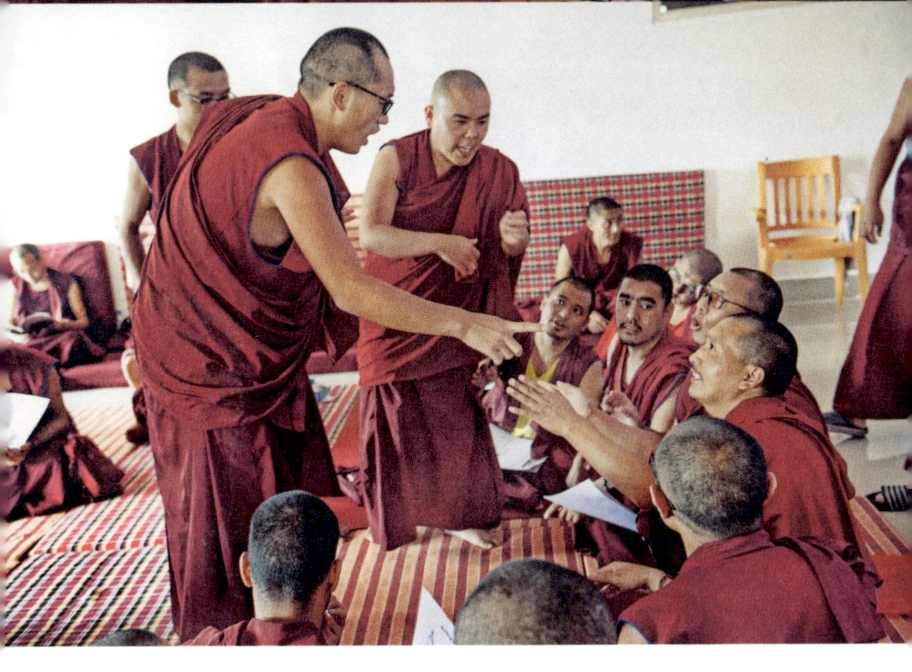

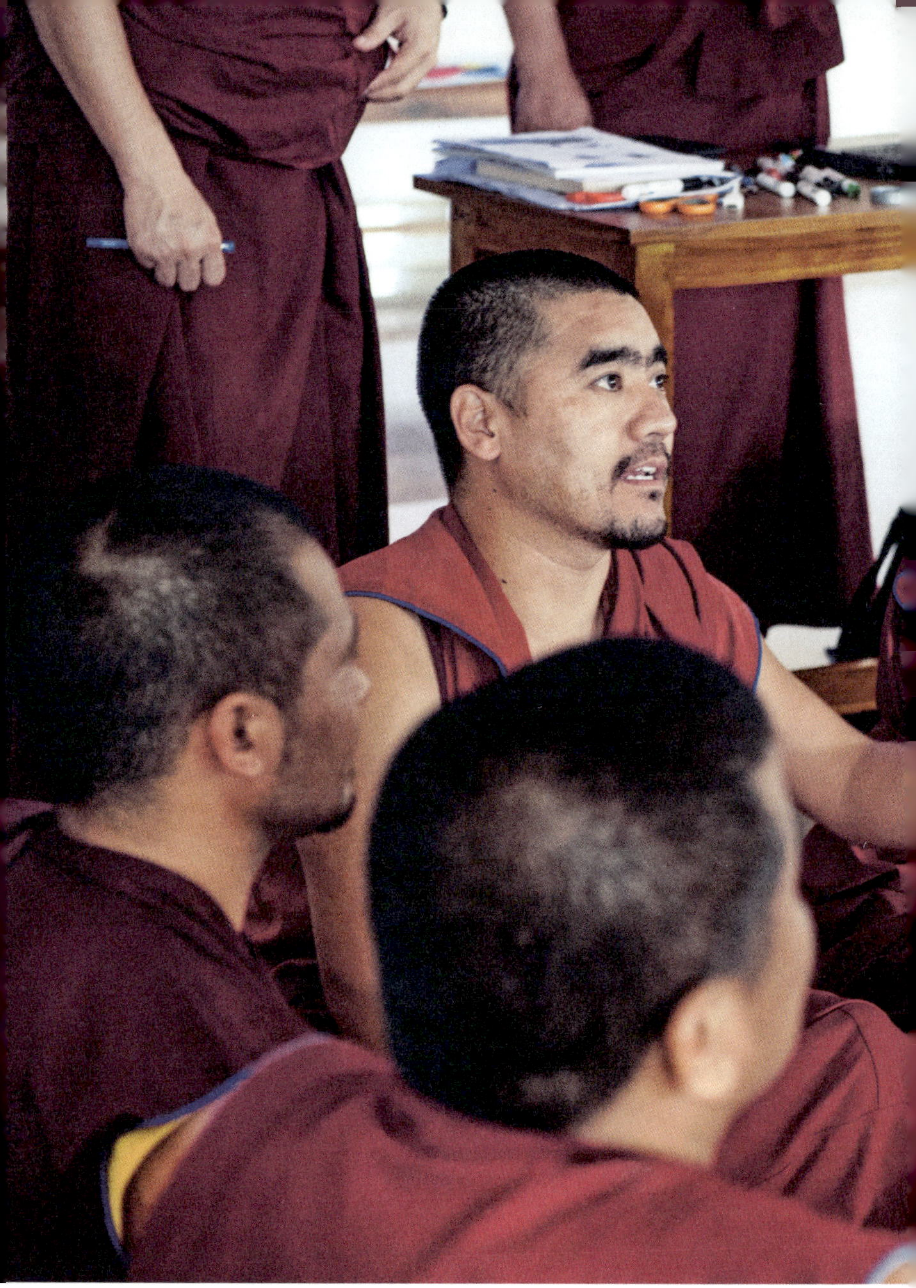

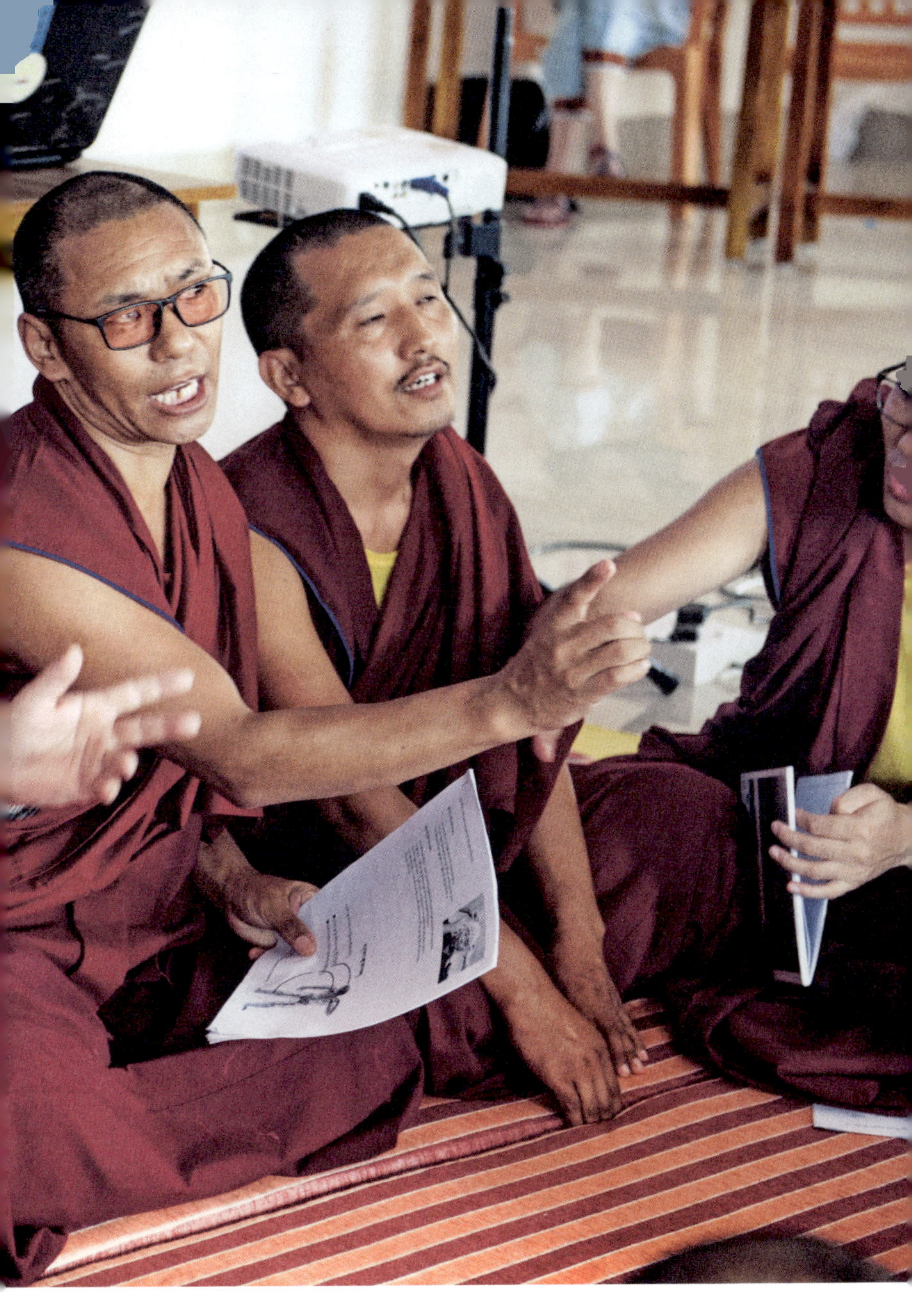

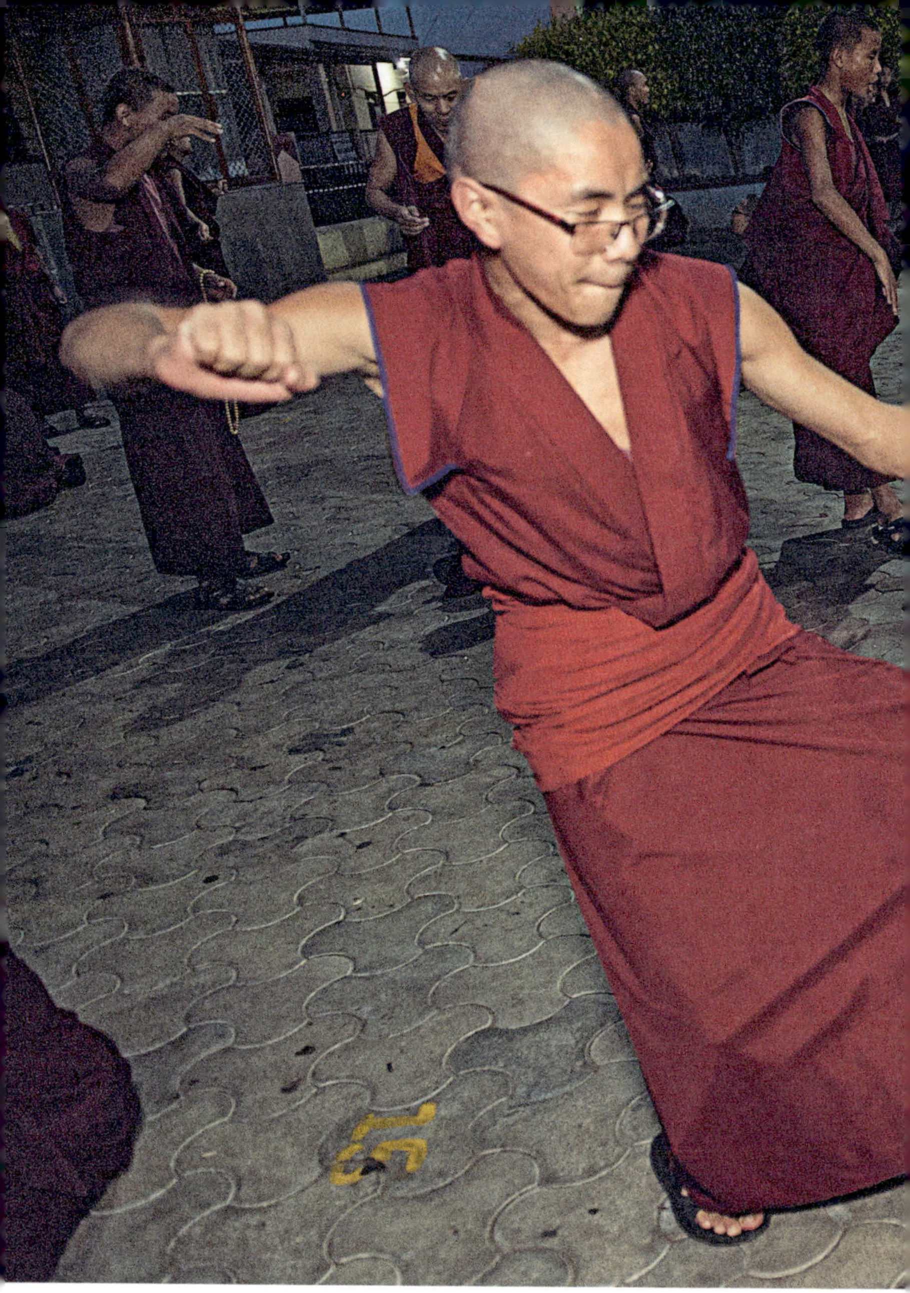

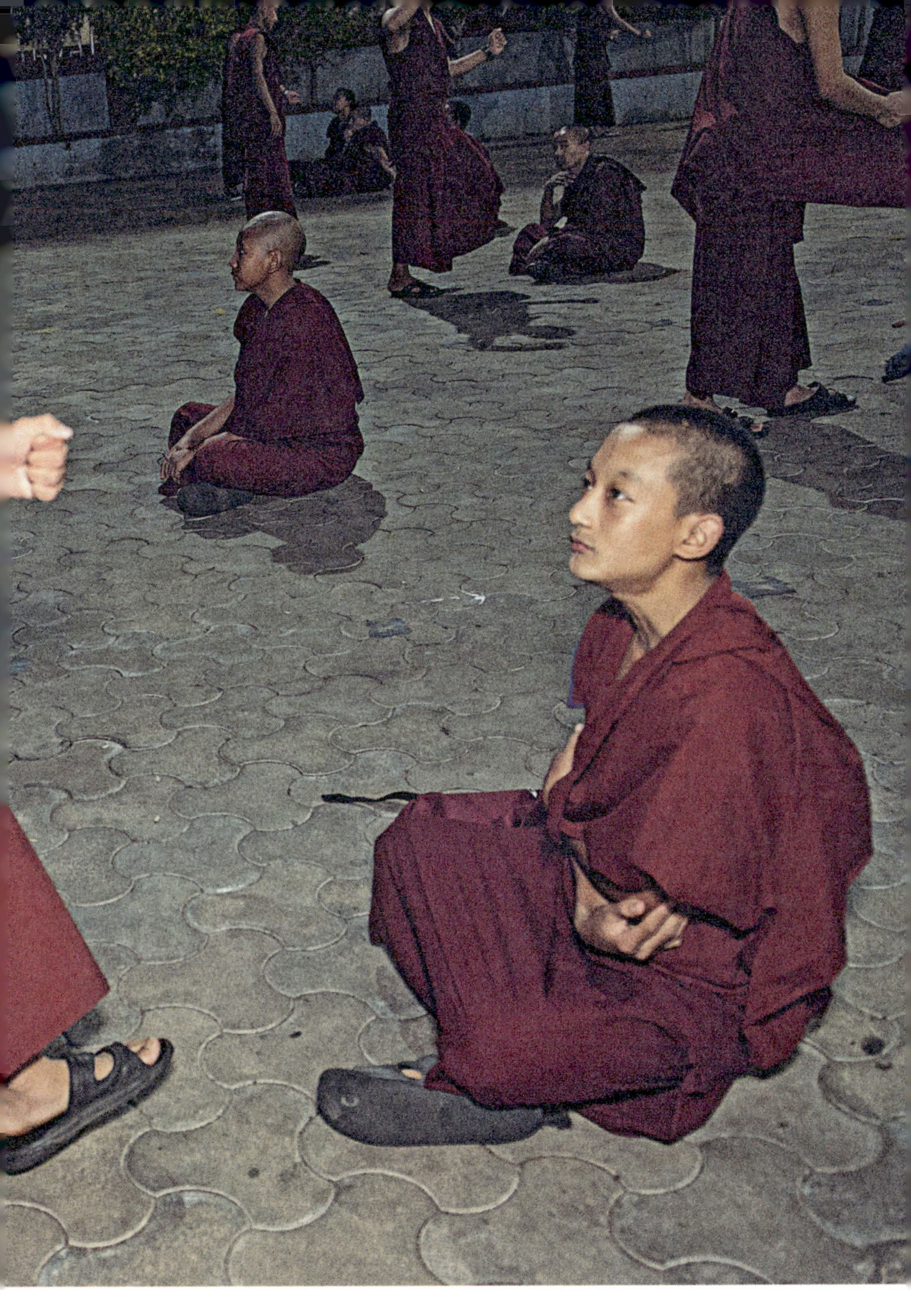

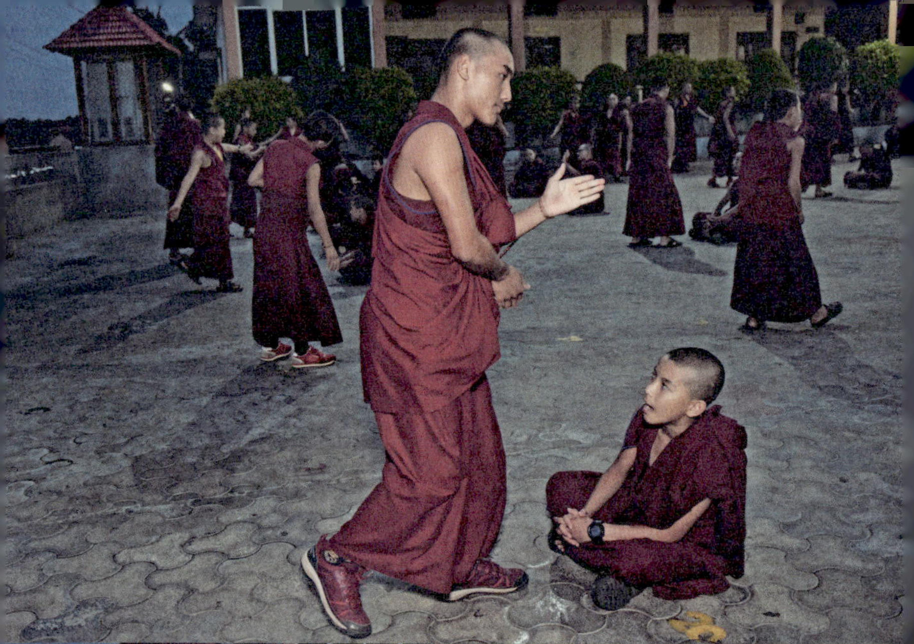

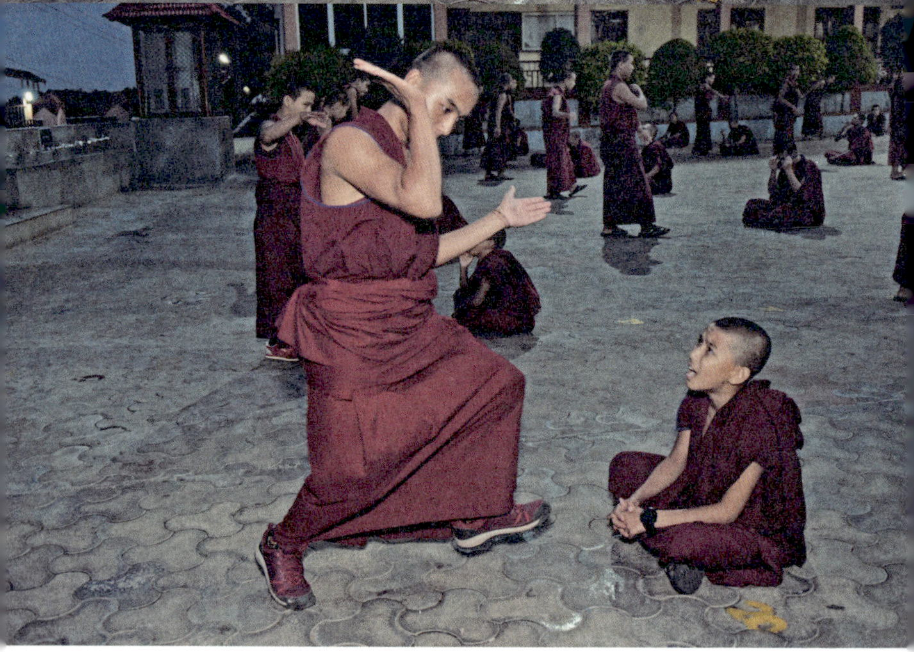

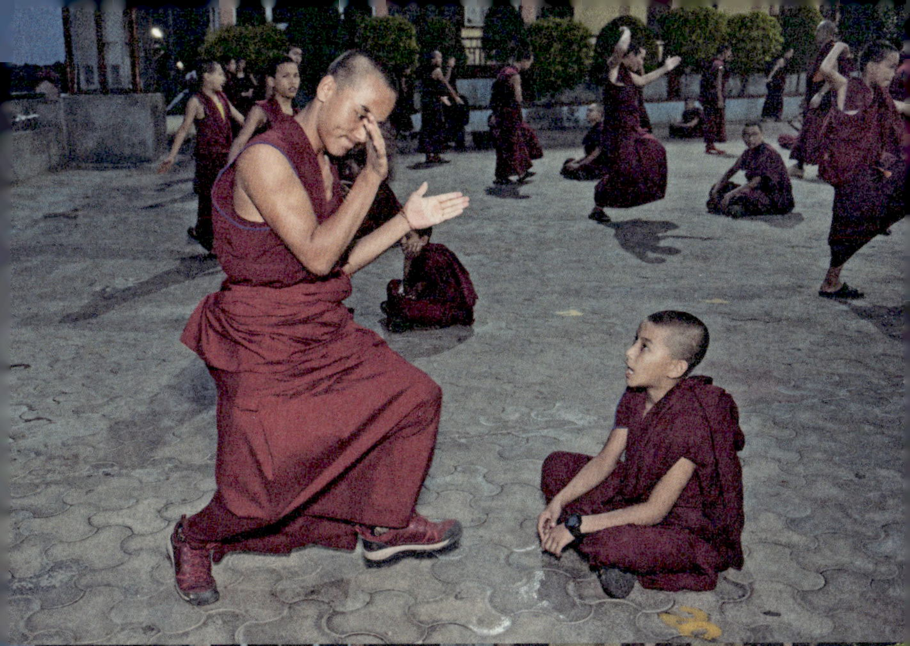

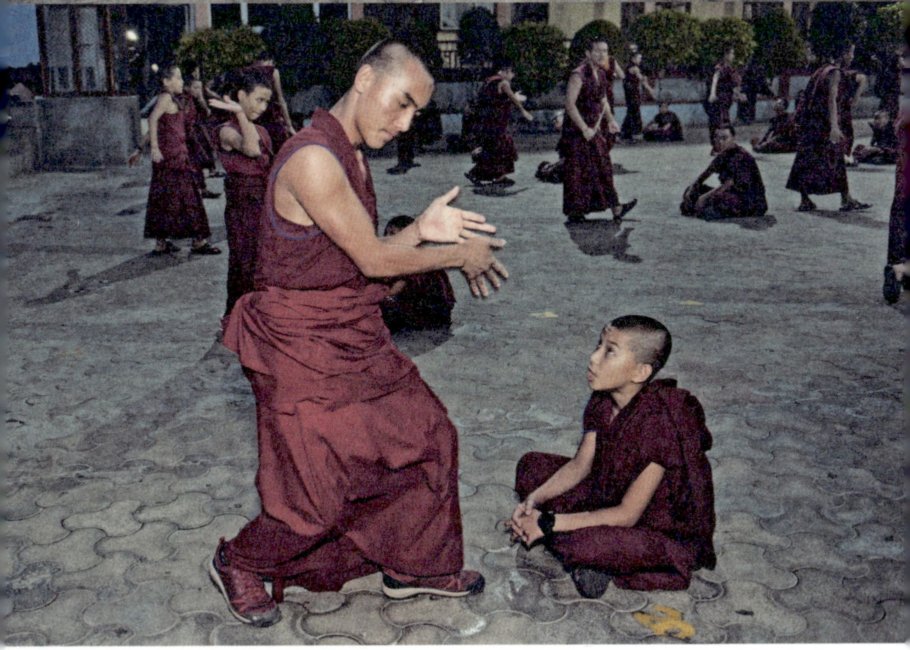

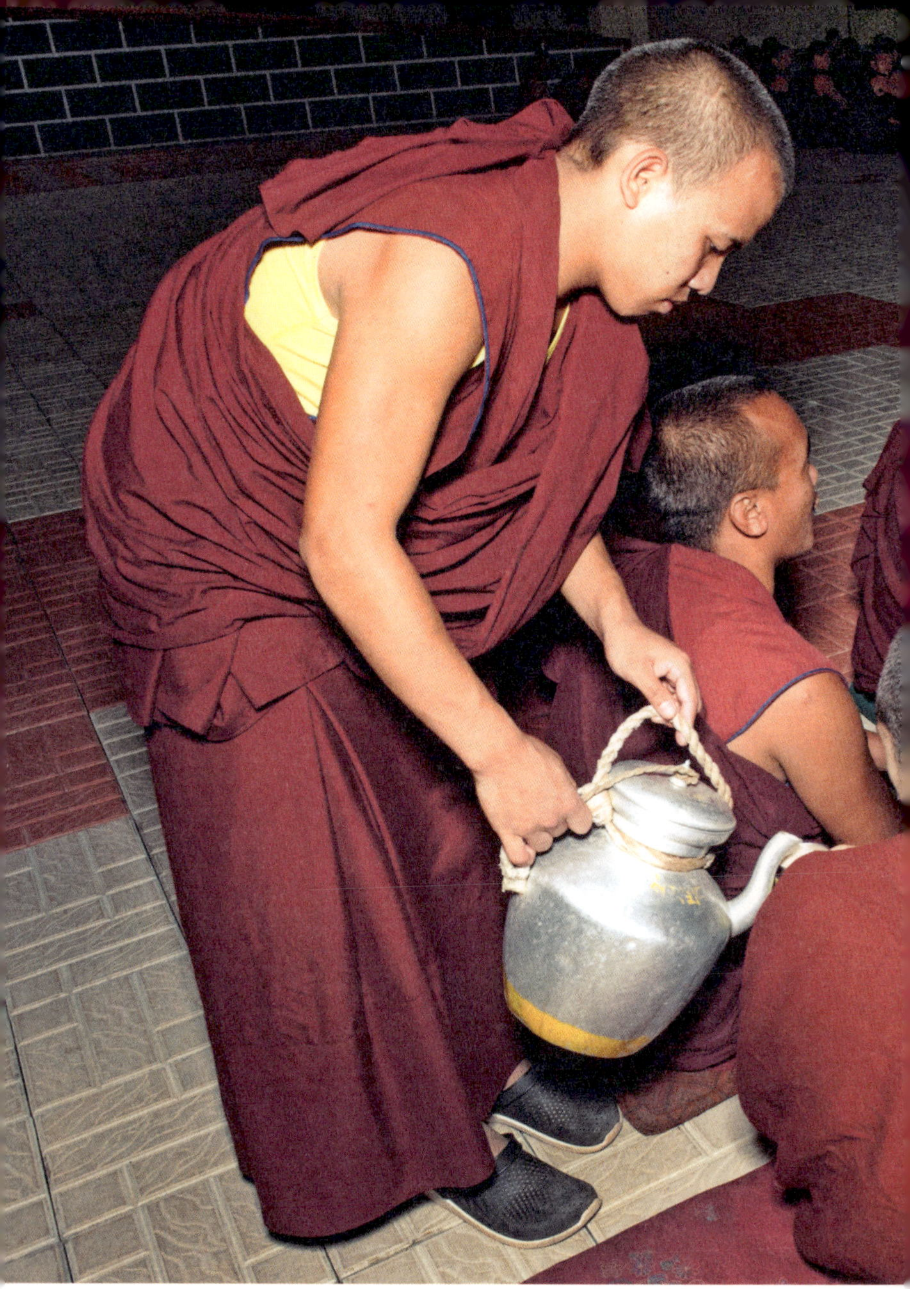

Monks and their teachers take a tea break during an evening debate in the monastery courtyard.

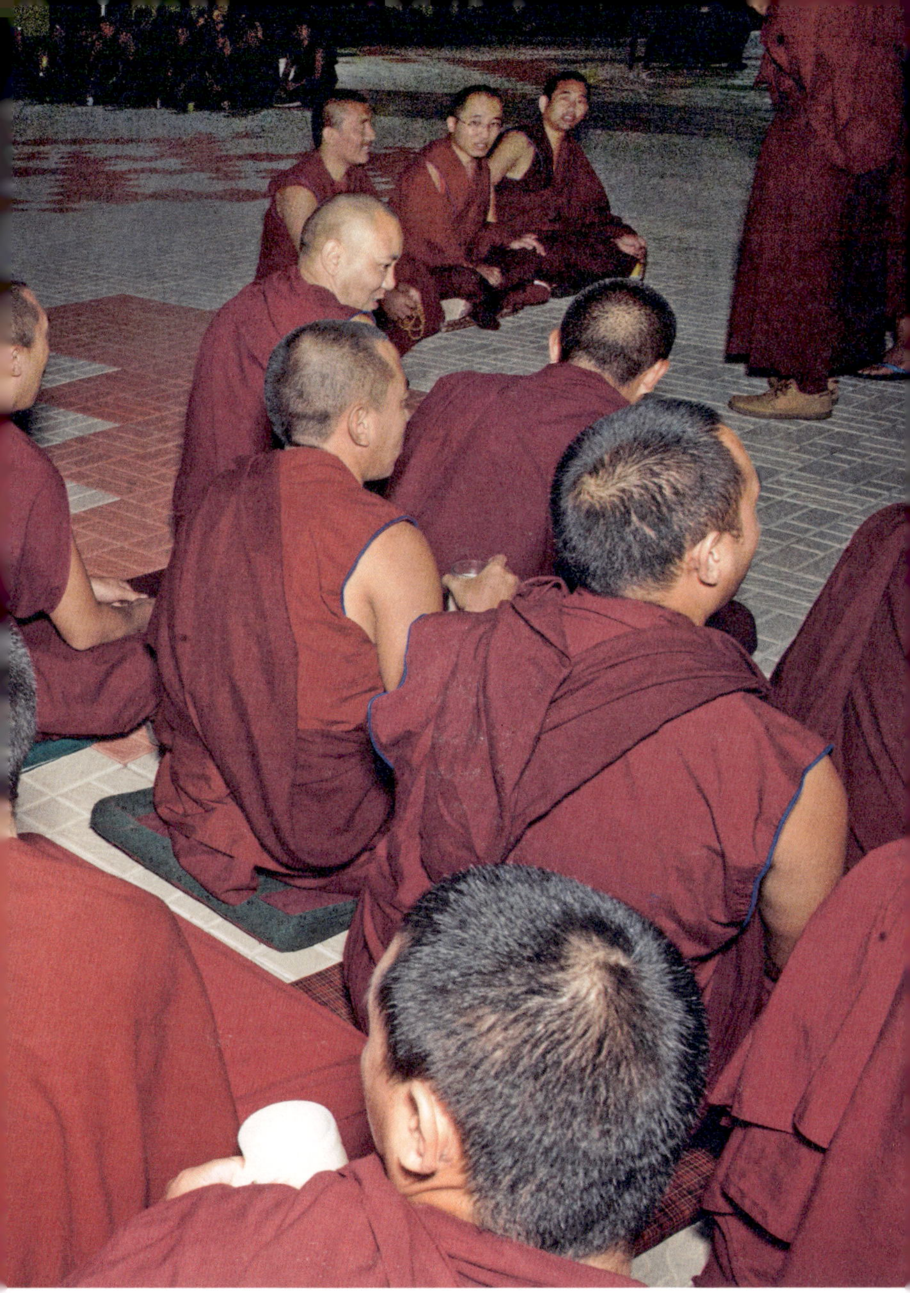

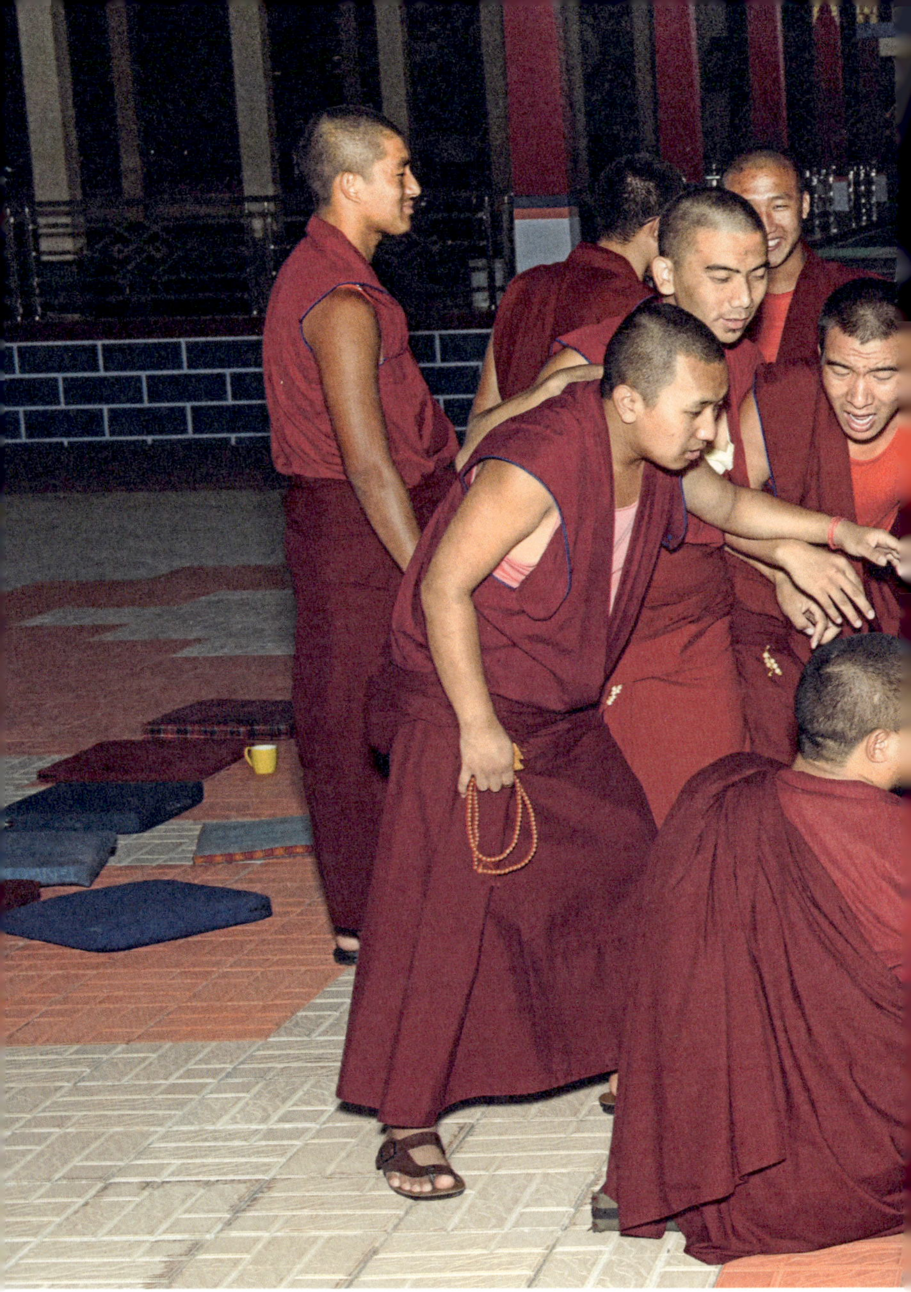

Emotions during a debate run the gamut from sedate to boisterous and heated, at times changing moment by moment as an argument unfolds.

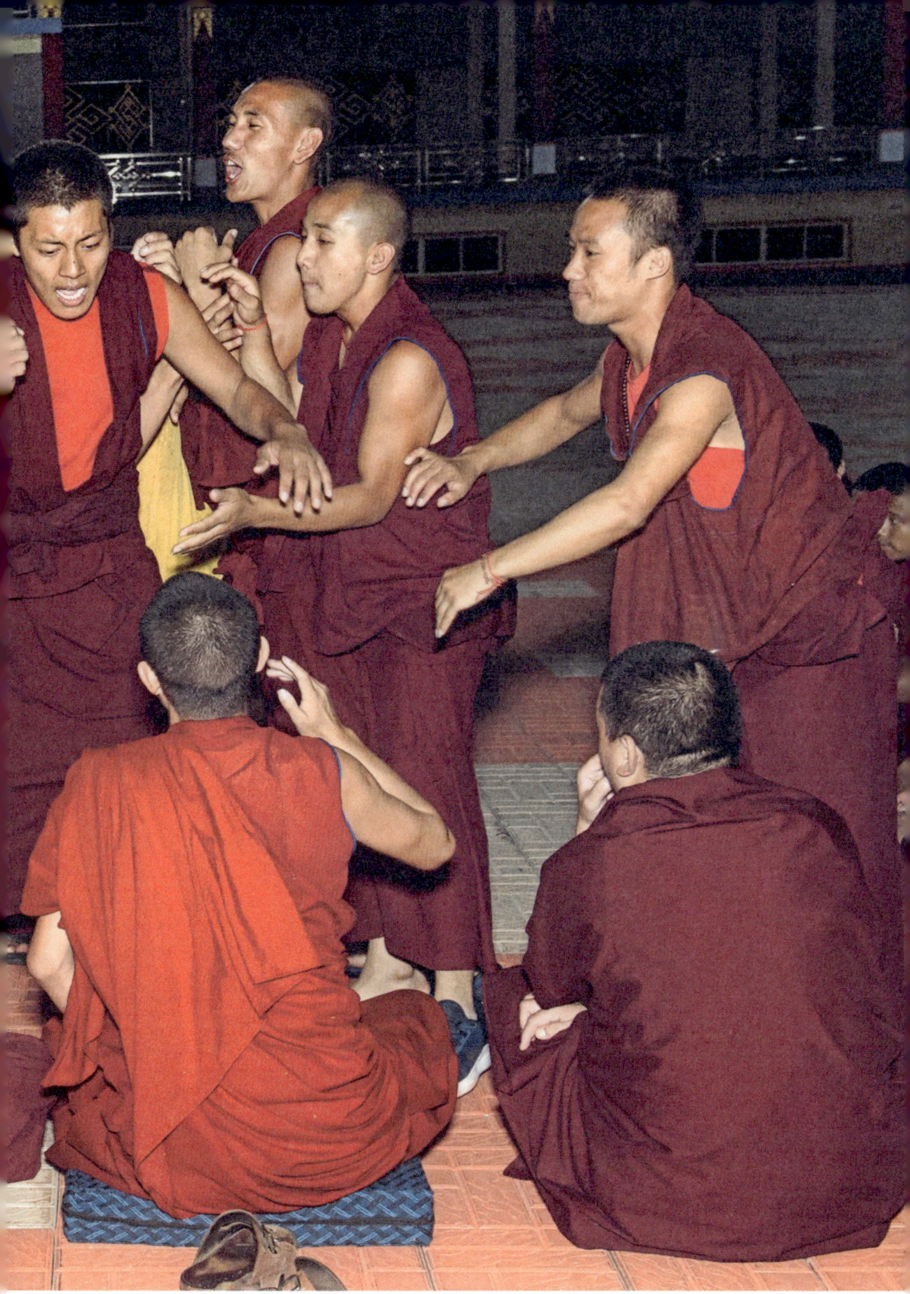

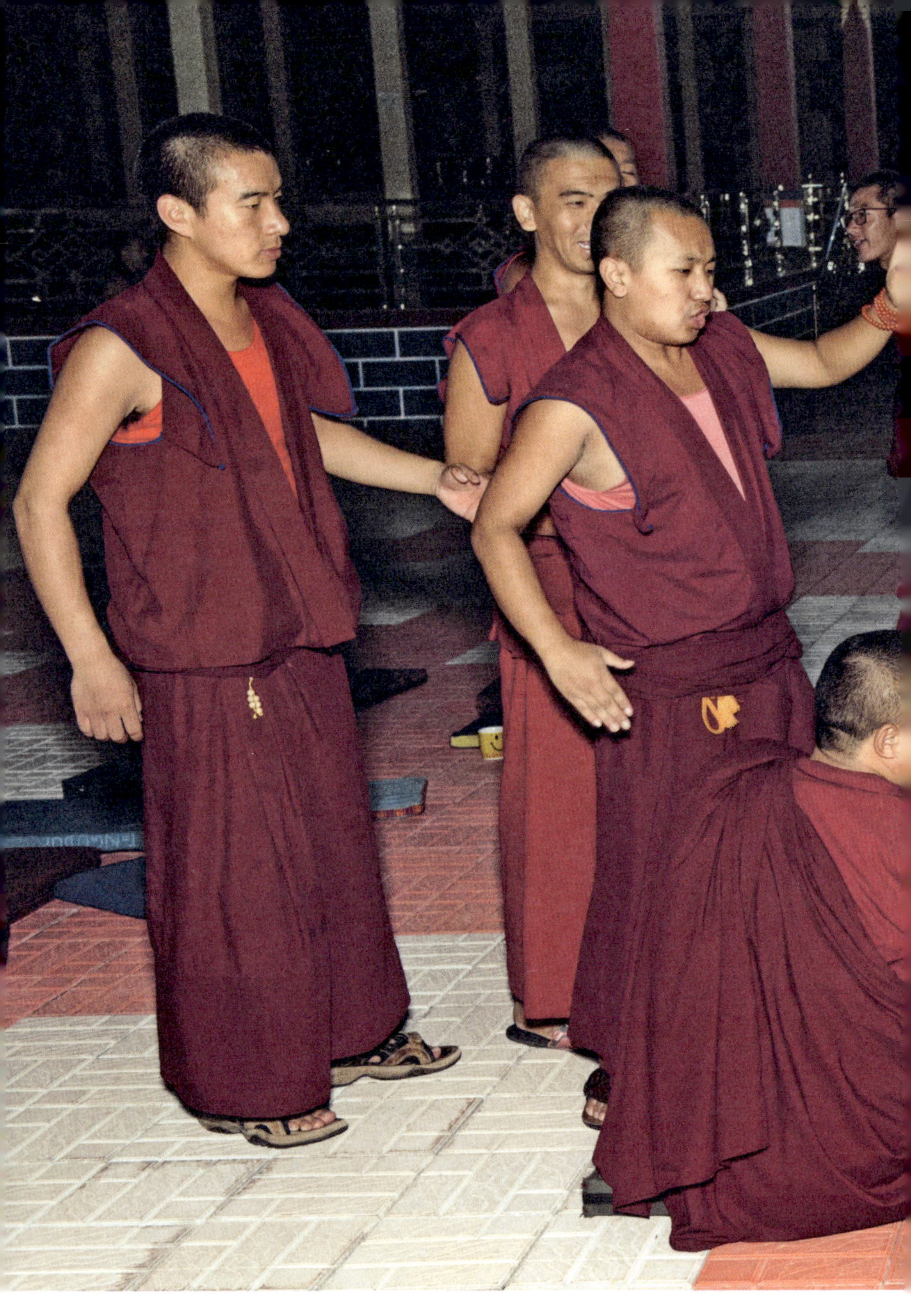

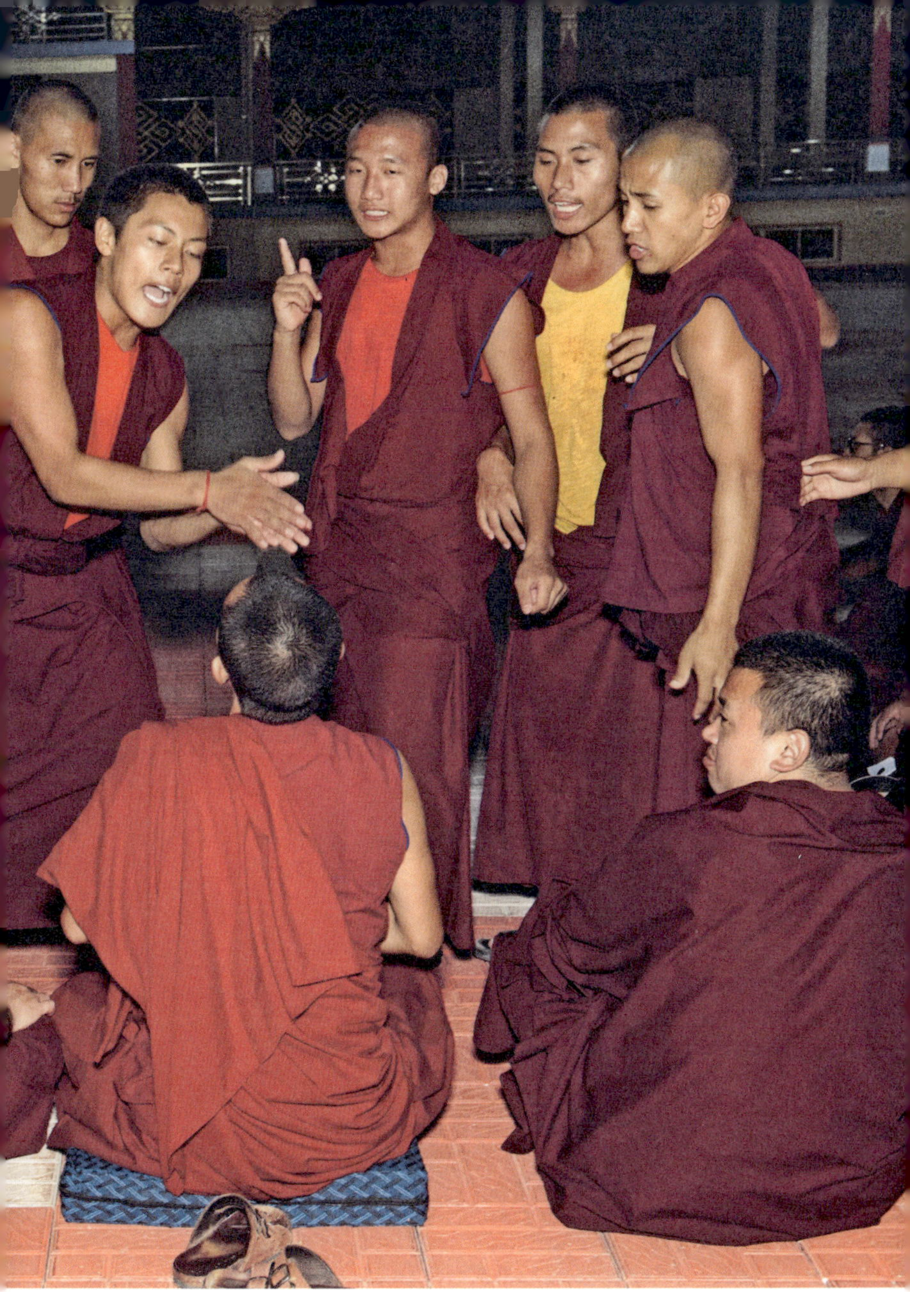

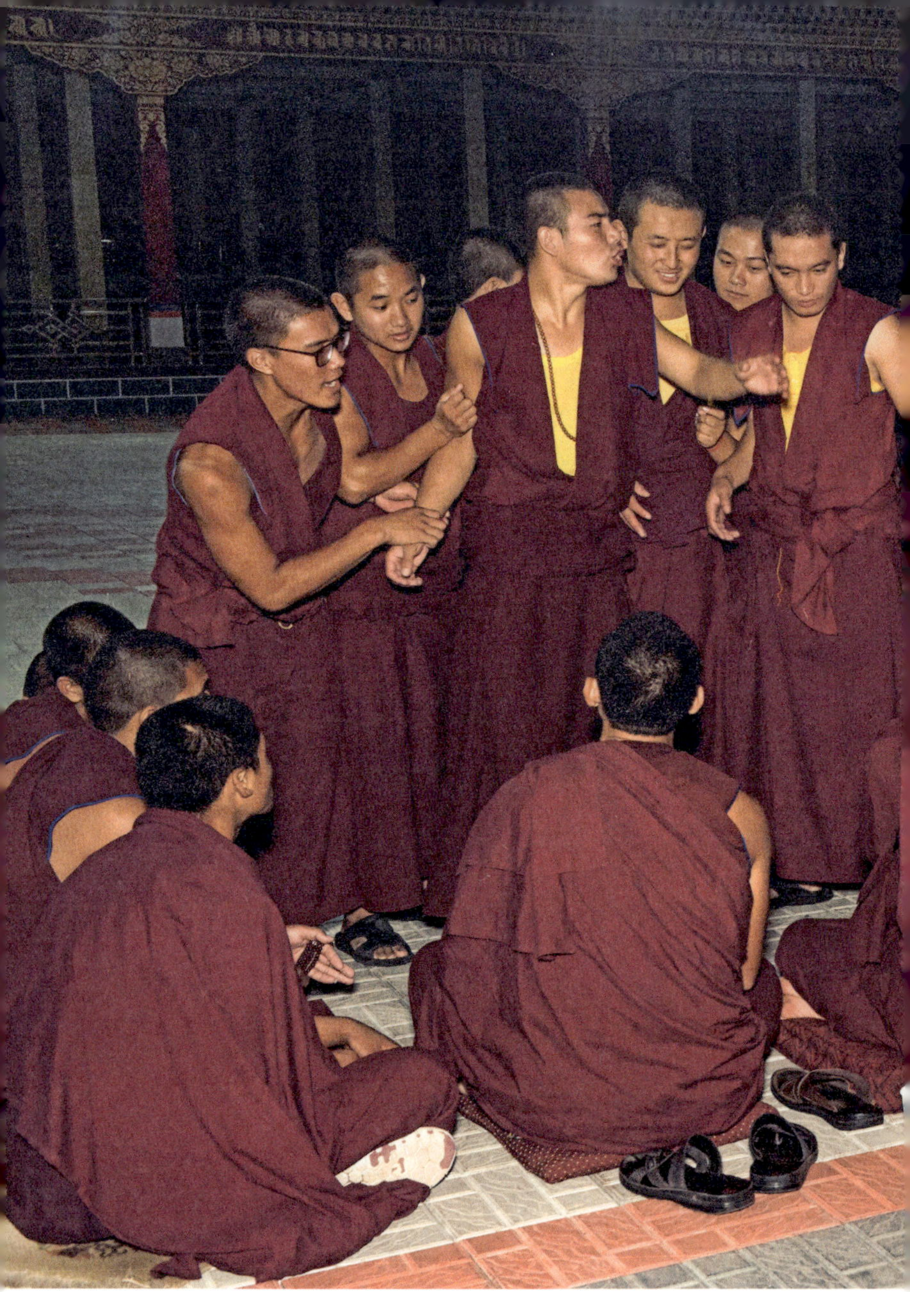

A senior monk, at far right, observes and listens as the standing group of challengers excitedly question the seated defenders.

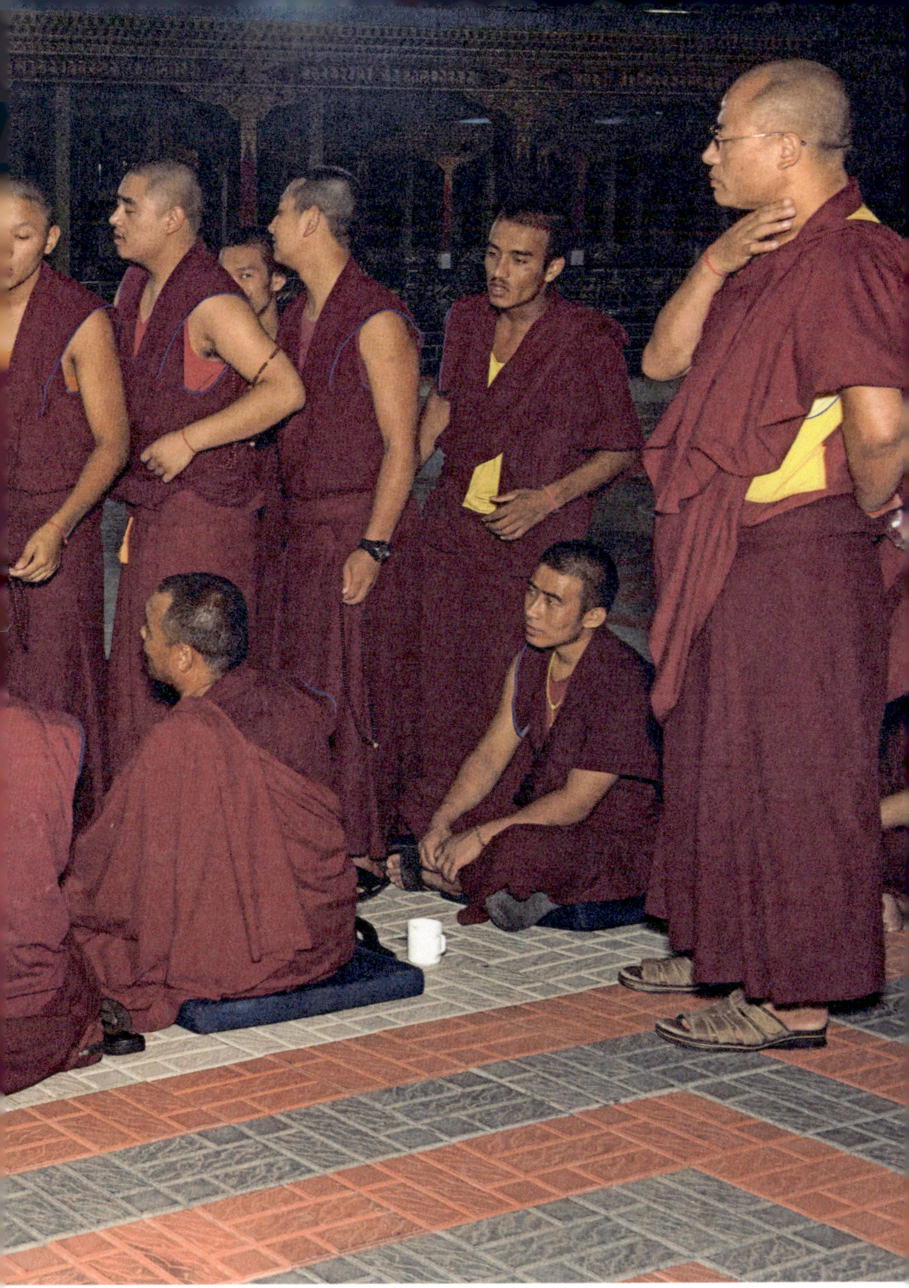

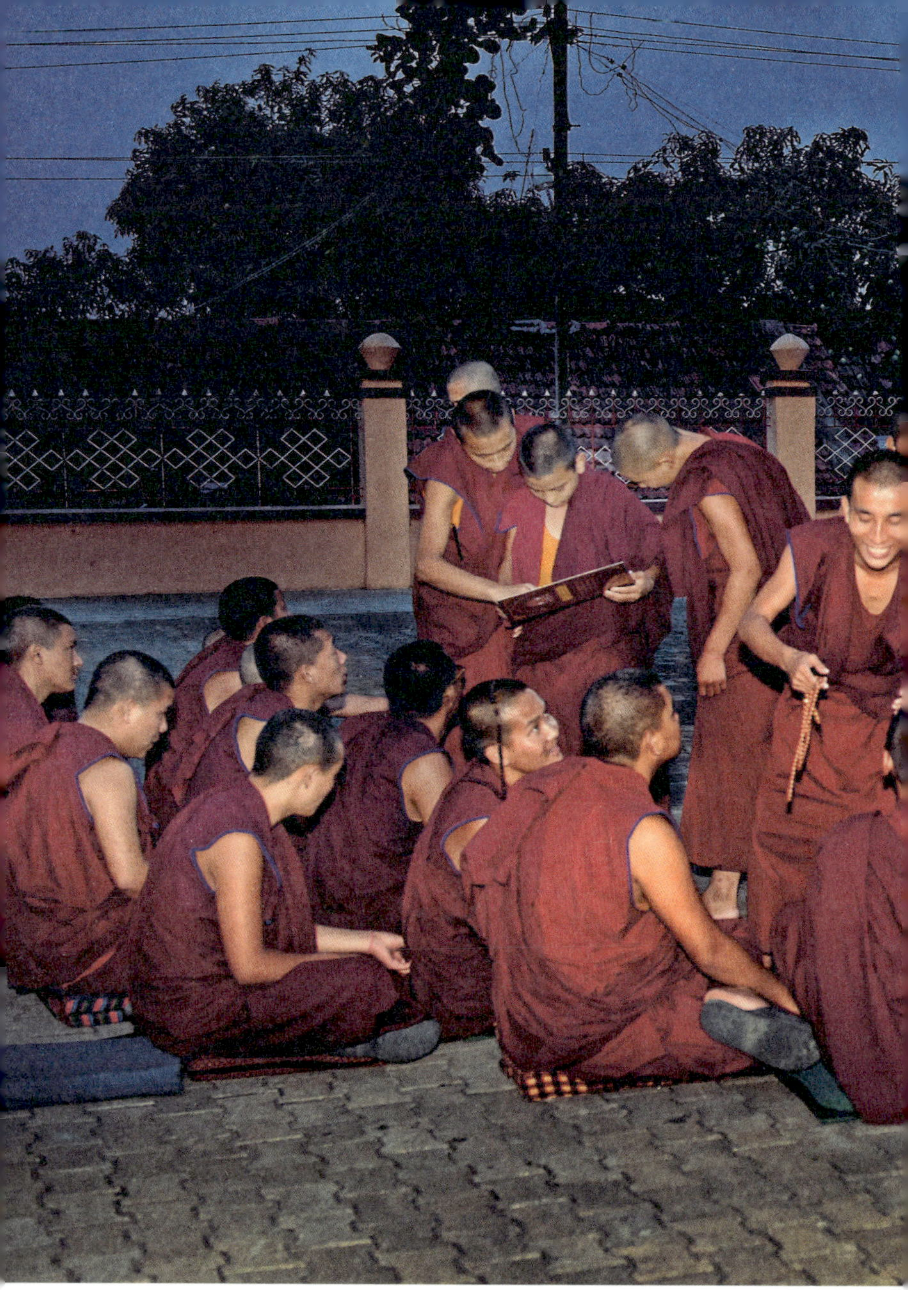

The courtyard transforms into an enchanted stage as challengers and defenders debate one another against the backdrop of the darkening sky and the silhouettes of Tibetan Buddhist temples.

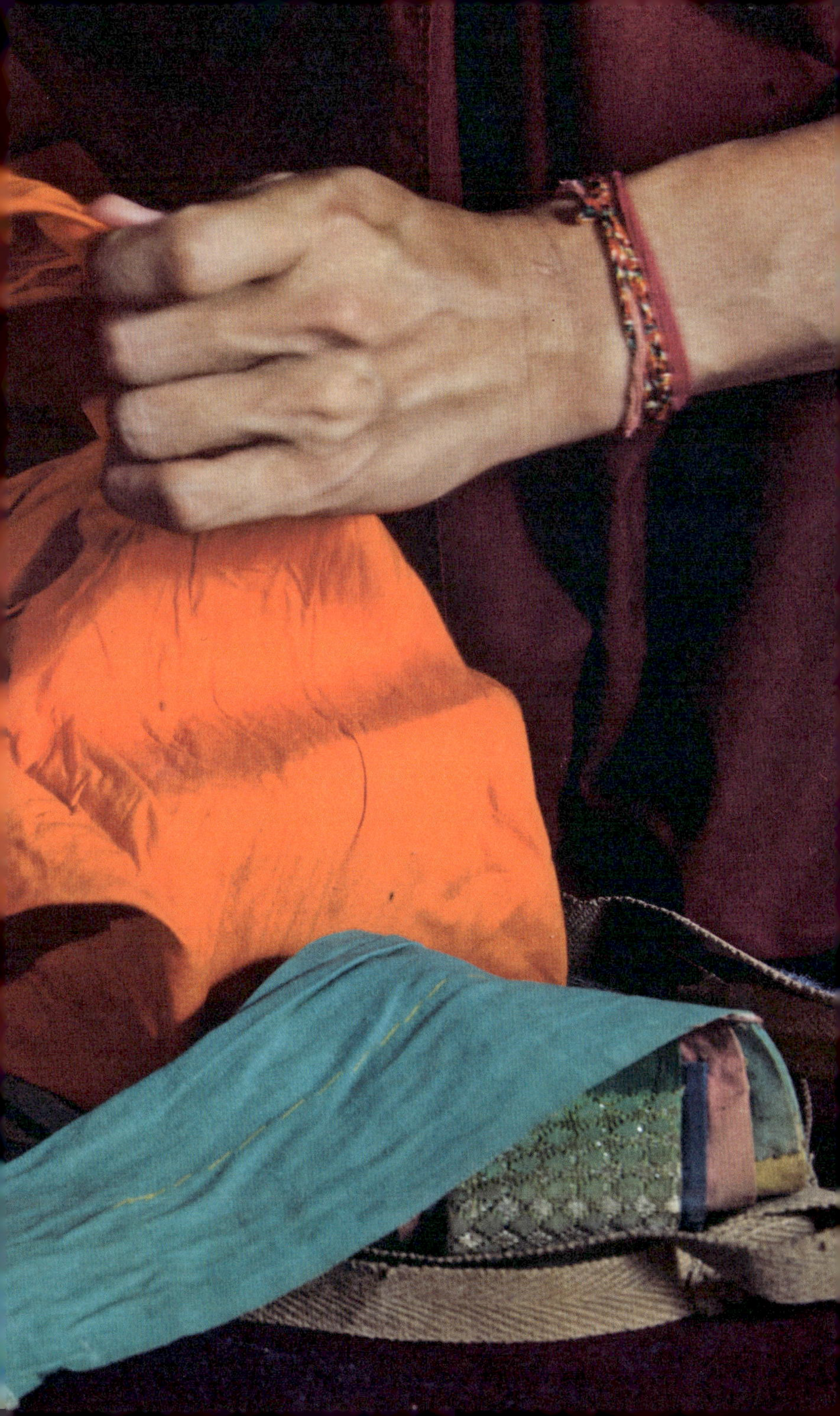

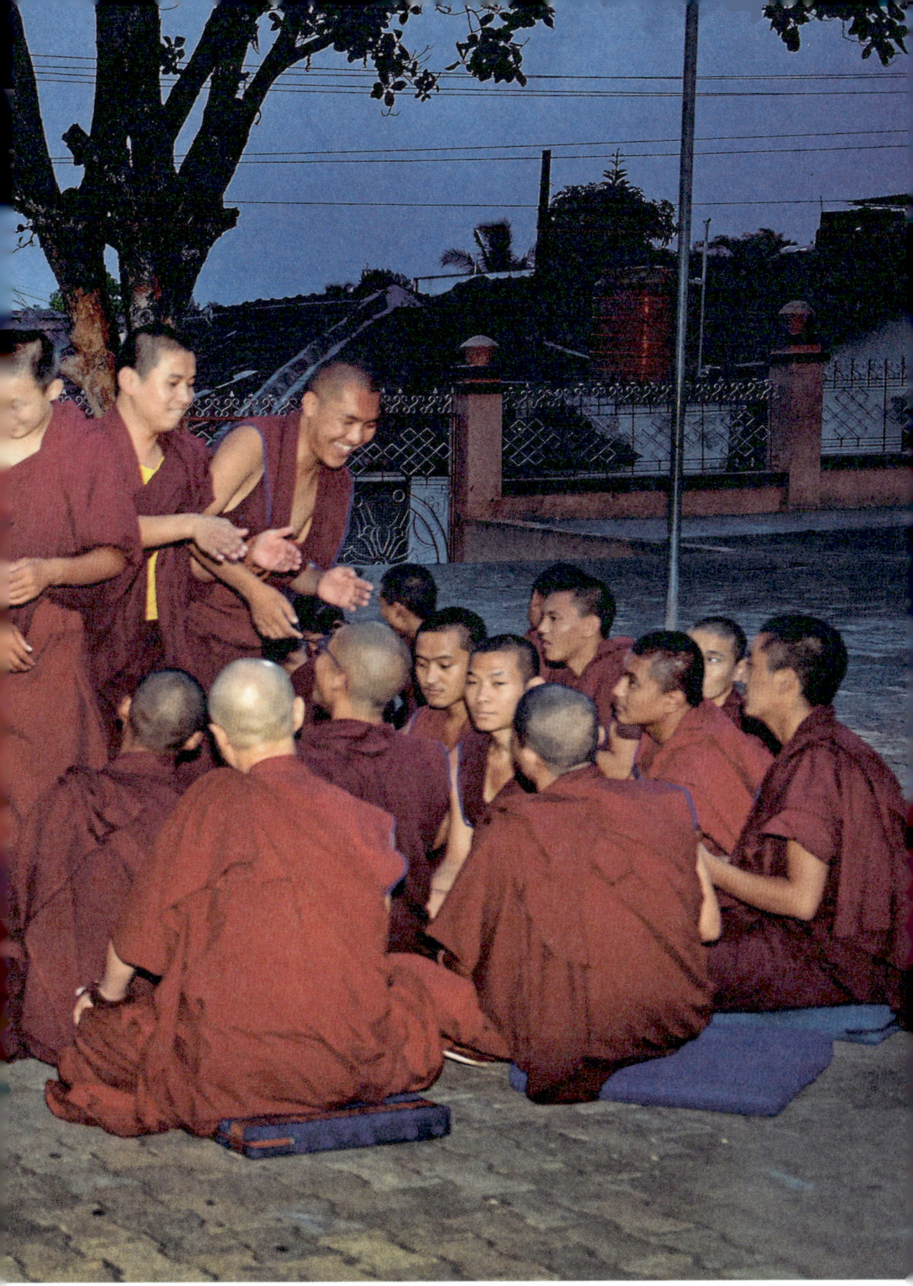

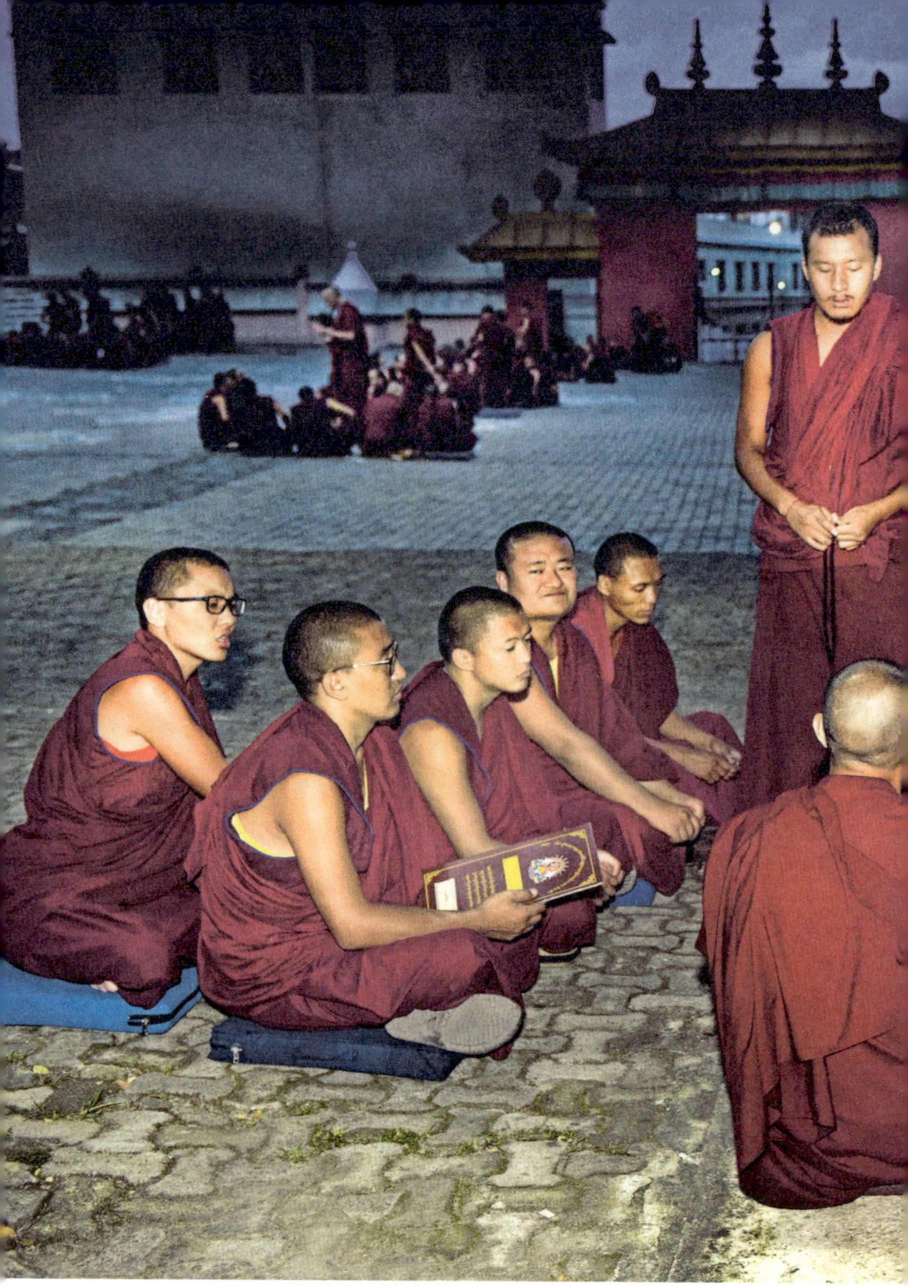

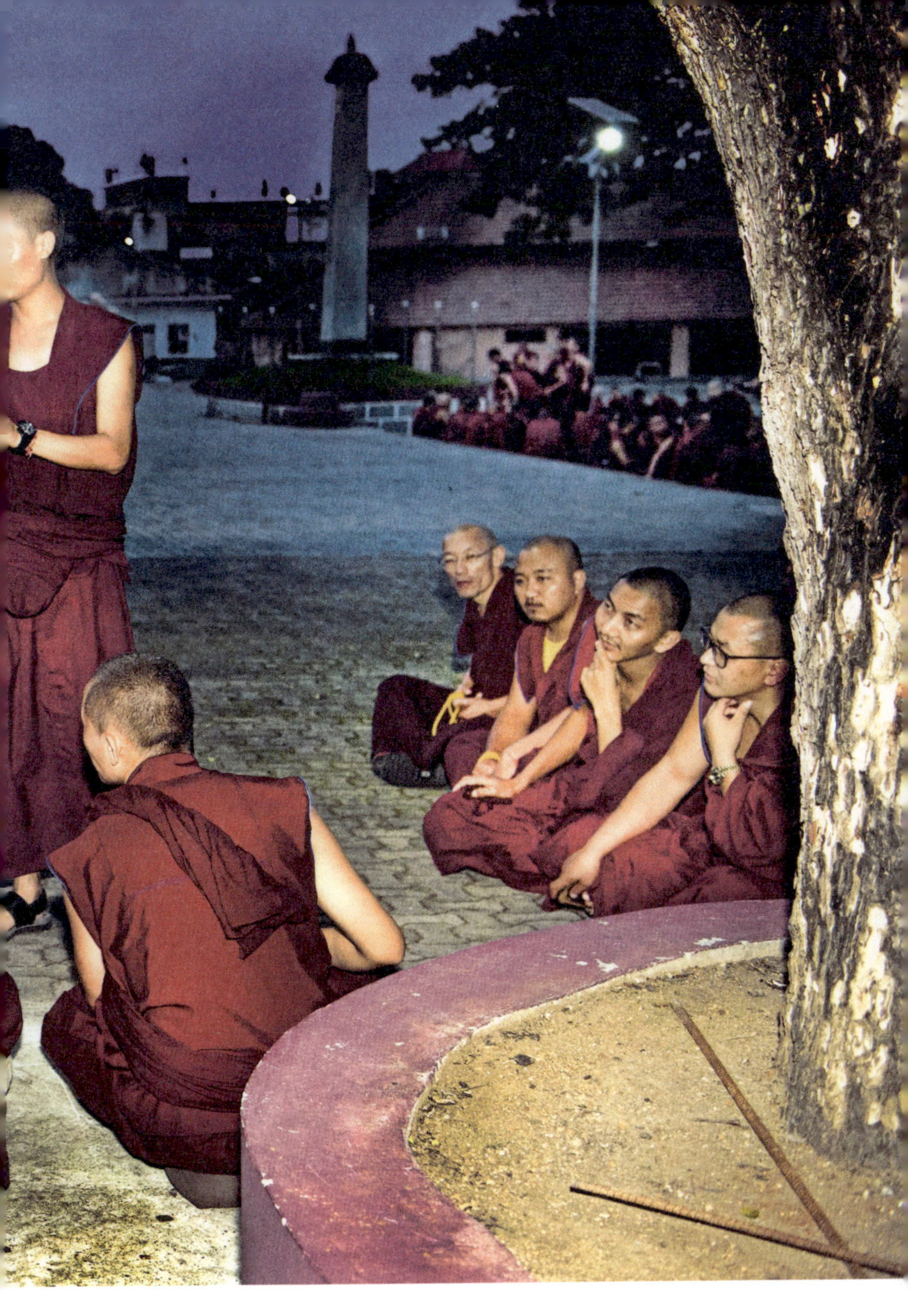

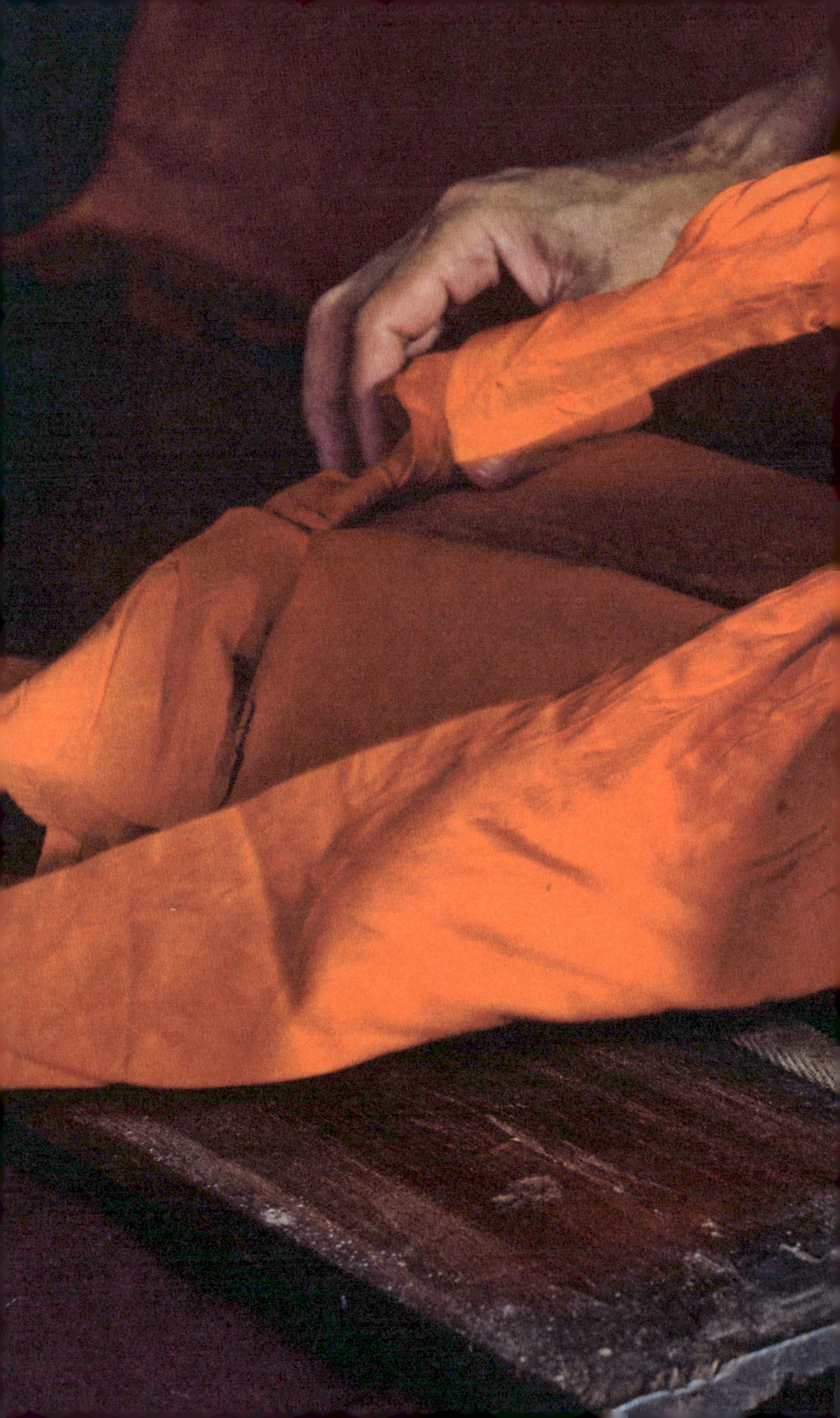

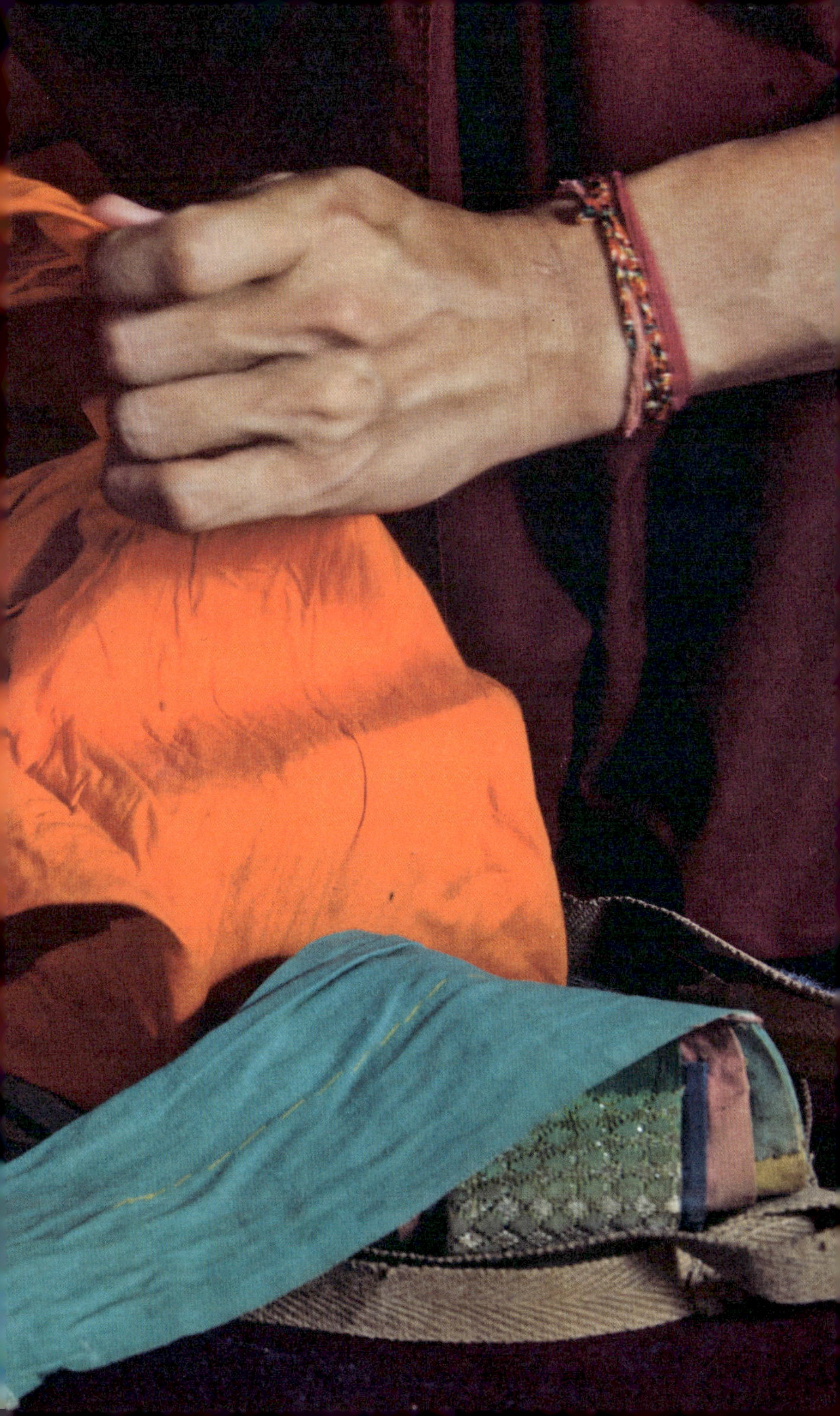

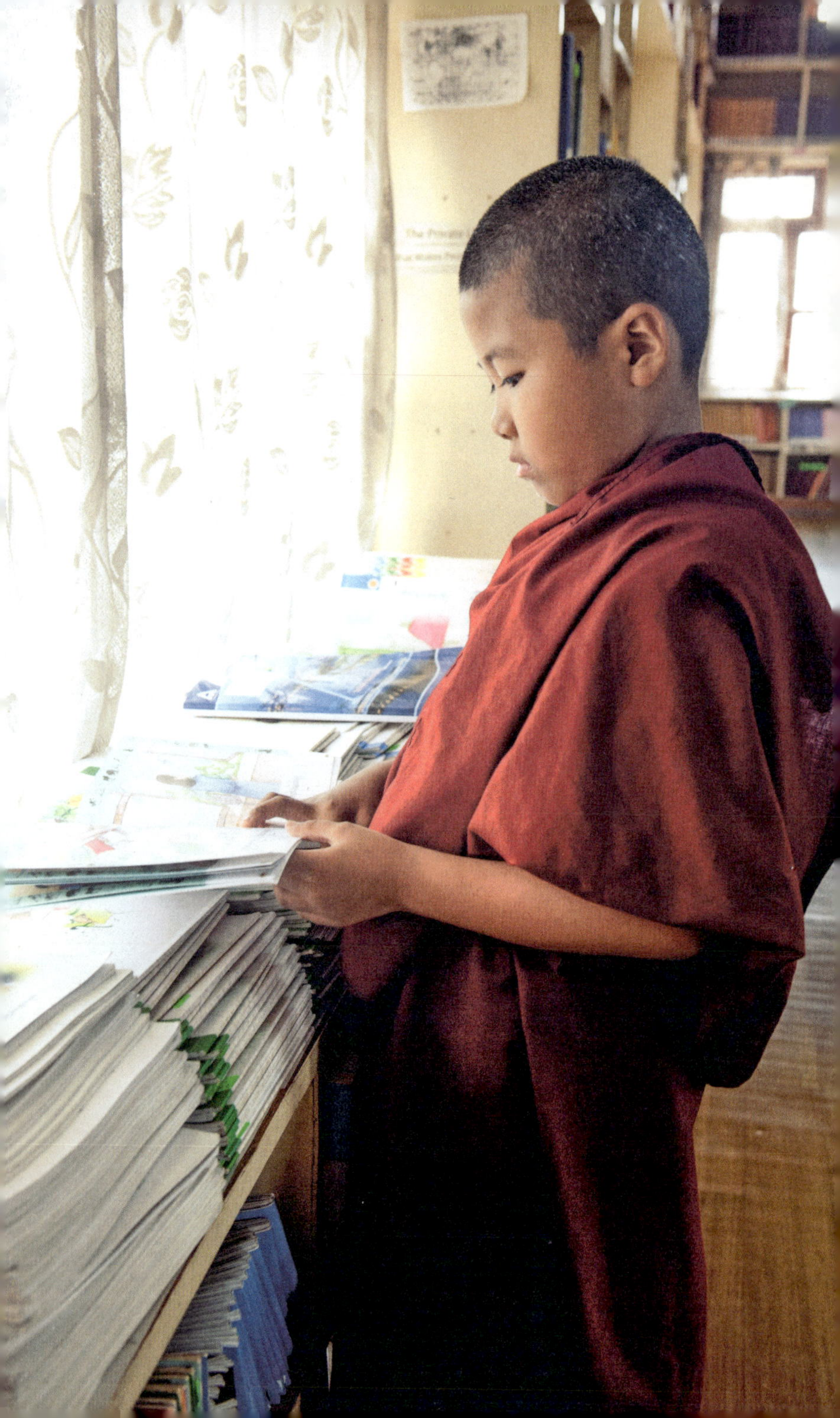

Contemplative Buddhist Tradition and Modern Science

Richard K. Raker

Buddhist contemplative tradition and modern science both investigate reality by recognizing and sharing the importance of empirical evidence, reason, and testimony. Yet there exists a tension between Buddhist scriptural absolutism and the scientific method. However, a common feature of Buddhist and scientific philosophies and methodologies—they each emphasize empiric observation—allows these two traditions to grow and flourish by influencing one another.

The 14th Dalai Lama's personal interest in and commitment to promoting Western scientific thought alongside Tibetan Buddhist practices has spurred several organizations to advance the addition of science curriculum into aspects of the education and training that Tibetan Buddhist monks receive. One example is The Emory-Tibet Science Initiative (ETSI), a comprehensive science curriculum designed and implemented by Emory University in Atlanta specifically for Tibetan Buddhist monasteries at Sera Mey, Sera Jey, Drepung, and Gaden Monastic Universities, all in southern India.

I traveled to Bylakuppe, in Karnataka state, as a member of the faculty for the ESTI program in the summer of 2019 to teach neuroscience to a group of monks. I came prepared with lectures, PowerPoint slides, and questions, which had already been translated into Tibetan by the time I arrived at the monastery. On the first day of class, I stood before sixty-five monks who sat on the floor cross-legged, facing me, with eyes, ears, and pens at the ready. I began to speak, but immediately I slowed down, as a monk who had science training conducted simultaneous translation. (The translator spent two years at Emory as a Tenzin Gyatso Science Scholar, taking courses alongside undergraduate students while also receiving individualized instruction in English, science, and mathematics from ETSI faculty members.)

Hands went up seeking answers to questions, which were motivated in part by the monks' traditional educational approach of memorization, constant review, questioning, and debate. I proposed that the class take up a question like "what is consciousness?" and debate it. Within a few minutes, the monks formed groups, with the challenger and defender taking turns. As the debate continued, the number of debaters increased. I witnessed a display of highly stylized, physical movements, with specific hand motions and gestures, verbal utterances, and body action and positioning such as shoving, mixed with teasing and humor. During the constant questioning, they defended their positions, finding both inconsistencies and consensus. The debaters and onlookers engaged each other throughout, so there was never a moment of silence. Unlike western debate, Tibetan monastic debate is dialectic and serves to question the consequence of the conclusions—not to win or lose but to help the interlocutors develop a clear understanding of what the logic proves.

Time will tell what impact have I made on their education and the impact these monks have made on me. The Tibetan Buddhist debate tradition shows that there is tremendous opportunity for transformation to occur in all of us.

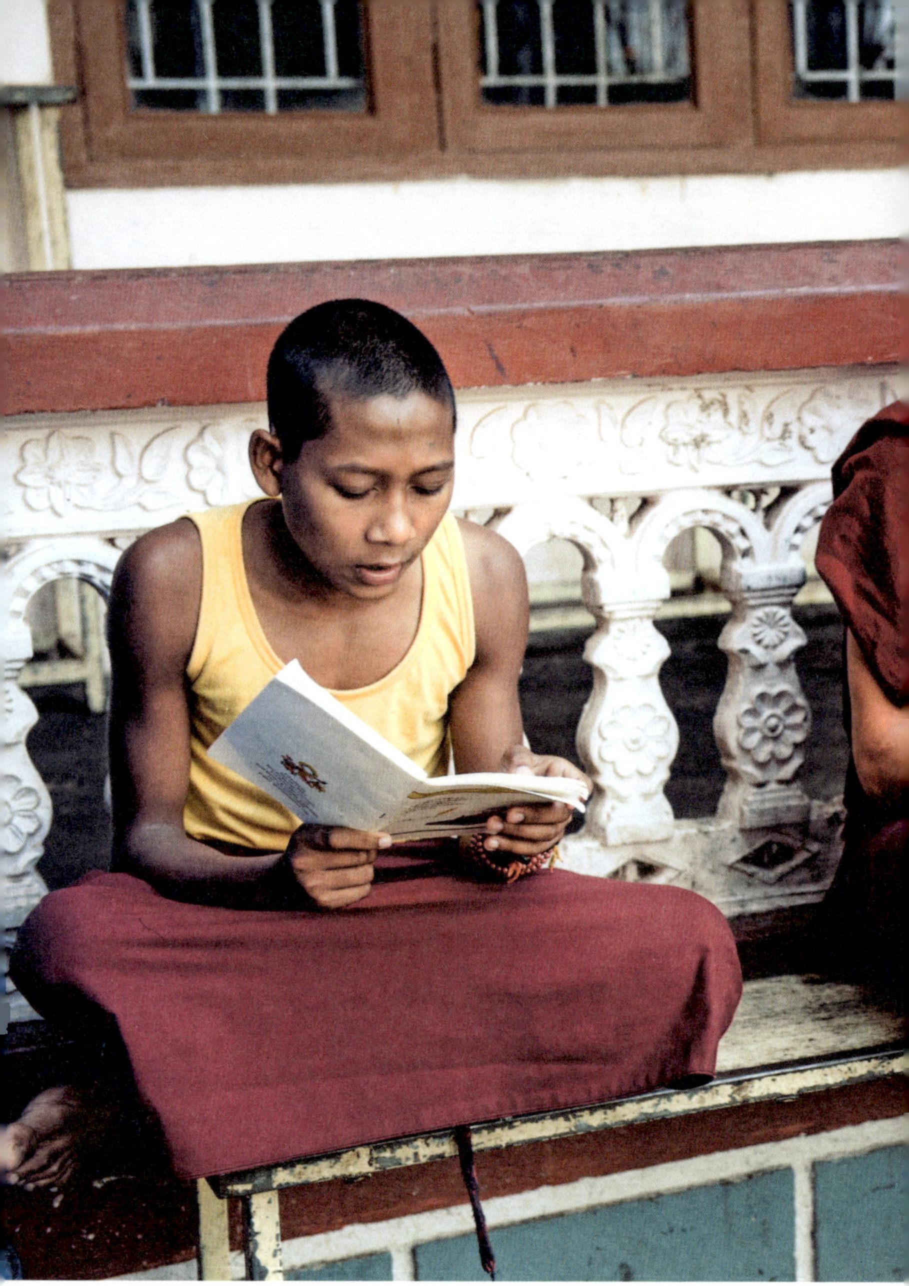

Scripture studies occur throughout the day.

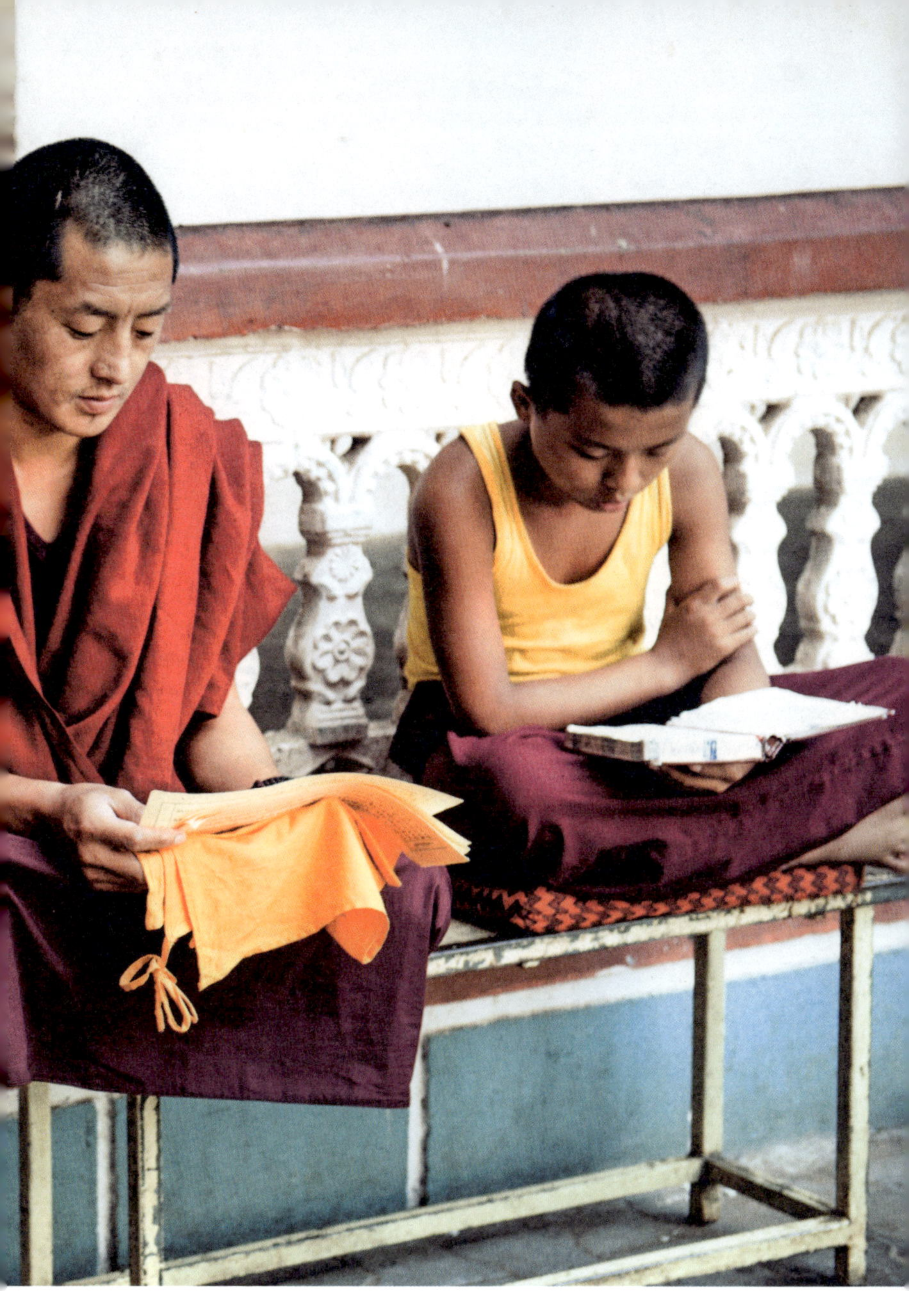

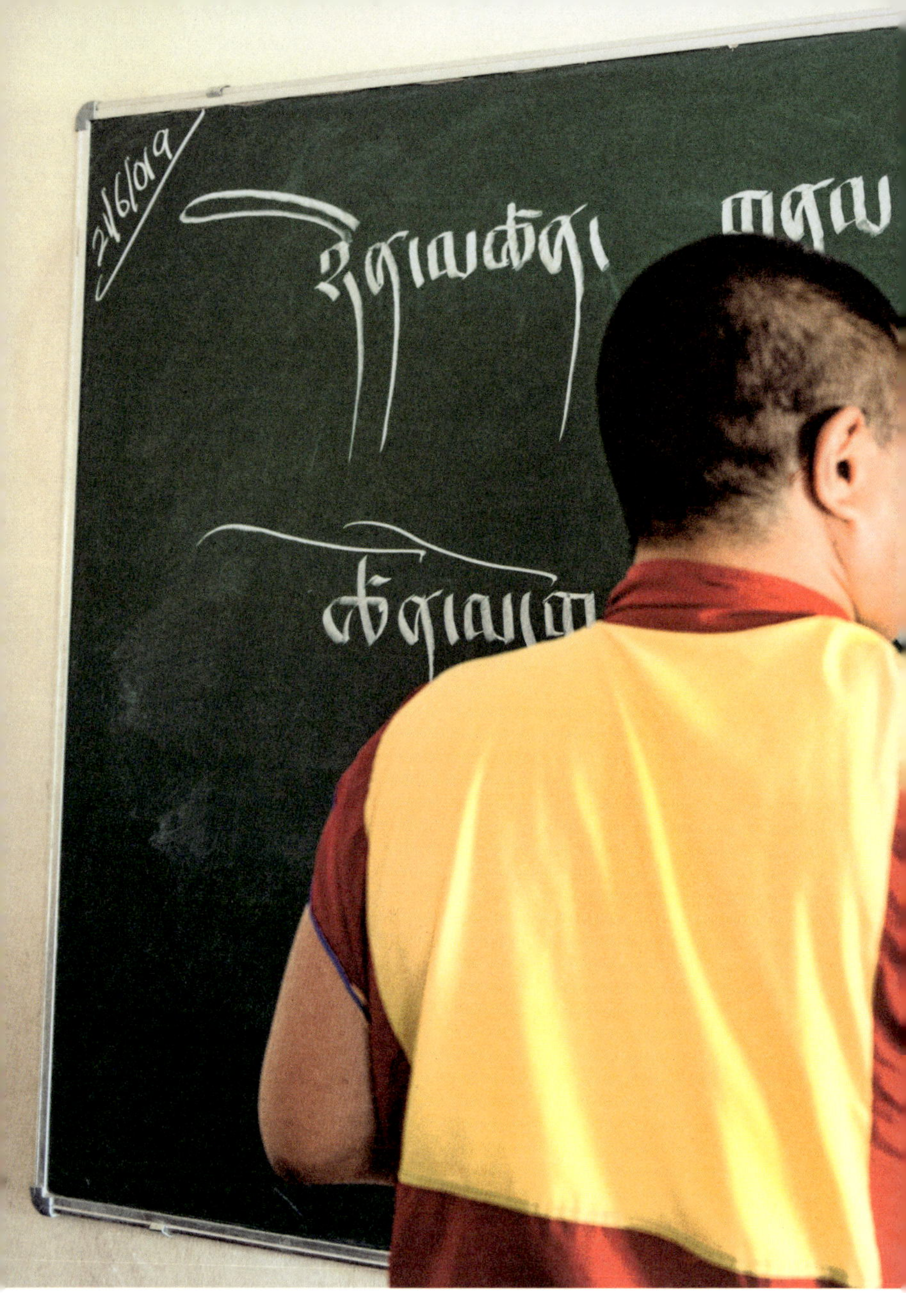

A teacher takes his time to write ornamental script legibly for a beginner grammar and calligraphy class.

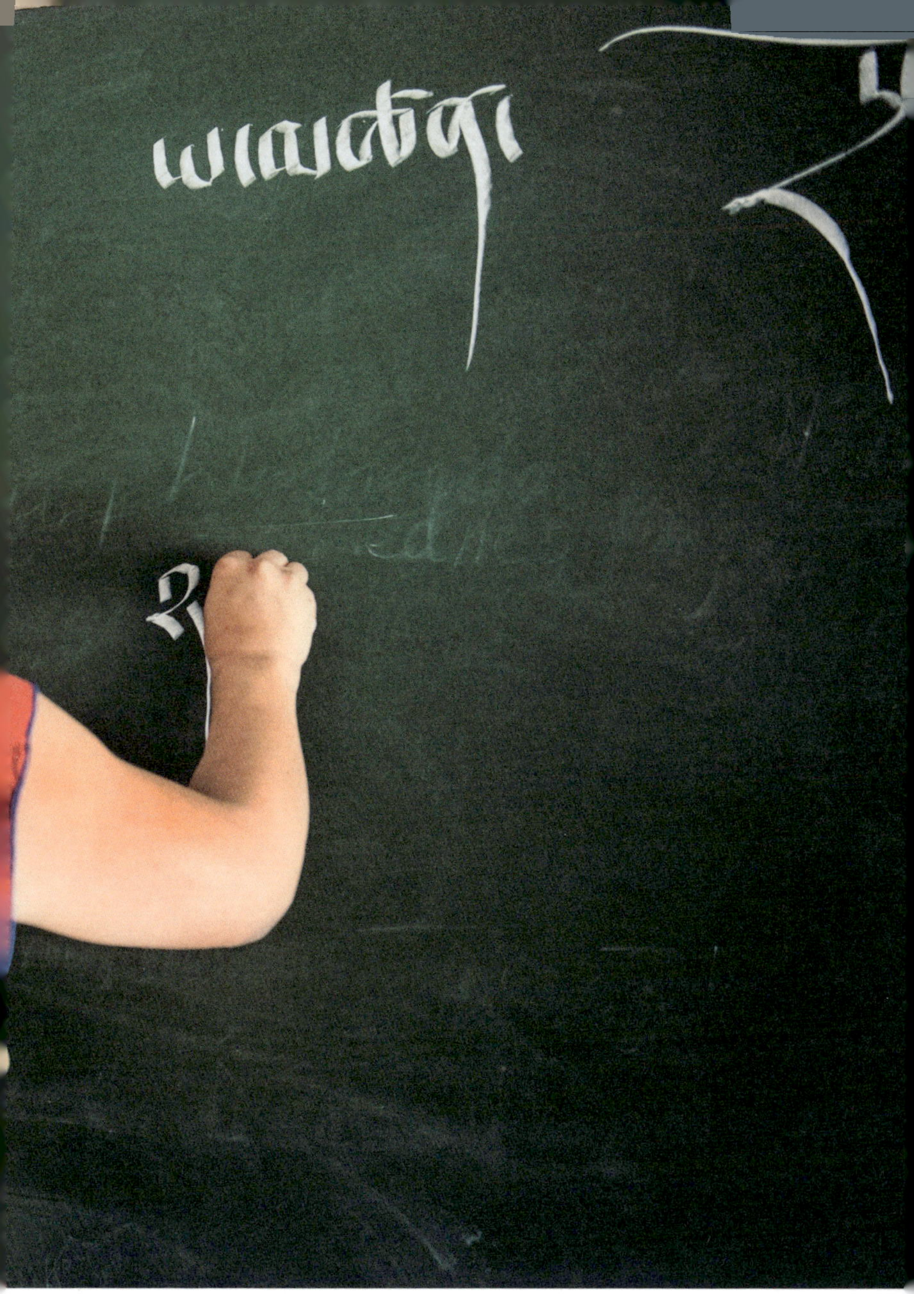

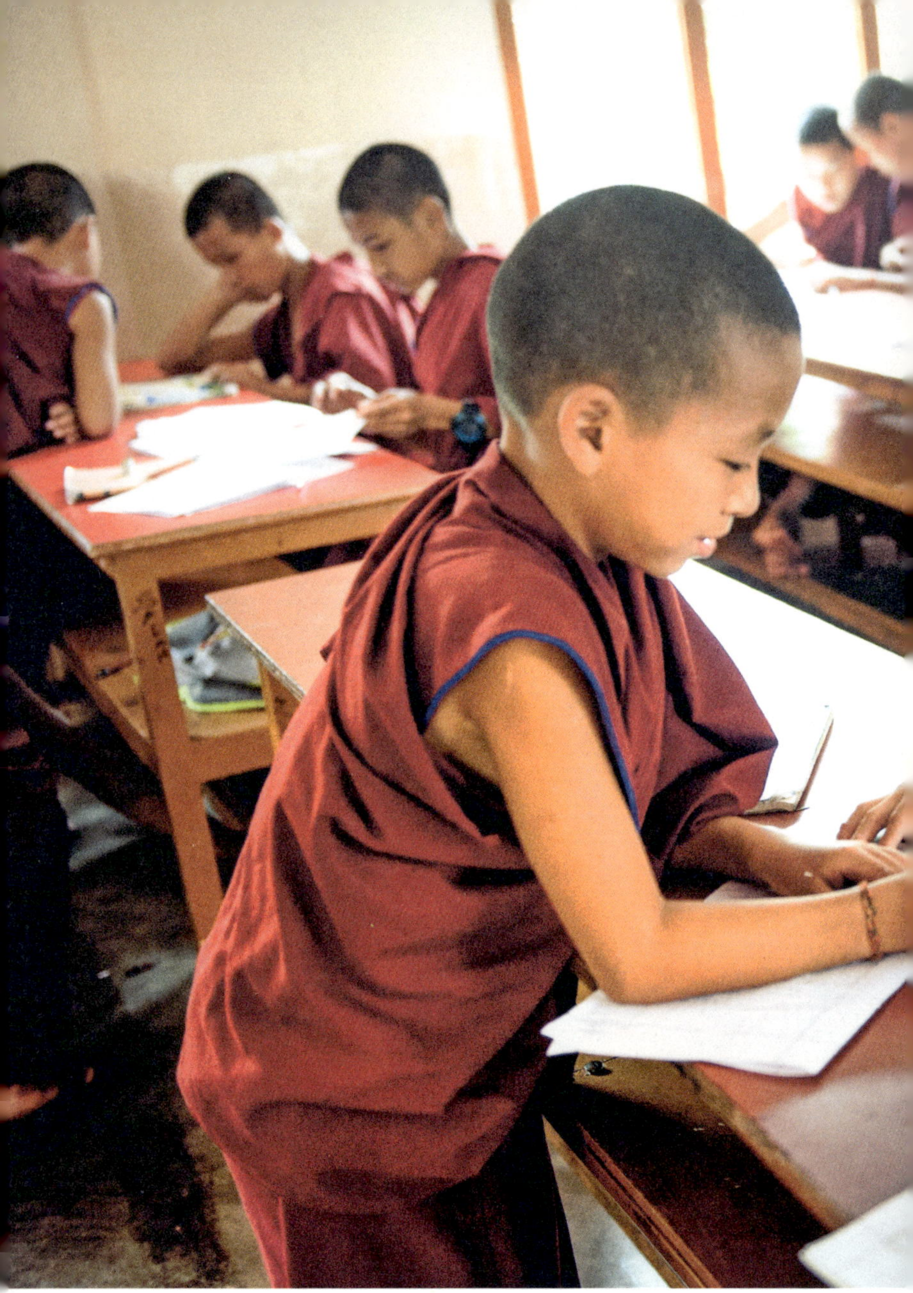

Like students everywhere, young monks work together during their lessons.

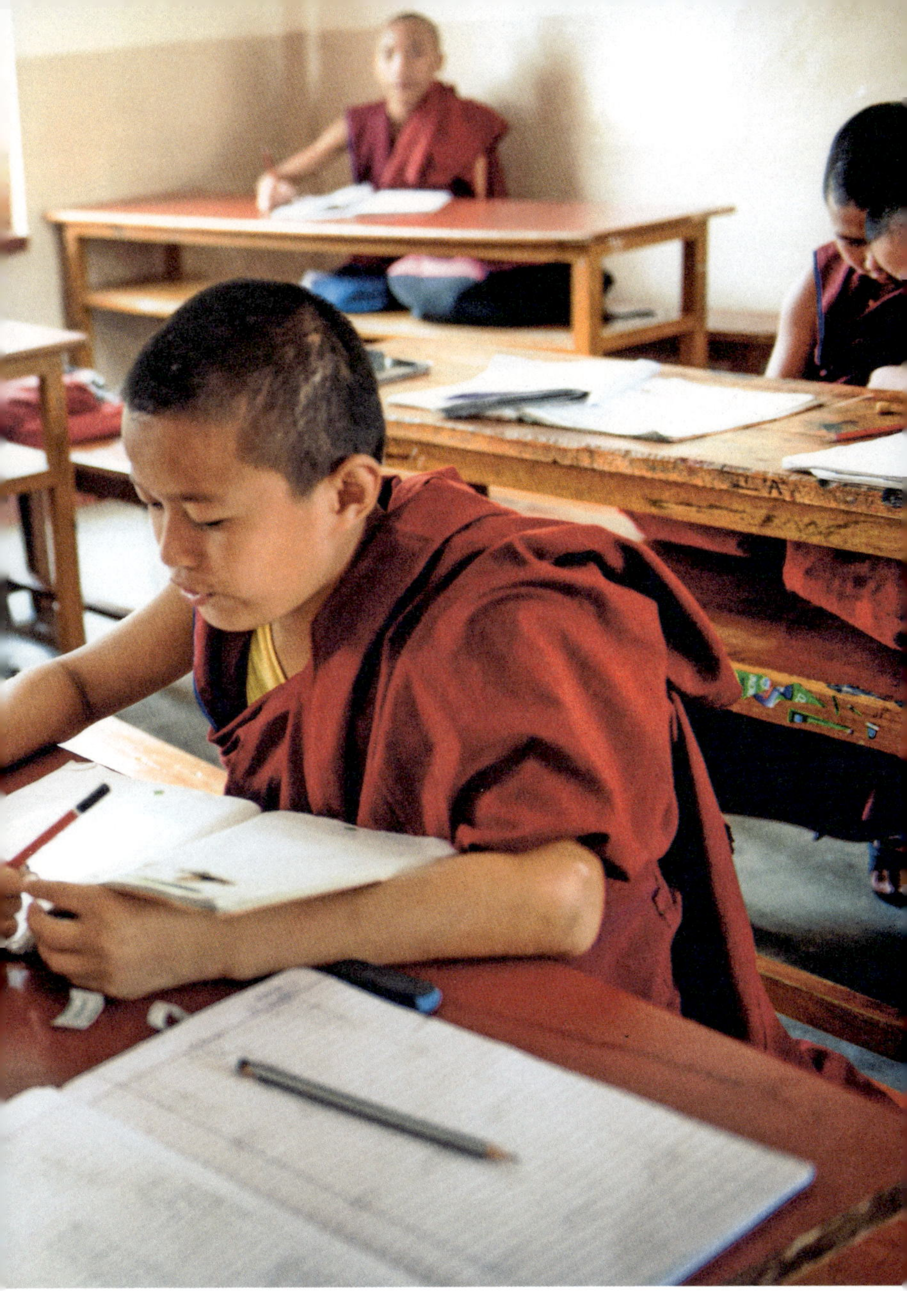

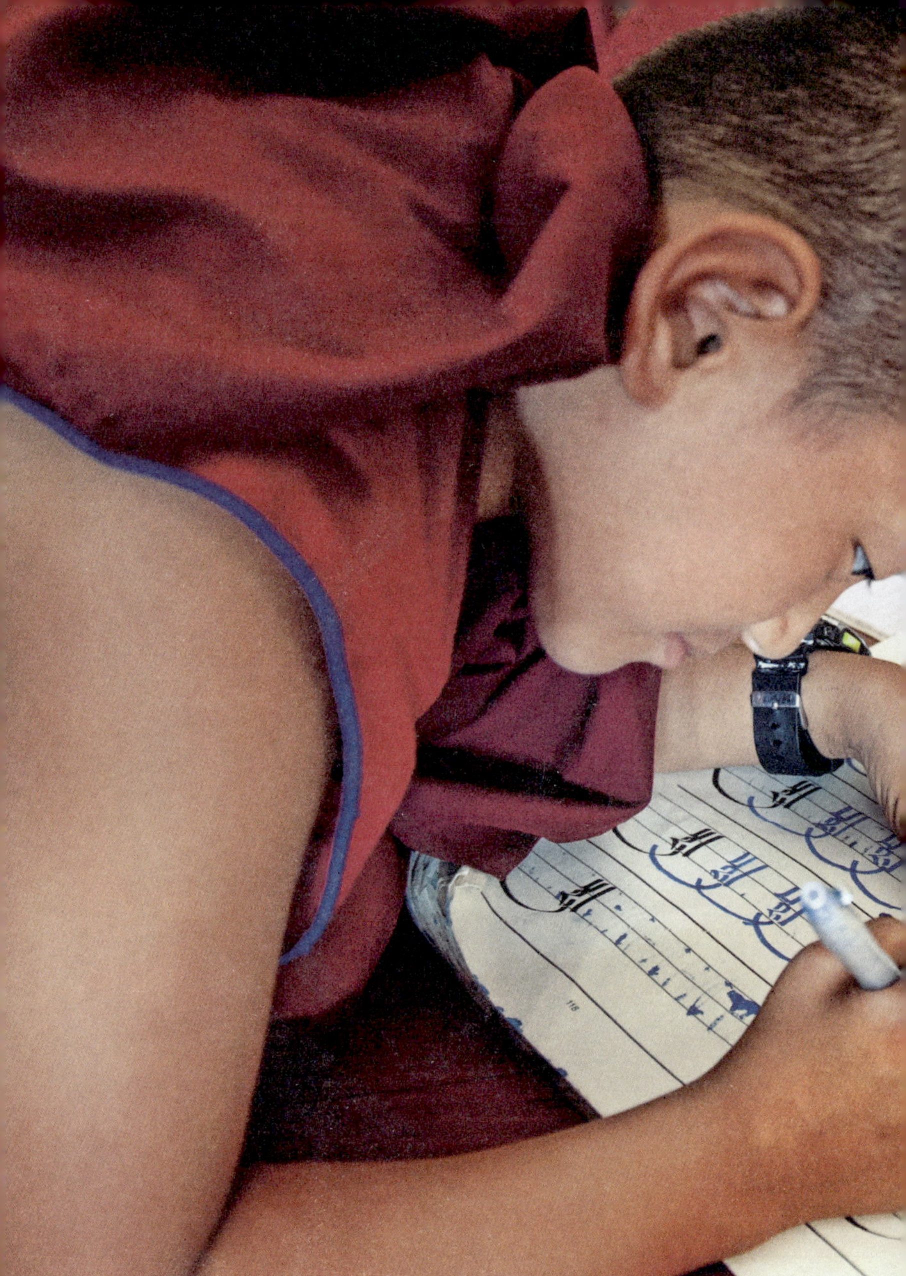

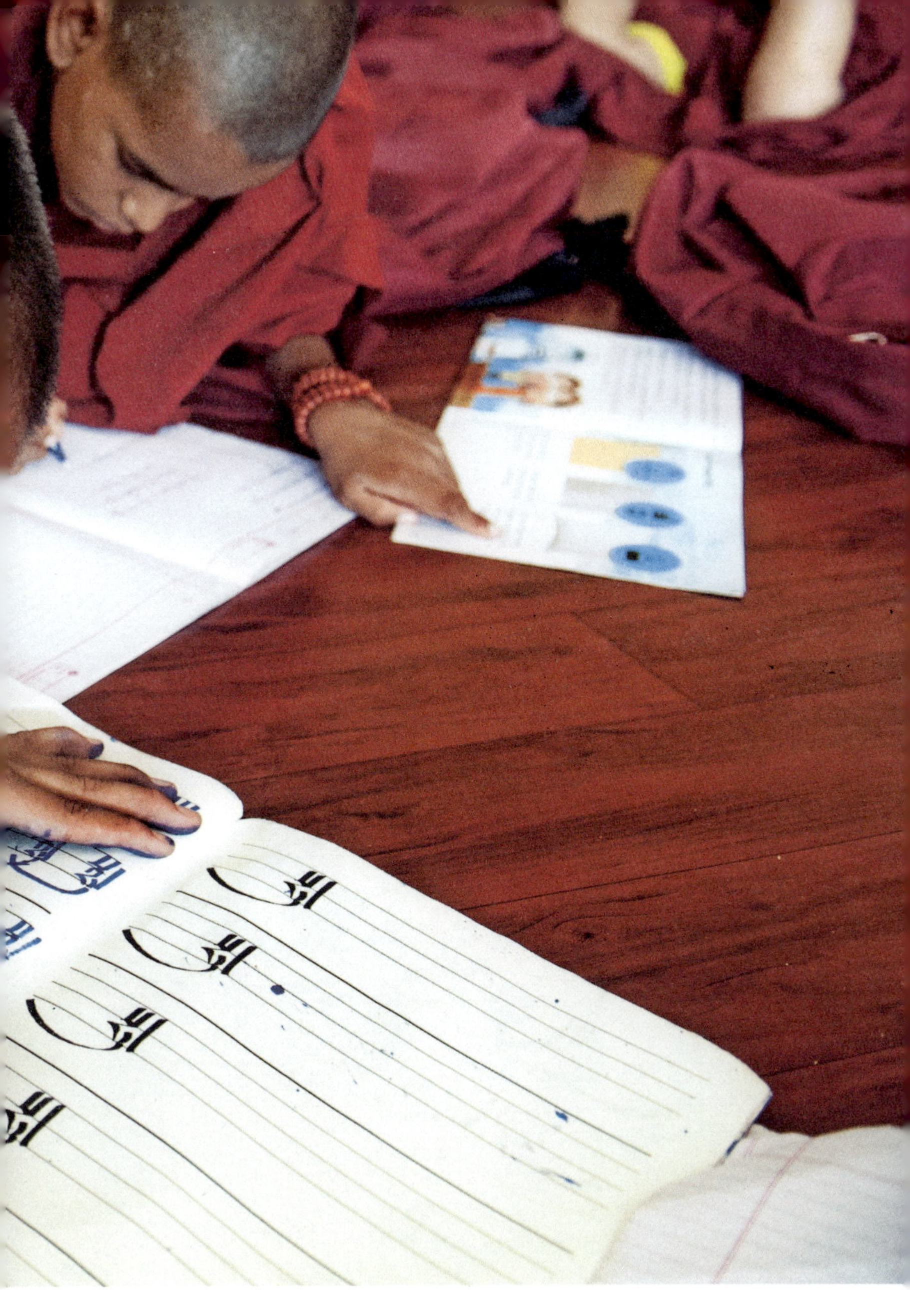

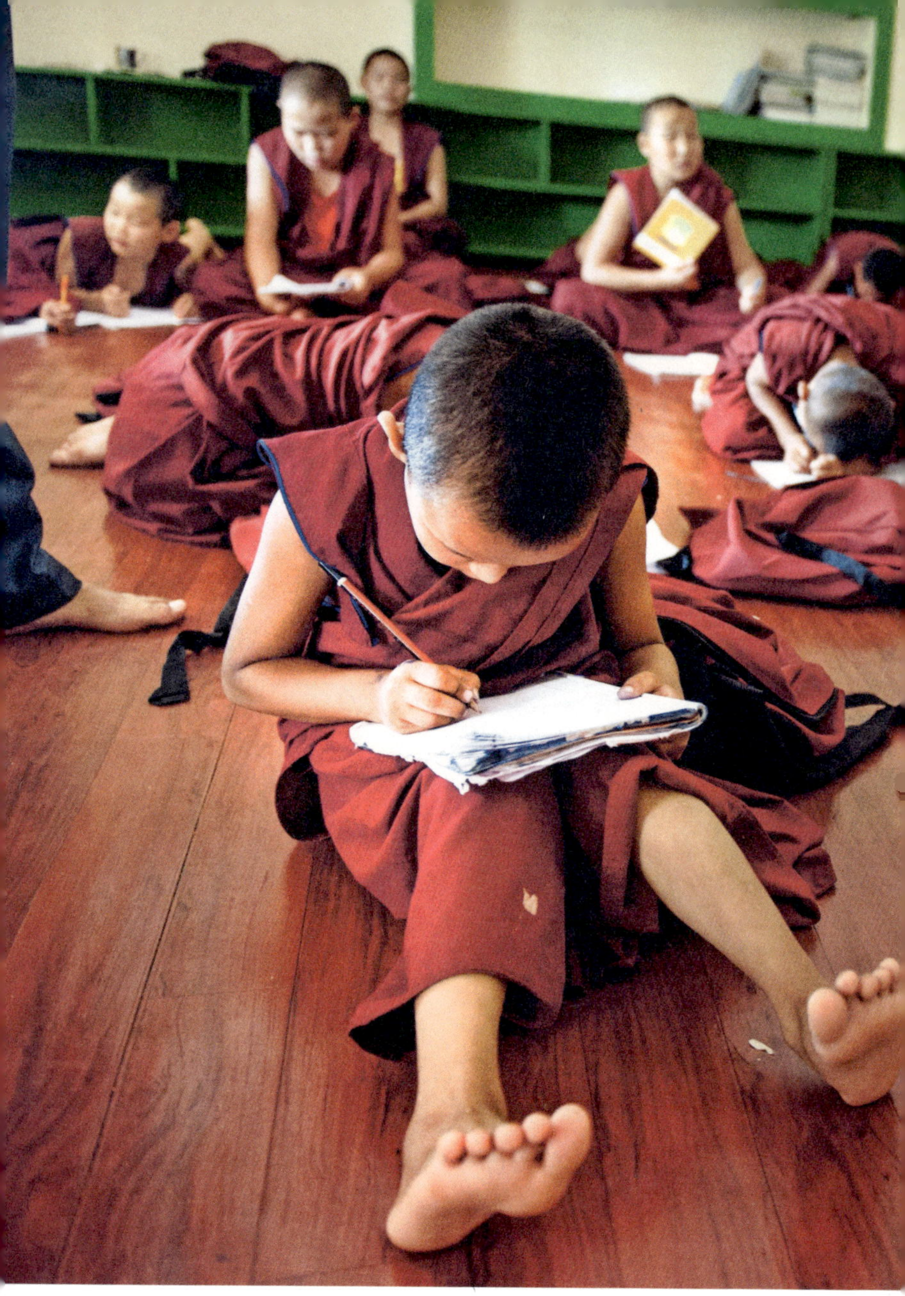

Monks attentively engage with their teacher's lesson.

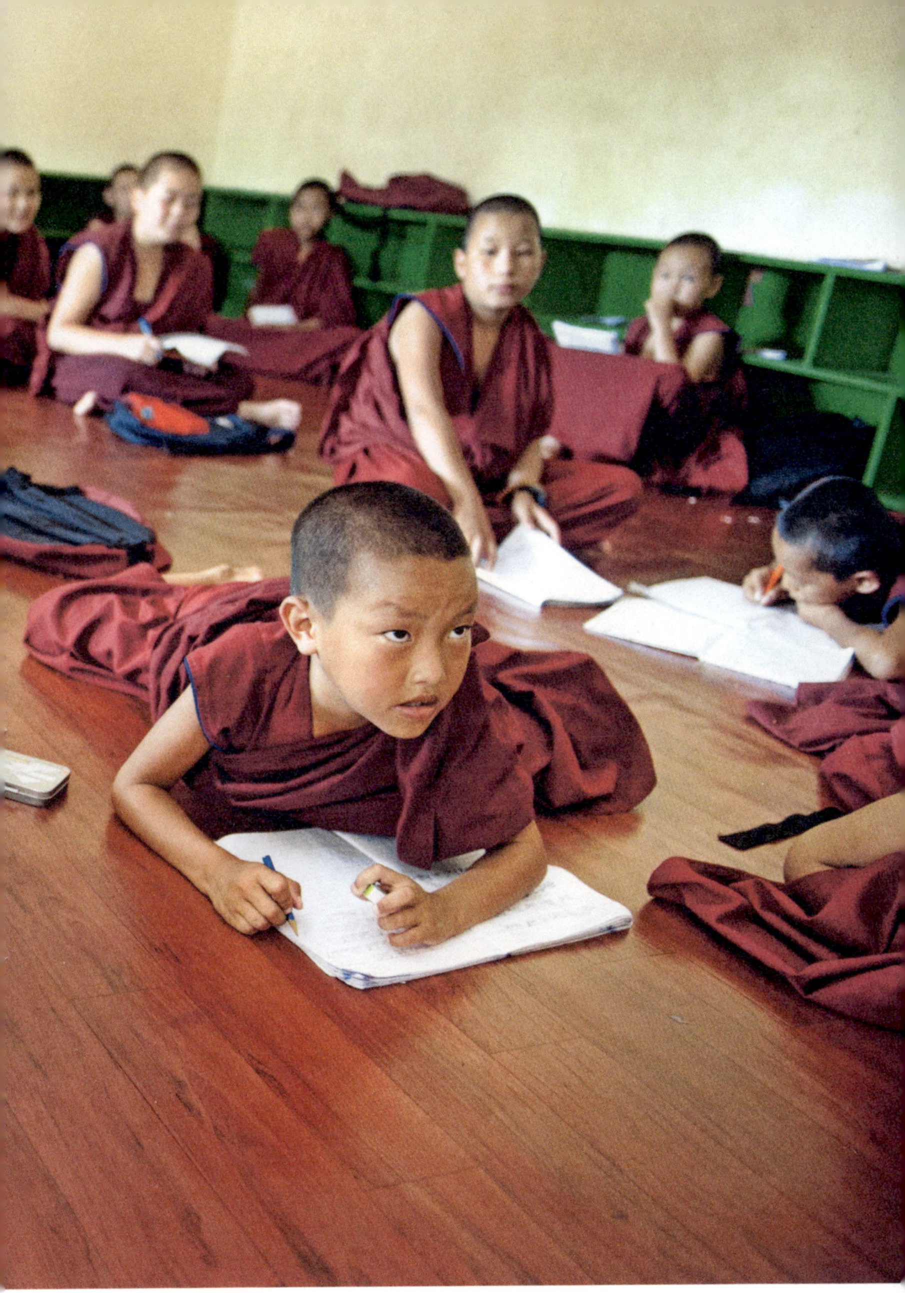

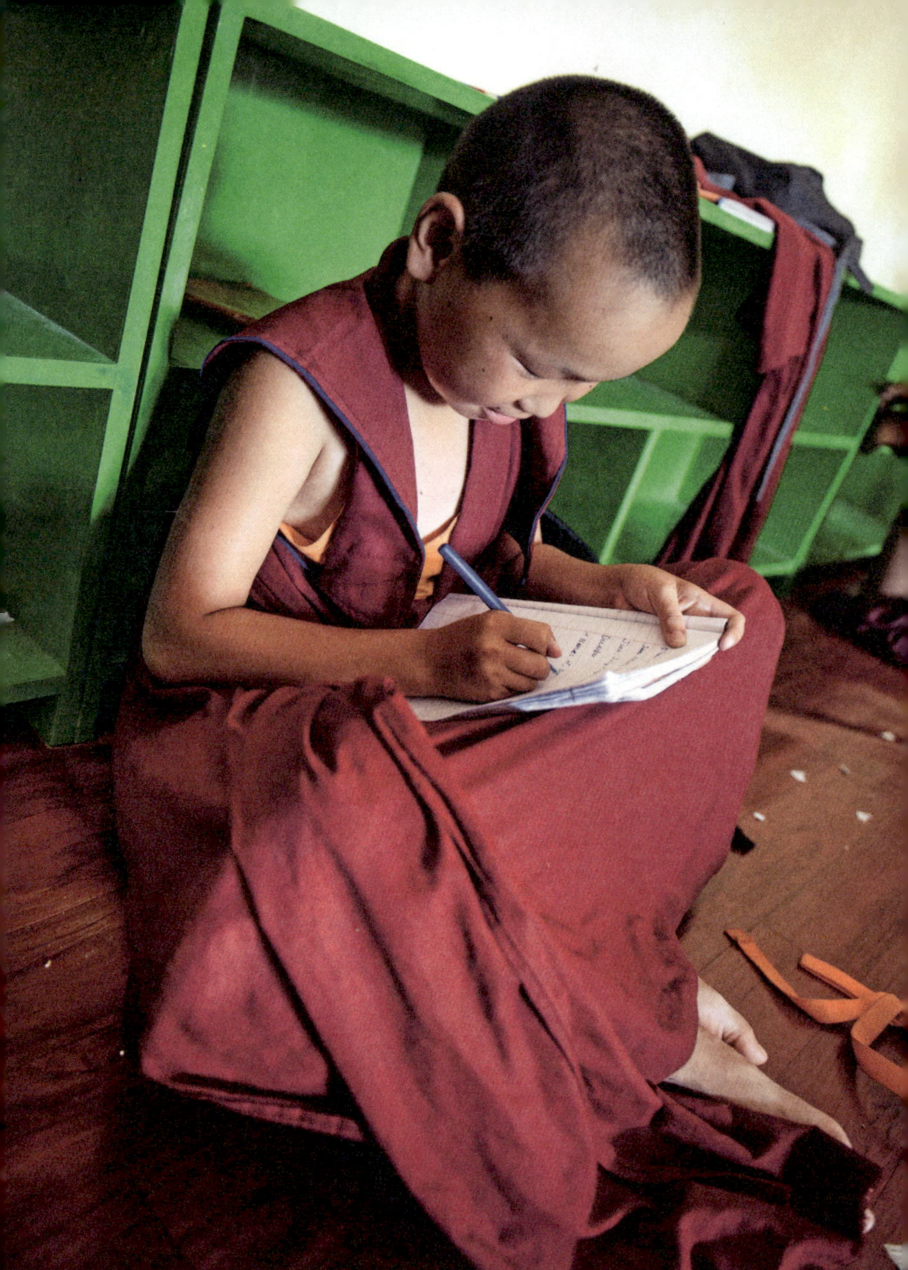

The debates that I've had with my classmates on generating *bodhicitta*—the aspiration to become Buddha to liberate all sentient beings—made a lasting impact on me. In these debates we used the Buddhist technique *tonglen*, in which you imagine taking in the suffering and pain of others and at the same time extending happiness, peace, and positivity to them. This practice cultivates compassion, empathy, and love. It's part of the larger *bodhicitta* practice, which strives to free beings from suffering. Through debating and practicing these techniques, I developed love and compassion for other beings, including animals. This transformation inspired me to adopt a vegetarian lifestyle, promising not to harm animals.

Debate has taught me how to engage in critical inquiry. When you know how to use logical reasoning, you can engage in any subject with depth and openness, be it philosophy, science, or religion, without relying on blind faith. I apply my debate experience daily to work through problems and look for truth by using reasoning, logic, and thinking from different perspectives to understand the multiple causes and conditions for any given issue.

— Kalden Gyatso

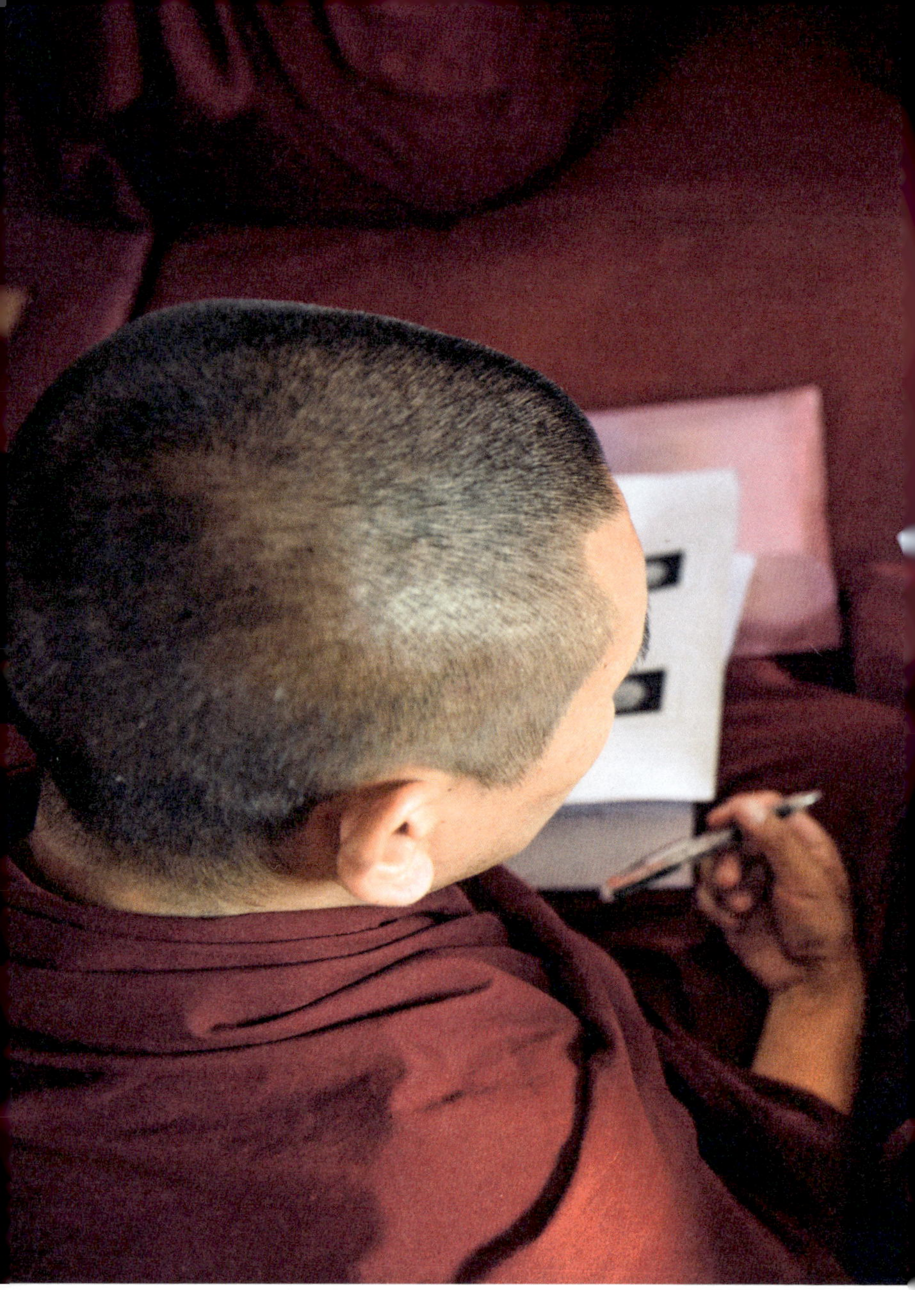

Tibetan monks share notes in a neuroscience class.

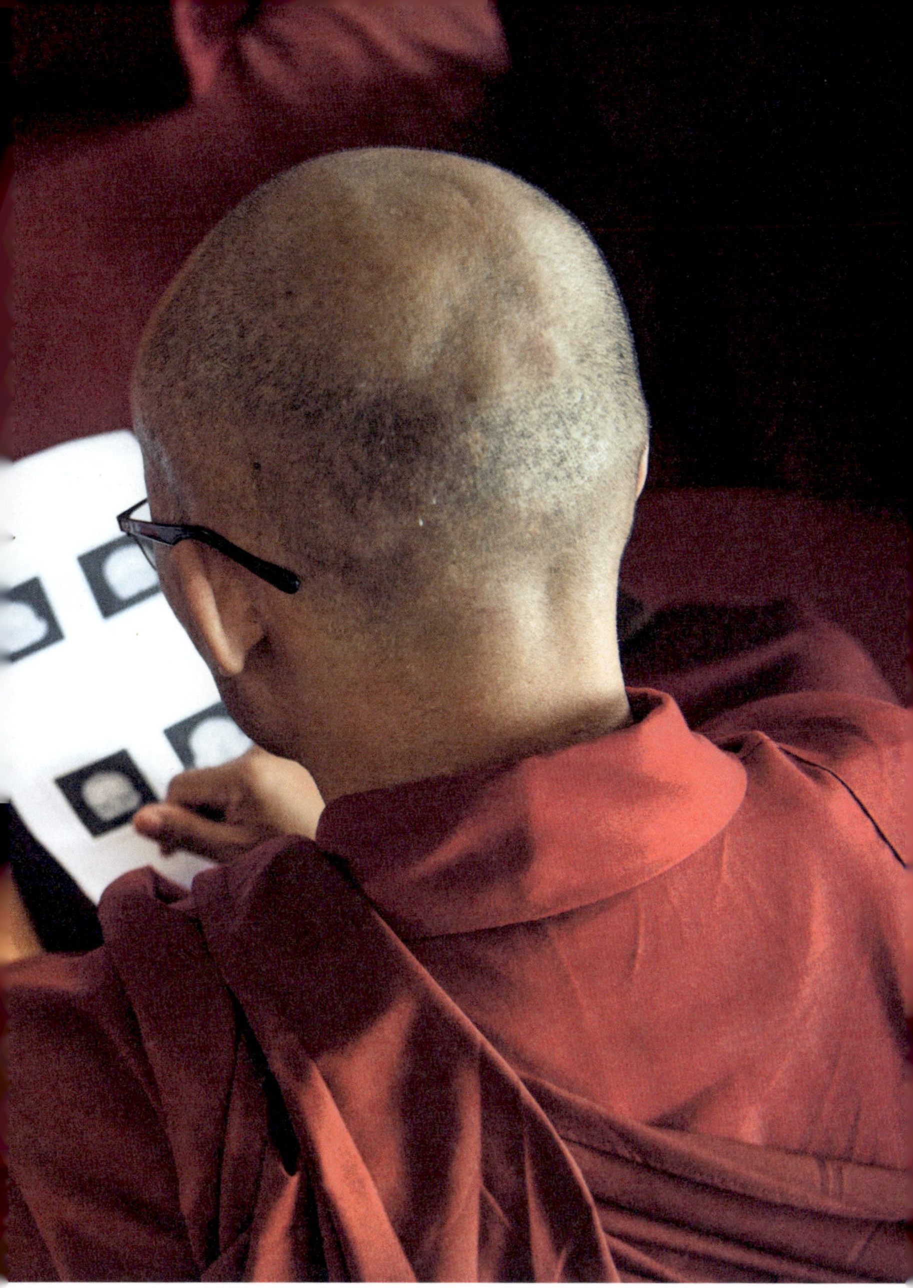

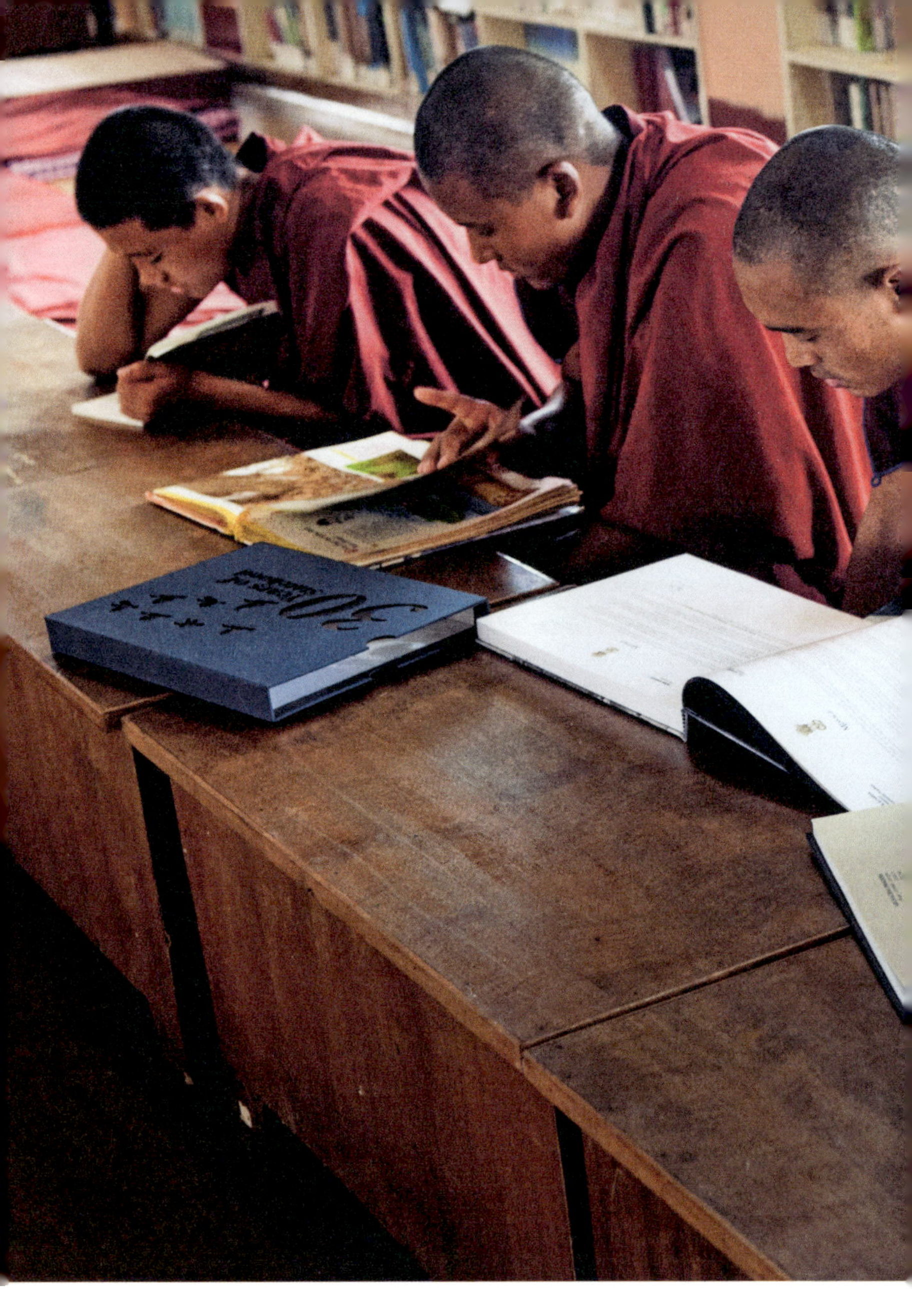

Students gather during their library period to study modern subjects—geography, mathematics, general science, world history, Tibetan grammar, and English.

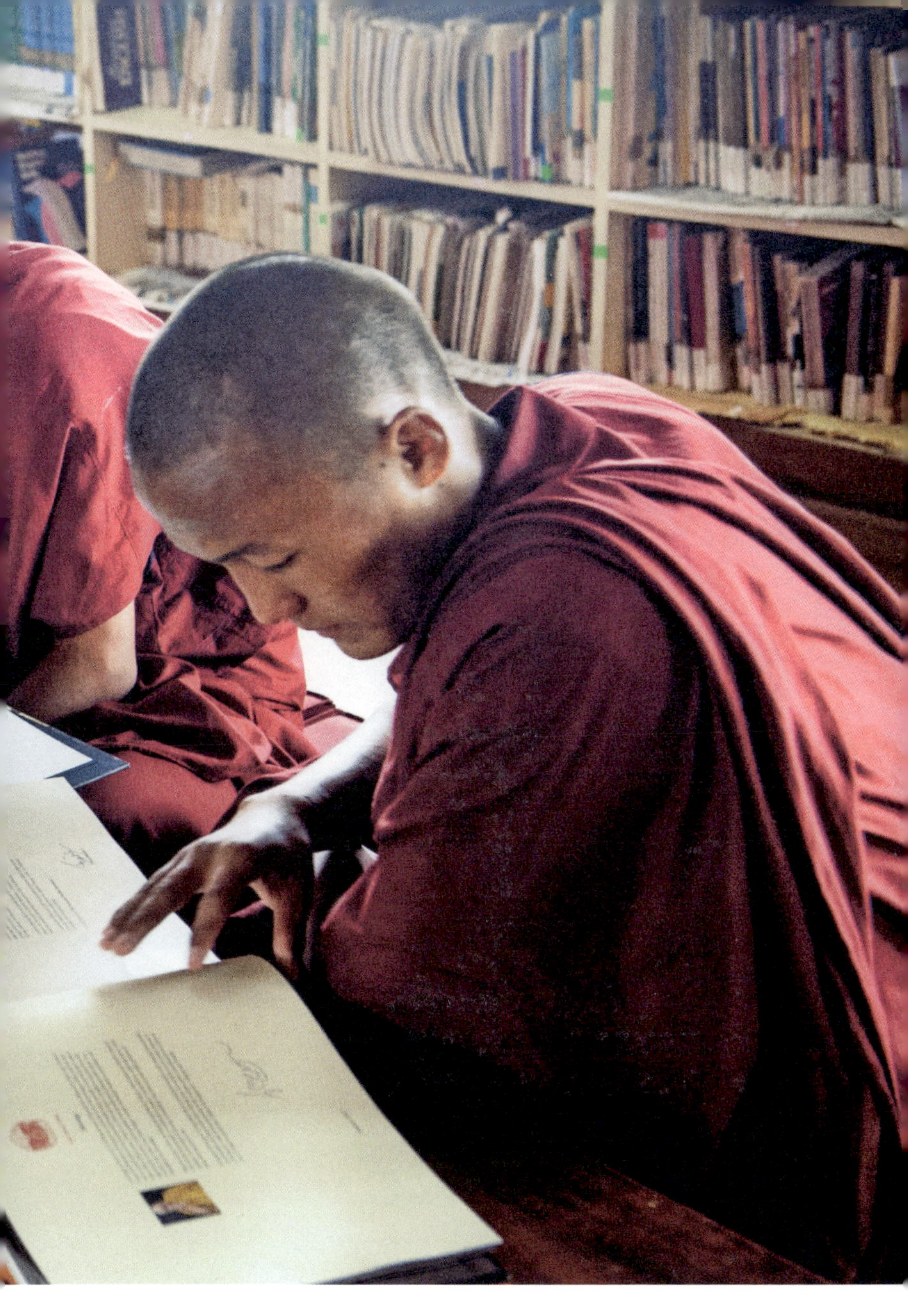

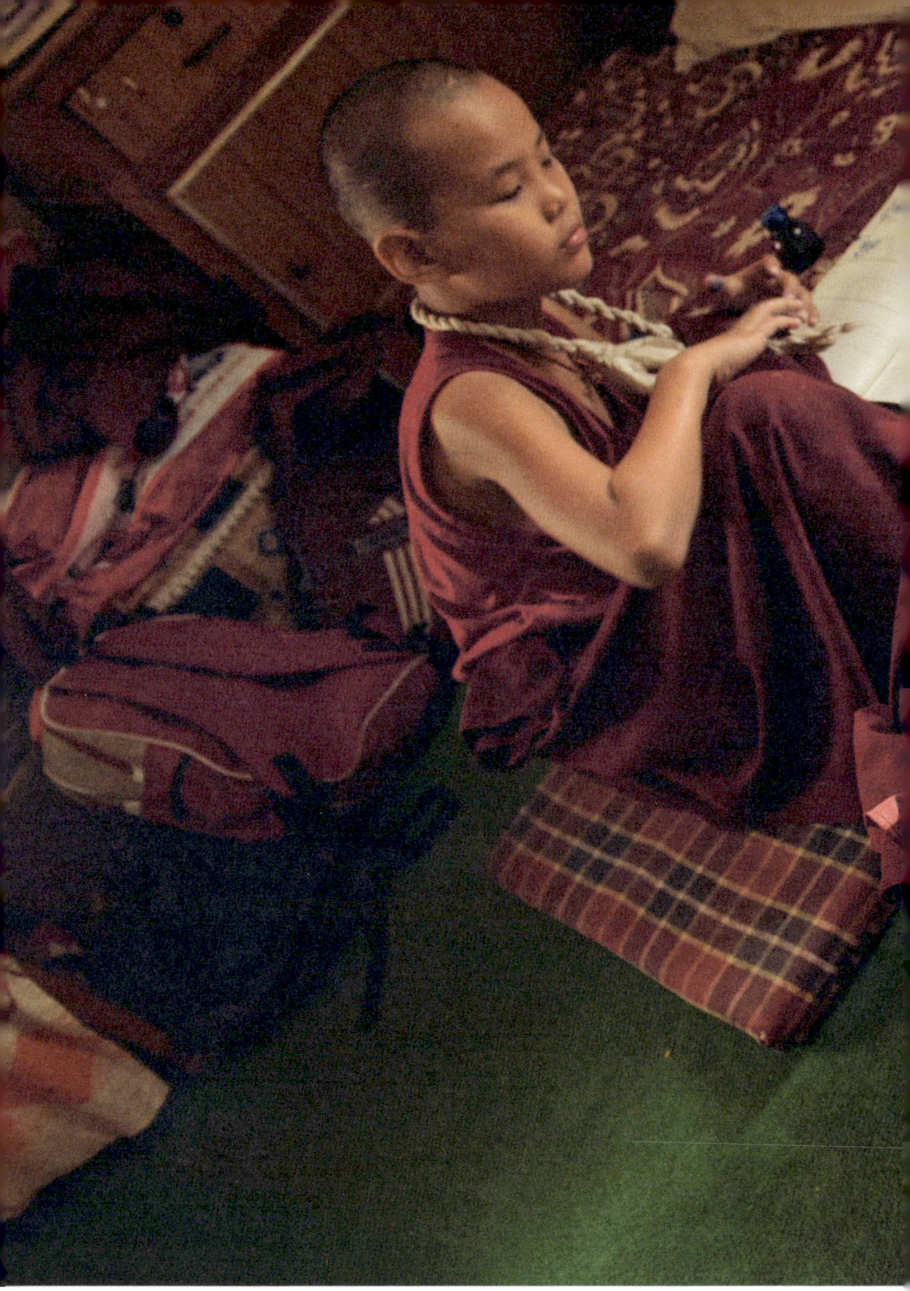

Young monks meet in their mentor's house to practice their calligraphy lessons.

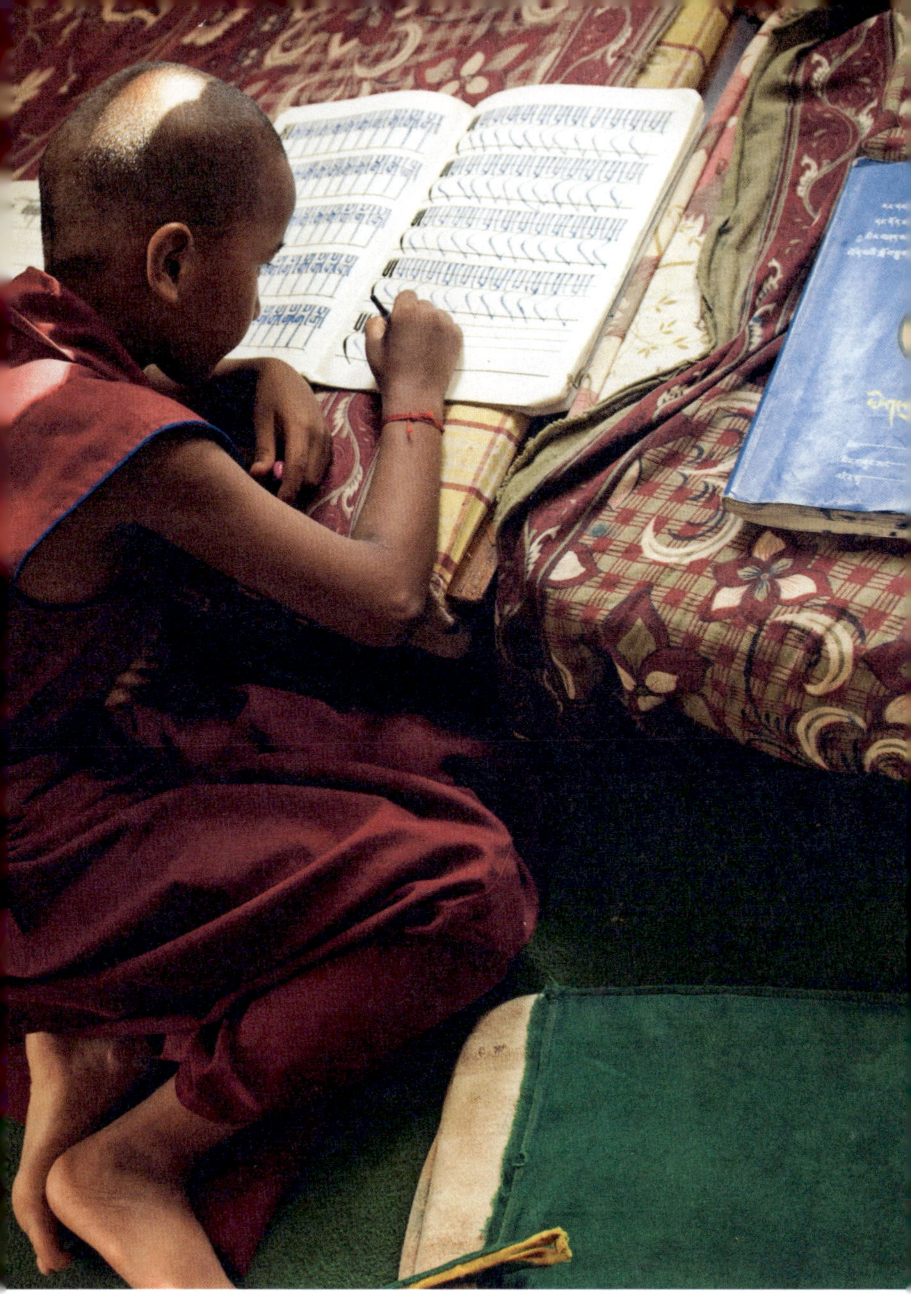

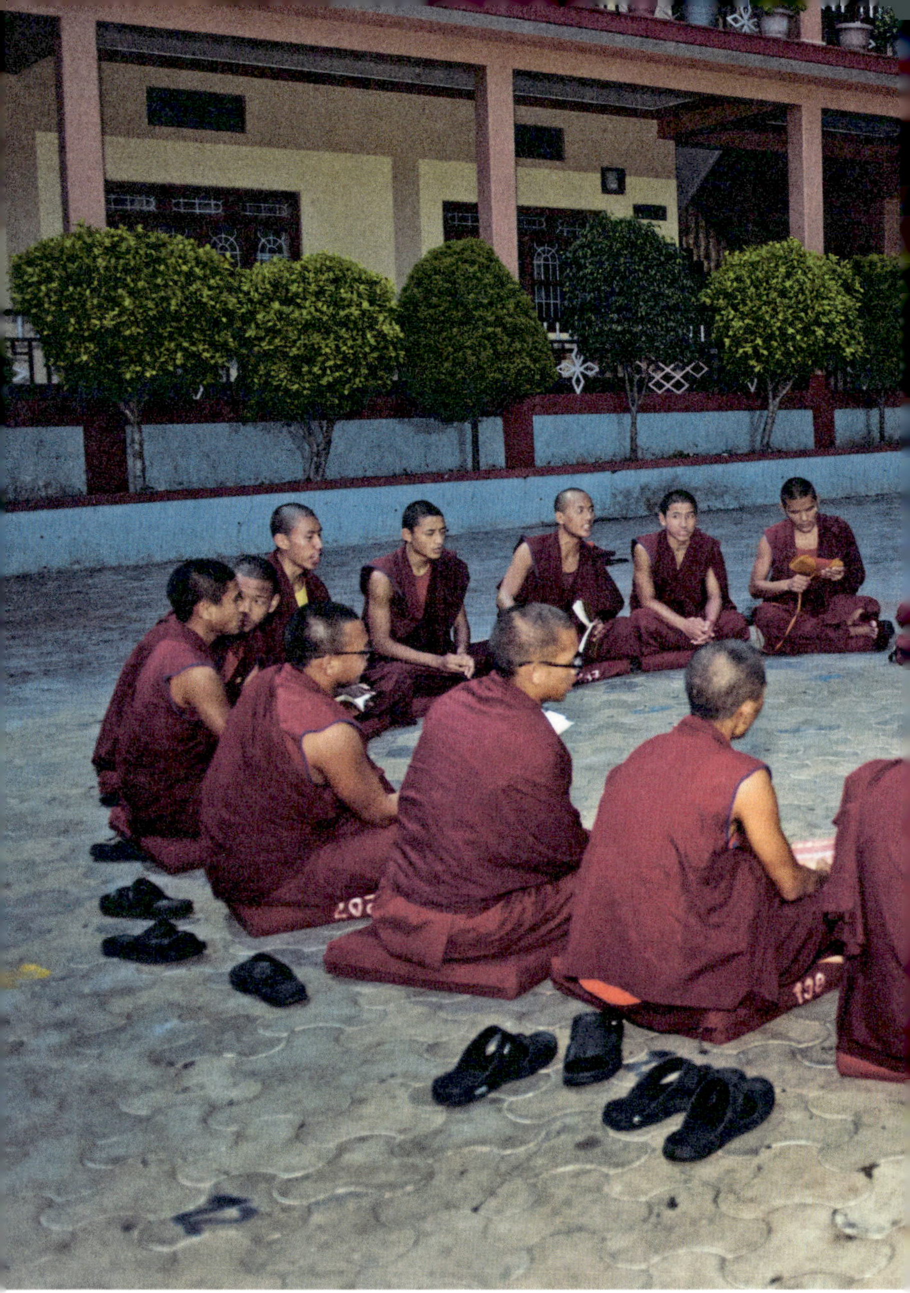

Practice recitation is held in a group courtyard setting to reinforce memorization of essential Buddhist texts.

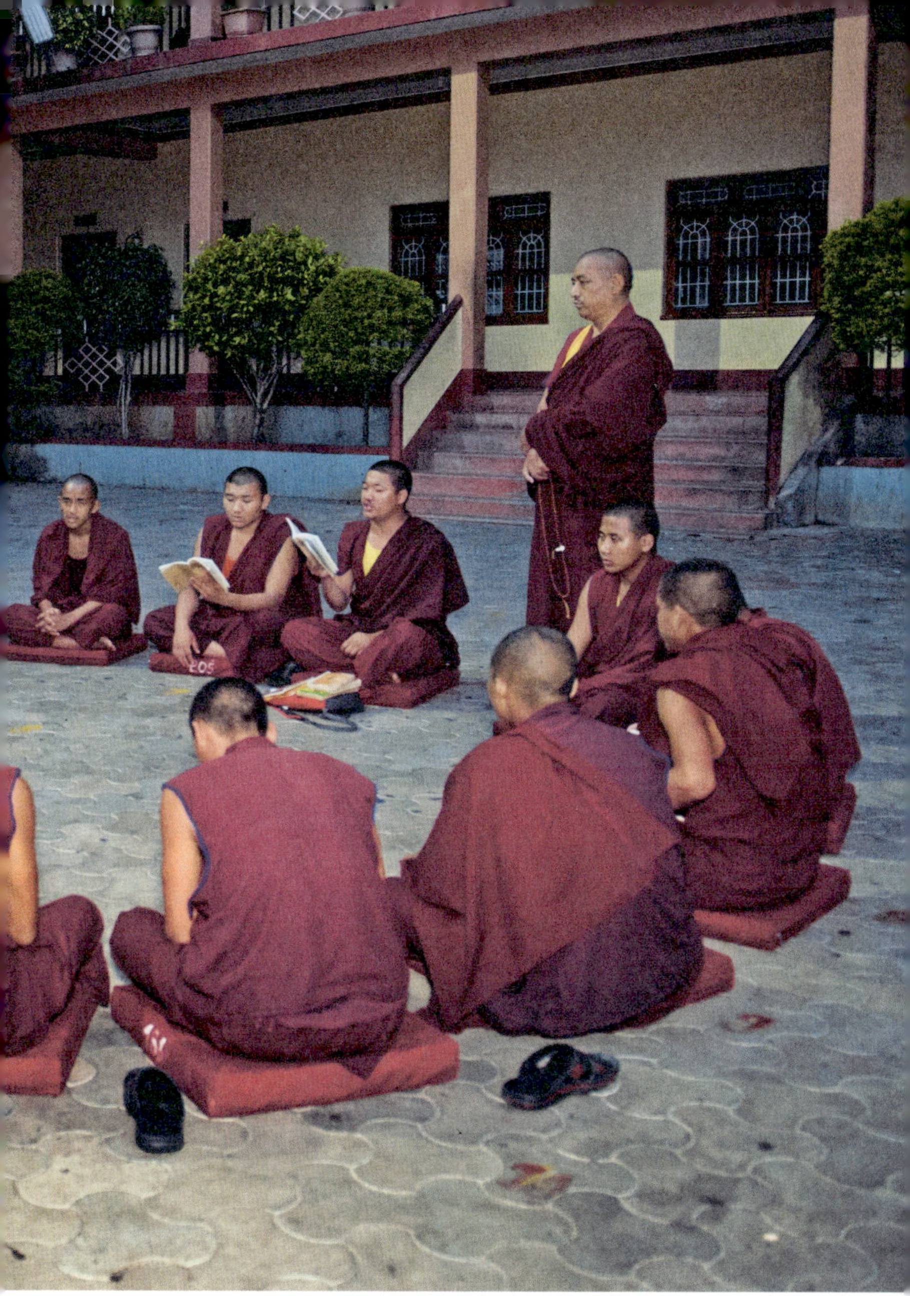

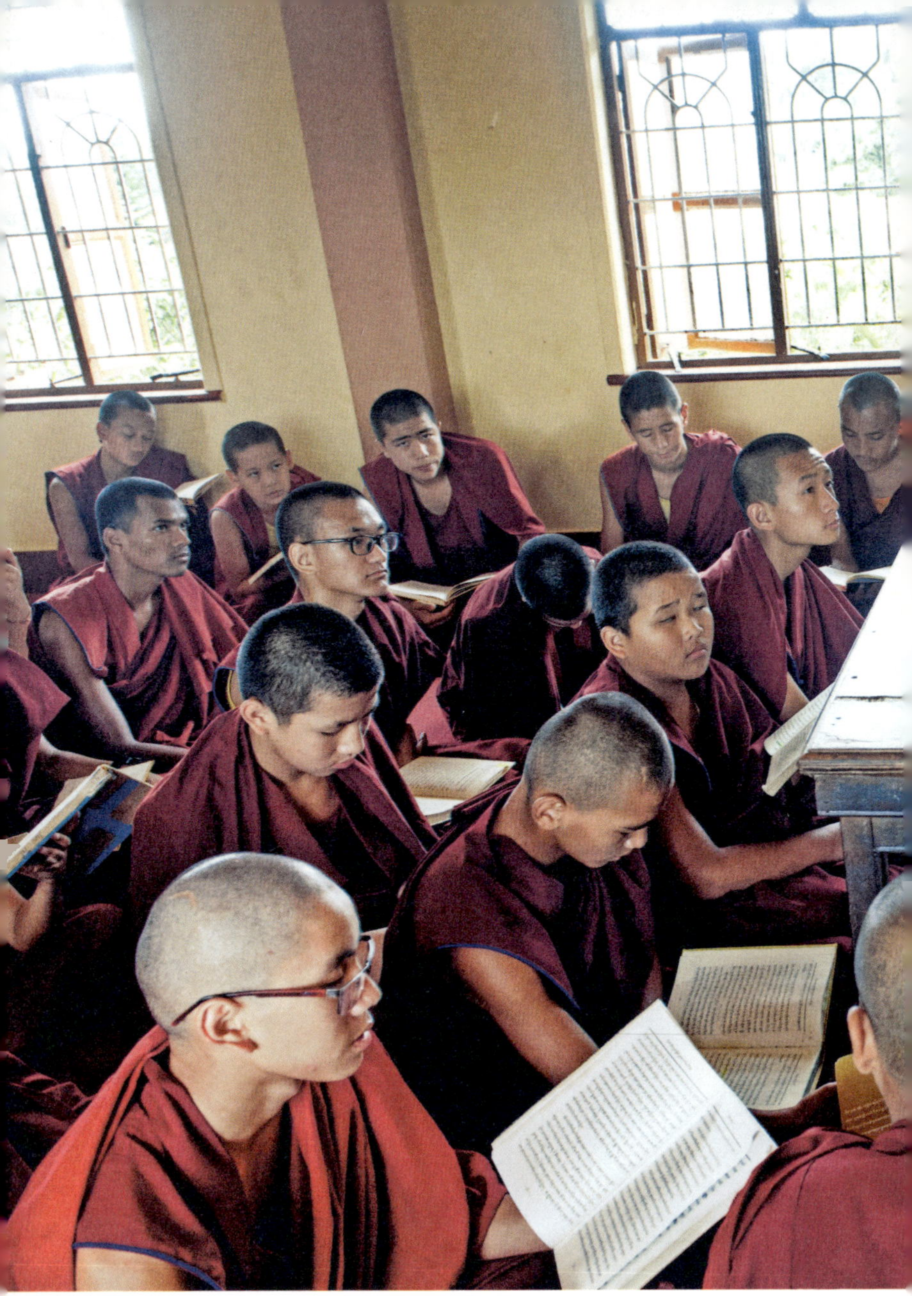

In this dialectic scripture class, students learn how to formulate and defend their logic, which helps prepare them for formal debate.

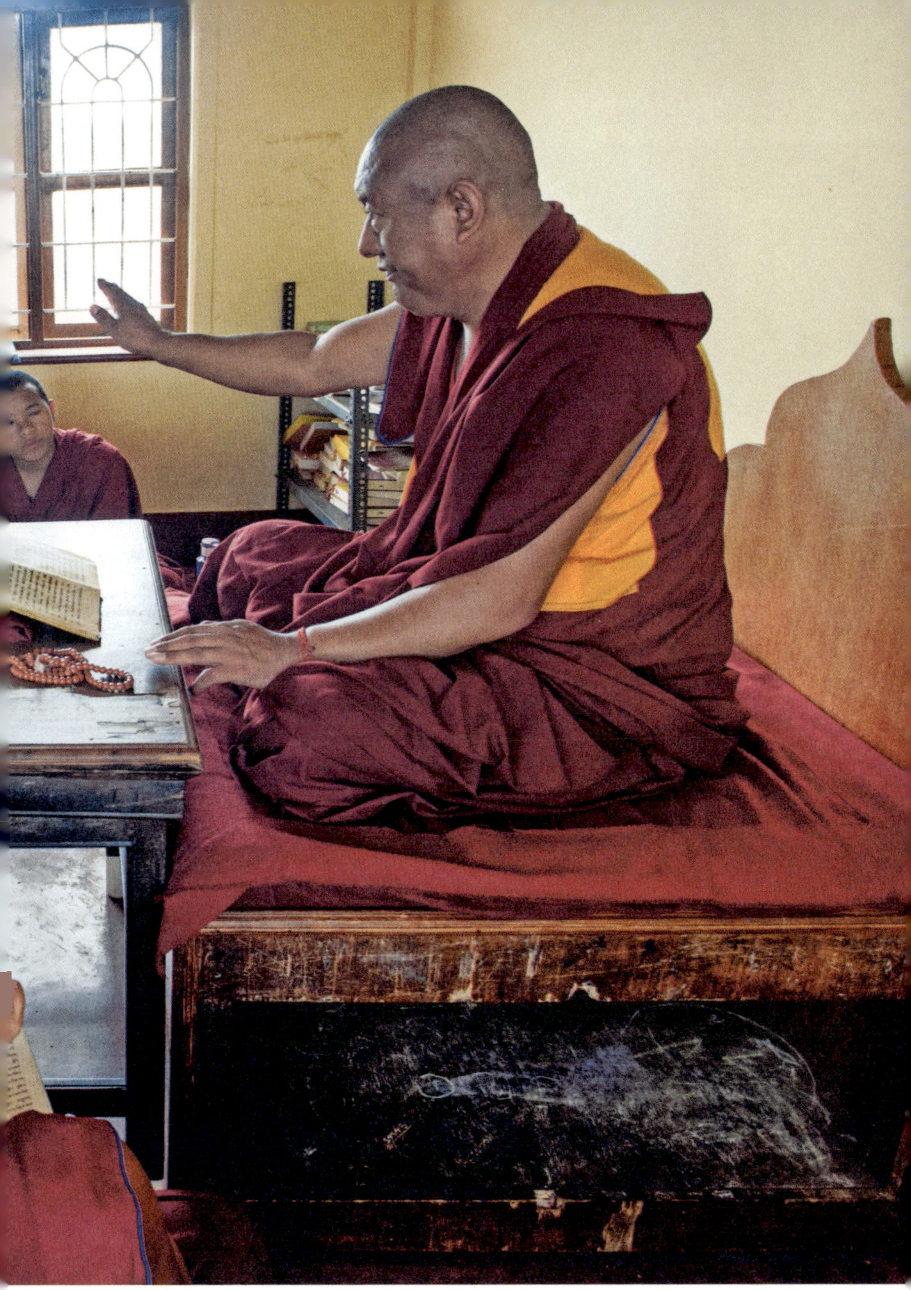

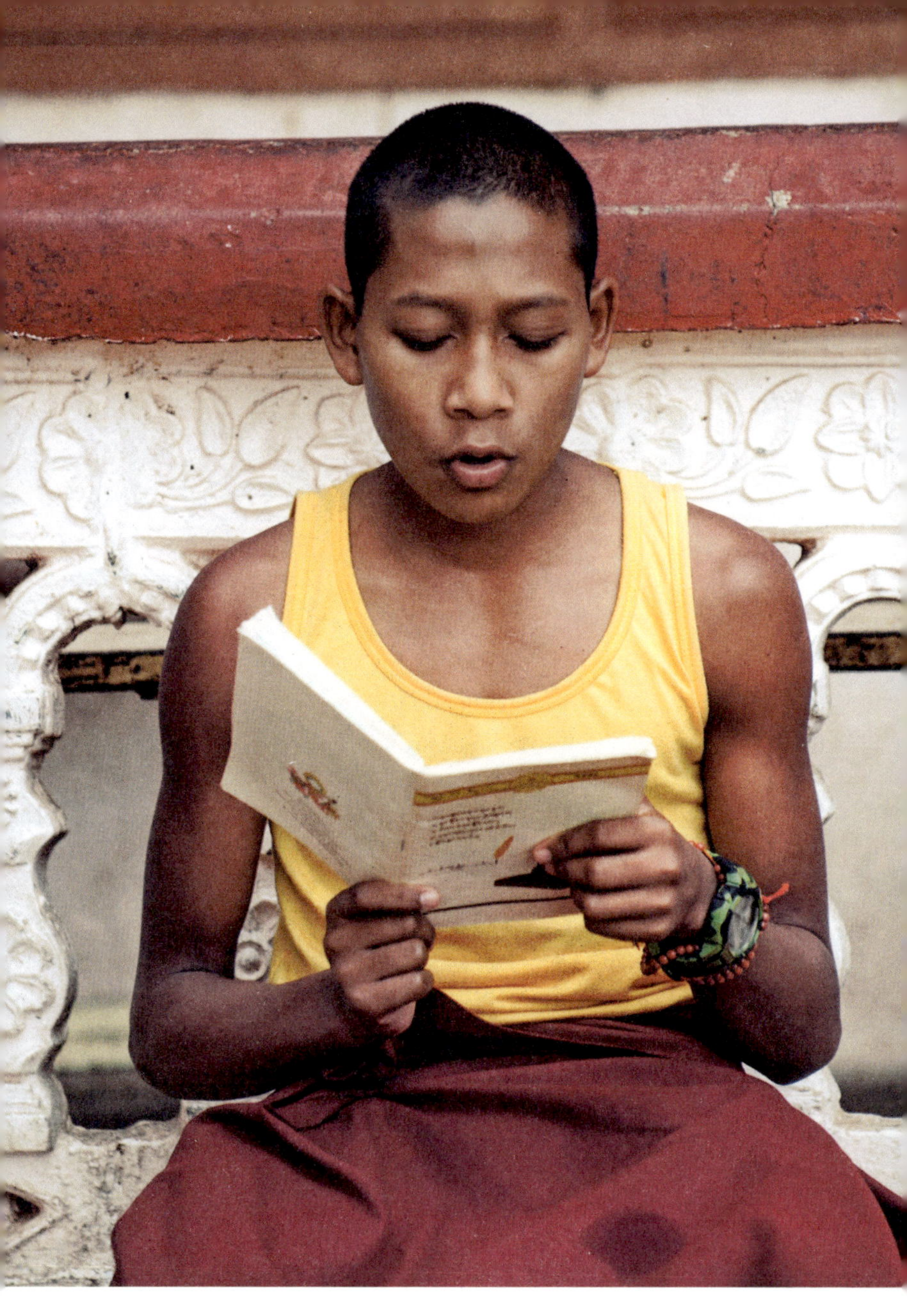

Freshly graduated from school and sporting my Beatles-style hairdo and bell-bottom trousers, I was eighteen years old when I first joined monkhood at what was then called the Buddhist School of Dialectics in Dharamsala. There, I was introduced to the traditional debate system as the mainstay of Buddhist monastic education. Perhaps just six months into our debate training, I found myself stubbornly holding on to my position, fully confident in it, while the rest of my classmates were debating against it. It took a couple of days of pondering before I realized my folly. My error was starkly clear to me now, yet I had been blinded by my belief and false confidence. This experience taught me that some of our false beliefs can have much deeper roots than one might imagine. During my years of study and in life, this insight allowed me to approach novel topics with open-mindedness.

The Tibetan Buddhist debate system improves your grasp of the problem at hand, facilitating the prospect of a meaningful solution. Debate practice equips you with tools for philosophical inquiry that help in examining a problem and providing perspective by situating it within its factual context but removing conceptual and philosophical baggage. It is even more rewarding when applied to the themes of well-being and prosperity, which involves looking at our emotions, attitudes, perspectives, habits, and actions, as the scriptures guide us to do. Debate is a wonderful tool to cultivate a well-rounded wisdom, one that is powerfully original, limitlessly deep, discriminatingly clear, and unhesitatingly quick in handling any situation.

— Dadul Namgyal

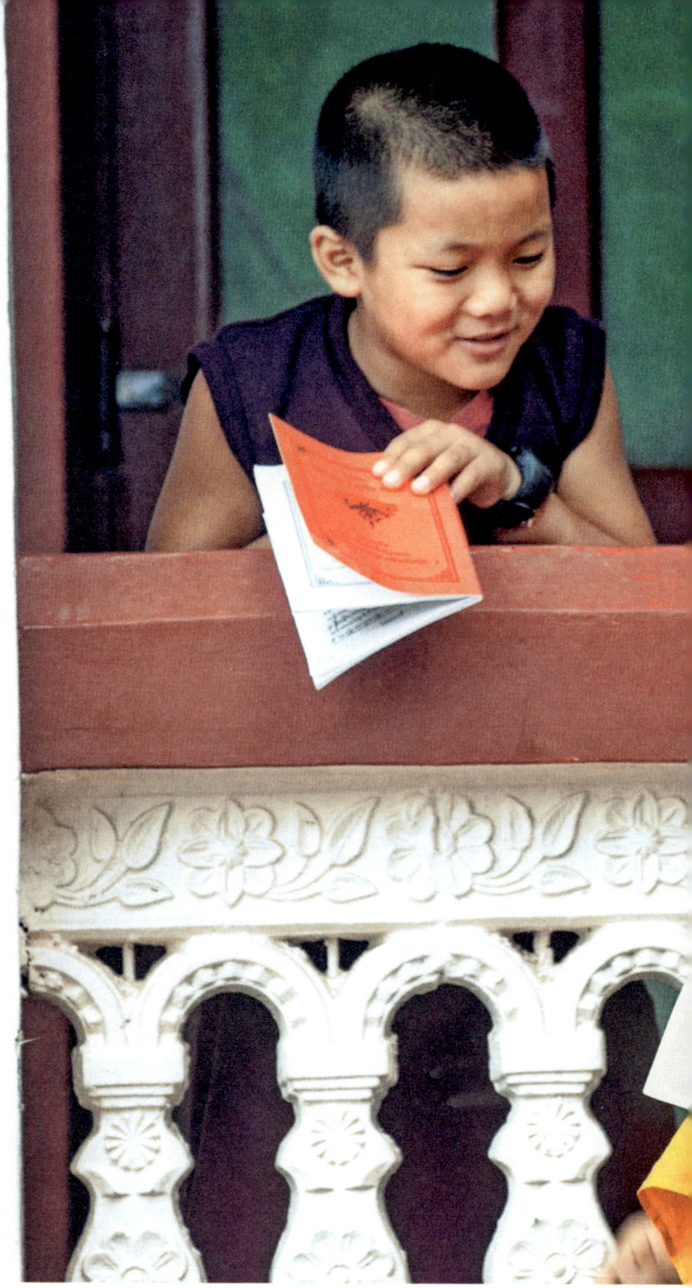

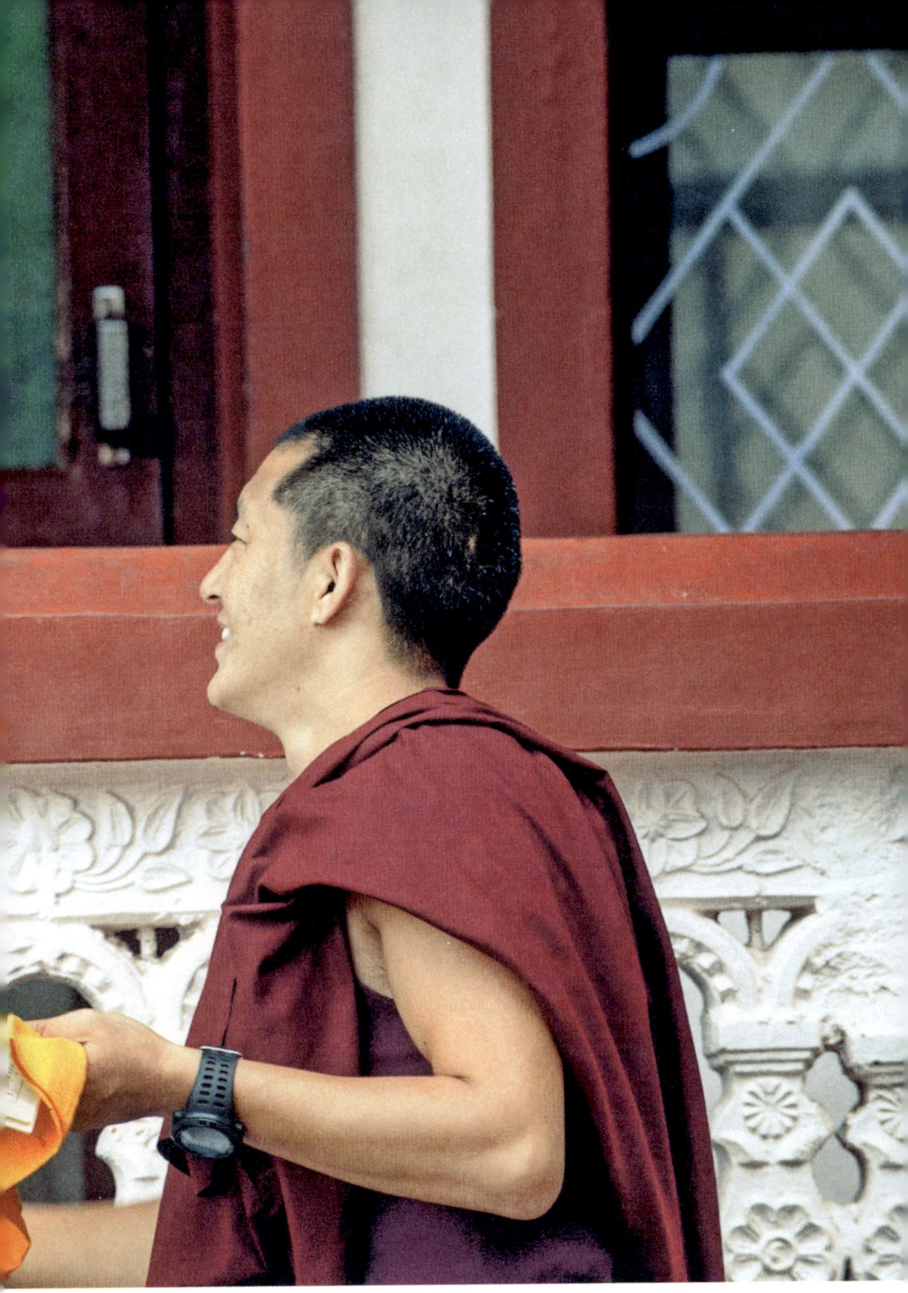

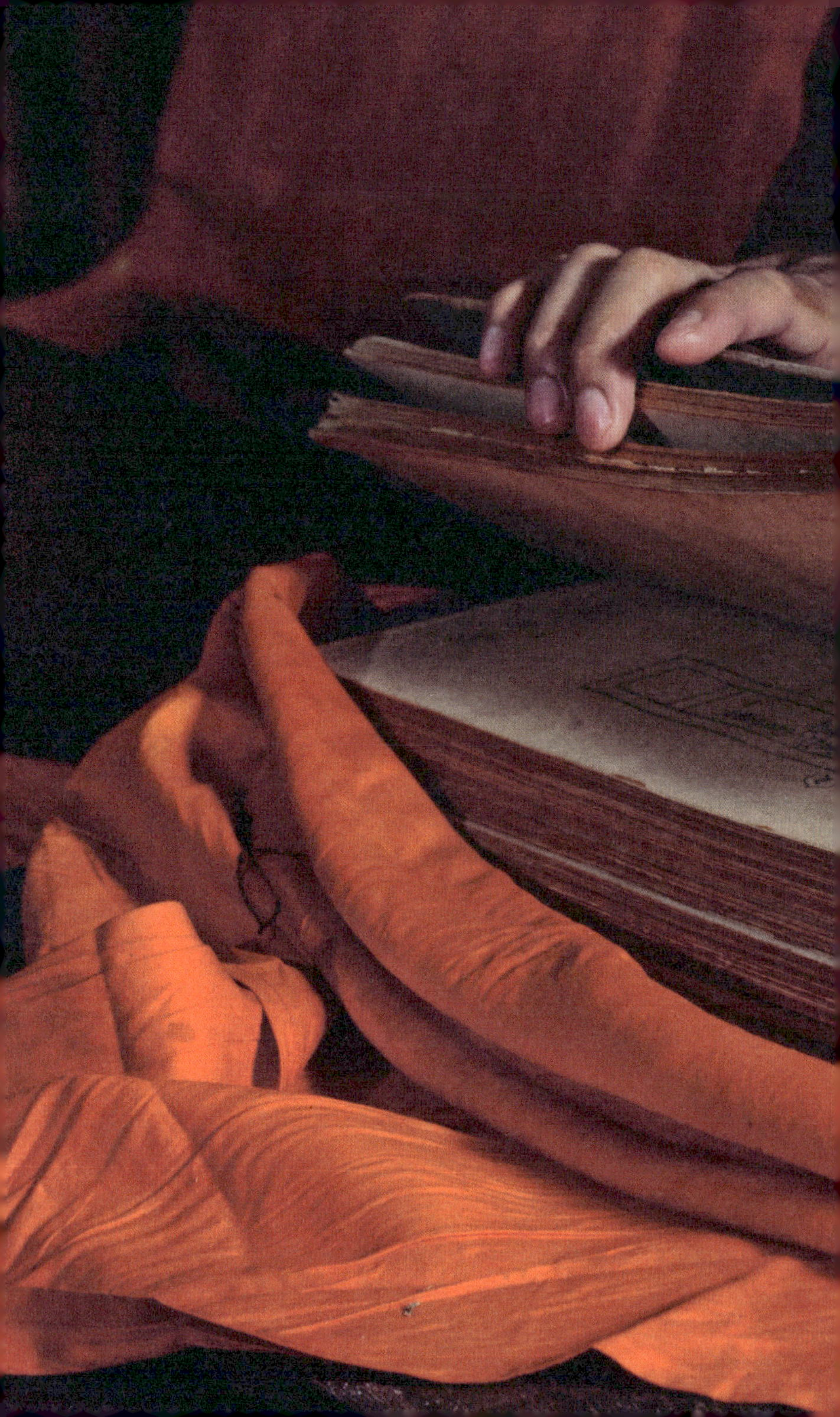

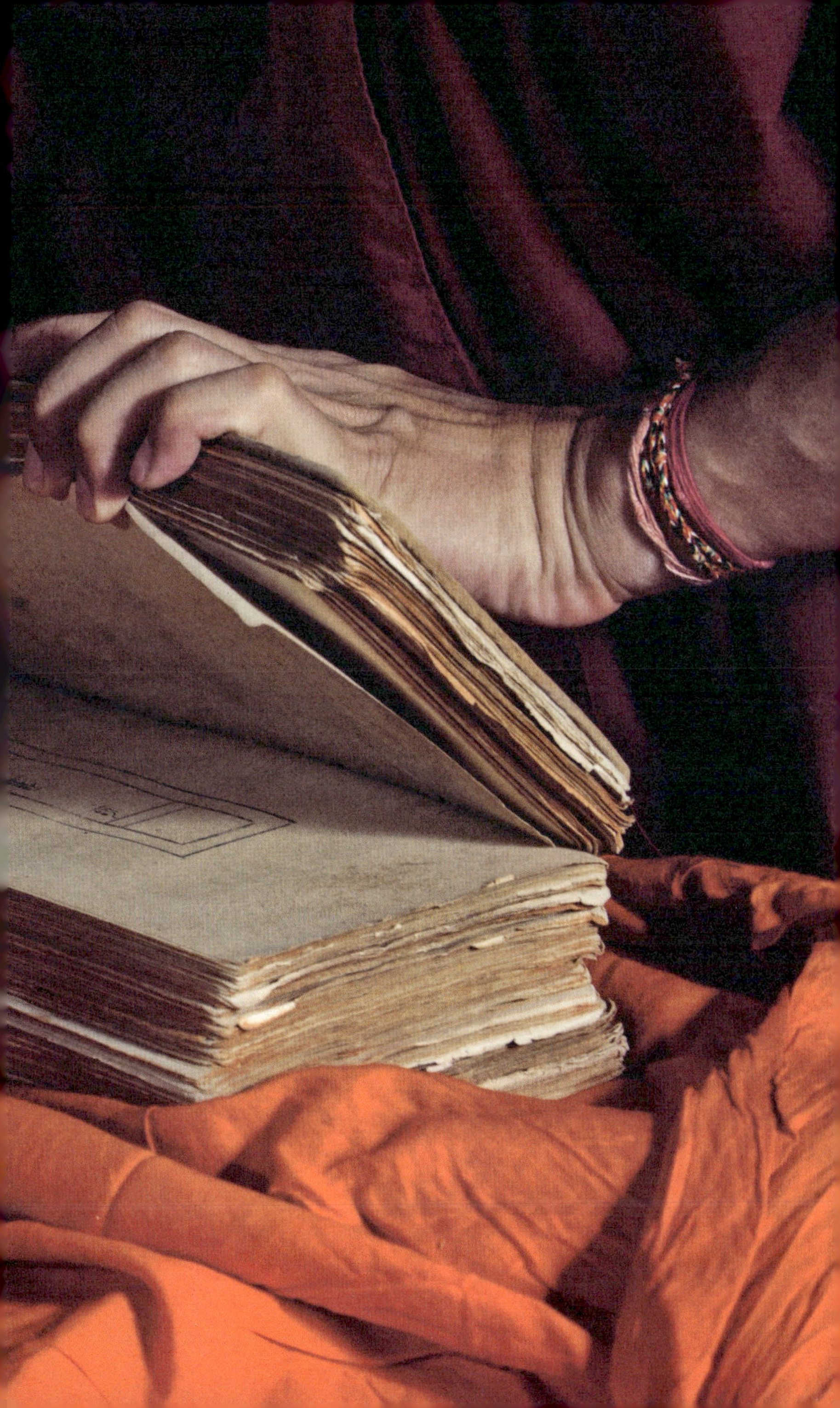

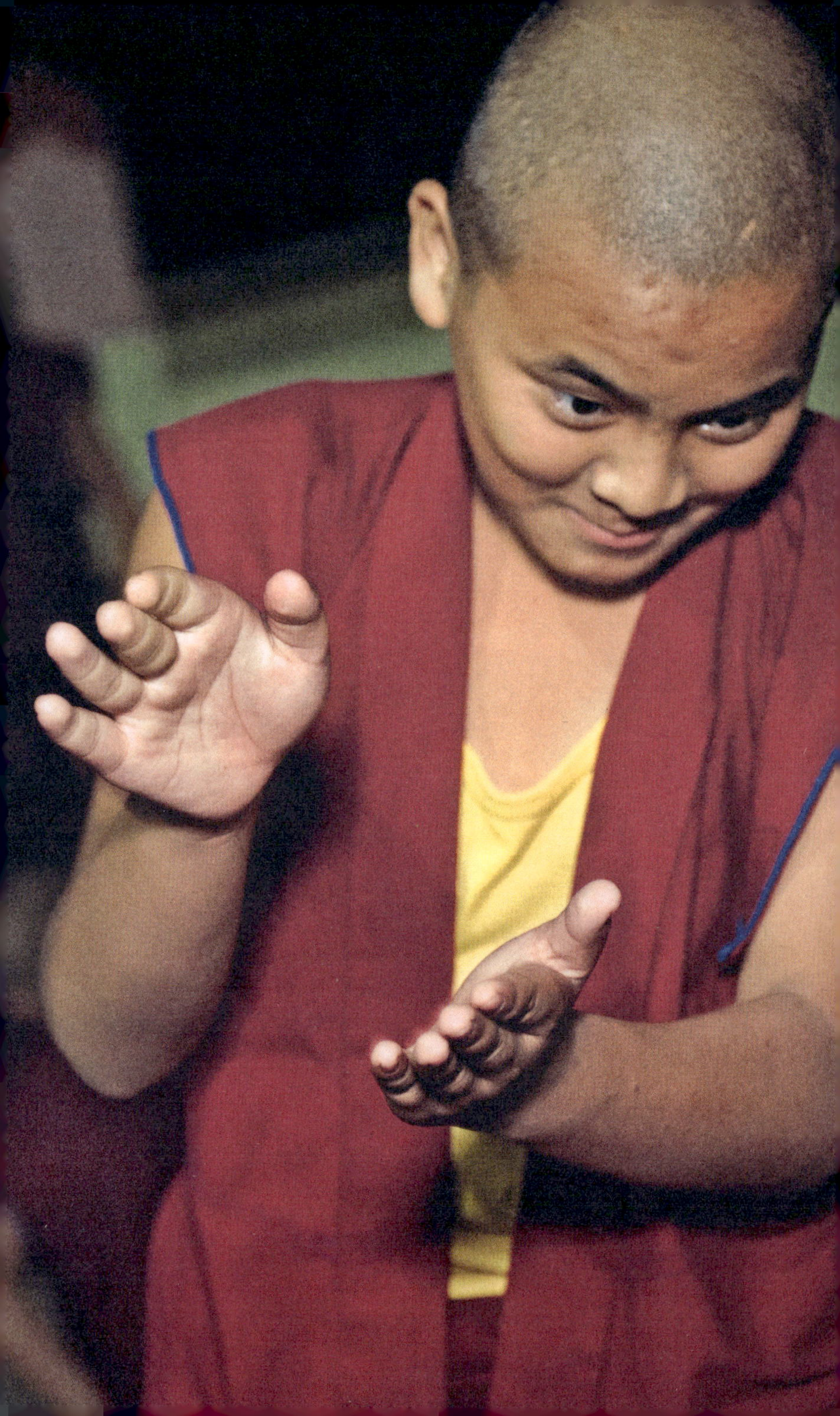

Clap and Hold—A Mantra for Scientific Discourse

Paul García

If you walk near the monasteries of southern India in the evening, the debates sound like soft murmurs in the distance. The peaceful night atmosphere dissipates as you draw closer to hundreds of saffron robes vividly animated. These are not ordinary conversations. The younger monks are in pairs while the older monks are clustered in groups. Standing monks, the challengers, aggressively pose queries to a solitary, seated defender. An opening question might be: "Is this tree permanent?" If the defender takes the affirmative position, the challenger follows up with questions about the plant's life cycle; if the defender takes the negative position, the challenger may use counterexamples such as memories or historical references to a specific tree. Even if you don't speak Tibetan, the ebb and flow of majority versus minority opinion is obvious. One-upsmanship is abundant, laughter not infrequent. The scene resembles any other unstructured gathering of people in many conversations, except one feature stands out—the dramatic handclap. Synchronous with the last syllable of the challenger's question is a dramatic "thwack" of the right hand on the left, menacingly close to the defender's face. After the clap, the right hand is purposefully kept palm-down and low. A brief half-moment of silence occupies the space as all involved parties wait in anticipation for the resonance of the hand-clap to fade, before the seated monk calmly states his response.

This theatrical punctuation of the verbal challenge serves many purposes. Monks rise very early in the morning, and in addition to their hours of monastic study, they have many assigned daily duties. After a long day of meditation, singing, chanting, reciting, cooking, and cleaning around the monastery, the startling clap helps to keep everyone's attention. But the position of the hand after the clap is equally important, as the right hand of the challenger subtly slides lower and to the side. This is the challenger's reminder to the defender to maintain composure by suppressing negative emotions that undermine their defended position. The debates are an excellent way to practice tamping down overt expressions of anger, jealousy, pride, humiliation, and fear. As a Western scientist with medical training, I am familiar with how experiencing negative emotions related to anxiety and public humiliation are an effective memory aid (although not a pleasant one). When outfitted with physiologic monitors, seated challengers have been recorded exhibiting hypertension, hyperventilation, and tachycardia (approximately 180 beats per minute). Training to experience these emotions with minimal outward reaction helps eliminate their destructive energy.

On occasion, the defender misremembers an important point in the logical narrative, and several monks will stand with the challenger, vigorously reciting a series of memorized statements that invalidate the position taken by the defender. Each monk fastens his robe before dynamically windmilling his right arm around to enthusiastically slap his left in unison, emphasizing the lesson. Or, if the seated defender describes his position persuasively enough, other monks begin to sit in silence beside him. At other times, the challenger gets tripped up and cannot continue along his rational trajectory. But most of the time, the large monastery bell rings and it is time for the debate to end and evening prayers to begin.

Often the debates focus on core Tibetan Buddhist concepts, such as emptiness (*śūnyatā* in Sanskrit). The main purpose is to deepen the understanding of specific concepts and use conviction for a meditative purpose. A challenger will sharpen his critical reasoning skills while trying to come up with counterexamples that might delegitimize a core concept. Similarly, if the defender has not grasped the concept well, he may lose the foundation of his stance, forcing him to rethink central themes. This inquiry, known as analytical meditation, is crucial to overcoming ignorance and afflictive emotions.

The monks believe that it is impossible to attain enlightenment without knowing the true nature of reality, and so an emphasis on understanding the disparity of an object's appearance with the genuine nature of that object is pivotal. Universal application of this dualism to all things—trees, individuals, groups, and even idcas—is necessary to eradicate misconceptions and negative emotions. Failing to recognize the existence of a deeper reality while focusing on appearance can lead to great suffering. Winning a debate is not the goal. Debates are merely an effective tool for acquiring knowledge critical for progression to enlightenment. Symbolically, both the superficial and the deeper parts of the activity are reflected in the handclap and hold.

I can't help but think how our scholarly communication at academic conferences and in scientific institutions would be different had we been trained in a similar debate style. How often have we expressed frustration based on the opinions of an anonymous reviewer? How many scientific feuds do we have in our fields? Maybe we have been too focused on the staccato slap while ignoring the importance of the intended natural rest symbolized by a low hand extended palm-down.

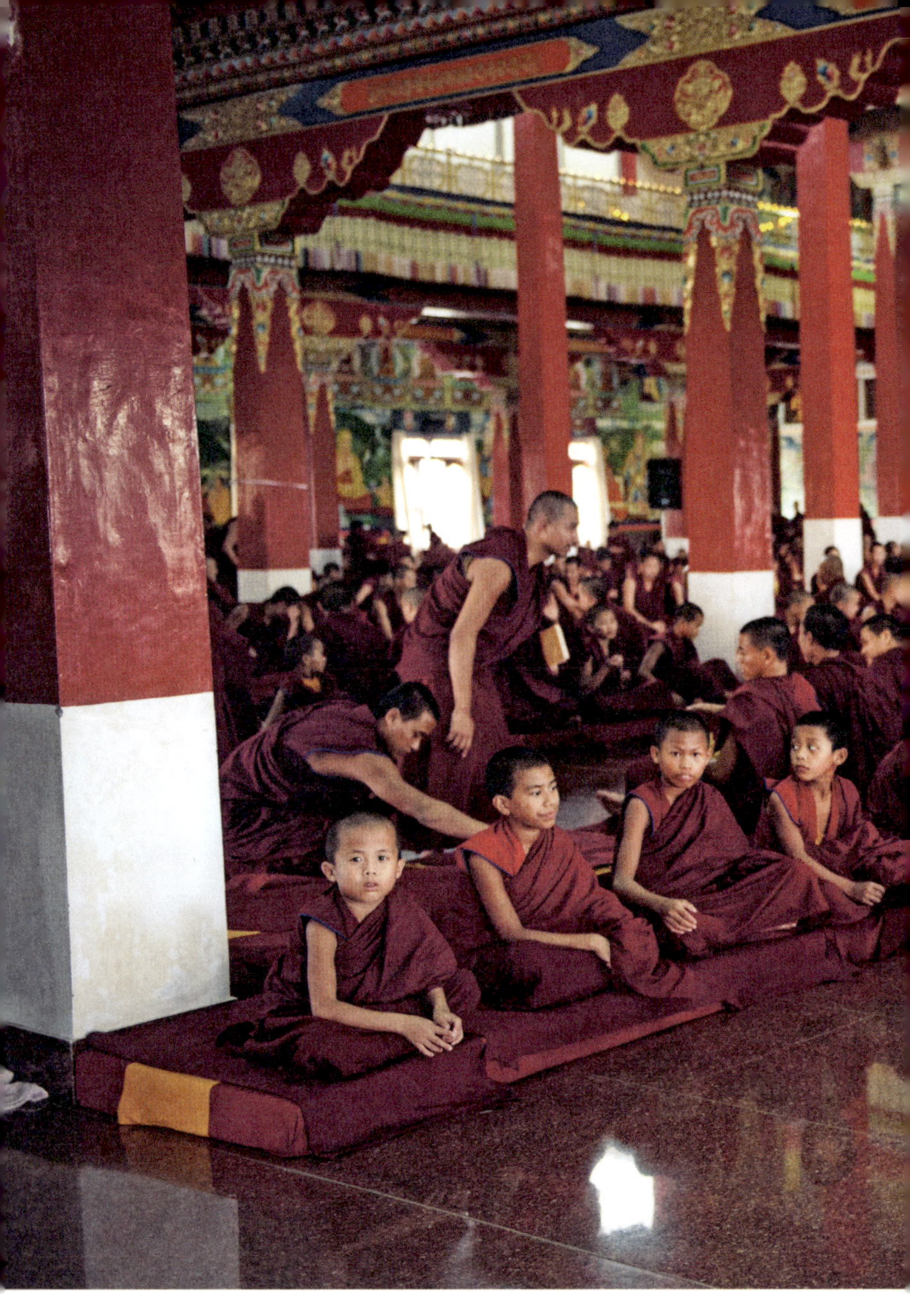

Monks assemble in the temple for chanting and meditation practice.

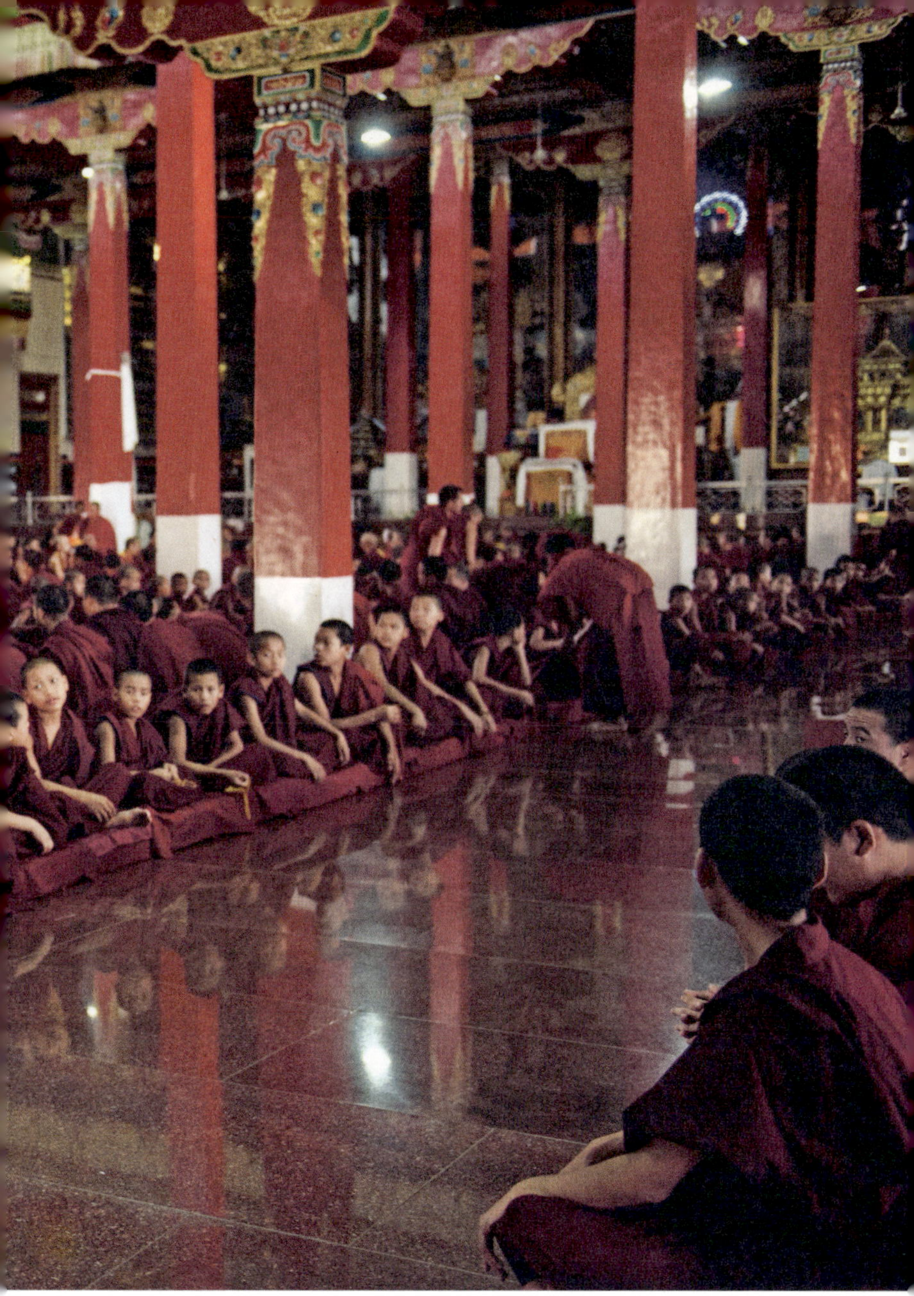

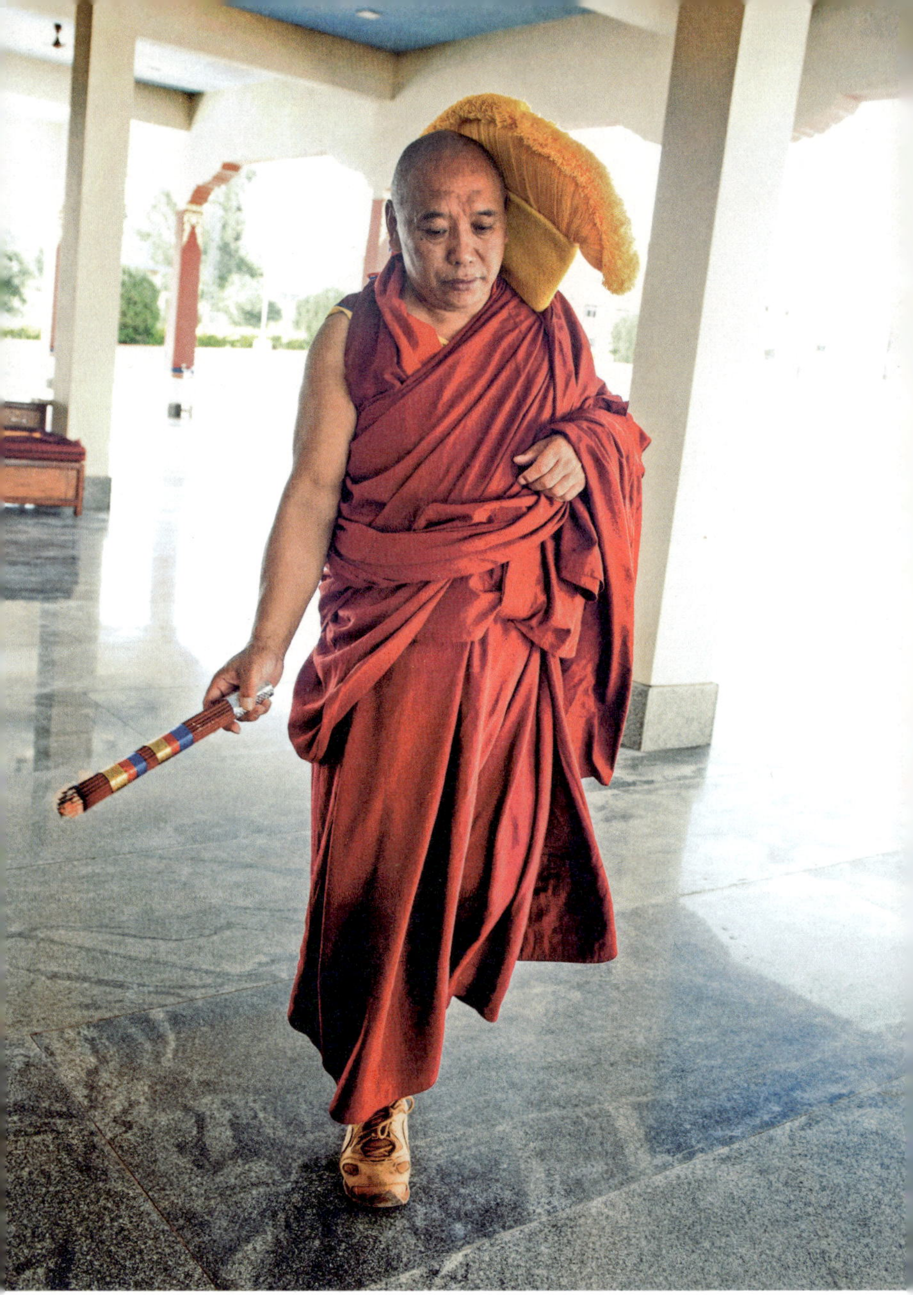

A senior monastic official, with his yellow hat resting on his shoulder, sanctifies a monastic space using colorfully bound incense. The yellow hat is a reminder of ethical discipline as the foundation of their study and practice.

The Venerable Lobsang Dorjee, my cousin and mentor, has played a crucial role in my life. When I was ten years old, and I was still quite small and naughty, I asked him to bring me with him to Tashi Lhunpo Monastery in Bylakuppe, where he was studying Buddhist philosophy. He introduced me to Buddhism, and from the beginning he taught me everything, even how to do laundry, until I could do things on my own. He mentored me even more than my parents did—I spent my first ten years with my parents and the next twenty-two with him.

I remember watching my cousin debating when I was young. After a debate, I would ask him questions. I learned how important it was to read and memorize the scriptures and their commentaries and to spend time interpreting them and understanding their meaning. Watching my cousin during debates inspired me to debate and to form my own points of view so that I could defend my own ideas.

— Rigzin Nurbu

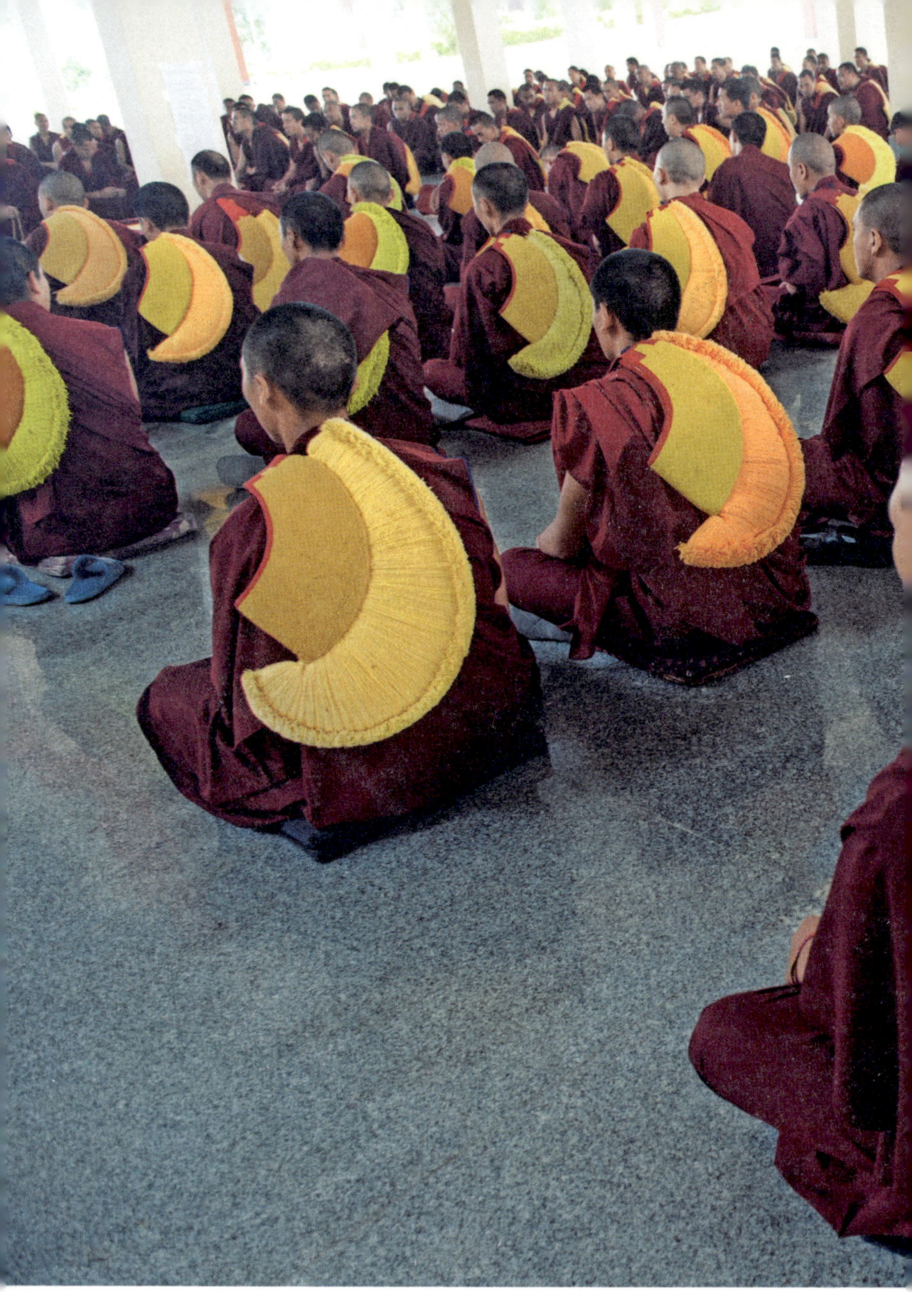

Monks of the Yellow Hat order, another name for the Gelug school of Tibetan Buddhism. Tsongkhapa, founder of the Gelug school, emphasized ethical practice.

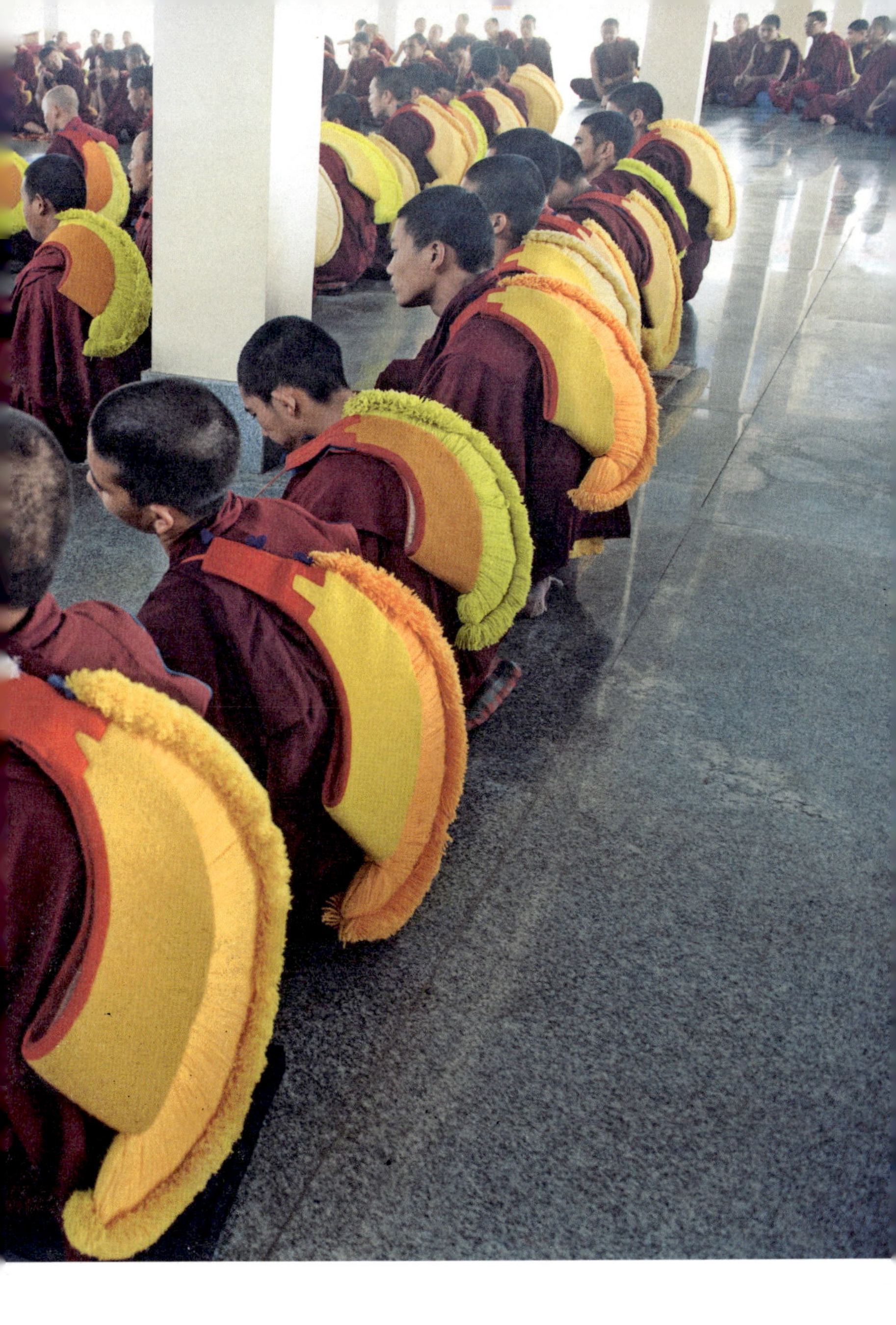

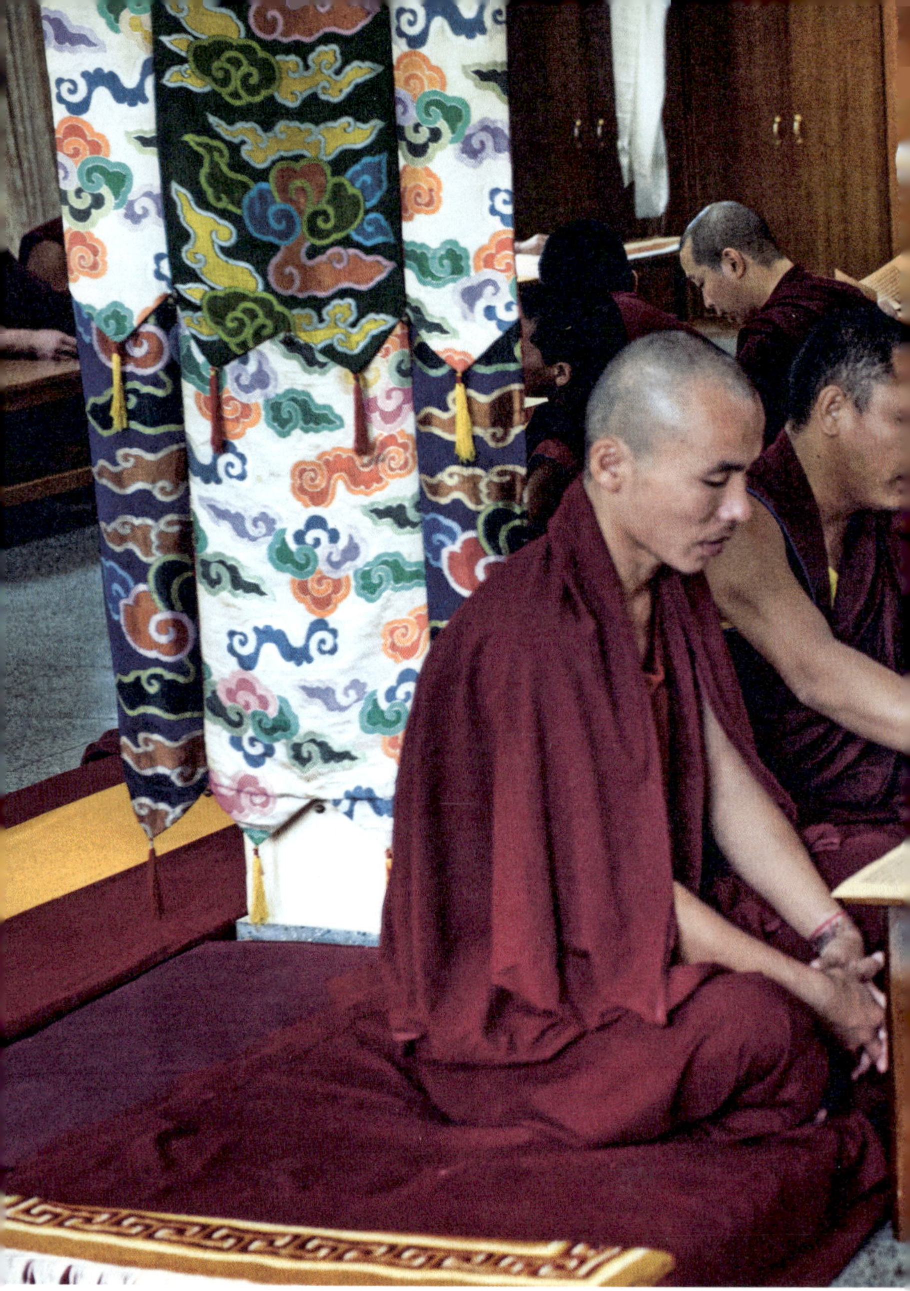

Monks conducting an annual ceremonial reading of the complete Buddhist canons in a temple. The canons, which contain the Buddha's words along with commentaries by his early Indian disciples, number over three hundred volumes, and the reading takes several days to complete.

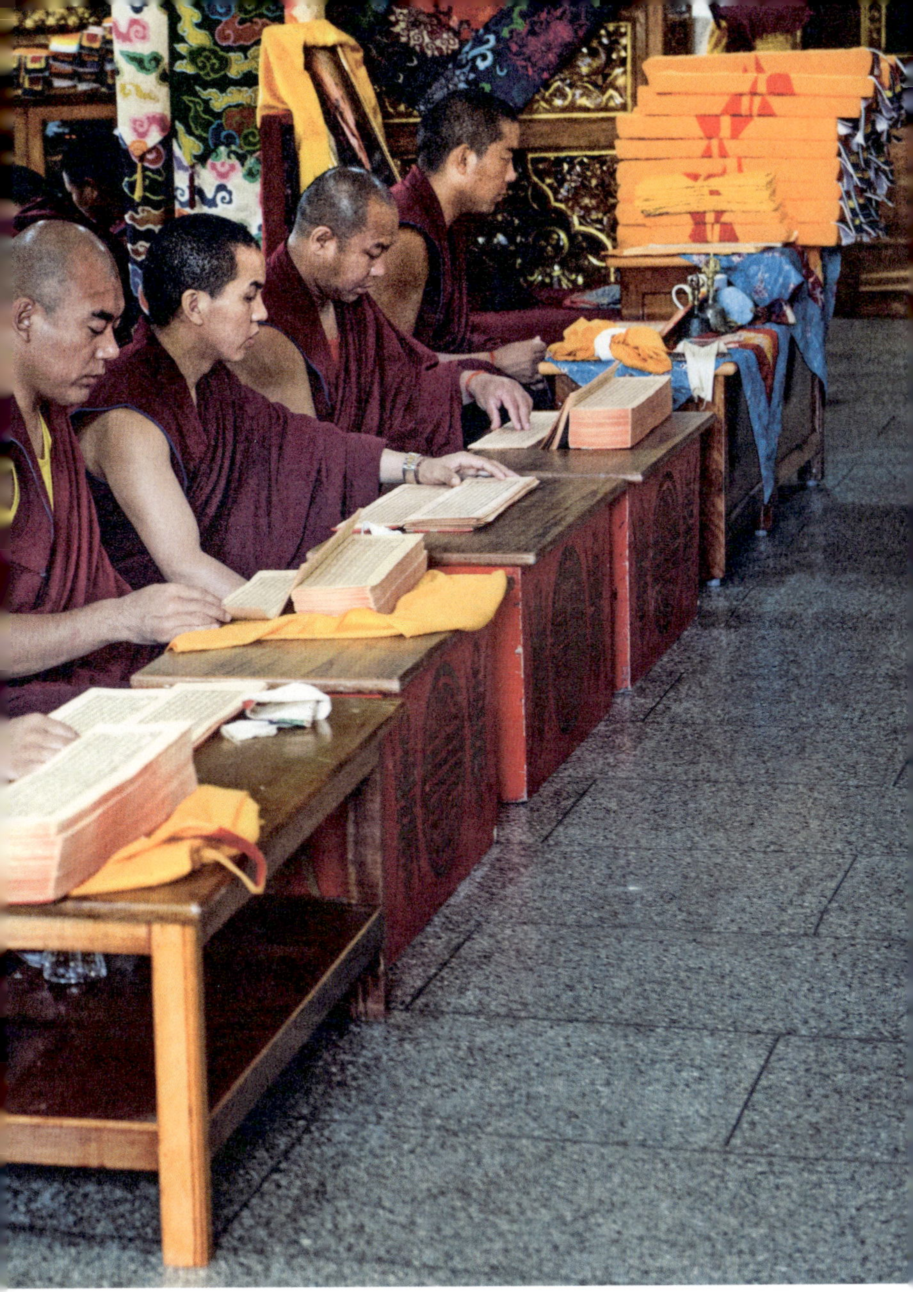

Monastic debate is necessary for monks, but it is also useful for any person in pursuit of knowledge. It can be viewed as a key that both allows you to differentiate between true and false and opens your intelligence.

I once debated the topic of impermanence as a subtle change that never ceases. As explained in the *pramana* text, anything that comes into existence owing to its cause and conditions must be impermanent and subject to change. For instance, if we look at an eighty-year-old man, right from the moment of his birth he begins to undergo gradual but ceaseless changes that are outside of his control. Change is a constant—sometimes for the better, sometimes for the worse. Realizing that change is inevitable revealed a new way of looking at the world for me and thus helped me to be more resilient when facing challenges.

I have been studying Buddhist logic for more than ten years, and one of the things that has moved me most profoundly is the concept of interdependence as explained in the Madhyamaka texts, which show that everything is interdependent, and therefore everything—our welfare, our happiness, our community, our environment—is dependent on others.

— Lobsang Dhondup

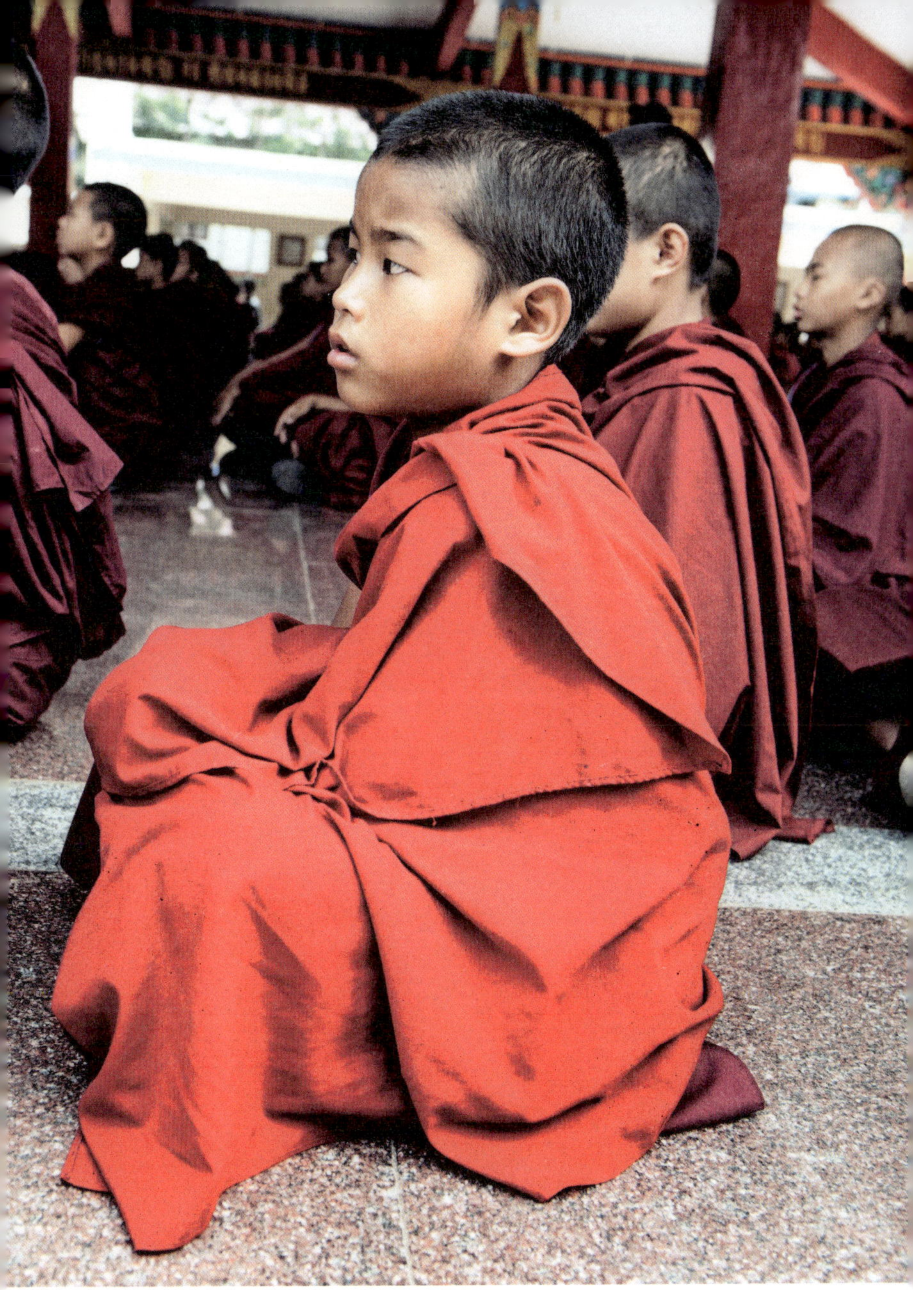

A young monk listens intently during a large group training in Buddhist practice.

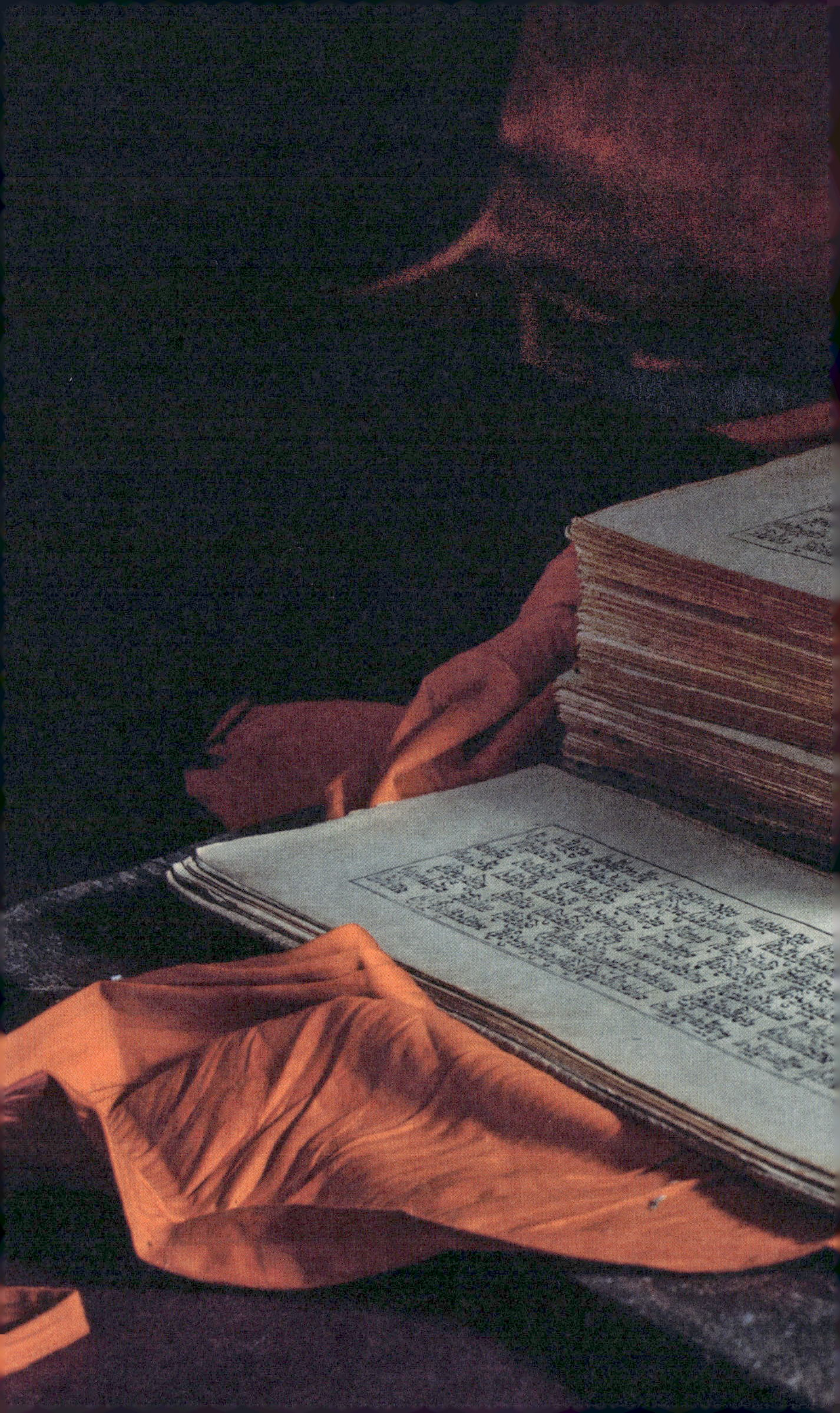

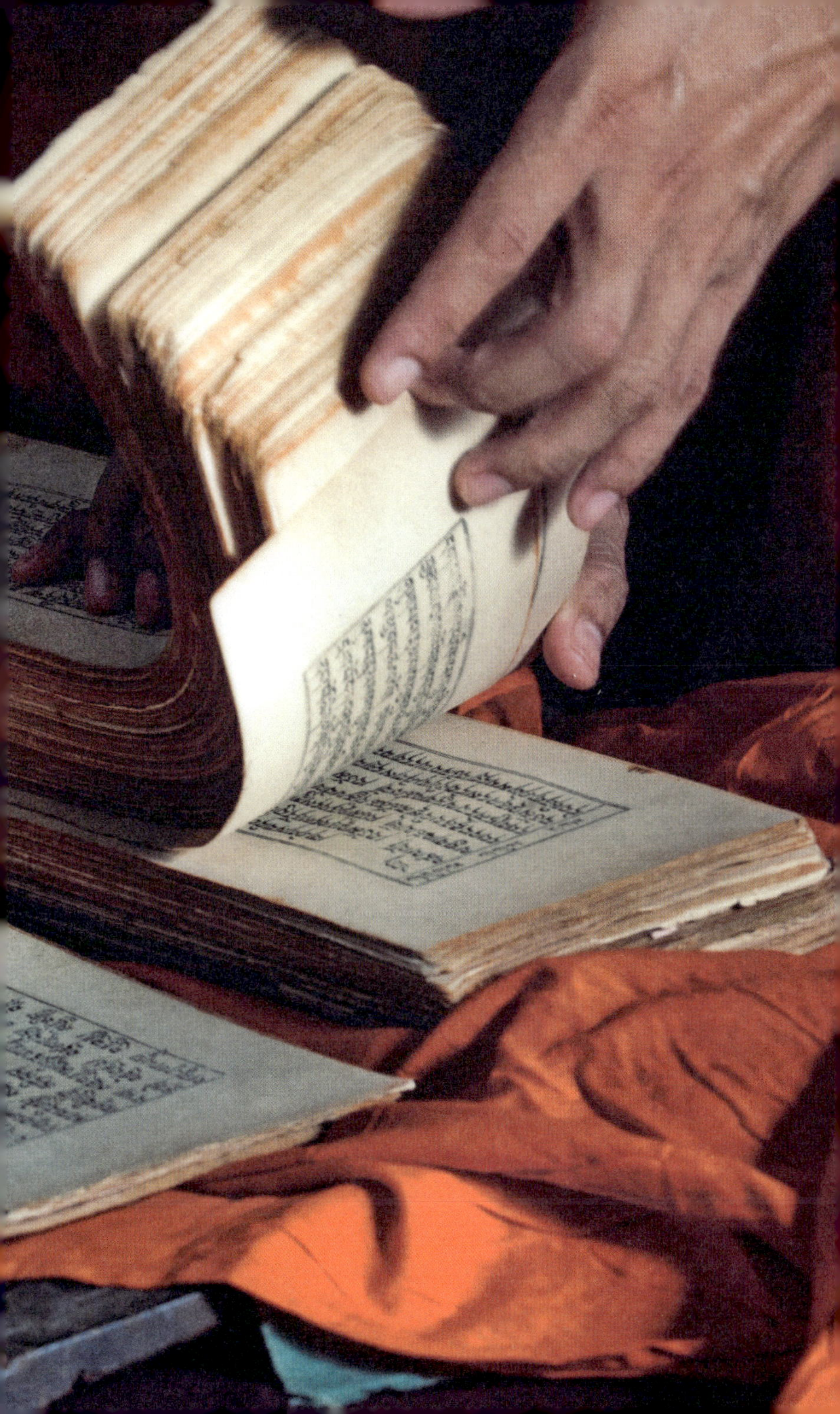

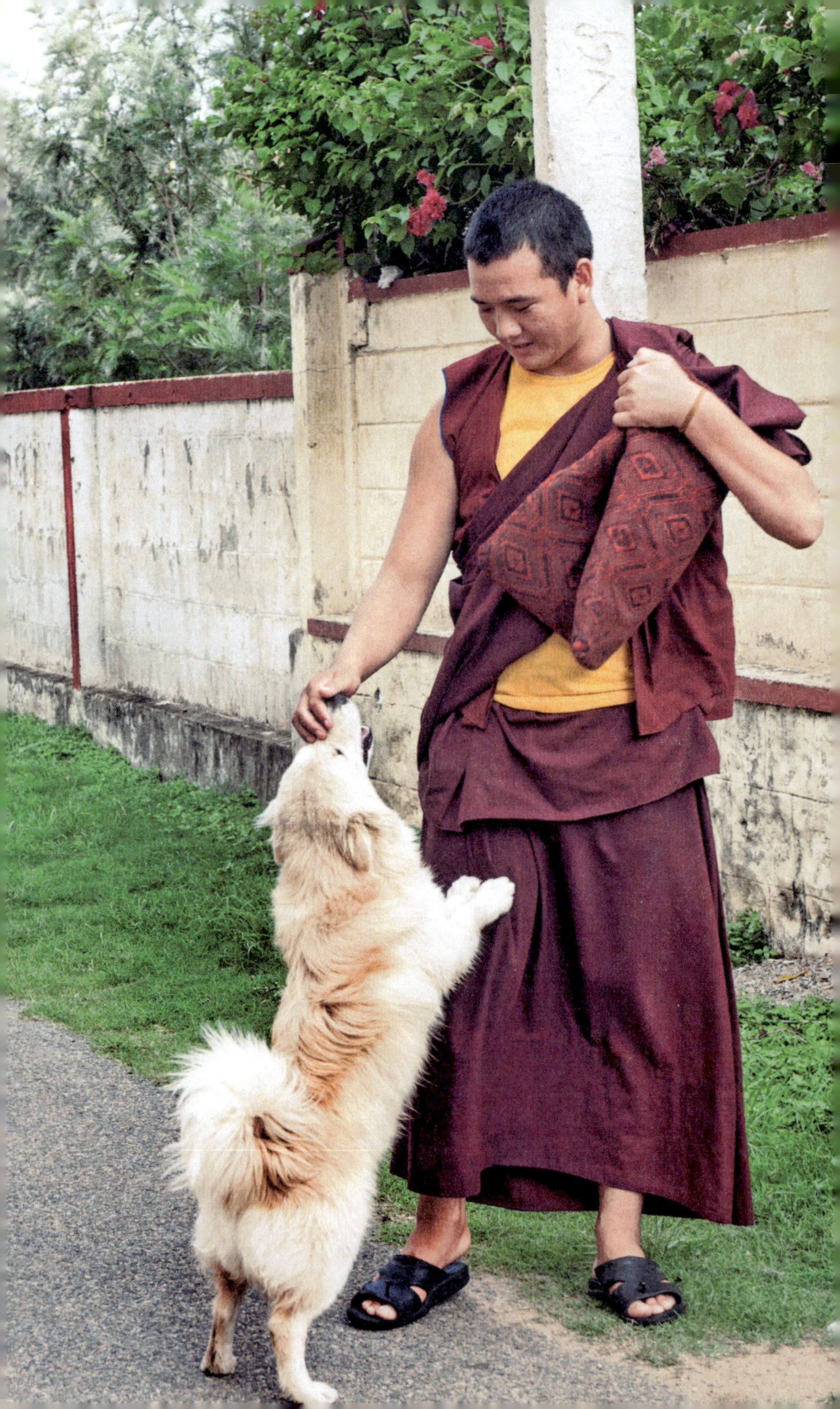

Are Bacteria Sentient? And Why You Should Care

Arri Eisen

I have been teaching biology to Tibetan monks and nuns for over a decade. I thought I knew everything there was to know about teaching science well, but this experience has entirely reshaped the way I think about teaching and doing science—even though I had been engaged in both for twenty years prior. Witnessing Tibetan Buddhist debate and everything it represents about learning in the Tibetan Buddhist monastic tradition was key to my transformation.

One day during my first year as a visiting scientist among the Buddhist monks in Dharamsala, an ancient city that sits in the shadow of the Himalayas in northernmost India and is the home to the Tibetan government in exile, I had taken a group of monks to various elevations so they could test the theory they had developed (with Darwin's help) that environments affect the characteristics of organisms and vice versa. I was walking down from the tree line above the city, which is nearly a mile above sea level, with Dhondup, who was at the time one of the few monks fluent in English. Dhondup and I had connected over basketball, of all things, which turns out to be a great love of Tibetans.

I asked him why he was there with me learning science rather than doing what I thought were monastic activities. First, he said, because the Dalai Lama said learning science is good, and then he commented, "I study modern science so I can understand my own Buddhism better." His statement drew me up short; I couldn't imagine anyone from my Judeo-Christian world ever saying such a thing in relation to their own religious tradition.

I found out later that Dhondup was succinctly summarizing a central tenet of the Nalanda tradition of Buddhism that he studies, which originated in India centuries ago but is now practiced only by Tibetans. The premise is that you cannot fully understand your own self, knowledge, and traditions until you understand everyone else's. So, studying science, a major modern knowledge system, would enrich, not erase, Dhondup's Buddhism.

This moment helped me recognize an unstated, perhaps unconscious, bias in Western education—especially in science education—that I know, and you don't, and that I'm here to convert you to what I know. An alternative interpretation of my role as educator, suggested by Dhondup's statement and the Nalanda tradition, is that my job is not to convert students, but rather to facilitate their becoming better versions of who they already are.

Debate as practiced in the Tibetan Buddhist monastic tradition animates this central concept, since it is a living practice that creates a communal rapport among the practitioners. Because every debate is choreographed yet spontaneous, the opportunity to contextualize new with traditional knowledge arises, exploring how they fit together and how they don't, challenging conceptions in a dance of verbal exchange that results in dynamic learning: "Go ahead, make me better, prove me wrong. . . No, you're wrong! Time's up." Now, relax and reflect.

Authentic teaching is the ultimate challenge. How to reach a roomful of unique individuals of different genders, with different background knowledge, and disparate experiences? The task is to synthesize the new with what they already may know, while considering a variety of learning styles. My classrooms at Emory University are far more diverse than in Buddhist monastery classrooms in India, but it took my teaching there, in a radically different setting, for me to arrive at a deeper understanding of how best to teach.

How does one teach monks about cells and genes? These structures are hard for anyone to imagine and are certainly far from the monks' daily ruminations over Buddhist philosophy focused on enlightenment. We approached it through the lens of this question: Are bacteria sentient? You may not care whether bacteria feel or perceive anything, but to a Buddhist, if bacteria are sentient, an ethical dilemma arises, since any sentient being can be reincarnated as any other. So, for a Buddhist, considering whether we should kill bacteria, either intentionally or not, is a serious question.

During our classes at the monastery, the monks grew their own bacteria, which they collected from door handles, ears, and other sources. They designed experiments to test for sentience in these bacteria. We used a special setup that allowed us to project what we saw under the microscope onto the wall as the monks introduced sugar water or dilute acid to the bacteria cultures. When the solutions were added, the microorganisms would suddenly dance. The experience of watching the bacteria respond must have been as magical and exhilarating for the monks as it was for the pioneers of microscopy—Antoine von Leeuwenhoek, Lazzaro Spallanzani, and Louis Pasteur—when they first observed microbes centuries ago. Imagine realizing that a great majority of living things had gone unseen and unknown for nearly all of human history. The monks were amazed, and they danced and chattered at the dramatic display of these tiny organisms.

Observing the cavorting bacteria with the monks, feeling the glee and awe of the students, I saw the bacteria anew. I recognized that how we see things is deeply shaped by culture. I wondered how human history might have been dramatically different if, instead of bacteria being discovered in the context of disease by Westerners who then spent the next several centuries trying to kill them, Tibetan Buddhists had discovered bacteria, seeing them as sentient, and learned to alter their environment so the organisms were no longer harming us. As it turns out, what we Westerners didn't realize was that in killing harmful bacteria with antibiotics, we were also extinguishing a vast trove of beneficial organisms, an essential brotherhood of good bacteria that we now know as our microbiome. We have seen the light perhaps too late: our microbiomes are key to our development, our immune systems, our digestion, and our mood. Many of the chronic and fatal diseases suffered by Westerners in the twenty-first century, including heart disease, diabetes, autoimmune diseases, depression, and others, are linked to the microbiome. Only now are some scientists taking Buddhist approaches like using good bacteria to neutralize the bad. It all could have been so different.

The monks and I spent a week in conversation and conducting experiments, learning the parts of cells, how genes work, the genotypes and phenotypes, and trying to figure out how it all works together to answer our big question about bacterial sentience. The final test was a debate. We divided the class in half, assigned one group to the affirmative proposition and the other group to the opposite viewpoint. They parried back and forth in vigorous argument, posing probing questions. How do our new knowledge and experiments fit into what we know about Buddhist philosophy? Is Buddhism wrong? Is science wrong? Are both right? What is sentience? What is the nature of the bacteria's sentience? The room grew so heated, so fast, the energy so frenetic and absorbing that the translator could barely communicate to me what was going on. "Okay!" I said, "Time to stop."

As if I had flipped a switch, everyone resumed being monks—relaxed and laughing quietly. Our week together was done.

"So," I asked, "How many of you think bacteria are sentient?" Half voted yes, half no. Clearly the debate is not finished.

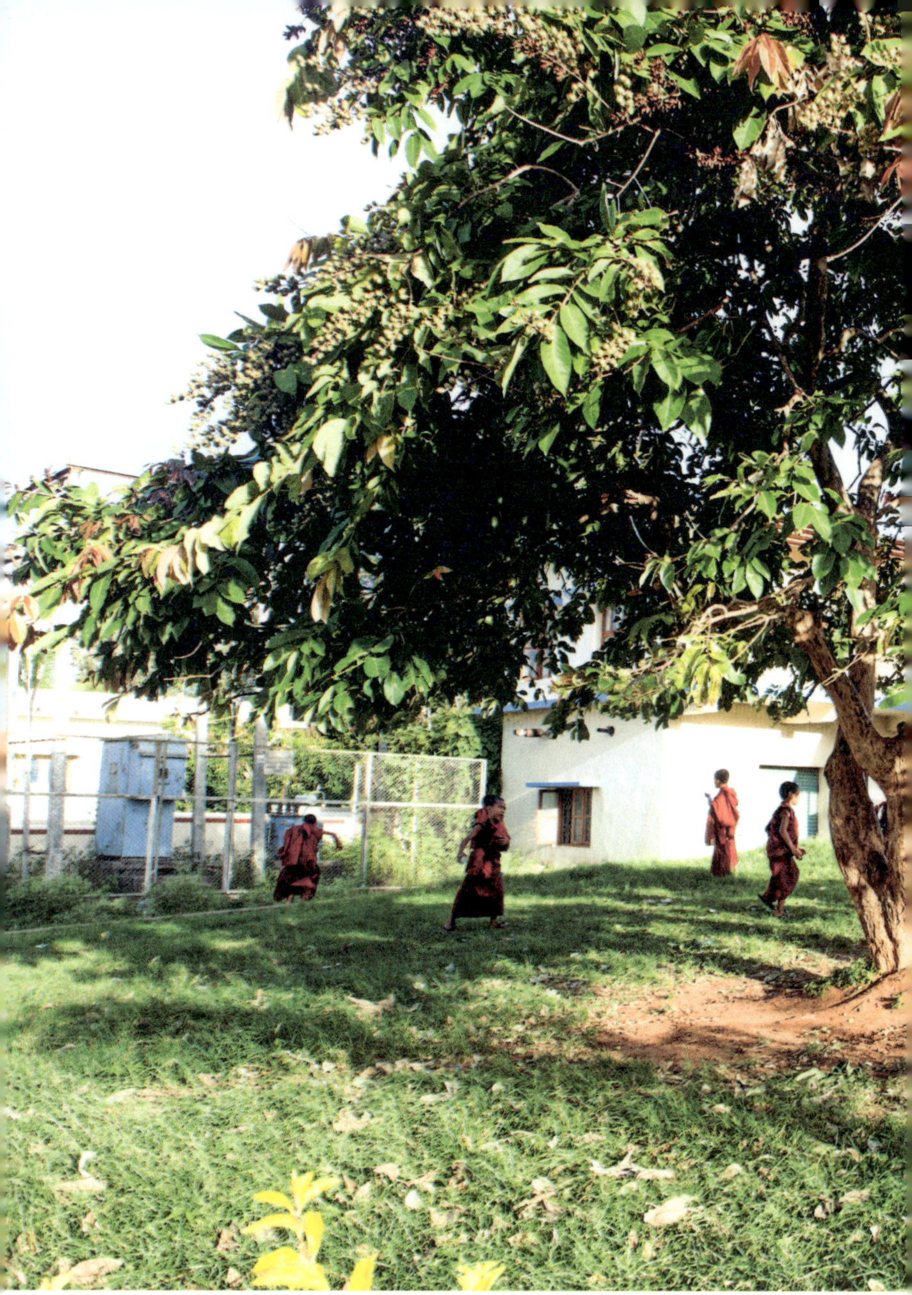

During a break from formal scripture lessons and other studies, young monks play with a rubber ball, toss a frisbee, or just enjoy the weather.

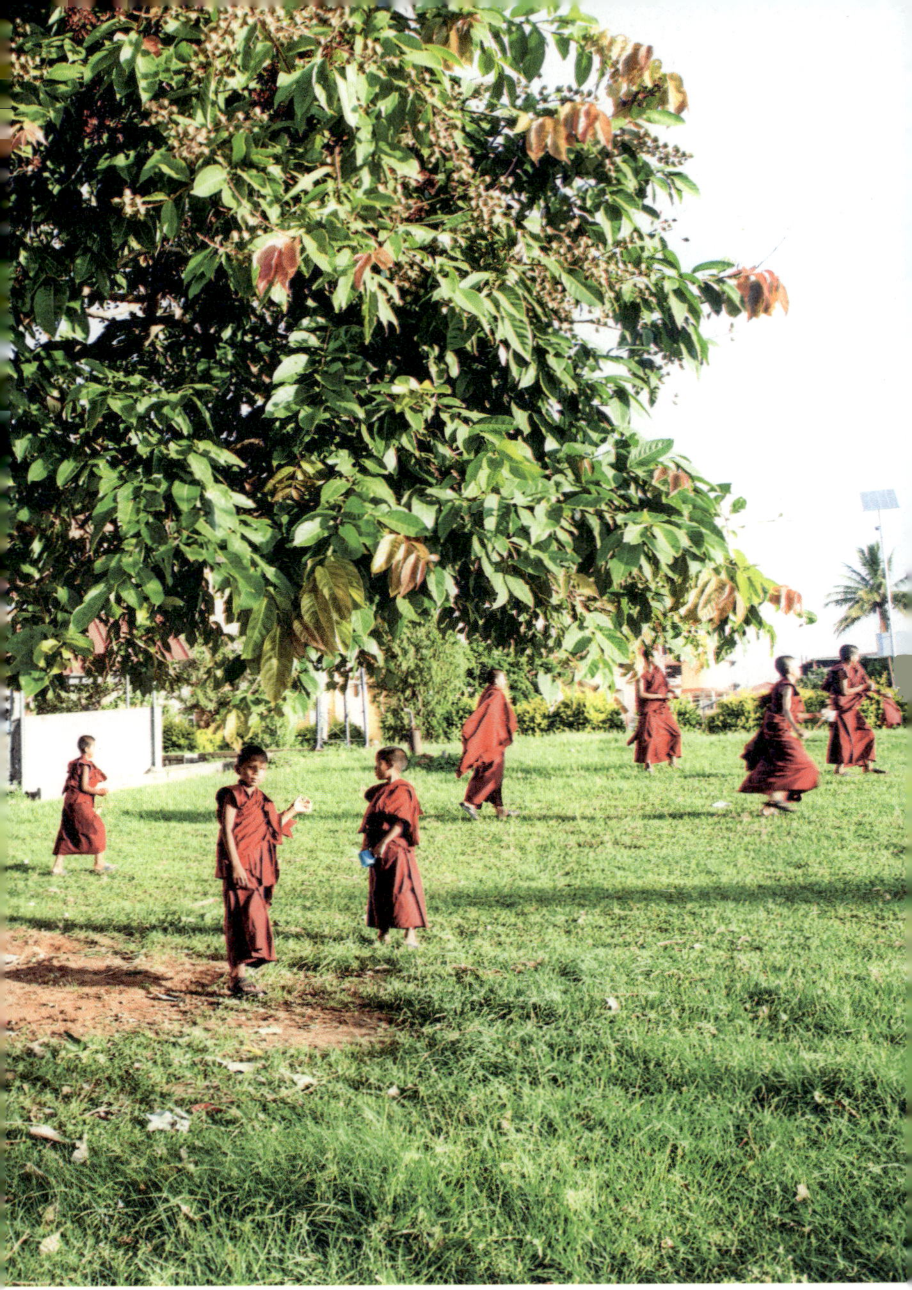

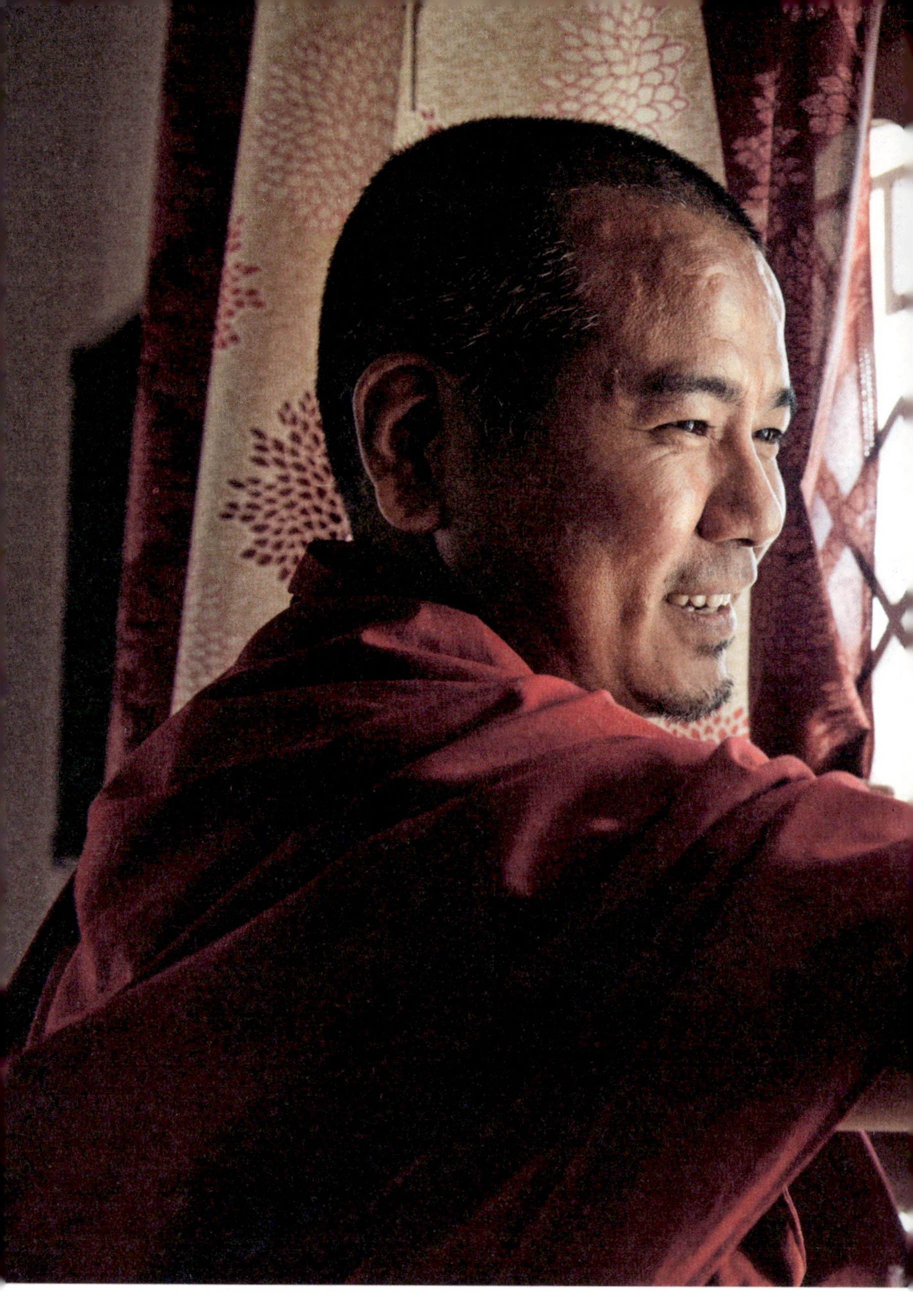

A senior monk looks out from a monastery window and watches junior monks during their morning debate in the courtyard.

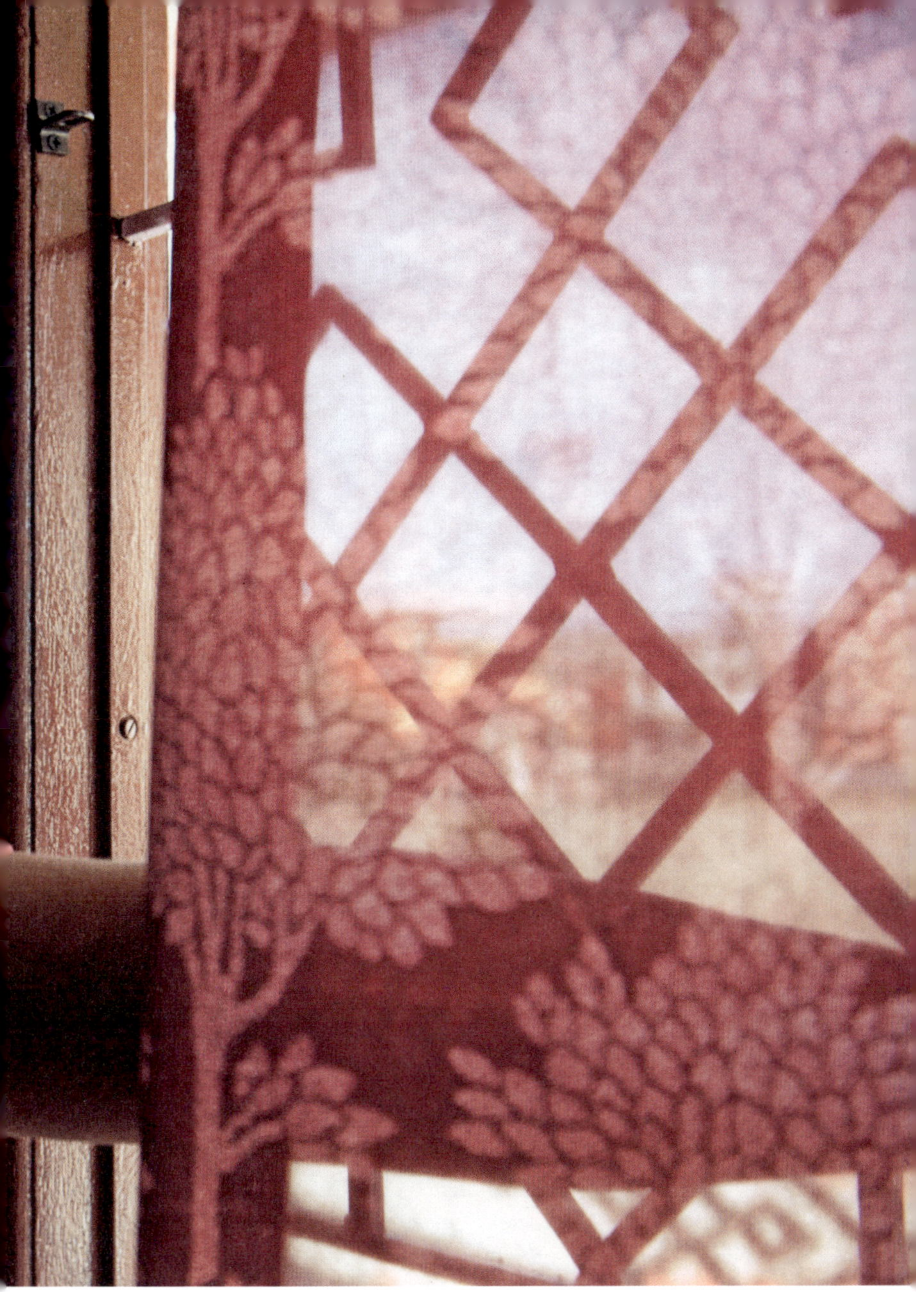

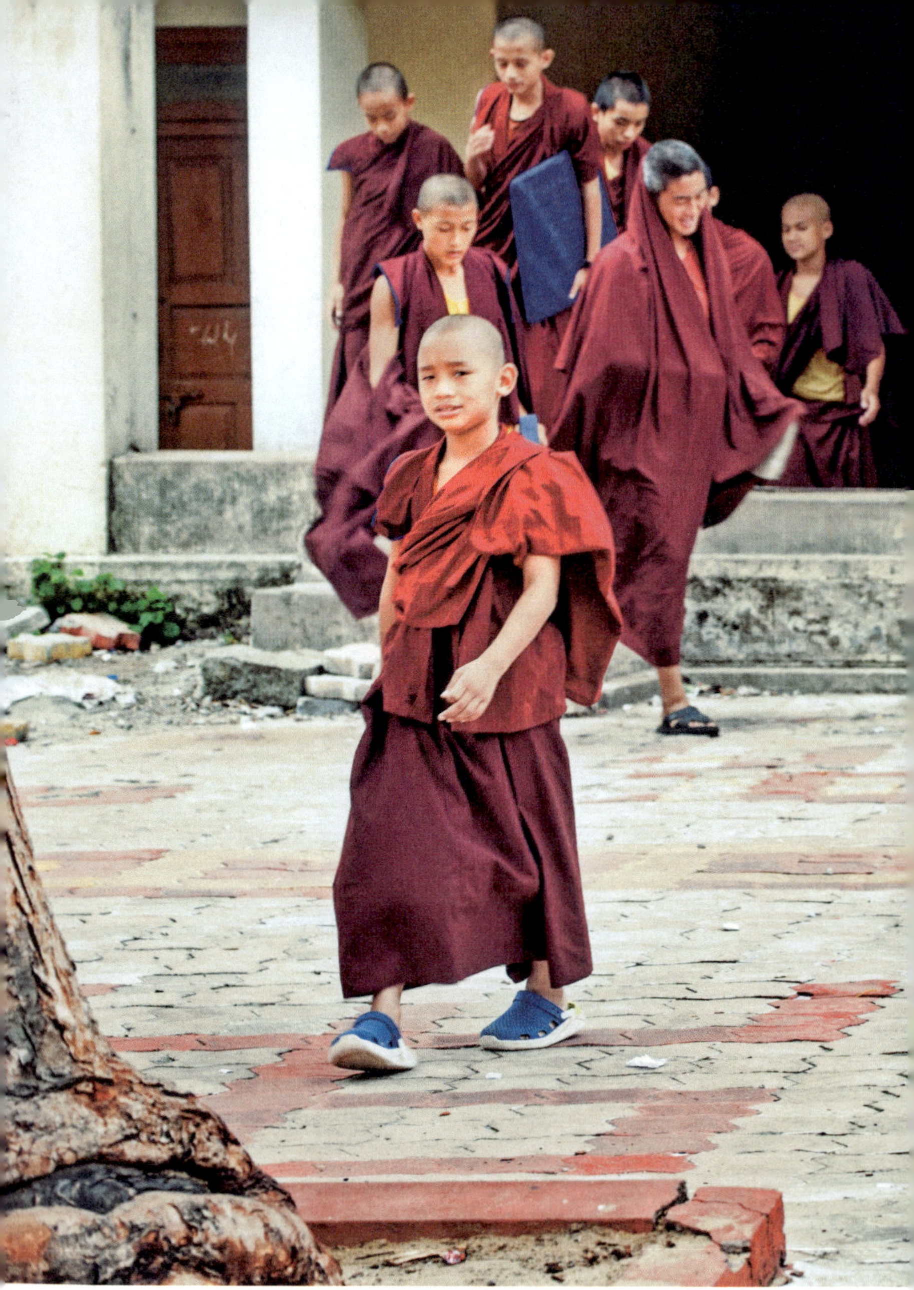

Students leaving their classes for the day.

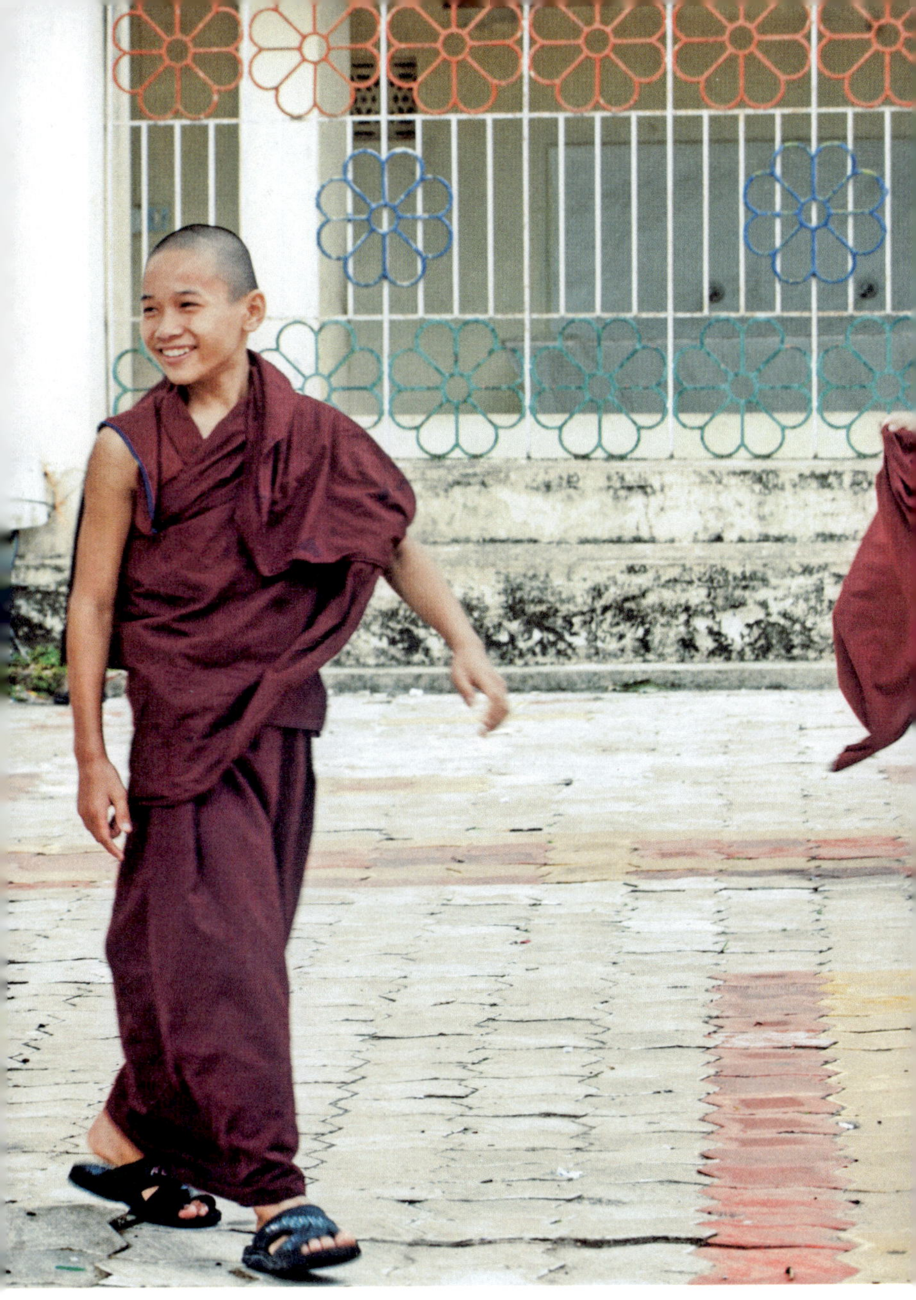

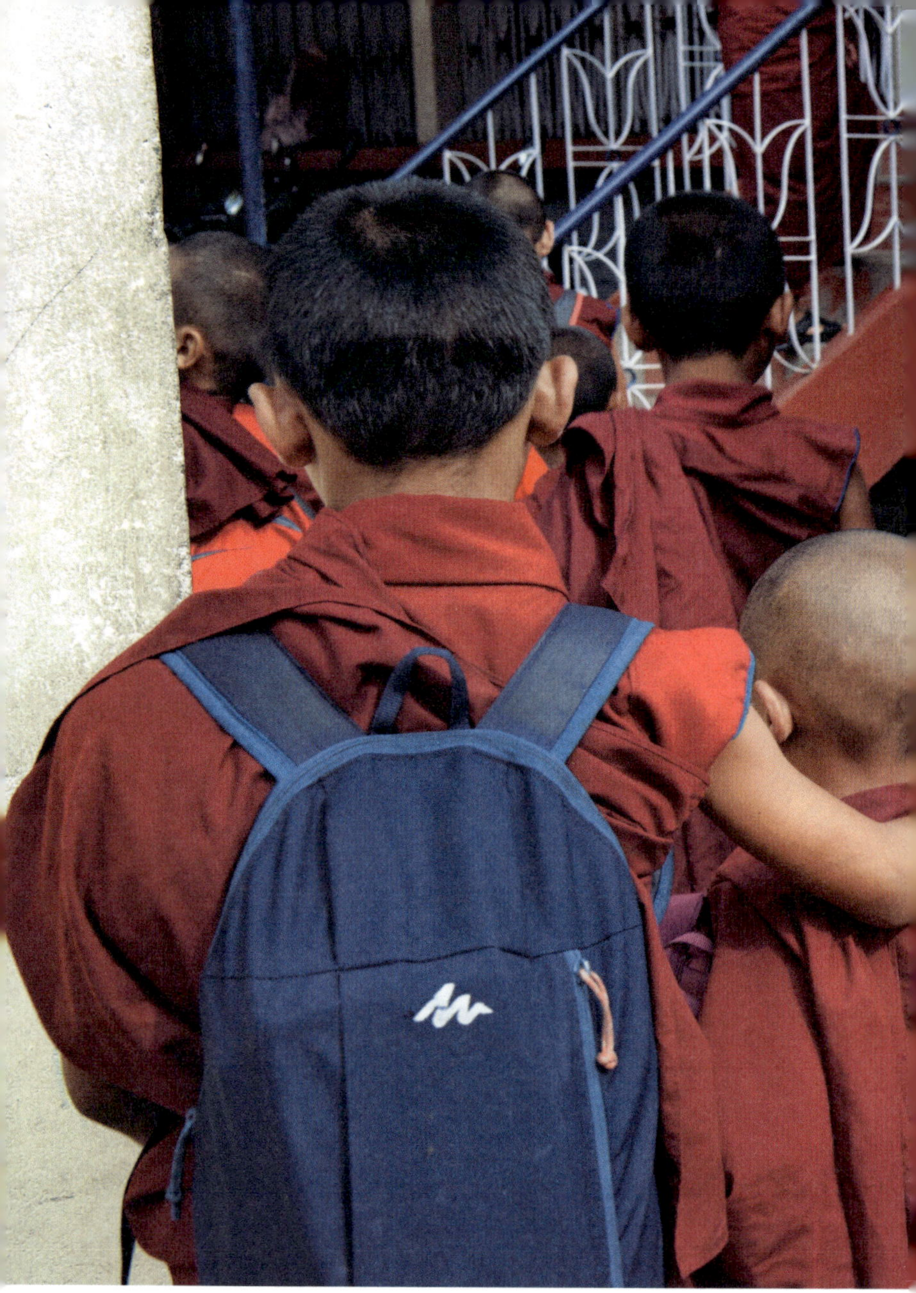

Monks watch over those younger than themselves with kindness and care.

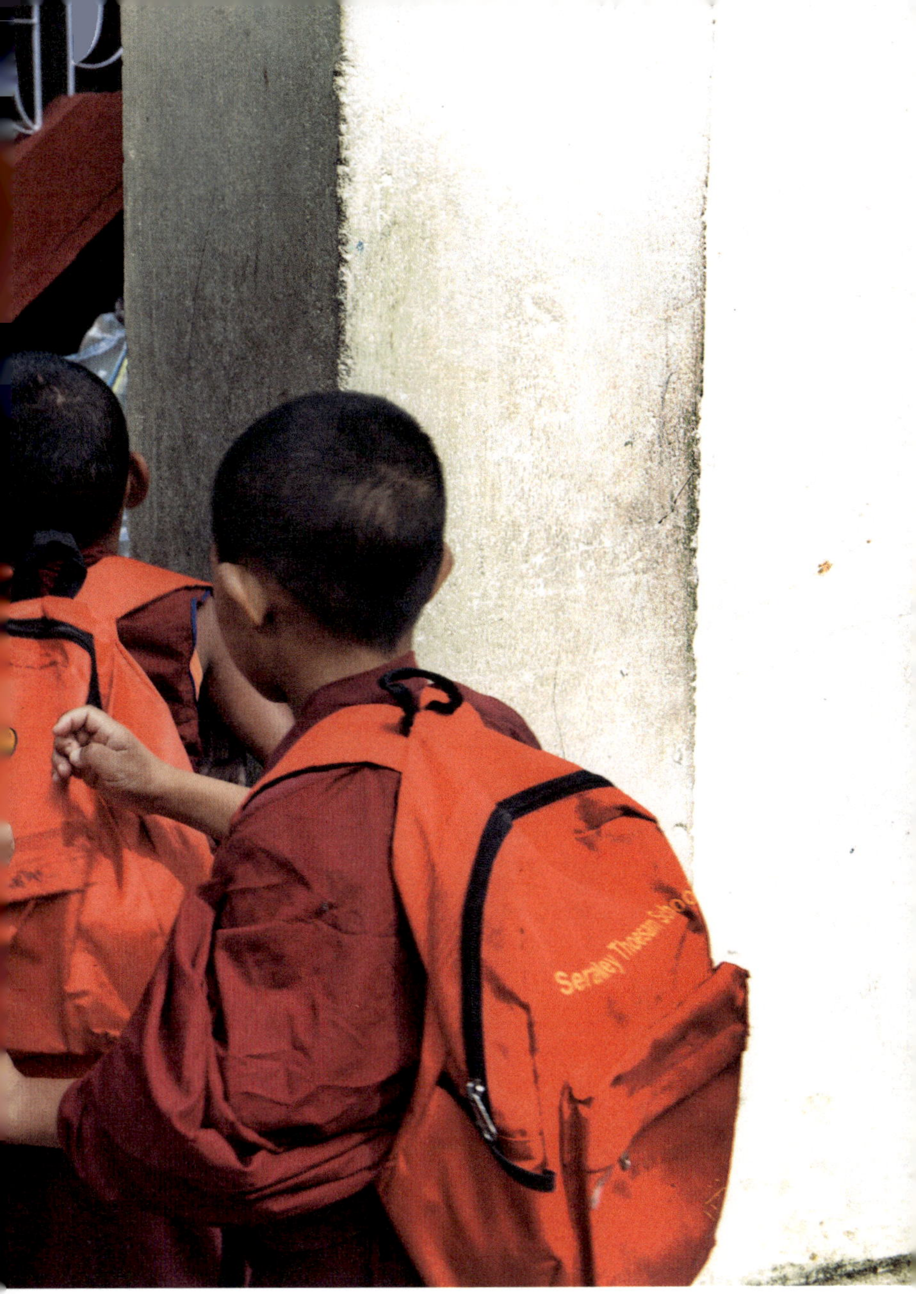

I was eight years old when I joined a monastery, before which I was in a boarding school far from home for three years. At the boarding school, I was alone and endured many challenges that harmed my intellectual development. I was extremely fortunate to have a very loving and caring mentor, who guided me to become a better human being. I don't think I would have achieved this maturity if I had not had his nurturing attention. I always cherished days under my mentor's care, and I forever feel gratitude for his kindness.

I use scriptures to overcome the challenges that I face in my life, because they contain methods to confront negative emotions through insightful logic and easy to apply stories. The study of scripture and practice of debate helps to quell the fodder for negative emotions and prevent them from overtaking your mind.

— Ngawang Norbu

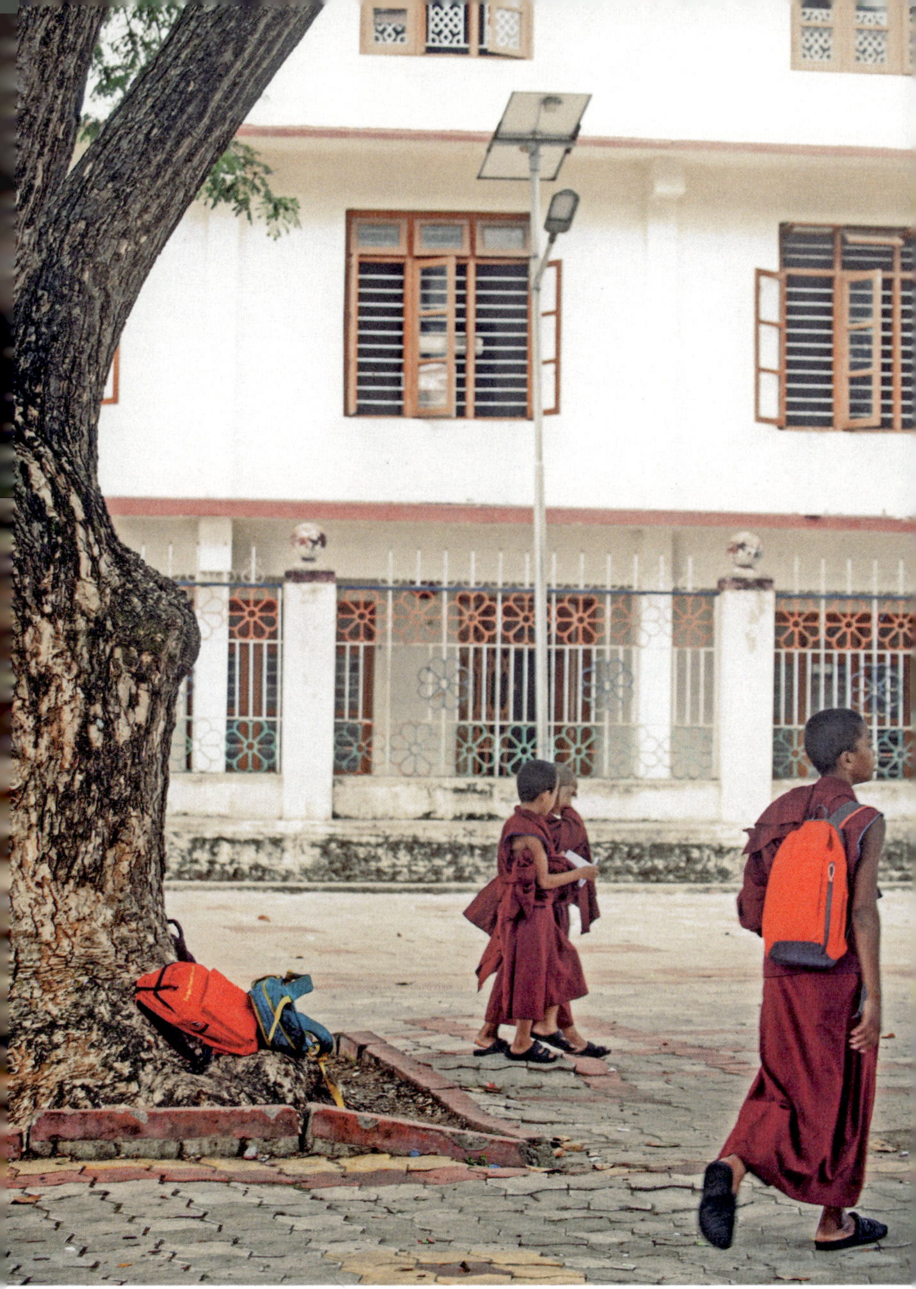

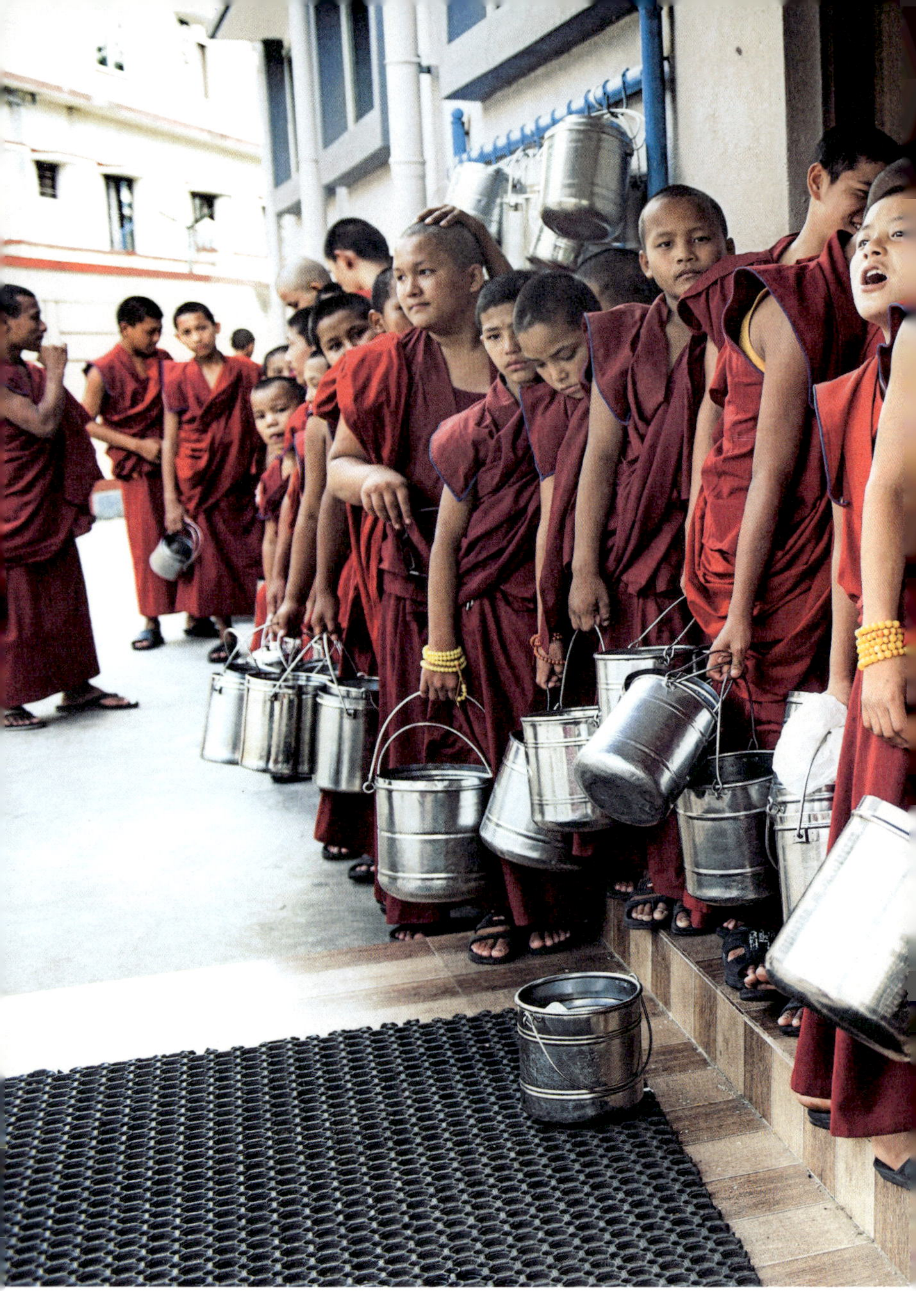

Lining up at the monastery's main kitchen for a meal that the young monks will take back to their dorms.

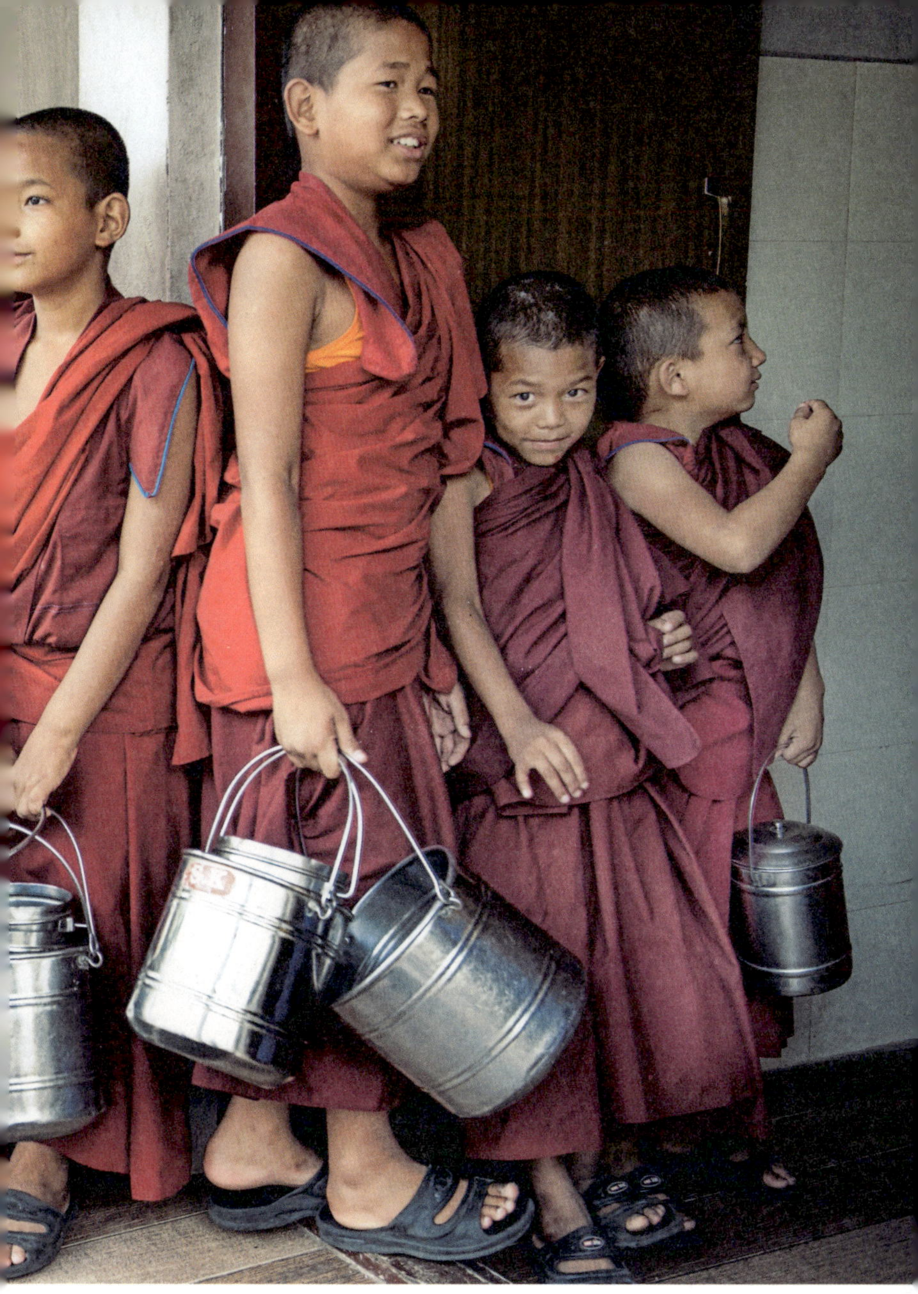

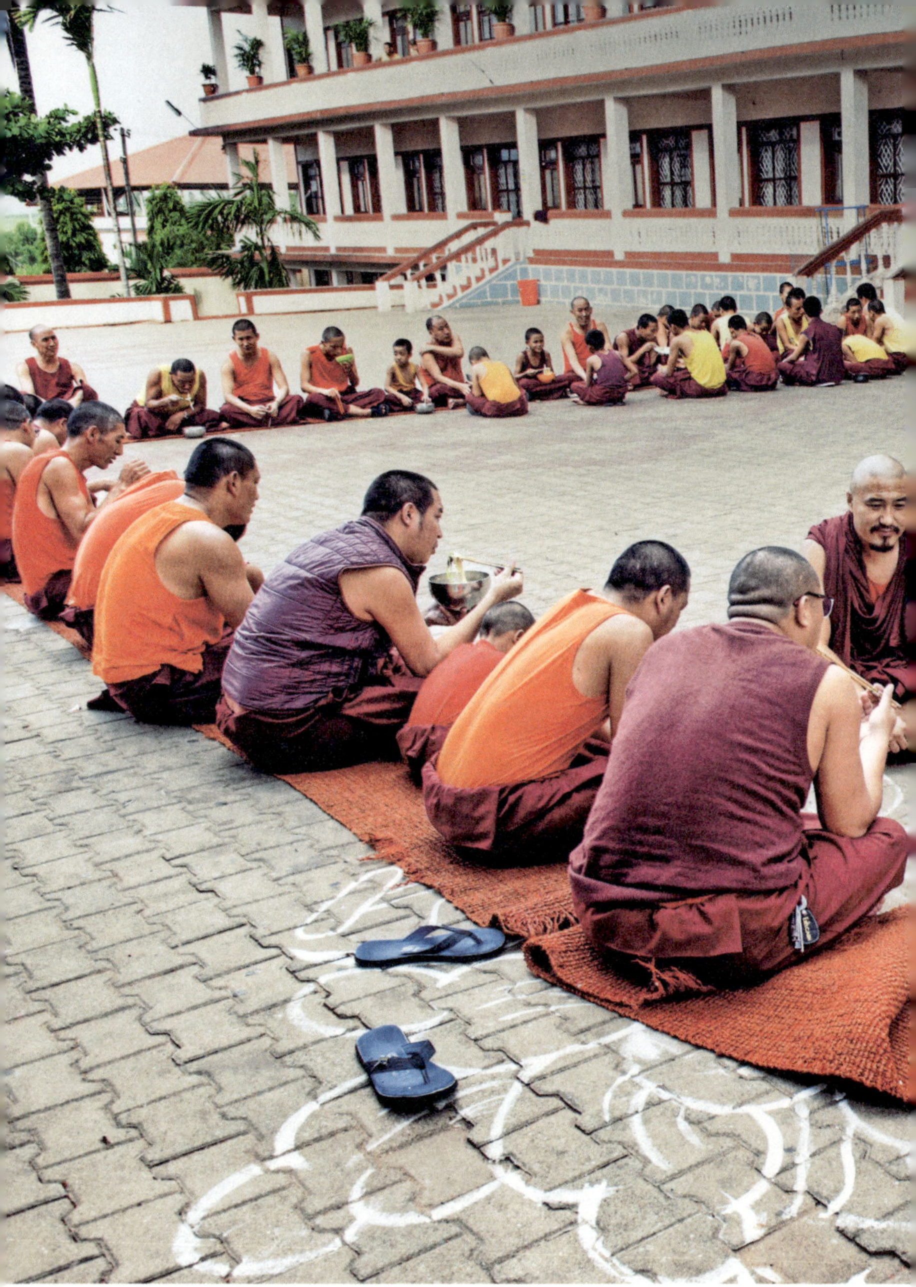

Sharing a meal in the courtyard of the monastery dormitory.

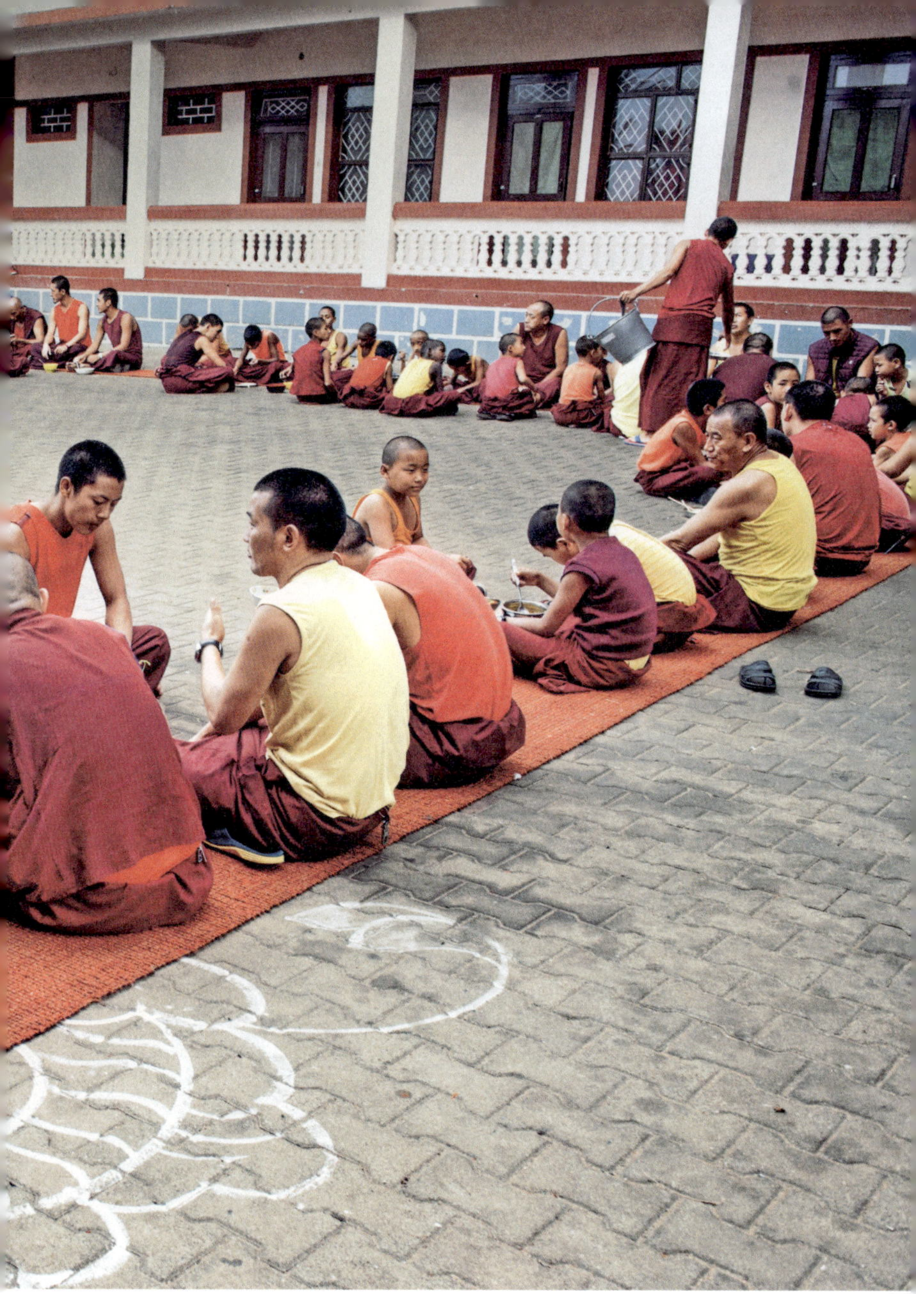

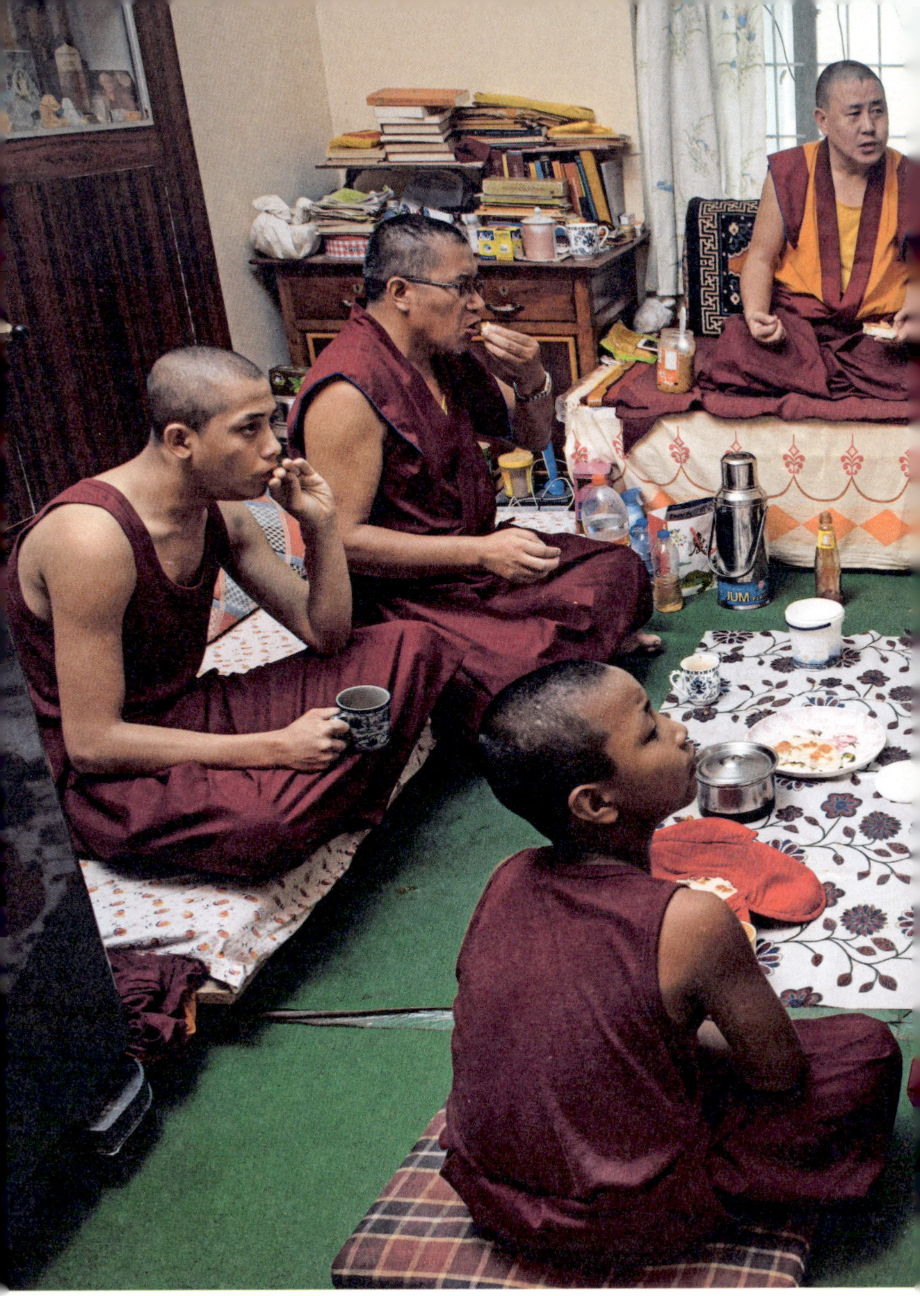

A mentor hosts his disciples at his home for a breakfast of Nutella on chapati and hot tea.

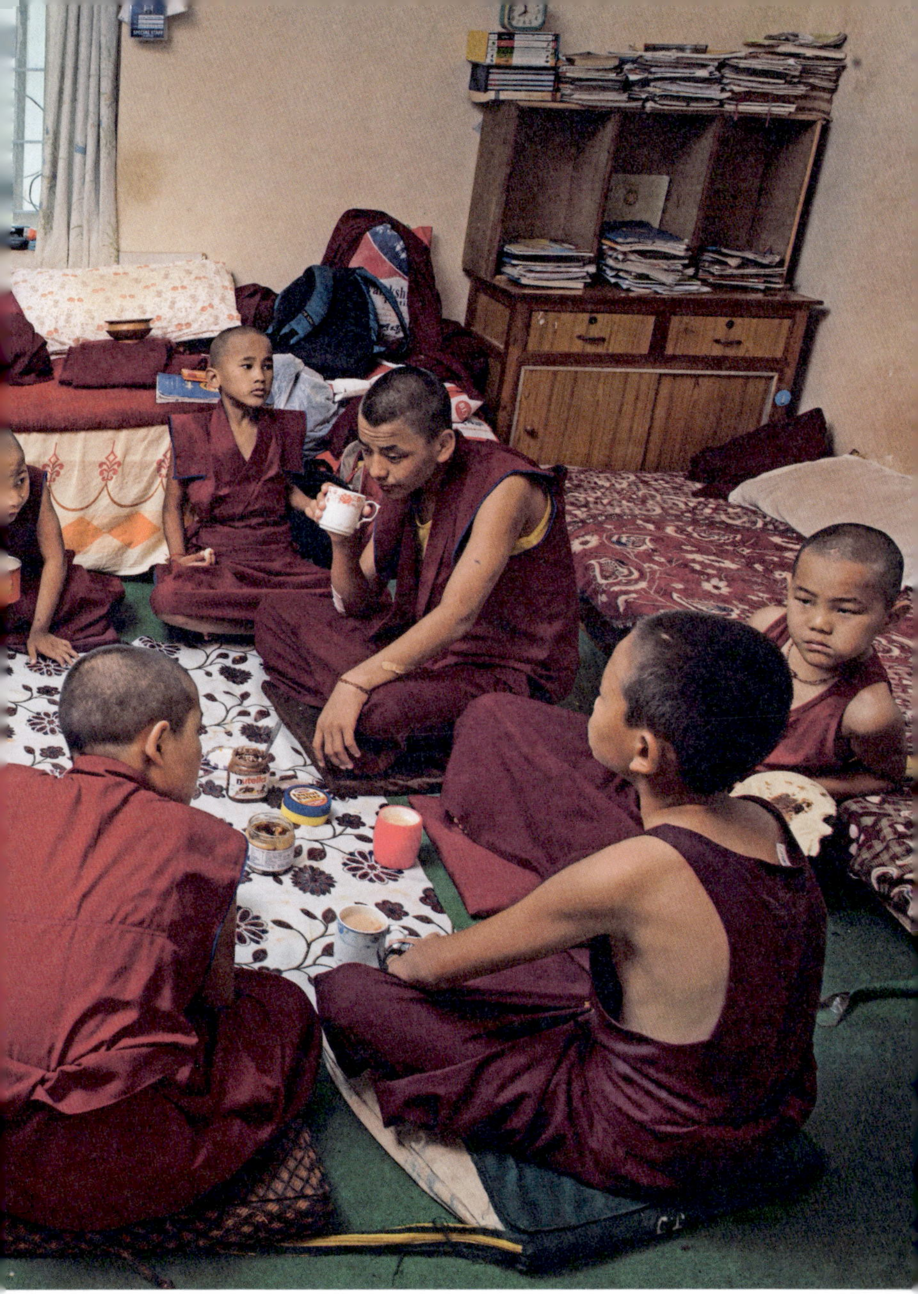
nutella

I began studying Buddhist philosophical debate when I was fifteen years old. For me, learning the art of debate broadened my thinking, helped me become more open-minded, and taught me not to blindly accept my beliefs. The debate process encouraged me to apply logical reasoning to analyze my observations.

There are various debate methods taught within this tradition, and one that has had significant impact on me is the concept of correct evidence, which emphasizes the authority of experiential knowledge in validating the existence of the object under observation. A common example of this is inferring the existence of fire from observing smoke. This inference is based on prior experience of witnessing smoke emanating from fire. This demonstrates the importance of experiential knowledge, which is central to Buddhist philosophy and has left a lasting impression on my life.

— Tenzin Topden

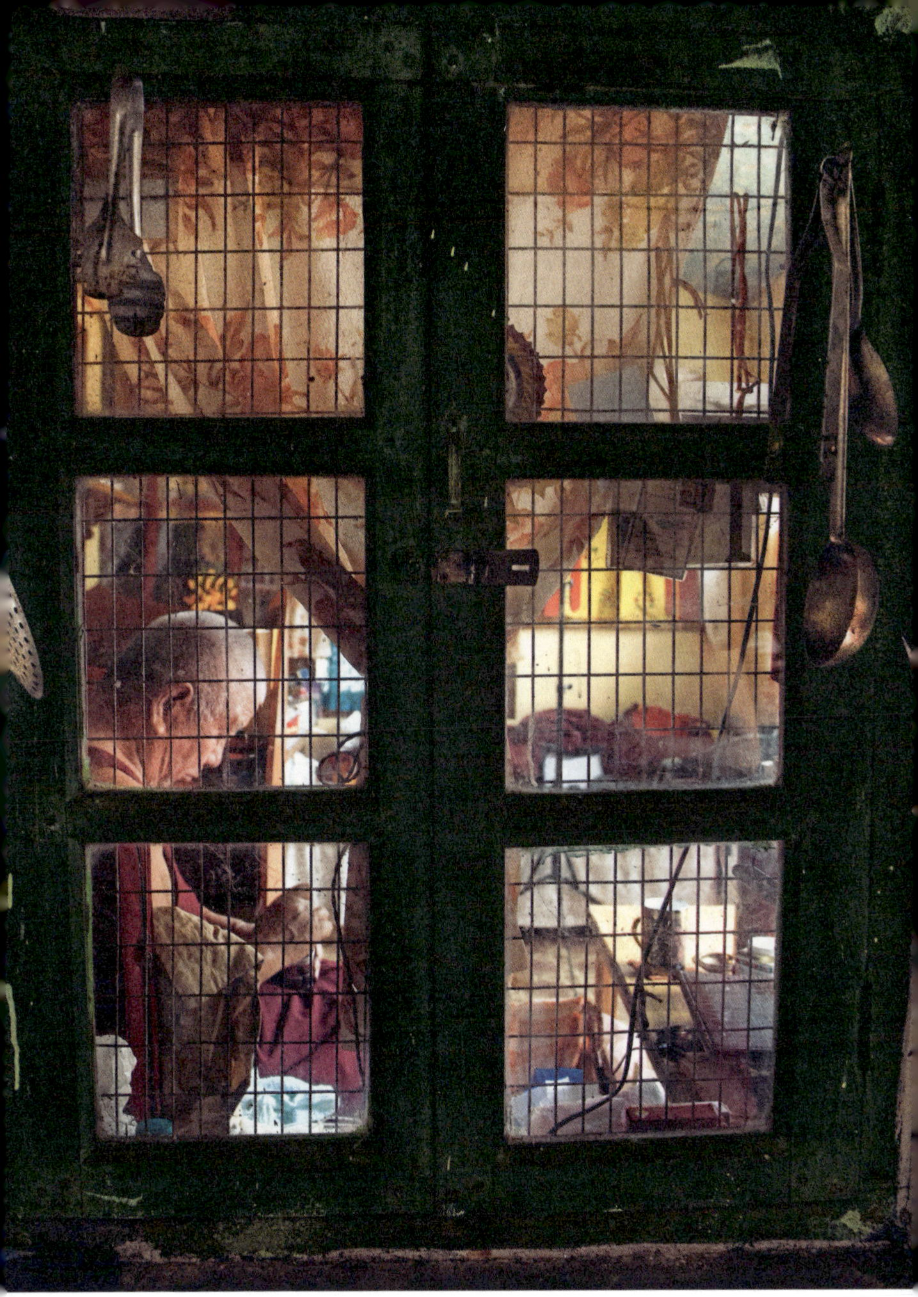

An elder monk prepares his medicine while his disciple prepares lunch in the next room. The mentor-disciple relationship for Tibetan Buddhist monks forges a lifelong bond.

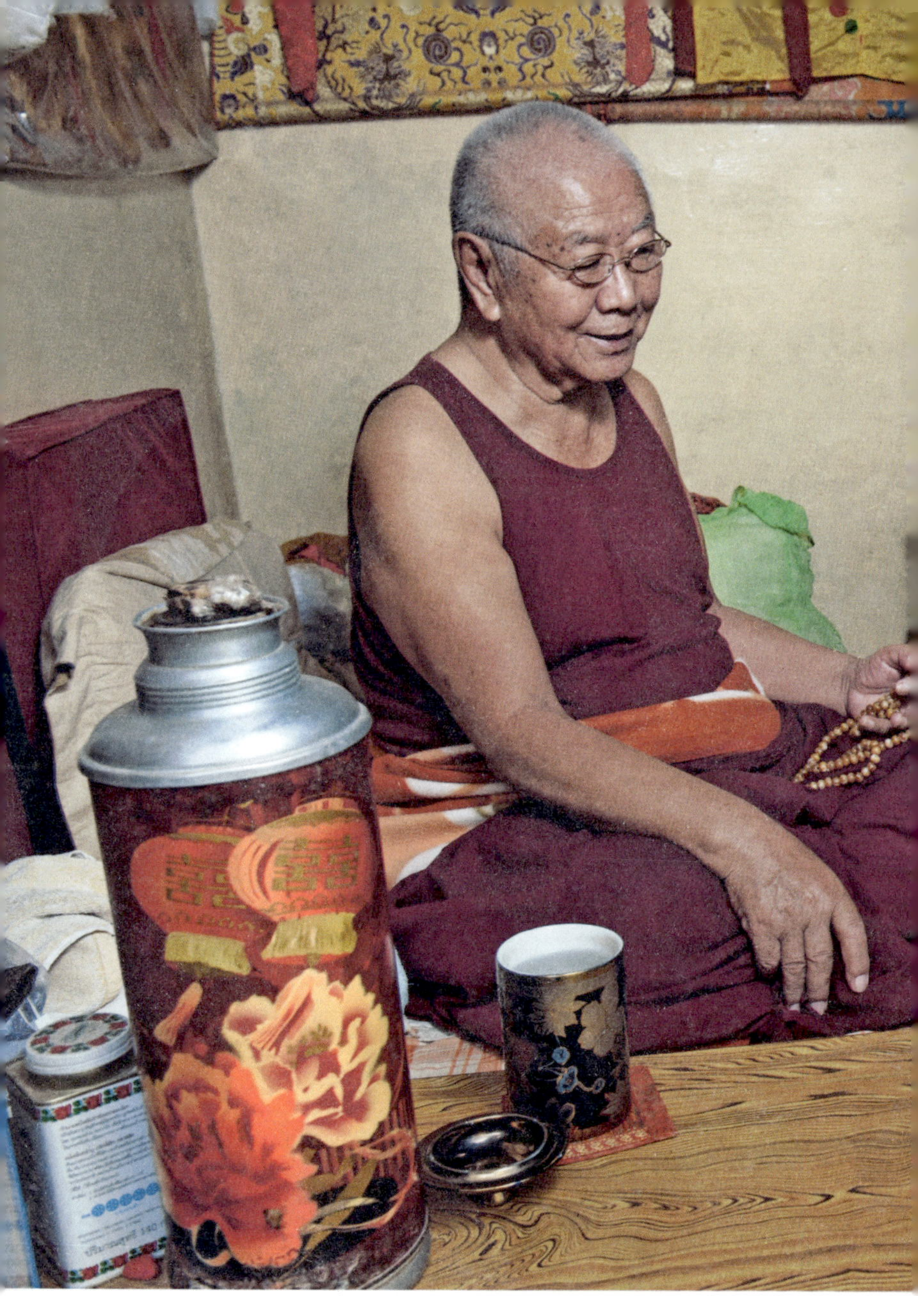

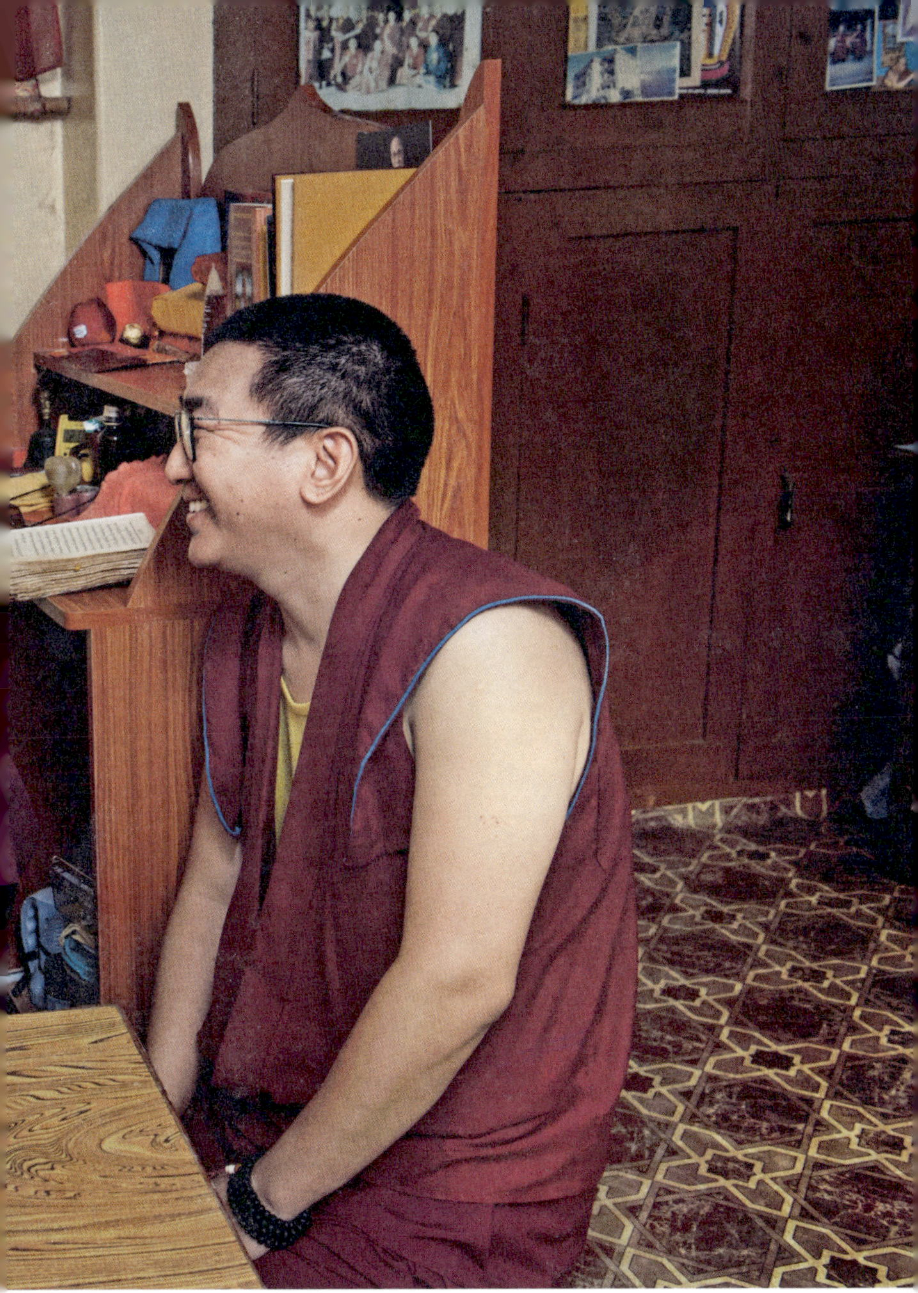

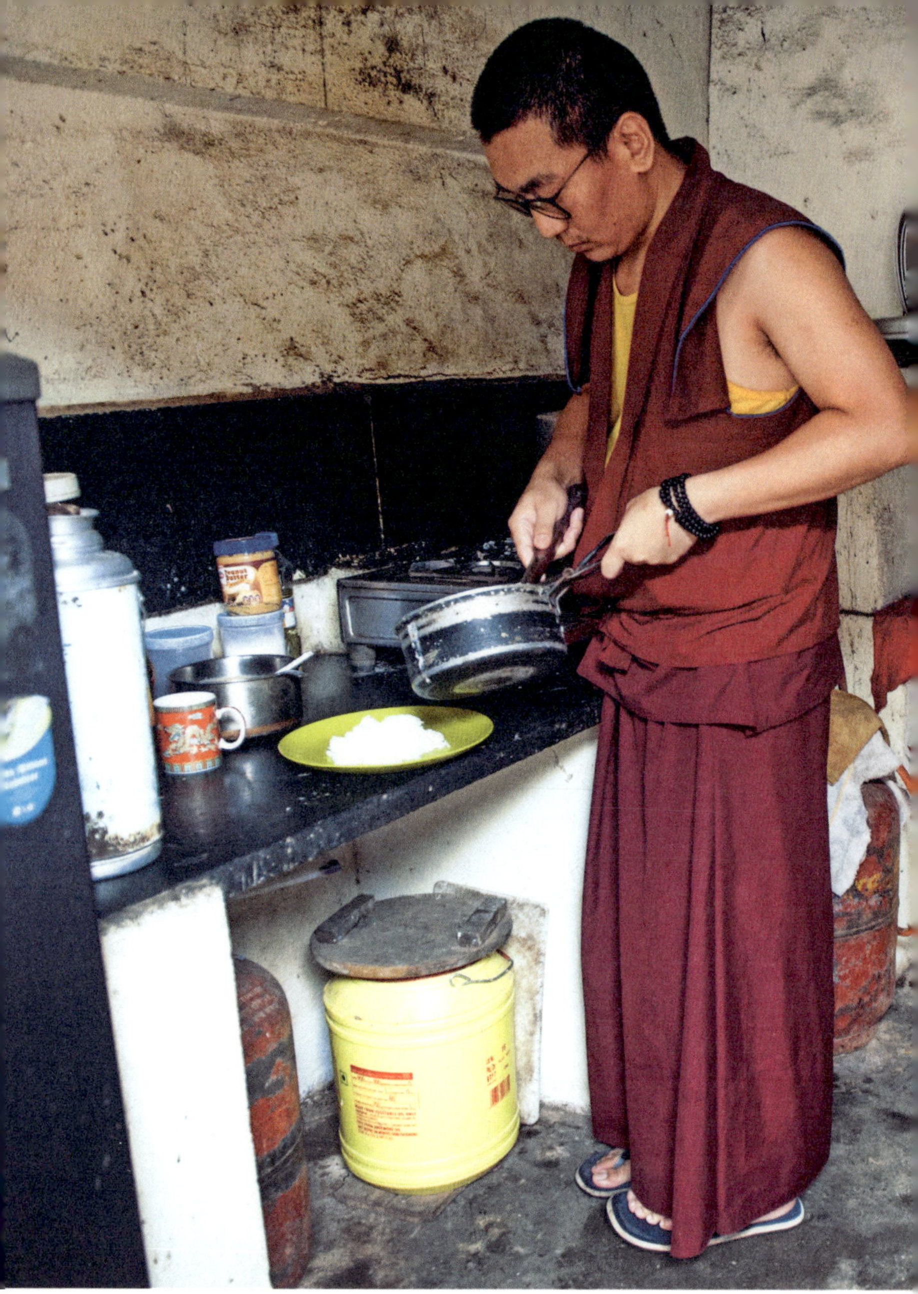

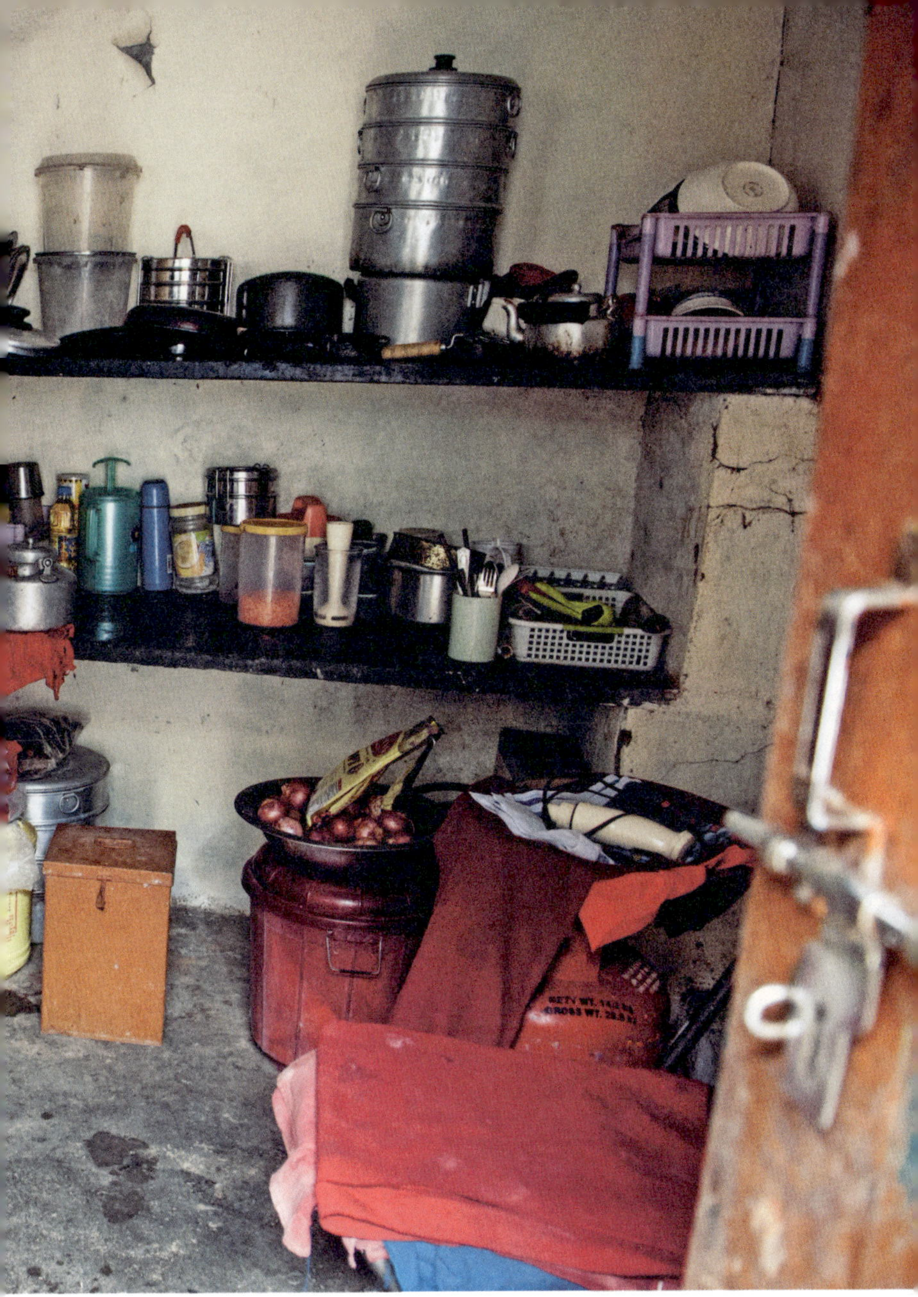

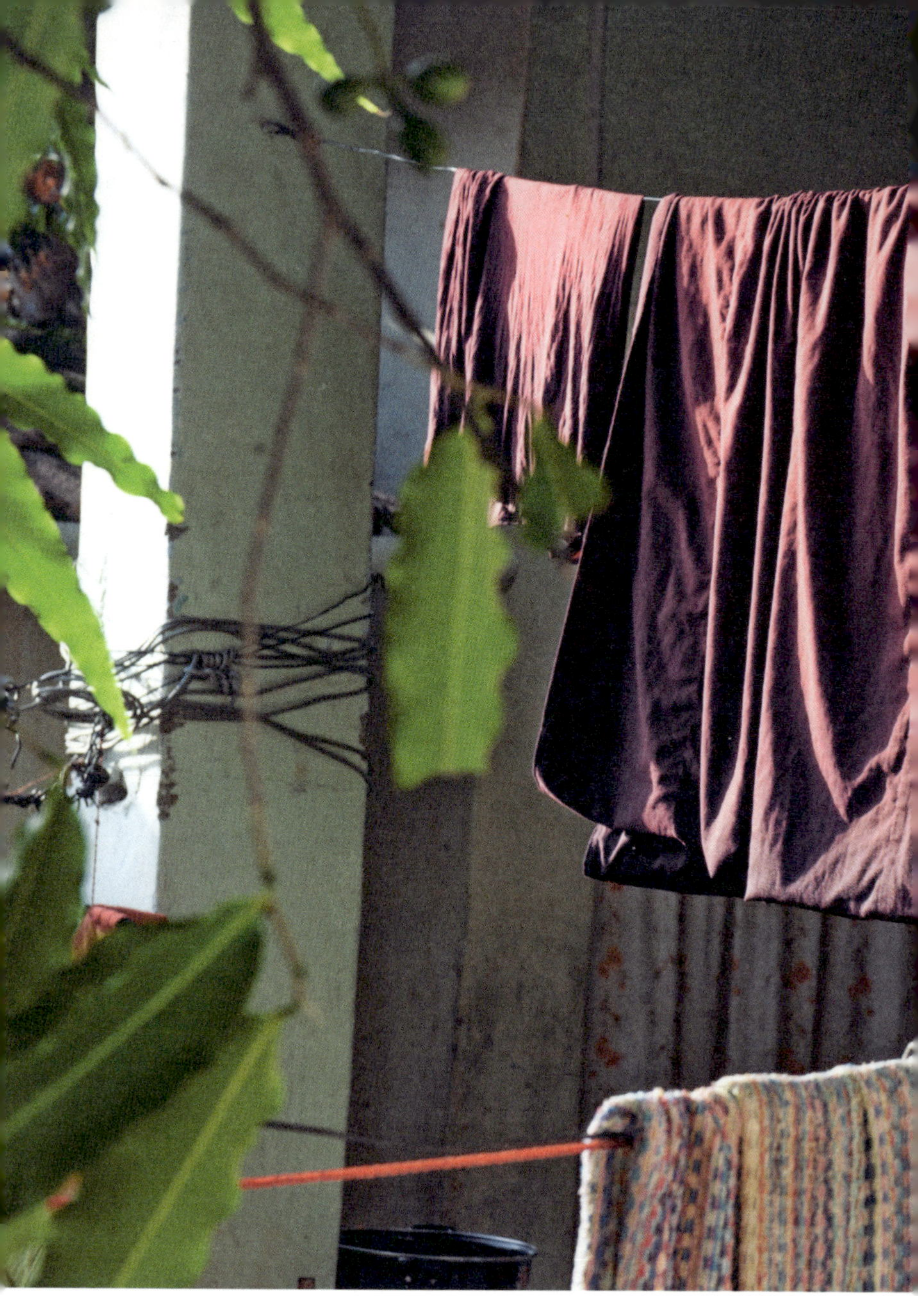

Drying laundry in the monks' quarters at the monastery.

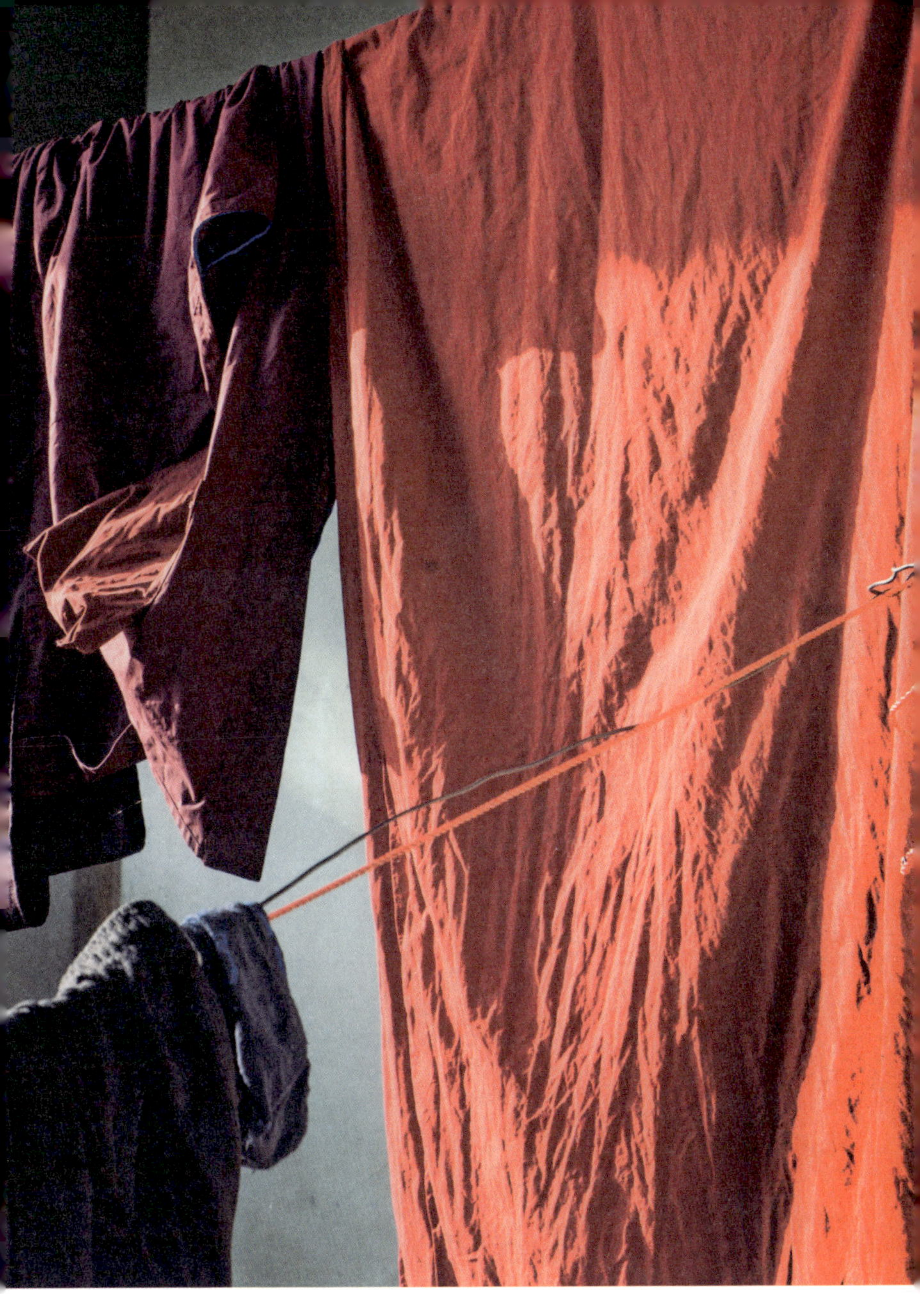

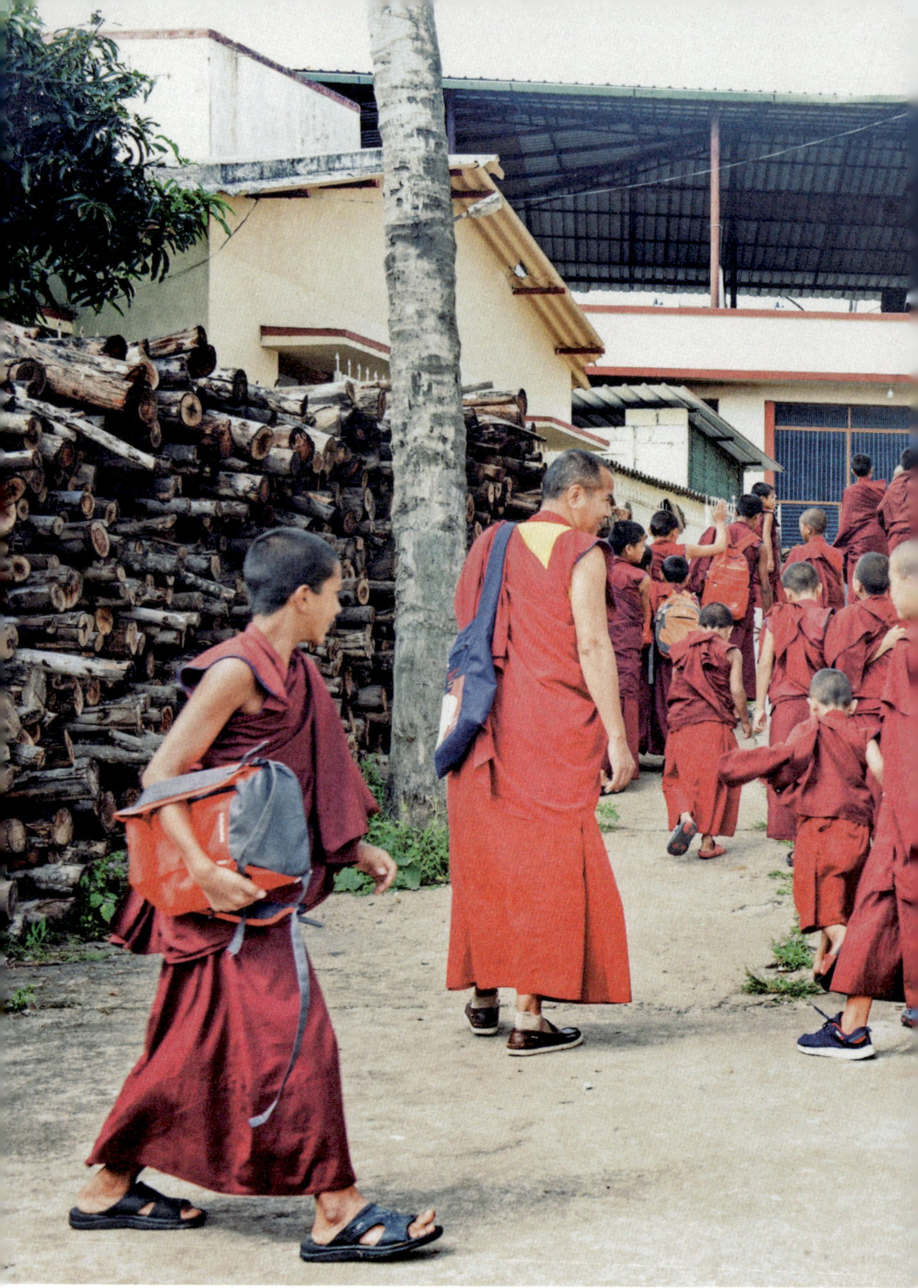

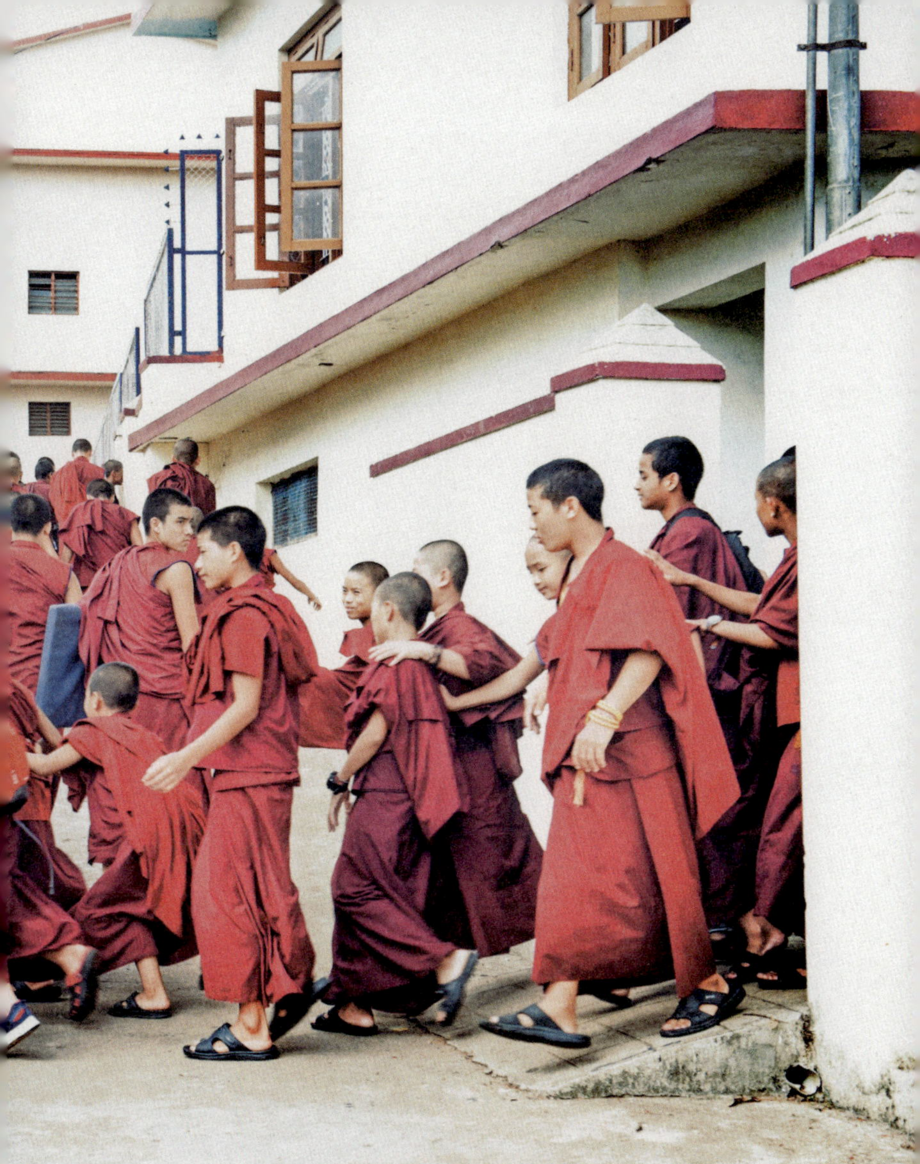

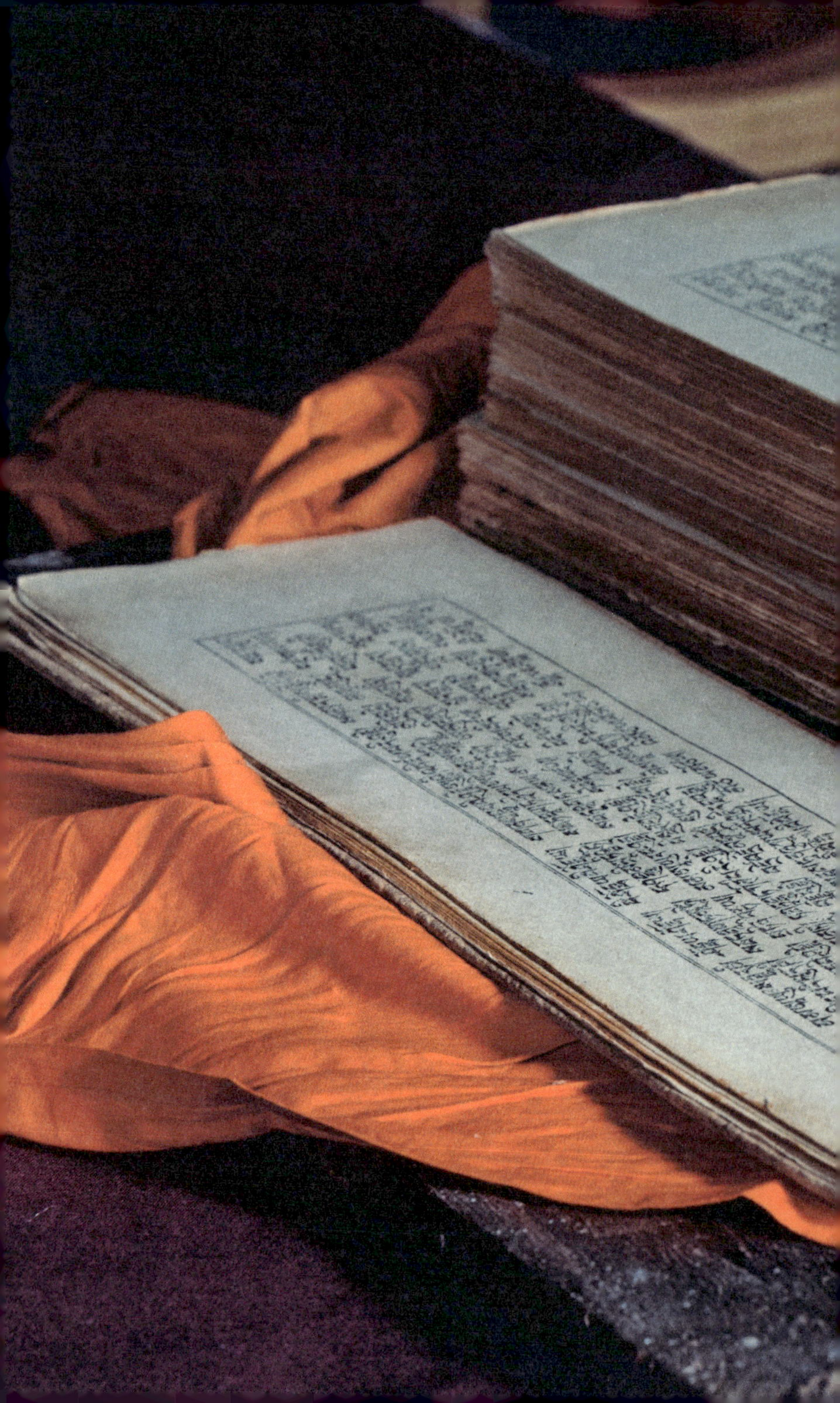

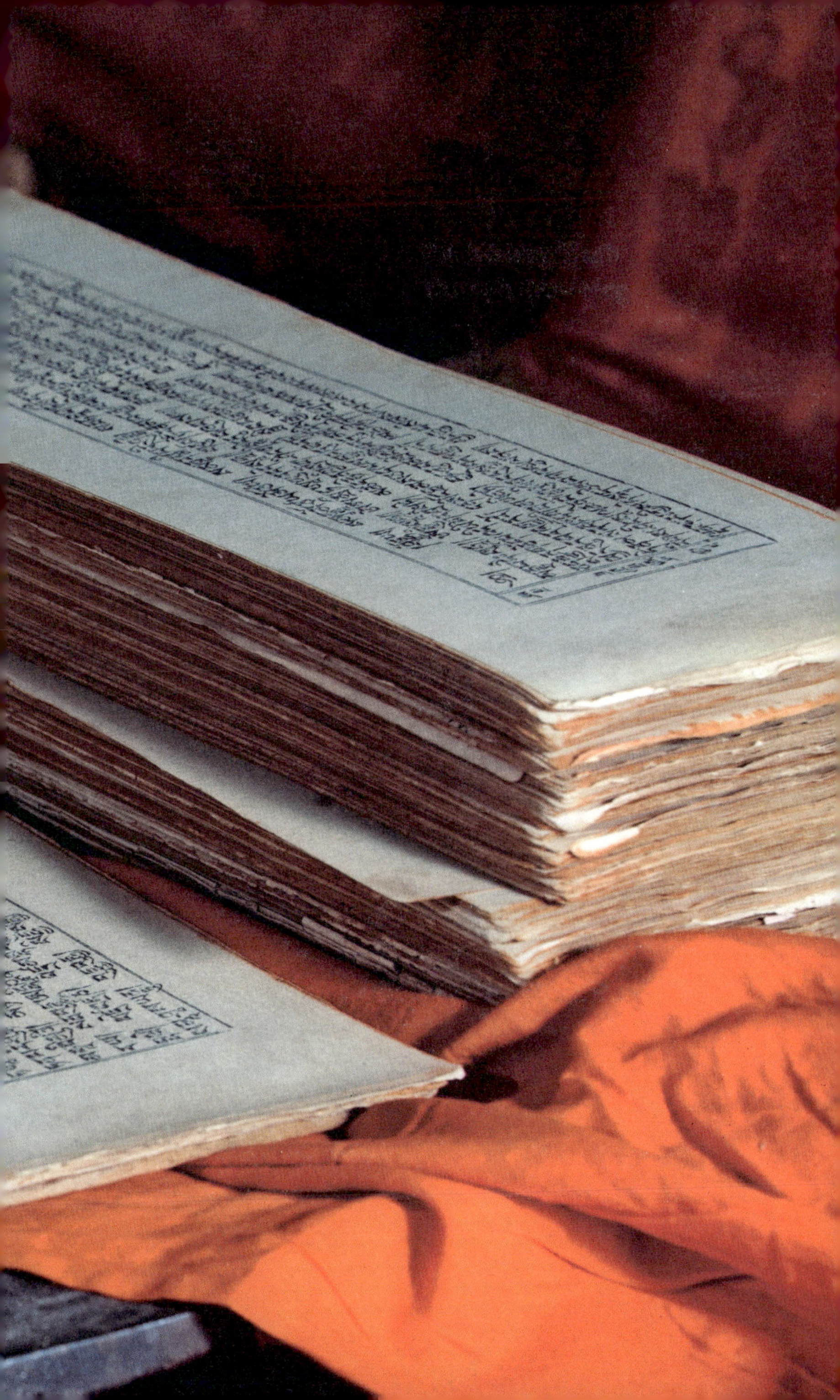

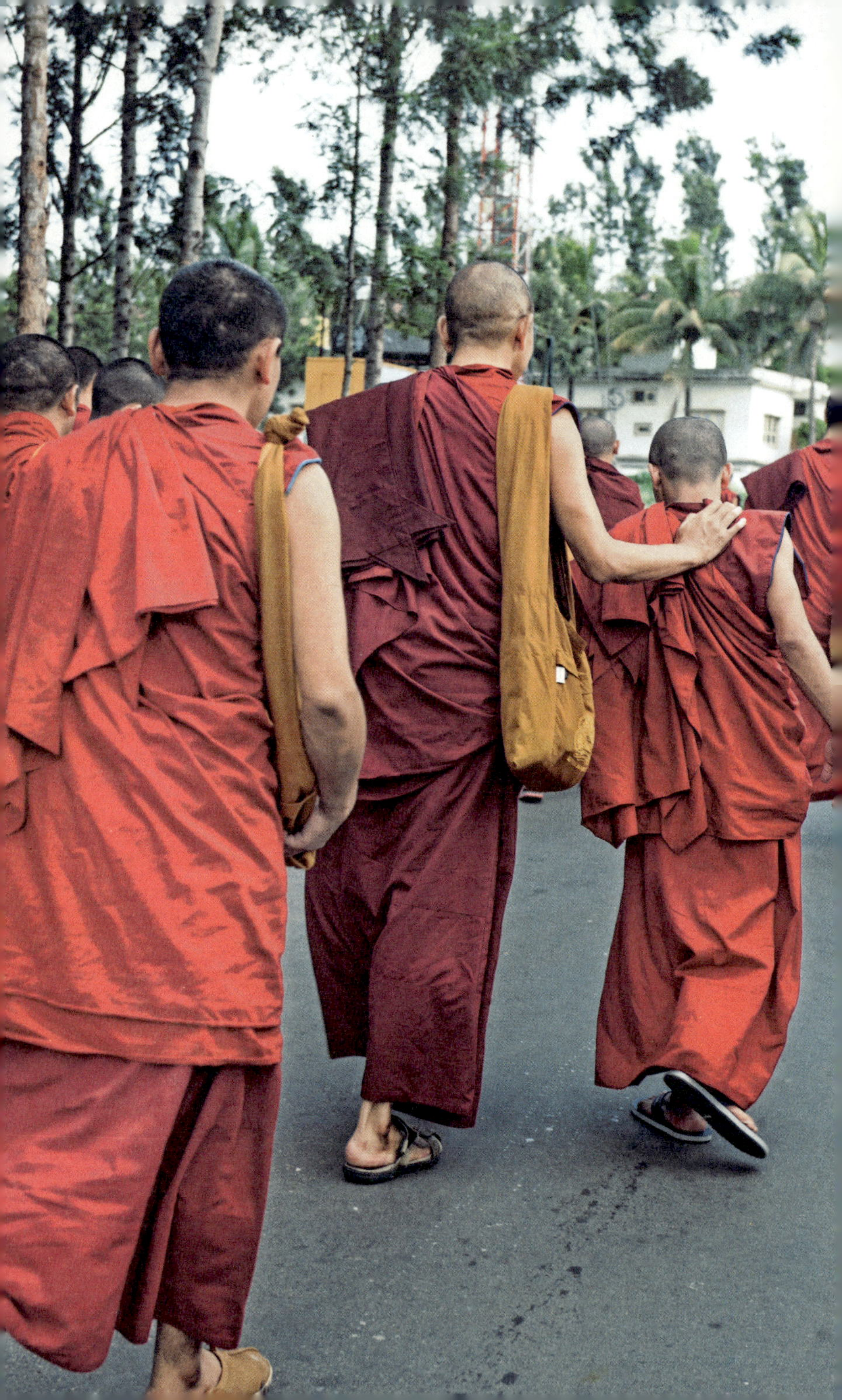

Contributors

His Holiness the 14th Dalai Lama, Tenzin Gyatso, describes himself as a simple Buddhist monk. At the age of two, then named Lhamo Dhondup, he was recognized as the reincarnation of the 13th Dalai Lama, Thubten Gyatso. He is the spiritual leader of Tibet.

Khensur Nicholas Vreeland is the director of The Tibet Center in New York City and was the abbot of Rato Dratsang Monastery in Mundgod, India, from 2012 to 2022. Born in Geneva to American parents, he was educated in Europe, North Africa, and the United States and pursued a career in photography before joining Rato Dratsang in 1985.

Khensur Tashi Tsering is a scholar who has taught internationally and has written six books on Buddhist philosophy and practices. In 2018, His Holiness the 14th Dalai Lama appointed him the abbot of Sera Mey Monastic University in Bylakuppe, India, and he served in this position until 2024. Khensur Tsering was awarded the British Empire Medal in 2019 for his service to Buddhism in the UK, where he lived for over twenty years. He is currently the director of the Dalai Lama Center for Tibetan and Indian Ancient Wisdom in Bodhgaya, India.

Geshe Dadul Namgyal (1959–2024) was the senior resident teacher at Drepung Loseling Monastery, Atlanta. He was also the senior translator and interpreter for the Emory-Tibet Science Initiative at Emory University, Atlanta, until April 2023, when he joined Sravasti Abbey in Newport, Washington.

Carol M. Worthman, PhD, is the Samuel Candler Dobbs Professor of Anthropology Emerita at Emory University, Atlanta, and a founder of the Emory-Tibet Science Initiative at Emory University, where she led the neuroscience section. She is a member of the American Academy of Arts and Sciences and a Fellow of the American Association for the Advancement of Science.

Richard K. Raker, MD, has practiced and taught anesthesiology for more than thirty years at Columbia University Irving Medical Center/New York-Presbyterian in New York City. An American Society of Anesthesiology Global Health Organization volunteer, he has trained Guyanese anesthesiology residents at the Georgetown Public Hospital. He has also volunteered as a neuroscience faculty member for the Emory-Tibet Science Initiative at Sera Mey Monastery in Bylakuppe, India.

Paul García, PhD, MD, leads the Division of Neuroanesthesiology at Columbia University Medical Center in New York City, where he conducts laboratory, translational, and clinical research focused on transitions between conscious and unconscious states. He has taught for two years as a member of the faculty team for the Emory-Tibet Science Initiative at Emory University, Atlanta.

Arri Eisen, PhD, is a teaching professor at Emory University, Atlanta. He is a founder of the Emory-Tibet Science Initiative and was the leader of its Biology section for many years.

Thupten Khetsun joined Dzongkar Choede Monastery in Hunsur, India, at age eight. He was a Tenzin Gyatso Science Scholar at Emory-Tibet Science Initiative at Emory University, Atlanta, from 2019 to 2021. He is the vice principal of Dzongkar Choede Secondary School.

Venerable Lobsang Dhondup joined Gaden Shartse Monastic University in Mundgod, India, in 2006. He was a Tenzin Gyatso Science Scholar at Emory-Tibet Science Initiative at Emory University, Atlanta. Currently, he teaches science at the Gashar Center for Contemplative Science and Studies at Gaden Shartse Monastery.

Kalden Gyatso joined Sera Jey Monastic University in Bylakuppe, India, at age eleven. He served as translator for the Emory-Tibet Science Initiative at Sera Jey for six years, after which he attended the Emory-Tibet Science Initiative at Emory University, Atlanta, as a Tenzin Gyatso Science Scholar. He is currently studying for his Geshe degree.

Rigzin Nurbu is the director of Tashi Lhunpo Science Center in Bylakuppe, India. He spent two years as a Tenzin Gyatso Science Scholar at the Emory-Tibet Science Initiative at Emory University, Atlanta. In 2023, he was awarded a Kachen degree and is pursuing a Laharampa degree from Tashi Lhunpo Monastic University.

Jampa Gyaltsen joined Shang Gaden Choekhor Ling Monastery in Pokhara, Nepal, at age eight. In 2004, he began his studies at Sera Jey Monastic University in Bylakuppe, India, where he has served as the head of the English Translation Centre since 2016.

Geshe Ngawang Norbu joined Sera Jey Monastic University in Bylakuppe, India, at age eight. In 2010, he studied as a Tenzin Gyatso Science Scholar at the Emory-Tibet Science Initiative at Emory University, Atlanta. Currently, he is secretary of the Buddhist Institute of Geluk International Foundation in Mundgod, India.

Geshe Tenzin Topden joined Sera Mey Monastic University at age twelve. He spent two years at Emory University, Atlanta, as a Tenzin Gyatso Science Scholar, after which he returned to Sera Mey to serve as the program coordinator for the Emory-Tibet Science Initiative summer intensive program. He was the director of the Sera Mey Science Center and principal of the monastery's school and currently serves on the board of the Thosesam Dratsang Trust.

About the Author

Nancy A. Scherl is a fine art portrait photographer based in New York City. Stylistically, she uses social commentary or social documentary, often blurring the boundaries between the two genres. Nancy completed an MFA in Photography, Video, and Related Media at New York City's School of Visual Arts, following her undergraduate studies in documentary and fine art photography at the University of Wisconsin-Madison. She is a life member of the American Society of Media Photographers, where she served as a board member from 2016 to 2019. Scherl served on the board at the Katonah Museum Artists Association from 2017 to 2024. She is the recipient of many awards, including a two-time Photolucida Critical Mass Top 200 Finalist (2019 and 2023) and the Arthur Griffin Legacy Award (2023). Her work has exhibited globally, including at FotoNostrum Mediterranean House of Photography, Barcelona; PX3 Espace Beaurepaire, Paris; A Smith Gallery, Johnson City, TX; Praxis Gallery, Minneapolis; South X Southeast, Molina, GA; Katonah Museum of Art, NY; Hammond Museum and Japanese Stroll Garden, North Salem, NY; and Griffin Museum of Photography, Winchester, MA.

Acknowledgments

I am profoundly honored and forever grateful to His Holiness the 14th Dalai Lama for his inspiring words and gracious advocacy in writing the preface for this book. His Holiness has championed modernization, democracy, and science education in Tibetan Buddhist monastic training, which led to the creation of the Emory-Tibet Science Initiative (ETSI) at Emory University, Atlanta. He is the force of perseverance for the Buddhist contemplative tradition, which includes debate training, and his visionary thinking forges connections with the West through science and contemplative practices.

My gratitude extends to all those at Emory University, where I had the privilege of speaking with Geshe Lobsang Tenzin Negi, Director and co-founder of the Center for Contemplative Science and Compassion-Based Ethics (Emory Compassion Center). Dr. Negi developed ETSI's innovative six-year science curriculum, tailored specifically for Tibetan monks and nuns, enabling them to teach and conduct research in science while remaining deeply rooted in their contemplative traditions.

I shot the photographs in this book at Sera Mey and Sera Jey Monastic Universities in Bylakuppe, India, which I visited in 2019 as a guest of ETSI. I was captivated by the Tibetan Buddhist tradition of monastic debate and came to appreciate the profound importance of this ancient practice, where monks and nuns hone their critical thinking skills in a dynamic and rigorous exchange of ideas. Through this tradition, I witnessed something that transcends both science and contemplative practices—a meeting of two cultures with distinct orientations towards logic and reasoning, brought closer together by using debate as a powerful tool to engage with each other's minds.

I would like to extend my gratitude and appreciation to Khensur Tashi Tsering for his beautiful foreword and to each author who contributed an essay or an insight to this publication. The richness of the ancient tradition of Tibetan Buddhist debate has been eloquently described through texts by these contributors, which my photographs alone simply could not express: Khensur Nicholas Vreeland, Dadul Namgyal and Carol M. Worthman, Richard K. Raker, Paul García, Arri Eisen, Thupten Khetsun, Lobsang Dhondup, Kalden Gyatso, Geshe Rigzin Nurbu, Jampa Gyaltsen, Geshe Ngawang Norbu, and Geshe Tenzin Topden.

Additional thanks to the following people and institutions: His Eminence Lobsang Tenzin; Tseten Chhoekyapa; Sera Jey and Sera Mey Monastic Universities; Tashi Lhunpo Monastery and the Science Center at Tashi Lhunpo; Geshe Lodoe Sangpo; Tsetan Dolkar; Karma Tenzin; the monks at Sera Mey, Sera Jey, and Tashi Lhunpo Monasteries; Tsondue Samphel; Jamyang Khetsun; Venerable Thupten Tharchin; Venerable Lobsang "Paljor" Dorjee; Kalsang Tashi; Tenzin Dhargye; Tenzin Dorjee; Geshe Lobsang Narayal Namgyal; Geshe Tenzin Khedup; Lobsang Tsultrim; Tenzin Namdol; Yeshi Thenlay; Ngawang Dhondup; Tsering Choegyal; Kalsang Choden; Tenzin Gyalsten;

Tenpa Choephel; Jampa Topgyal; Lobsang Phuntsok; Thupten Chemi; Geshe Ngawang Sherab; and Jampa Monlam.

And my deepest thanks go to all the people who contributed to this publication: Amy Wilkins, Robin Brunelle, Takaaki Matsumoto, Elizabeth Avedon, Nancy Wolff, Joan Brookbank, Bonnie Briant, and Sherry Edwards.

I had envisioned making gold-leaf vellum prints on wooden panels of my imagery to replicate the beautiful Tibetan Buddhist scriptures that I saw in the Sera Jey library. I extend my appreciation to the following mentors who helped me to bring my vision to fruition: Marcy Palmer, Charles Douglas, and Debra Klomp Ching.

Thank you to Hannah Smith, Art Linton, Magdalena Sole, and Joanna Hurley.

I extend my appreciation to the photography community at large, and to my entire family.

My heartfelt thanks go to Richard K. Raker, without whom I would likely not have had this extraordinary experience. I had the privilege of photographing the monks in their monastery home while Rich taught neuroscience classes alongside other visiting faculty. Being among this community of monks was a rare and profoundly special experience that has left an enduring impression on me, and I continue to draw upon it, especially in moments of distraction in my daily life. I hold vivid and fond memories of how effortlessly the monks maintained their focus, even as I worked to capture with my camera the intensity and passion of their debate practice. I am forever grateful for this transformative experience and for the life I share with Rich, whose support and presence have made this journey even more meaningful.

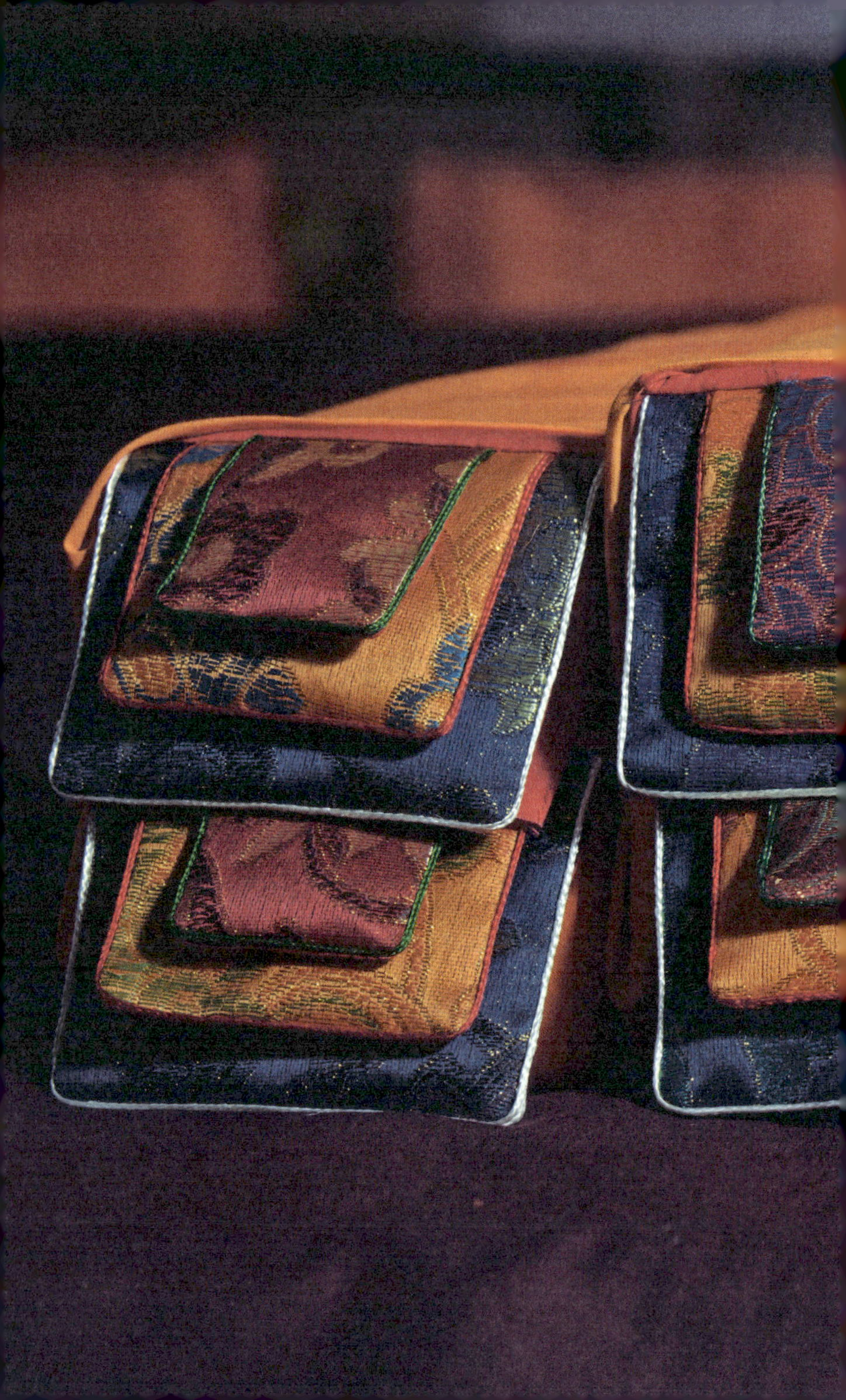

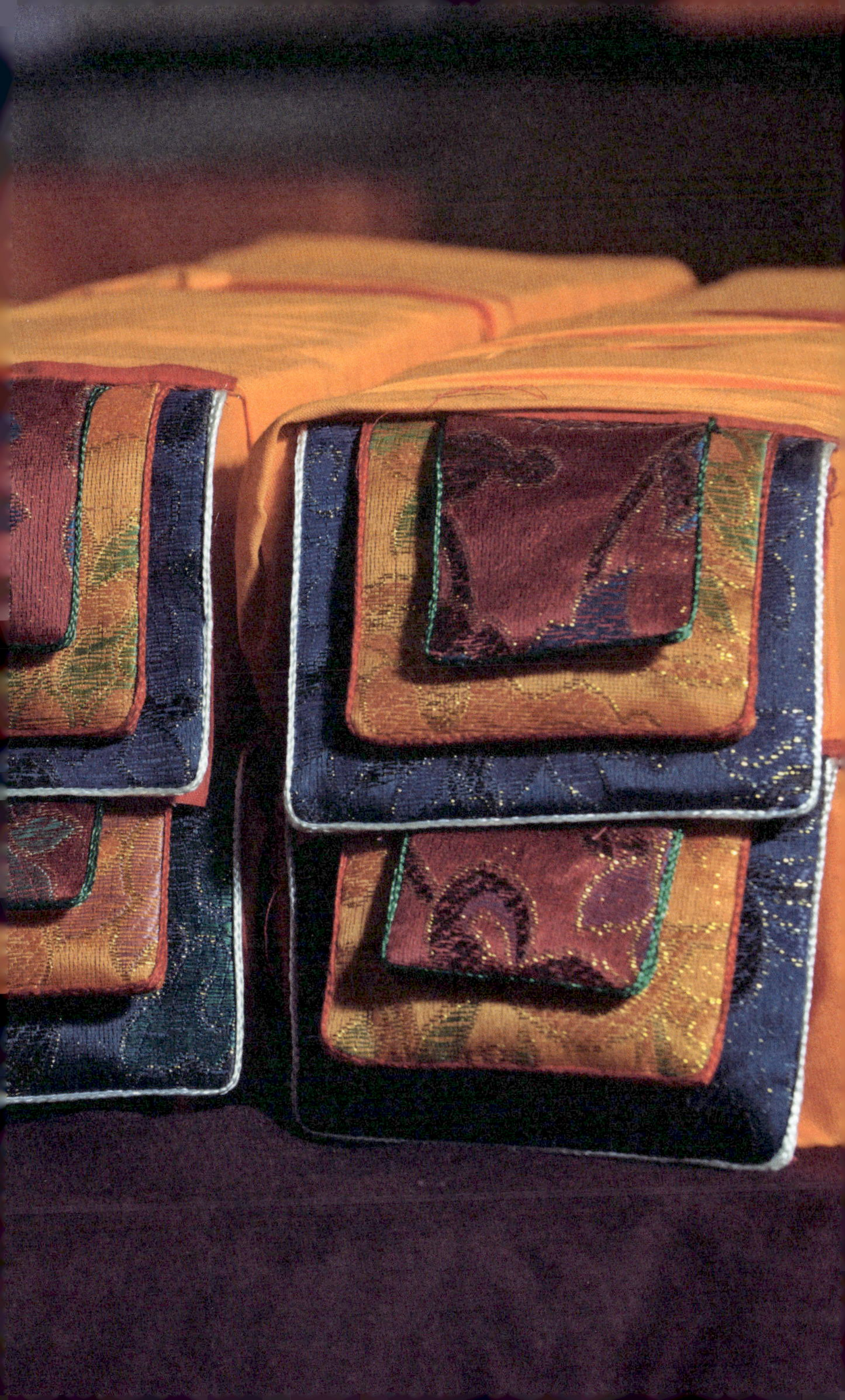

༄༅། །དགོང་ས་ཏཱ་ལའི་བླ་མས་བསྩལ་བའི་སྔོན་གླེང་།

ནེན་སི་ཤེར་ལི་ལགས་ཀྱིས་བརྩམས་པའི་ "བོད་བརྒྱུད་ནང་བསྟན་གྱི་དགོན་པའི་རྩོད་རིག་སློལ་རྒྱུན་ཆེན་མོ་སྡེ་རྩོལ་དང་ཕྱིར་རྩོལ།" ཞེས་པའི་དཔེ་དེབ་འདི་པར་སྐྲུན་བྱས་པར་ངོས་རང་དགའ་པོ་བྱུང་། རྒྱ་གར་གྱི་ནཱ་ལེནྡྲའི་སློལ་རྒྱུན་སྙིང་པ་ནས་བྱུང་བའི་རྩོད་པ་ནི་བོད་ཀྱི་དགོན་པའི་ཤེས་ཡོན་སློབ་གསོའི་ནང་དཔྱད་ཞིབ་ཕྲ་མོའི་ལག་ཆ་གལ་ཆེན་ཞིག་ཏུ་གྱུར། དཔེ་དེབ་འདིས་དུས་རབས་མང་པོའི་རིང་ཉམས་ལེན་བྱས་པའི་དགོན་པའི་རྩོད་པའི་ཐབས་ལམ་རྣམས་གསལ་སྟོན་དང་འགྲེལ་བཤད་བྱས་ཡོད།

ངོས་རང་གི་ཉམས་མྱོང་ལ་གཞིགས་ན། རྩོད་པས་ངོས་ཀྱི་བསམ་བློ་གཏོང་སྟངས་གྲུང་པོ་བཟོ་བ་དང་། ནང་པའི་ལྟ་གྲུབ་དང་ཚད་མ་རིག་པའི་ནང་གི་རྟོག་འཛིང་ཆེ་བའི་བརྗོད་གཞི་རྣམས་ལ་གོ་རྟོགས་འཕེལ་བར་ཤུགས་རྐྱེན་ཟབ་མོ་ཐེབས་ཡོད། རིགས་ལམ་གྱིས་དཔྱད་པའི་བརྒྱུད་རིམ་འདིས་ངོས་ཀྱི་ཉིན་རེའི་འཚོ་བའི་ནང་དུའང་ཕན་ཐོགས་ཆེན་པོ་ཡོད་པ་མཐོང་གི་འདུག

དེང་སང་རྩོད་པ་ནི་དགོན་པའི་ཤེས་ཡོན་སློབ་གསོ་གཅིག་པུའི་ནང་དུ་ཕུས་མེད། དེ་ནི་བཙན་བྱོལ་ནང་གི་བོད་པའི་སློབ་གྲྭ་ཁག་གི་སློབ་ཁྲིད་ཐབས་ལམ་ནང་དུ་བཙུག་ཡོད་ལ། རྒྱ་གར་གྱི་ས་ཁུལ་ཁག་གི་ཧི་མ་ལ་ཡའི་མི་རིགས་འགའ་ཤས་ཀྱིས་ཚན་རིག་ལྟ་བུའི་སློབ་ཚན་གཞན་དག་ལ་དཔྱད་ཞིབ་བྱེད་སྐབས་སུའང་བེད་སྤྱོད་བྱེད་བཞིན་པ་མཐོང་གི་འདུག

ཤེར་ལི་ལགས་ཀྱིས་"རྩོལ་སྡེ་རྩོལ་ཕྱིར་རྩོལ་"ནང་ལེགས་པར་བཤད་པའི་རྩོད་པའི་རིན་ཐང་ལ་དེང་རབས་ཀྱི་ཤེས་ཡོན་སློབ་སྟོན་པ་རྣམས་ཀྱིས་དགའ་མོས་བྱེད་པའི་རེ་བ་ཆེན་པོ་ཞུ་བཞིན་ཡོད།

ཕྱི་ལོ་ ༢༠༢༡ ཟླ་ ༣ ཚེས་ ༥ ལ།

སྔོན་གླེང་།

དགེ་བཤེས་བཀྲ་ཤིས་ཚེ་རིང་།

ཨ་རིའི་སྒྱུ་རྩལ་པར་པ་བུ་མོ་ནེན་སི་ཤེར་ལི་ཡིས་ཕྱོགས་སྒྲིག་བགྱིས་པའི་བོད་པའི་གདན་ས་ཁག་གི་ཐུན་མིན་སློབ་གཉེར་བྱེད་ཕྱོགས་སྐོར་གྱི་བརྙན་དེབ་ཡིད་དུ་འོང་བ་འདི་ལ་སྔོན་གླེང་ཞིག་འབྲི་རྒྱུར་དགའ་སྤྲོབས་ཆེན་པོ་བྱུང་། ཡིད་དུ་འོང་བའི་དཔེ་དེབ་འདིས་གནའ་བོའི་ནང་བསྟན་གཞུང་ལུགས་ལ་བོད་ཀྱི་སློབ་གཉེར་དང་འབྲེལ་བའི་རྩོད་པའི་ཐབས་ལམ་རྣམས་གསལ་སྟོན་བྱས་ཡོད། བརྙན་པར་འདི་དག་གི་བརྒྱུད་ནས་གདན་སའི་སློབ་གཉེར་བ་རྣམས་ཀྱིས་གཞུང་གི་དགོངས་དོན་རྟོགས་ཐབས་སུ་སློབ་གཉེར་ཇི་ལྟར་བྱེད་ཚུལ་སྐོར་བློ་ཡུལ་དུ་གསལ་པོར་འཆར་ཐུབ།

སྟོན་པ་སངས་རྒྱས་བཅོམ་ལྡན་འདས་ཀྱི་ཟབ་རྒྱས་ཀྱི་ཆོས་ཚུལ་ལ་བརྟེན་ནས་སྤྱི་ལོའི་དུས་རབས་གཉིས་པར་བྱོན་པའི་དཔལ་མགོན་འཕགས་པ་ཀླུ་སྒྲུབ་དང་ཐུགས་སྲས་འཕགས་པ་ལྷ་གཉིས་ཀྱིས་ཟབ་མོའི་ལྟ་གྲུབ་དཔྱད་པའི་འཕགས་ཡུལ་གྱི་ལམ་སྲོལ་ཕུན་སུམ་ཚོགས་པ་ཞིག་གསར་གཏོད་མཛད། སངས་རྒྱས་ཀྱིས་ང་ཚོས་རང་གི་སེམས་དང་ཚོར་བའི་རང་བཞིན་ལ་དཔྱད་པ་བྱེད་དེ་གོ་རྟོགས་གོང་འཕེལ་གཏོང་བ་ལ་བརྟེན་ནས་ང་ཚོའི་མི་ཚེར་འགྱུར་བ་འགྲོ་ཐུབ་པའི་ལམ་སྟོན་གནང་ཡོད་ལ། དེའི་རྗེས་ཐོགས་སུ་རྗེས་འཇུག་འཕགས་ཡུལ་མཁས་པ་རྣམས་ཀྱིས་མིའི་སེམས་ཀྱི་རང་བཞིན་ལ་དཔྱོད་པའི་ལྟ་གྲུབ་དེ་འཕེལ་རྒྱས་སུ་བཏང་ནས། ནང་པའི་མཚན་ཉིད་རིག་པ་དང་། ནང་པའི་སེམས་ཁམས་རིག་པ། ནང་པའི་ཚད་མ་རིག་པ་ལྟ་བུའི་རིག་གནས་སྣ་ཚོགས་དར་རྒྱས་བྱུང་། སྲོལ་རྒྱུན་འདི་ལས་རང་གི་སེམས་བསྒྱུར་བཅོས་གཏོང་བ་དང་། བྱམས་པ་དང་། སྙིང་རྗེ། བཏང་སྙོམས། ཞི་གནས། ལྷག་མཐོང་བཅས་གོང་འཕེལ་གཏོང་བའི་ཉམས་ལེན་བྱུང་བ་སྟེ་མཐར་ཤེས་རབ་ཐོབ་པའི་དམིགས་ཡུལ་བཟུང་ཡོད། གསུང་རབས་དགོངས་འགྲེལ་དང་བཅས་པ་འདི་ཚོ་ལ་ནང་པའི་སློབ་དཔོན་རྗེས་འཇུག་དང་བཅས་པས་དུས་རབས་མང་པོའི་རིང་སློབ་གཉེར་ཞིབ་ཏུ་བྱས་ཡོད་ལ། ལྷག་པར་དུ་ནཱ་ལནྡཱའི་ཆོས་བརྒྱུད་རྒྱུན་འཛིན་བྱེད་མཁན་ནང་ལ་སློབ་

གཉེར་ཞིབ་འཇུག་གཏིང་ཟབ་བྱས་པ་རེད། དམིགས་ཡུལ་གཙོ་བོ་ནི་ནང་སེམས་ལ་འགྱུར་བ་གཏོང་ཐབས་བྱེད་རྒྱུ་དེ་ཡིན་པ་དང་། དེ་ཡང་དད་པ་ཙམ་གྱིས་མི་ཚོག་པར། ནང་སེམས་འགྱུར་བ་གཏོང་བར་བྱེད་པའི་སྤྱོད་ལམ་ཚུལ་མཐུན་དང་ལྷན་དུ་སྦྲེལ་ཏེ། དགག་སྒྲུབ་ཀྱི་བརྟག་དཔྱད་ཞིབ་འཇུག་གཏིང་ཟབ་ཀྱི་ངང་ནས་འགྱུར་བ་གཏོང་ཐབས་བྱེད་བཞིན་ཡོད།

སྤྱི་ལོའི་དུས་རབས་བདུན་པའི་སྨད་དང་བརྒྱད་པའི་འགོ་སྟོད་ནང་ནཱ་ལནྡྲའི་ཆོས་བརྒྱུད་འདི་བོད་དུ་དར་བ་དང་། ལྷག་པར་དུ་ཆོས་བརྒྱུད་འདི་བོད་ནང་ཡོངས་སུ་ཁྱབ་པའི་དུས་རབས་བཅུ་གཅིག་པའི་སྐབས་དེར། བོད་ཀྱི་མཁས་པ་ཆོས་ལུས་ཀྱི་རྣམ་འགྱུར་གྱི་ཐོག་ནས་རིག་རྩལ་རྣམས་སྟོན་པར་བྱེད་པའི་རྟགས་གསལ་གྱི་ལམ་ལུགས་དར་སྤེལ་བྱས་པ་ལ་བརྟེན་ནས་བོད་ཀྱི་སློབ་གཉེར་བྱེད་ཚུལ་ཡོངས་སུ་བཅོས་སྒྱུར་བྱས། ཁོང་ཆོས་ལུས་ཀྱི་རྣམ་འགྱུར་དྲག་པོ་དང་། ཐལ་མོ་རྡེབ་པ། གདོང་གི་རྣམ་འགྱུར་བཅས་ལ་བརྟེན་ནས་རྩོད་པ་མཚོན་པའི་ཐབས་ལམ་གསར་གཏོད་གནང་། རྣམ་འགྱུར་འདི་དག་ནི་ངག་ཐོག་ནས་དམ་བཅའ་འཛུགས་པ་དང་། རིགས་པའི་ལམ་ནས་དེ་བཀྲོལ་བྱེད་ཀྱི་ཐལ་བ་འཕེན་པ། བྱ་བའི་ལམ་ནས་མཐོང་སྲིད་པའི་དགག་སྒྲུབ་ཀྱི་རྩོད་པའི་འཕེལ་རིམ་དེ་དག་མཇུག་བསྡོམས་གསལ་བར་བྱེད་པ་བཅས་ཀྱི་དོན་དུ་ཡིན།

སློབ་གཉེར་ལམ་ལུགས་འདིའི་ནང་ཞུགས་པའི་དམིགས་ཡུལ་ནི་དེས་གཞི་རྩའི་ལྟ་གྲུབ་ལ་གོ་རྟོགས་ཟབ་མོ་རྙེད་པ་ཙམ་དུ་མ་ཟད། ལུས་ཀྱི་རྣམ་འགྱུར་གྱི་ཐོག་ནས་རྩོད་པ་དང་དགག་སྒྲུབ་ཀྱི་རིམ་པ་དང་འགྲོས་རྣམས་གཟུགས་སུ་བཀོད་ནས་སེམས་སུ་འཛིན་པའི་ཆེད་དུའང་ཡིན། ནེན་སེའི་པར་རིས་རྣམས་ཀྱིས་ཐབས་ལམ་དེ་དག་མཛེས་སྡུག་ལྡན་པའི་སྒོ་ནས་མཚོན་ཐུབ་པ་བྱུང་ཡོད།

པར་རིས་འདི་དག་བཟོ་སྐབས། ནེན་སི་ཡིས་དགེ་འདུན་པ་རྣམས་ཀྱི་སྒེར་གྱི་གནས་ཁང་དུའང་བཅར་ཏེ་ཁོང་ཚོས་རང་གི་སྤྱི་ཚོགས་ནང་འཚོ་བ་ཇི་ལྟར་སྐྱེལ་བ་དང་དར་རྒྱས་འགྲོ་ཚུལ་ལ་རྒྱུས་ལོན་བྱས། མོས་སློབ་མ་རྣམས་ཀྱིས་ཁོང་ཚོའི་དགེ་རྒན་དང་མཉམ་དུ་འབྲེལ་བ་བྱེད་སྟངས་དང་། གྲྭ་པ་གཞོན་

པ་དང་རྒྱན་པའི་བར་གྱི་འབྲེལ་བ། དེ་བཞིན་སློབ་ཁྲིད་དང་སློབ་སྦྱོང་གི་སྒྲོམ་གཞི་འདི་དག་བརྒྱུད་ནས་སྤྱི་ཚོགས་ཀྱི་འབྲེལ་བ་སྲུག་ཏུ་གཏོང་བའི་རྩོད་པའི་སྒྲིག་ལམ་བཅས་ཀྱི་སྐོར་ཞིབ་ཁྲ་བཟོས་ཡོད། མོའི་པར་རིས་བརྒྱུད་ནས་ཀློག་པ་པོ་རྣམས་ཀྱིས་བོད་ཀྱི་ཐུན་མོང་མ་ཡིན་པའི་སྲོལ་རྒྱུན་འདི་དག་དགོན་སྡེ་ཁག་ཏུ་ཇི་ལྟར་གསོན་པོར་གནས་ཚུལ་གྱི་ཚོར་བ་གསལ་པོ་ཞིག་འཐོབ་ཐུབ། བོད་ཀྱི་དགོན་སྡེའི་སྤྱི་ཚོགས་བཙན་བྱོལ་གྱི་གནས་སྟངས་སུ་གནས་ཡོད་ནའང་། ད་དུང་དར་རྒྱས་འགྲོ་བཞིན་པ་མ་ཟད། དུས་རབས་ཉེར་གཅིག་པའི་འཚོ་བའི་རྣམ་པར་ཡང་འཇུག་བཞིན་ཡོད།

ངས་ཧེན་སི་ལ་སྙིང་ཐག་པ་ནས་བཀའ་དྲིན་ཆེ་ཞུ་རྒྱུ་ཡིན། ཁོང་གིས་པར་རིས་འདི་དག་ཕྱི་ཕྱོགས་ཀྱི་འཛམ་རྟེན་དང་། ཁྱད་པར་དུ་རྒྱ་གར་ནང་གི་སློབ་གཉེར་དང་ཉམས་ལེན་གྱི་གནས་འདི་དག་ཏུ་བསྐྱོད་མི་ཐུབ་མཁན་རྣམས་ལ་ལེགས་སྐྱེས་སུ་འབུལ་བར་འབད་བརྩོན་དང་དུས་ཚོད་ཏ་ཅང་མང་པོ་བཏང་ཡོད།

རྒྱུ་མཚན་གྱི་སྒོ་ནས་བདེན་པ་གཏན་ལ་འབེབས་པ།

དགེ་བཤེས་ཊེ་ཀོ་ལ་སི། ཕྲིར་ལེཊ་ཊ།
ར་སྟོད་གྲྭ་ཚང་གི་མཁན་པོ།

སངས་རྒྱས་ཀྱིས་རང་གི་སློབ་མ་རྣམས་ལ་ཐུབ་པ་ཉིད་ཀྱི་གསུང་ཁས་ལེན་མ་བྱེད་གོང་དཔྱད་པ་ལེགས་པར་བྱ་དགོས་པར་བཀའ་གནང་བ་བཞིན། ང་ཚོས་ཀྱང་རང་ལ་བསླབས་པའི་དོན་རྣམས་བདེན་པ་ཡིན་མིན་ངེས་པའི་ཆེད་དུ་ངེས་པར་དུ་བརྟག་དཔྱད་བྱེད་དགོས། རྩོད་པ་ནི་ང་ཚོ་ནང་པའི་དགེ་འདུན་པ་རྣམས་ཀྱིས་དེ་ལྟར་བྱེད་པའི་ཐབས་ལམ་ཞིག་ཡིན། ང་ཚོས་སློབ་གྲོགས་དང་ལྷན་དུ་རིགས་པ་དང་རྒྱུ་མཚན་གྱི་སྣང་བའི་བརྒྱུད་ནས་རང་གིས་ཤེས་པ་རྣམས་ཀྱི་འཇུག་འབྲས་ཡང་དག་པ་ཡིན་མིན་འཚོལ་ཞིབ་བྱེད་ཀྱི་ཡོད། ང་ཚོས་སྐབས་འགར་དོགས་སློང་བྱེད་པ་དང་། སྐབས་རེ་ལན་འདེབས་བྱེད་པ་ཡིན། གང་ལྟར་ང་ཚོས་རང་ཉིད་ལ་ཡོད་པའི་གོ་བ་ལོག་པ་རྣམས་ཇེ་ཉུང་དུ་གཏོང་བཞིན་དུ་བརྟན་ཞིང་ཟབ་པའི་གོ་རྟོགས་ཤིག་འཕེལ་རྒྱས་སུ་གཏོང་། བརྩོན་པ་ལ་བརྟེན་ནས་རིམ་བཞིན་གོ་རྟོགས་རྣམས་ཕྲ་རུ་དང་བློ་སྐྱེས་ང་ཚོས་ཐོབ་པའི་བློ་ཤེས་བྱ་རྣམས་ལ་དད་པ་འཕེལ་བར་འགྱུར། འདི་ནི་རྨོངས་པའི་དད་པ་ཞིག་མིན་པར་མ་ཟད། དཔྱད་པ་ལས་བྱུང་བ་དང་གོ་རྟོགས་ལ་གཞི་བཅོལ་བའི་དད་པ་ཞིག་ཡིན། འདི་ནི་ང་ཚོས་བློ་གཏད་ཆོག་པའི་དད་པ་ཞིག་ཡིན།

རྩོམ་སྒྲིག་པའི་གཏམ།

ཉེན་སི་ཤེར་ལི།

གུས་བརྗེ་དང་། ཆེ་མཐོང་། སྙིང་རྗེ་བཅས་ནི་རྣེལ་ཀོབ་ཏུ་ཡོད་པའི་སེ་ར་བྱེས་སྨད་ཀྱི་གཙུག་ལག་སློབ་གཉེར་ཁང་གི་མཁས་མང་འདུ་བའི་ཁོར་ཡུག་ལ་ཡོངས་ཁྱབ་ཏུ་གྱུར། ངས་ཨེ་མོ་རི་གཙུག་ལག་སློབ་གཉེར་ཁང་གི་མངའ་འོག་ཏུ་ཡོད་པའི་ཨེ་མོ་རི་བོད་ཀྱི་ཚན་རིག་ལས་འཆར་ (ETSI) གྱི་ཆ་ཤས་སུ་༢༠༢༡ལོར་དགོན་པ་ཁག་ལ་བལྟ་སྐོར་བྱེད་པའི་གོ་སྐབས་བྱུང་། ཨེ་མོ་རི་བོད་ཀྱི་ཚན་རིག་ལས་འཆར་དེ་༢༠༠༨ལོར་འགོ་བཙུགས་པ་རེད། དེ་ཡང་༧གོང་ས་སྐུ་ཕྲེང་བཅུ་བཞི་པ་ཆེན་པོ་མཆོག་གིས་ཨེ་མོ་རི་གཙུག་ལག་སློབ་གཉེར་ཁང་ལ་བོད་ཀྱི་དཔེ་མཛོད་ཁང་དང་མཉམ་འབྲེལ་ཐོག་དགེ་འདུན་པ་རྣམས་ལ་སློབ་ཚན་གསར་བཟོ་གནང་རྒྱུགས་གསུངས་པ་ལྟར་རེད། དམིགས་ཡུལ་ནི་མི་རིགས་སྤྱིའི་ཁེ་ཕན་ཆེད་དུ་ནུབ་ཕྱོགས་ཀྱི་ཚན་རིག་དང་གནའ་བོའི་བོད་བརྒྱུད་ནང་བསྟན་གྱི་ཤེས་རབ་དབར་རྒྱུན་མཐུད་ཀྱི་འབྲེལ་བ་ཞིག་གསར་གཏོད་བྱ་རྒྱུ་དེ་ཡིན།

སྤྱི་ལོ་ ༡༩༥༩ ལོར་རྒྱ་ནག་སྲིད་གཞུང་གིས་བོད་བཙན་འཛུལ་བྱས་པར་བརྟེན་བོད་ཀྱི་ནང་པ་མང་པོ་ཞིག་བཙན་བྱོལ་དུ་འགྲོ་དགོས་བྱུང་བ་རེད། སྐྱབས་མགོན་ཏཱ་ལའི་བླ་མ་མཆོག་དང་ཡུལ་གྲུར་གྱི་ནང་པའི་དགེ་འདུན་པ་མང་པོ་ཞིག་བལ་ཡུལ་གྱི་ས་མཚམས་དང་། ལྷ་ཡུལ་ལྷ་བུའི་རྒྱ་གར་དུ་སློབ་སྦྱོང་བྱེད་པ་དང་། མདུན་བསྐྱོད་བྱེད་པ་བཅས་ཀྱི་ཆེད་དུ་བཤད་གྲྭ་ཁག་བཏབ་ཡོད།

ཞོགས་པ་དང་དགོང་དྲོའི་དུས་མཚམས་སུ་འབུ་ཙོག་ཙོག་པའི་ཐྲིག་སྒྲ་དང་། བྱིའུའི་སྐད་སྙན། ཕྱིའི་ཟུག་སྐད་བཅས་རྣ་བར་གོ་ཡོང་ལ། གཉུག་མར་གནས་པའི་དགེ་འདུན་པ་རྣམས་ཀྱི་ཉིན་རེའི་བྱེད་སྒོ་ཁག་འགོ་འཛུགས་ཅིང་མཇུག་སྒྲིལ་བར་བྱེད། མཐོང་སྣང་གི་ཚོན་ཐེར་དུ་གྱུར་པའི་དགོན་པའི་ས་གཞི་ནི་ཕུན་སུམ་ཚོགས་པ་ཞིག་སྟེ། ཉིན་རེའི་ལས་ཀ་དང་། བྱེད་སྒོ། ཚོ་ག་ཕྱག་ལེན་བཅས་ཆོས་ཕྱོགས་ཀྱི་བྱ་བ་ཁོ་ནས་དུས་འདའ་བར་བྱེད། ལས་བྱའི་དུས་མཚམས་རིང་པོའི་ནང་དུ་ནང་པའི་ཆོས་ལུགས་ཀྱི་འདོན་པའི་དབྱངས་དང་

སློབ་ཁྲིད་ཀྱི་སྒྲ་དབྱངས་བཅས་སྦྱོད་ཤག་དང་། སློབ་གྲྭའི་བར་ཁྱམས། རྩེད་གྲྭའི་ར་བ། གཙུག་ལག་ཁང་བཅས་སུ་བསྐྱོད་མར་གྲག

ཉིན་མོའི་སྣང་བ་ནི་ཉི་མ་མ་ཤར་གོང་ནས་འགོ་འཛུགས་ཤིང་། དགེ་རྒན་དང་སློབ་མ་རྣམས་སྨོན་ལམ་འདེབས་པ་དང་སྒོམ་ཉམས་ལེན་བཅས་ལ་འཇོམས་ཏེ། དེ་ནས་ཞོགས་ཇ་དཀྱུས་མ་ཞིག་དང་། སློབ་སྦྱོང་། ཉིན་རེའི་བྱེད་སྒོའི་རྣམ་གཞག་གྲ་སྒྲིག་བཅས་བྱེད། དགེ་རྒན་གྱི་འགན་འཁྲི་ནི་རང་གི་སློབ་མ་རྣམས་ལ་གྲོགས་པོ་དང་། ཆོས་ཀྱི་སློབ་དཔོན། ཤེས་ཡོན་སྦྱིན་མཁན་བཅས་ཀྱི་འདུ་ཤེས་འཛིན་རྒྱུ་དེ་ཆགས་ཡོད།

དགེ་འདུན་པ་ལོ་གཞོན་རྣམས་ནི་སློབ་འབྲིང་ལ་འགྲིམས་ཏེ་ཨང་རྩིས་དང་། སྦྱོར་གློག །སྐད་ཡིག །ཡིག་གཟུགས་དང་། རི་མོ་བཅས་སྦྱོང་བཞིན་ཡོད། འཛིན་གྲྭའི་མིང་རྣམས་ནི་འཛིན་ཁང་སོ་སོའི་སྒོ་བྱང་དུ་བཀོད་ཡོད། མཚན་ཉིད་སློབ་ཚན་ནི་ངའི་སློབ་ཚན་དགའ་ཤོས་དེ་ཡིན། རྒྱུ་མཚན་ནི་སློབ་ཚན་དེའི་སྐབས་སུ་རྩོད་པའི་རིག་པ་སློབ་པས་སོ། །དཔེ་ཆ་ནི་དགེ་འདུན་པ་སོ་སོའི་ཤེས་ཡོན་གྱི་གཞི་རྩར་གྱུར་ཡོད་ཅིང་། དེ་ཡང་སོ་སོའི་མི་ཚེའི་ནང་བློ་འཛིན་དང་རྩོད་རིག་བཅས་ཀྱི་ཐོག་ནས་འདྲིས་པར་བྱེད། རྩོད་རིག་ནི་གཞན་གྱི་ལངས་ཕྱོགས་དང་ལྟ་བ་རྣམས་ལ་བརྒལ་ལན་བྱེད་པ་དང་སོ་སོའི་འདོད་ཕྱོགས་སྲུང་བར་བྱེད་པ་ལ་སྐྱོད་ཆོག་པའི་ཐབས་ལམ་དམིགས་བསལ་ཅན་གྱི་ནུས་པ་ཞིག་རེད།

དགེ་འདུན་པ་རྣམས་འཛིག་རྟེན་གྱི་བསམ་བློ་དང་བྲལ་ཏེ། ཕན་ཚུན་མཉམ་རུབ་དང་། འཚོ་བ་དཀྱུས་མའི་རྣམ་པ་བཅས་ལ་འཇུག་པས་ངའི་ཡིད་དབང་འཕྲོགས་སོང་། ཁོང་ཚོའི་ཉིན་རེའི་བྱེད་སྒོ་ཁག་ལ་འཆར་གཞི་དང་གོ་རིམ་ཡོད་པས། ཐ་དགོང་གི་རྩོད་པ་རྣམས་ལ་དམིགས་བསལ་དུས་བཅད་ཡོད། དགེ་འདུན་པ་རྣམས་རྩོད་པའི་སྐབས་དྲག་ཤུལ་དང་ཆུར་ཟིང་གི་རྣམ་པ་ཇི་ཙམ་ཆེ་ན་ཡང་། རྩོད་པ་ཚར་བ་དང་ལབ་གླེང་ཡང་ཚར་བར་བྱེད་པ་ཡིན། འཁྲབ་སྟོན་གྱི་རྣམ་པ་ཅན་གྱི་རྩོད་པ་རྩོད་སྟངས་ཀྱི་སྐབས་སུ་ཡང་ཡང་འབྱུང་བའི་དྲག་ཤུལ་གྱི་རྣམ་པ་ནི་དོན་དངོས་ཐོག་དཔྱད་པ་བྱ་སའི་བརྗོད་

བྱའི་རིགས་ལམ་ལ་གོ་རྟོགས་བྱུང་བའི་སྐབས་ཀྱི་ཕྱི་རྒོལ་དང་སྔ་རྒོལ་གང་རུང་གི་འདོད་ཕྱོགས་ཀྱི་མཚོན་བྱེད་རྟོན་པོ་ཞིག་རེད། རྩོད་པ་ཚར་བའི་རྗེས་སུ་དགེ་འདུན་པ་རྣམས་ཉིན་རེའི་བྱ་གཞག་དང་། ཞལ་ལག་མཉམ་མཆོད། སློབ་ལམ་མཉམ་འདེབས། སློབ་སྦྱོང་དང་གོམས་བགྲོད་བཅས་ཞི་བདེའི་ངང་ནས་ལྷན་དུ་བྱེད་པ་མཐོང་ཆོས་སུ་ཡོད། རྩོད་པས་མི་ཚེའི་གོ་རྟོགས་ལ་འགྱུར་པ་ཐེབས་ཤིད་ཀྱང་། ཕན་ཚུན་གུས་བརྩི་དང་གཅེས་སེམས་ལ་འགྱུར་བ་མི་ཐེབས།

ངས་སྤྱི་ཚོགས་དཔྱད་བརྗོད་དང་སྤྱི་ཚོགས་ཀྱི་ཡིག་ཆ་གཉིས་མཉམ་བསྲེས་བྱས་ནས་སེམས་ཁམས་དང་རིག་གཞུང་གི་གནད་དོན་ཞིབ་འཇུག་བྱེད་པའི་མི་སྣའི་པར་རིས་བཟོ་བཞིན་ཡོད། ངའི་སྤྱི་ཚོགས་དཔྱད་བརྗོད་ཀྱི་བྱ་བའི་ནང་དུ། ངས་གློག་བརྙན་དངོས་བདེན་ལས་བླངས་པའི་སྣང་བ་གཞི་འཛིན་དང་གནས་ཡུལ་བདམས་ནས་མི་སྣའི་པར་རིས་བཟོ་ཀྱི་ཡོད། ངའི་སྤྱི་ཚོགས་ཀྱི་ཡིག་ཆའི་ལས་ག་དེ་ཙུང་ཟད་རང་བཞིན་ལྡན་པ་ཞིག་ཡིན་པ་དང་། གར་ཏེ་ཡེར་རྡི་རེ་སོན་གྱི་"དུས་སྐབས་གཏན་འབེབས"ཀྱི་བསམ་བློ་ལས་ཤུགས་རྐྱེན་ཐེབས་ཡོད། སྐབས་རེར་ངས་རྒྱབ་ལྗོངས་བཟོས་པའམ་སྣང་བ་ཆོད་འཛིན་བྱེད་ཀྱི་ཡོད་ནའང་། ཕྱིར་བཏང་དུ་ངས་བརྙན་པར་གྱི་རྒྱབ་ལྗོངས་ནང་དུ་ཡུལ་རྣམས་རང་བཞིན་གྱིས་འཛུལ་བར་སྒུག་གི་ཡོད་པ་ལས་ལྷག་པར་ཆས་ཀྱི་ཁ་ཕྱོགས་སྒྱུར་ཀྱི་མེད།

དགོན་པའི་ཁོར་ཡུག་དེ་ང་ཡི་པར་གྱི་སྣང་བརྙན་དང་སྒྱུ་རྩལ་གྱི་རྣམ་པའི་ཆེད་དུ་ཧ་ཅང་འོས་འཚམས་ཤིག་ཏུ་ཆགས་སོང་། དགོང་མོ་ཆོས་རྭའི་ནང་མུན་པ་རུབ་པའི་སྐབས་སུ་དགེ་འདུན་པ་རྣམས་གཅིག་གིས་གཅིག་གམ། གཉིས་ཀྱིས་གཅིག་གམ། གཅིག་གིས་གཉིས་སམ། རྩེ་ཚན་བཅས་སུ་བགོས་ཏེ། གྲིབ་ནག་གི་ནང་ལ་ཡང་གསོན་ཤུགས་དང་དྲག་ཤུགས་བཅས་ཀྱི་ཐོག་ནས་ཕར་རྒོལ་ལམ་སོ་སོའི་འདོད་ཕྱོགས་སྲུང་བའི་ཆེད་དུ་རིགས་ལམ་བེད་སྤྱོད་གཏོང་གི་ཡོད། ནམ་མཁའི་འོད་སྣང་ཉིན་ནས་སྲོད་དང་སྲོད་ནས་མཚན་དུ་འགྱུར་བའི་སྐབས་སུ་རྩོད་པ་དེ་དག་ནི་བོད་བརྒྱུད་ནང་བསྟན་གྱི་ལོ་རྒྱུས་འཁྱེར་བའི་ཟློས་གར་གྱི་འཁྲབ་སྟོན་གས་སྦུབས་མེད་པའི་རྣམ་པ་ཞིག་ཏུ་འགྱུར་བ་ཡིན། སེམས་ངར་ཆེན་པོའི་ཐོག་ནས་ཕན་ཚུན་རྩོད་པ་རྩོད་པའི་དགེ་འདུན་པ་དེ་དག་གི་ཡིད་

ངོའི་གཟུགས་བརྙན་དང་སྐད་སྒྲ་ཁྱད་པར་ཅན་དེ་དག་གིས་ངའི་ཡིད་དབང་འཕྲོགས་སོང་།

རིག་གཞུང་ཕྱུག་པོ་འདི་ལ་རྒྱབ་སྐྱོར་དང་ཁ་འཐོར་དུ་ཕྱིན་ནས་ཉེན་ཁའི་གནས་སུ་གྱུར་ཀྱང་ནང་པའི་ཚོགས་སྡེ་ད་དུང་དར་རྒྱས་སུ་འགྲོ་བཞིན་པའི་སྐོར་གྱི་ངའི་གོ་རྟོགས་བཅས་རེད། ངའི་རེ་བ་ལ་ཤར་ཕྱོགས་པ་དང་ནུབ་ཕྱོགས་པ་གཉིས་ཀས་མཉམ་དུ་བོད་བརྒྱུད་ནང་བསྟན་གྱི་རྫོང་པའི་རིག་པ་འདི་གཅེས་འཛིན་བྱས་ནས། ལག་བསྟར་གྱི་ཐོག་ནས་སྤྱངས་ཏེ། ང་ཚོའི་བསམ་བློ་གཏོང་སྟངས་དང་ལྟ་བའི་ཁ་ཕྱོགས་ཇི་ལྟར་འཛིན་པ་བཅས་ནི་རྟག་ཏུ་བསམ་ཚུལ་དང་ཉམས་མྱོང་སྣ་ཚོགས་པ་ལ་འཇུག་བཞིན་དུ། སྙིང་རྗེའི་སྐོར་སློབ་སྦྱོང་བྱེད་པ་དང་ཉམས་ལེན་བྱེད་པ་བཅས་ཀྱི་ལྷེ་མིག་ཏུ་གྱུར་པར་གོ་རྟོགས་ཡོང་བའི་རེ་བ་ཡོད། འདི་ནི་ང་ཚོས་སོ་སོ་དང་གཞན་དག་གི་བདེ་དོན་ཡར་རྒྱས་གཏོང་ཐུབ་པ་ནི་ལེགས་སྐྱེས་ཤིག་རེད།

བོད་བརྒྱུད་ནང་བསྟན་གྱི་རྩོད་པའི་ནང་གི་སྔ་རྒོལ་དང་ཕྱི་རྒོལ་གྱི་རྣམ་གཞག

དགེ་བཤེས་དགྲ་འདུལ་རྣམ་རྒྱལ་དང་། ཁྭ་རོལ། ཕྱོར་ཐི་མཊ།
ཨེ་མོ་རི་གཙུག་ལག་སློབ་གཉེར་ཁང་།

དེབ་འདིས་རྒྱ་ཆེའི་གློག་པ་པོ་རྣམས་བརྙན་མིག་གི་དྭངས་ཤེལ་ལས་མཐོང་བའི་བོད་ཀྱི་དགོན་སྡེའི་གཙུག་ལག་སློབ་གཉེར་ཁང་ཆེན་མོའི་སློབ་གཉེར་བ་ཚོའི་ཆོས་རྩོད་ཀྱི་རྣམ་པ་ལ་ཁྱུག་ཙམ་ཞིག་བལྟ་བར་འཁྲིད་པ་དང་། གསོན་ཉམས་ལྡན་པའི་བྱེད་སྒོའི་ཁྱད་ཆོས་དང་། མཉམ་ཞུགས་ཀྱི་ཚོར་བ་དྲག་པོས་རྩོད་པ་པོ་རྣམས་ཡིད་དབང་འགུག་པའི་སྦྱོང་བརྡར་འདི་ཡི་ནང་དོ་སྣང་དབང་མེད་དུ་འགུག་པར་བྱེད། མ་ཟད། ཡིད་དབང་འཕྲོག་པའི་མཐོང་ཆོས་ཀྱི་ངོས་དེའི་འོག་ཏུ་སློབ་སྦྱོང་གི་དགོས་པའི་རྨང་གཞི་ཆེན་པོ་ཞིག་དང་ལྡན་ལ་རྩོད་པ་ནི་བོད་ཀྱི་ནང་བསྟན་སློབ་གཉེར་གྱི་ཁ་བྲལ་ཐབས་མེད་པའི་བྱེད་སྒོ་ཞིག་ཏུ་འཁྱུམས།

འདིར་ང་ཚོས་རྒྱ་ཆེའི་གློག་པ་པོ་རྣམས་ལ་གོ་རྟོགས་གསལ་དུ་གཏོང་ཆེད་དུ་བོད་བརྒྱུད་ནང་བསྟན་གྱི་རྩོད་པའི་དགོས་དམིགས་དང་སྦྱོང་བརྡར་སྐོར་གྱི་བཤད་མདོར་བསྡུས་ཤིག་བཀོད་ཡོད།

རྒྱབ་ལྗོངས།

ཅིའི་ཕྱིར་རྩོད་པ་རྩོད་ཀྱི་ཡོད་དམ། བོད་ཀྱི་ནང་ཆོས་ཀྱི་དགོས་དོན་ནི་ཐུབ་ཕྱོགས་ཀྱི་སྲོལ་རྒྱུན་དང་ཆེས་མི་འདྲ་སྟེ། ཕྱི་མས་རྒྱལ་ཐབས་ལ་དམིགས་པ་དང་། སྔ་མས་སྐྱོང་ཐབས་ལ་དམིགས། གནད་དོན་འདི་ཅིའི་ཕྱིར་དང་གང་འདྲ་ཡིན་པ་ཤེས་པ་ལ་བོད་ཀྱི་དགོན་སྡེའི་སློབ་གཉེར་གྱི་དམིགས་ཡུལ་གྱི་ཁྱད་པར་ལ་སོམས་དང་། ཚེ་གང་པོར་སློབ་གཉེར་དང་ཉམས་ལེན་བྱས་ཏེ་ཐར་པ་དང་ཐམས་ཅད་མཁྱེན་པའི་དོན་དུ་བརྩོན་ཞིང་དཀའ་སྤྱོད་ཆེ་བའི་རྒྱུད་རིམ་འདིས་སྡུག་བསྔལ་གྱི་རྒྱུ་དང་མ་རིག་པའི་ལོག་རྟོག་སེལ་བར་འབད་ཀྱི་ཡོད། དེ་ལྟར་སྐྱེ་བ་མང་པོའི་རིང་ལ་སེམས་ཀྱི་གཏིང་རུམ་ན་གཞི་བཅས་པའི་སེམས་ཀྱི་རང་

གཤིས་ཀྱི་སྒྲིབ་པ་ངོས་བཟུང་ནས་དེ་དག་ལ་གཉེན་པོ་བསྟེན་ནས་མ་རིག་པ་སྤངས་ཏེ་སངས་རྒྱས་ཀྱི་གོ་འཕང་འཐོབ་པར་བྱེད་ཀྱི་ཡོད། སྟོང་པ་ནི། རང་ཉིད་དམ་གཞན་དང་མཉམ་དུ་སྟོང་པ་ན་གཉིས་ཀའི་སེམས་ཀྱི་ལོག་རྟོག་སེལ་བ་དང་། ཤེས་རབ་ཀྱི་རྣོ་ངར་བརྡར་བར་བྱེད་པས་སྟོང་པ་ནི་ནང་པའི་སེམས་ཀྱི་སྦྱོང་བརྡར་བྱེད་པའི་ཐབས་ལམ་རྩ་ཆེན་པོ་ཞིག་ཡིན།

དེབ་འདིའི་ནང་དུ་འཁོད་པའི་དེང་རབས་ཀྱི་སྟོང་པའི་ལག་ལེན་འདི་ལྷོ་ཨེ་ཤེ་ཡའི་ལོ་རྒྱུས་རིང་མོའི་ནང་བརྒྱུད་དེ་སངས་རྒྱས་མ་བྱོན་གོང་ནས་བྱུང་བ་ཞིག་རེད། དེ་དུས་སྟོང་པ་ནི་ནང་དོན་རིག་པའི་འཕེལ་རྒྱས་འཚོལ་མཁན་ཚོའི་ཁྲོད་དུ་ཁྱབ་གདལ་ཆེ། ནང་པའི་མངོན་སུམ་དང་། དཔྱད་པ། ཤེས་བྱའི་རྣམ་གཞག་གི་སྤྲོལ་གཏོང་དུས་སྐབས་སུ་ཆོས་ལུགས་ནང་ཁུལ་དང་ཕྱི་རོལ་གཉིས་ཀའི་དཀའ་ངལ་ལས་ཁེ་ཕན་བྱུང་ཡོད། སྟོང་པའི་མཇུག་འབྲས་ཀྱི་གལ་ཆེའི་རང་བཞིན་ནི་ཧ་ཅང་ཟབ་མོ་ཡོད་པས། མཁས་པ་ཞིག་དང་ཁོང་གི་རྗེས་འབྲང་པ་ཡོངས་རྫོགས་ཀྱིས་སྟོང་པ་བྱེད་མཁན་གྱི་ལྷ་བ་རྒྱལ་བ་ཡིན་ན། དེས་སྟོང་པ་བྱེད་མཁན་དེར་གནས་ལུགས་ཀྱི་སྐོར་ལ་ཡང་དག་པའམ་དགག་པར་མི་ནུས་པའི་ལྷ་བ་ཡོད་པ་གཏན་ལ་ཕབ་པ་ལ་བརྟེན་ནས་ཆོས་ལུགས་བསྒྱུར་བ་ཡིན། དོན་དངོས་སུ་སངས་རྒྱས་ཉིད་ཀྱིས་ཀྱང་སངས་རྒྱས་མ་ཐོབ་གོང་དང་སློབ་དཔོན་གྱི་མཛད་པ་མ་བཞེས་གོང་དུ་དེ་ལྷ་བུའི་སྟོང་པ་མཛད་ཡོད། དེ་ནས་བཟུང་ཕྱི་རོལ་པ་དང་མཉམ་དུ་སྟོང་པ་བྱེད་པ་ནི་ཁྱབ་གདལ་ཆེ་བ་བྱུང་ཞིང་། དེས་དུས་རབས་དྲུག་པའི་ཚད་མ་རིག་པའི་སློབ་དཔོན་ཕྱོགས་གླང་གིས་ཐོག་མར་ནང་པའི་གཏན་ཚིགས་རིག་པའི་འཕེལ་རྒྱས་དང་ཡིག་ཐོག་ཏུ་འགོད་པར་སྐུལ་མ་བྱས་པ་དང་། དུས་རབས་བདུན་པར་ལྷ་གྲུབ་ཟླ་བ་ཆོས་ཀྱི་གྲགས་པས་དེ་བས་རྒྱས་པར་མཛད། གཞི་རྩའི་རྣམ་གཞག་འདི་དག་ཚད་མ་སྟེ་"ཡང་དག་པའི་ཤེས་པ"འམ"ཡང་དག་པའི་ལྷ་བ"འཚོལ་བཞིན་པའི་ཕྱི་རོལ་པ་དང་མཉམ་དུ་ཐུག་འཕྲད་རིམ་པའི་བརྒྱུད་ནས་གོ་རིམ་སྒྲིག་པ་དང་། ལམ་ལུགས་སུ་བཀོད་པ། ལེགས་བཅོས་བྱས་པ་བཅས་བྱུང་ཡོད། བོད་ཀྱི་མཁས་པའི་སྤྲོལ་རྒྱུན་གྱི་རྨང་གཞི་དེ་རྒྱ་གར་གྱི་ནང་པའི་ཚད་མ་རིག་པ་དང་ཤེས་བྱེད་རིག་པའི་གཞུང་ལུགས་གཙོ་བོ་རྣམས་བོད་སྐད་དུ་བསྒྱུར་མཁན་རྔོག་བློ་ལྡན་ཤེས་རབ་

(༡༠༥༩-༡༡༠༩)དང་། དེང་སང་གནས་ཤིང་དར་རྒྱས་འབྱུང་བཞིན་པའི་བོད་ཀྱི་རྩོད་པའི་རིག་པའི་ལམ་ལུགས་གཏན་ལ་འབེབས་མཁན་ཕྱ་པ་ཆོས་ཀྱི་སེང་གེ་(༡༡༠༩-༡༡༦༩)བཅས་ཀྱིས་བརྟན་དུ་བཏང་ཡོད། རྒྱལ་ཁ་ལས་གསལ་བཤད་འཚོལ་བའི་རྩོད་པ་ནི་ཤེས་བྱ་དང་ཡེ་ཤེས་གཉིས་ཀ་གོང་འཕེལ་གཏོང་བའི་ནུས་པ་ལྡན་པའི་བརྒྱུད་ལམ་ཞིག་ཏུ་གནས་ཤིང་། དེ་དག་གིས་གདོན་མི་ཟ་བར་འགྱུར་བ་བསྐྲུན་པའི་ཤུགས་རྐྱེན་ཡང་ཐེབས་ཡོད།

རྩོད་པ་ནི་ཆེས་ཐོག་མའི་དགོན་སྡེའི་སློབ་གཉེར་གྱི་རྒྱུད་རིམ་གྱི་ཆ་ཤས་ཤིག་ཡིན་པ་དང་། སློབ་སློབ་གཉེར་བ་ཚོས་ཐོག་མར་གཏན་ཚིགས་རིག་པ་ནན་ཏན་དང་། ཁ་དོག་དང་དབྱིབས། སྤྱི་དང་བྱེ་བྲག འགོག་པ་དང་སྒྲུབ་པ། བཀག་པ་ཉིས་རིམ་དང་མང་རིམ་ལྟ་བུའི་ཉིན་རེའི་བརྗོད་གཞི་བེད་སྤྱོད་བྱས་ནས་རྩོད་པའི་རྨང་གཞིའི་སྒྲོམ་གཞི་དང་ལག་ལེན་གྱི་སྒྲིག་གཞི་རྣམས་སློབ་ཀྱི་ཡོད། དེ་ནས་རྒྱུ་དང་རྐྱེན། ཕན་ཚུན་སྤངས་འགལ་དང་འབྲེལ་བ། ཐལ་ཕྱིའི་ཁྱབ་པ། རྟོག་པ་དང་མངོན་སུམ། སྐད་ཡིག་དང་བྱེད་པ་པོ། རྗེས་དཔག་དང་ཐལ་འགྱུར། དེ་བཞིན་ནང་པའི་སེམས་ཁམས་རིག་པའི་གཞི་རྩ་ལྟ་བུའི་ཙུང་ཟད་དཀའ་བའི་རིག་པའི་གནད་དོན་རྣམས་ལ་འཇུག་གི་ཡོད། གཞུང་ལུགས་ཁག་ལ་ཞིབ་འཇུག་བྱེད་པར་སློབ་ཕྲུག་ཚོར་ཉུང་མཐར་ལོ་ཁ་ཤས་འགོར་གྱི་ཡོད། ཐོག་མའི་སྦྱོང་བརྡར་གྱི་དུས་ཡུན་འདིའི་རིང་ལ། ཁོང་ཚོས་མགྱོགས་པོ་དང་ཞིབ་ཚགས་ངང་ཀློག་རྒྱུ་སྦྱོང་གི་ཡོད་ལ། ཉིན་ལྟར་དུས་ཚོད་ཁ་ཤས་རིང་ནང་པའི་གཞུང་ཆེན་གཙོ་བོ་ལྔ་སྟེ། ཚད་མ་རིག་པ་དང་། ཤེར་ཕྱིན། དབུ་མའི་ལྟ་གྲུབ། འདུལ་བ། སེམས་ཁམས་རིག་པ་བཅས་རྩ་བའི་གཞུང་ལུགས་རྣམས་བློར་འཛིན་གྱི་ཡོད། དེ་ཡང་གཞུང་ལུགས་དེ་དག་དང་འབྲེལ་བ་ཁག་གི་བརྒྱུད་ནས་སློབ་ཚན་དེ་དག་གི་མཐོ་རིམ་སློབ་གཉེར་གྱི་གྲ་སྒྲིག་བྱེད་པའི་ཆེད་དུ་ཡིན་ཞིང་། དགོན་པ་སོ་སོའི་གཞུང་ལུགས་རྣམས་ཀྱང་དེའི་ཁོངས་སུ་གཏོགས། སློབ་གཉེར་བ་ཚོས་བརྡ་སྤྲོད་རིག་པ། གསོ་བ་རིག་པ། སྙན་ངག ཡང་ན་སྒྱུ་རྩལ་དང་ལག་ཤེས་ལྟ་བུའི་འཇིག་རྟེན་པའི་སློབ་ཚན་ཡང་སྦྱོང་སྲིད་མོད། འོན་ཀྱང་འདི་དག་ནི་སྦྱོང་གཞི་གཙོ་བོ་མིན།

རྩོད་པར་མཉམ་ཞུགས་པ་ཚོས་རང་གིས་སྦྱངས་ཟིན་པ་དག་གི་ནང་དོན་གཏིང་ཟབ་ས་ནས་ཀློག་འདོན་དང་ཡིད་ལ་དྲན་དགོས་པ་རེད། རྩོད་པའི་བརྗོད་གཞི་ལུང་ཚིག་གམ་གཞུང་ཚིག །དངོས་པོ་གང་ཞིག་ལ་ཚད་མ་རིག་པའི་ཐ་སྙད་དང་གོ་རིམ་ངེས་ཅན་ཞིག་གི་ཐོག་ནས་དཔྱོད་ཞིབ་བྱེད་ཀྱི་ཡོད། དམིགས་ཡུལ་ནི་ཚད་མའི་རིགས་ལམ་གྱི་ཐོག་ནས་ནང་དོན་ངོས་འཛིན་དང་། གསལ་ཁ་འདོན་པ། འདྲི་རྩད་བྱེད་པ། རྩ་གཞུང་ལས་བཀྲལ་བའི་ལྟ་ཚུལ་གྱི་ཤེས་བྱ་རྣམས་ལ་གོ་རྟོགས་ཡོང་ཆེད་རེད། གཏན་འབེབས་སློབ་ཚན་དེ་དག་ལ་བསླབས་པས་མཉམ་སྦྲེལ་གྱི་སློབ་སྦྱོང་དང་། ནང་པའི་ཤེས་རབ་དང་ཉམས་ལེན་ལ་གོ་རྟོགས་ཟབ་མོ་འཐོབ་པའི་ཐབས་ལམ་ཆགས་ཀྱི་ཡོད་ལ། རྩོད་པའི་རིགས་ལམ་གྱིས་ལོག་རྟོག་སེལ་བ་དང་། ནང་དོན་ཁ་གསལ་མེད་པ་དང་དཀའ་གནད་རྣམས་གསེད་བཀྲོལ་བྱེད་པར་ཕན་གྱི་ཡོད།

སློབ་ཕྲུག་ཚོས་རྩོད་པའི་རིག་རྩལ་དང་། དཔྱད་ཞིབ། གཏན་ཚིགས་འགྲོ་ལུགས་བཅས་ཀྱི་རྨང་གཞི་བརྟན་པོ་ཞིག་བཏིང་རྗེས། ནང་པའི་སློབ་ཚན་ལྷག་པོ་དེ་དག་གཅིག་རྗེས་གཉིས་མཐུད་ཀྱིས་མཐར་ཕྱིན་པར་སློབ་གཉེར་བྱེད་འགོ་འཛུགས་ཀྱི་ཡོད། ནང་པའི་གཞུང་ལུགས་ལ་གཞི་བཅོལ་བའི་སློབ་ཚན་གཙོ་བོ་རྣམས་སློབ་སྦྱོང་བྱེད་པ་དེས་སློབ་ཕྲུག་ཚོའི་མཉམ་འབྲེལ་སློབ་སྦྱོང་གི་ཆེད་དུ་སྤྱི་མཐུན་གྱི་རྨང་གཞི་ཞིག་བསྐྲུན་གྱི་ཡོད་ལ། ནང་པའི་ཤེས་རབ་དང་ལག་ལེན་ལ་གཏིང་ཟབ་ཅིང་ཡོངས་ཁྱབ་ཀྱི་གོ་རྟོགས་འཐོབ་པའི་ལམ་ཞིག་ཀྱང་སྟོན་གྱི་ཡོད།

མཐོ་རིམ་སློབ་གཉེར་གྱི་རིམ་པ་འདིའི་སྐབས་སུ། སློབ་ཚན་རེ་རེའི་ནང་གི་རིམ་པ་བཞིན་འཕེལ་རྒྱས་འགྲོ་བའི་བརྗོད་གཞི་རེ་རེའི་ཆེད་དུ། སློབ་ཕྲུག་ཚོས་ཐོག་མར་དགོན་པའི་གཞུང་ལུགས་དང་ངེས་པར་དུ་སློབ་དགོས་པའི་འགྲེལ་པ་གཞན་རྣམས་ལ་སློབ་སྦྱོང་བྱེད་འགོ་འཛུགས་ཀྱི་ཡོད། ཁོང་ཚོས་རང་གི་གཏན་ཚིགས་རིག་པ་དང་རྩོད་པའི་ཐབས་ལམ་གྱི་སྦྱོང་བརྡར་བེད་སྤྱོད་བྱས་ཏེ་གཞུང་གི་ནང་དོན་ལ་ཞིབ་འཇུག་བྱེད་པ་དང་། དེའི་གནད་དོན་གསལ་པོ་བཟོ་བ། ནང་པའི་གཞུང་ལུགས་རྒྱ་ཆེན་པོའི་སྐོར་ལ་རང་གི་འཕེལ་རྒྱས་འགྲོ་བཞིན་པའི་ཤེས་བྱ་རྣམས་བརྟན་དུ་གཏོང་གི་ཡོད།

དེ་ལྟར་བྱེད་འདོད་ཡོད་པ་རྣམས་ཀྱིས་དགོན་པ་གཞན་གྱི་མཁས་པའི་གཞུང་ལུགས་དང་། བོད་བརྒྱུད་ནང་བསྟན་ཆོས་བརྒྱུད་གཞན་གྱི་འབྲེལ་ཡོད་གཞུང་ལུགས། ཁ་སྐོན་གྱི་ཟུར་ལྟའི་གཞུང་ལུགས། དེ་ནས་མདོ་ཆ་ཚང་དང་དེ་ལས་གཞན་པ་བཅས་ལ་གློག་སྦྱོང་རྒྱ་སྐྱེད་གཏོང་ཤྲིད་པ་དང་། དེ་ལྟར་བྱས་ཏེ་དགོན་པའི་མི་ཚེའི་རིང་ལ་བརྗོད་གཞི་གང་འདྲ་ཞིག་ཡིན་རུང་(ནུབ་ཕྱོགས་ཀྱི་ཚན་རིག་གི་སློབ་ཚན་ཚུད་པ)དེར་འཇུག་པའི་ཤེས་ཡོན་དང་རིག་རྩལ་ལྡན་པའི་མཁས་པ་རང་སོས་ལྟར་འགྱུར་ཐུབ།

བྱ་བའི་རྒྱུད་རིམ།

རྩོད་པ་ལ་རྣམ་པ་འགའ་ཤས་ཡོད། སྤྱིར་བཏང་ཕལ་ཆེ་བ་གནས་ཚད་མཉམ་པའི་སློབ་གཉེར་བ་ཕན་ཚུན་བར་མི་གཉིས་གཉིས་རྩོད་ཀྱི་ཡོད། ཉིན་ལྟར་གྲྭ་དམངས་ཚང་མ་ཆོས་གྲྭའི་ནང་འཛོམས་ནས་དགེ་འདུན་པ་བརྒྱ་ཕྲག་མང་པོས་རྩོད་པ་རྩོད་པའི་ལྡིར་སྒྲས་དགོན་པའི་གཡས་གཡོན་ཁེངས་འགྲོ་བ་རེད། ཡང་རྩོད་པ་ལ་རྩོད་སྤྲུངས་དང་མང་ཚོགས་ཡོད་པའི་དམ་བཅའ་འཇོག་པ་ཡང་ཡོད་པ་རེད། དཔེར་ན། ཉིན་ལྟར་འཛིན་གྲྭའི་ནང་ཁུལ་དུ་སློབ་གཉེར་བ་དྲུག་གྲས་འགགས་རྩོད་སྤྲུངས་བརྒྱབ་ནས་དེ་ཉིན་གྱི་རྩོད་པ་མཇུག་སྒྲིལ་འགྲོ་བ་ལྟ་བུ་རེད། གཞན་ཡང་། འཛིན་གྲྭ་ཕན་ཚུན་དབར་རྩོད་འགྲན་དང་། གདན་ས་ཕན་ཚུན་བར་རྩོད་འགྲན་ཡོད་ཅིང་། དེའི་སྐབས་སུ་མི་རེ་རེ་བཞིན་རྩོད་ཟླ་དང་། མང་ཚོགས་ཡོད་སར་དམ་བཅའ་འཇོག་པ་བཅས་ཀྱང་ཡོད།

རྩོད་པ་རྩོད་པའི་བྱ་བའི་རྒྱུད་རིམ་ལ་གཏན་འབེབས་ཡོད་པས་ཆེད་ལས་ཀྱི་བརྡ་ཆད་སྤྱད་དེ་དྲི་བ་དང་ལན་འདེབས་བྱེད་དགོས་པ་རེད། གཤམ་གྱི་སྡེ་ཚན་ནང་ལ་དེ་དག་གི་རྒྱུད་རིམ་མདོར་བསྡུས་ཤིག་འགྲེལ་བཤད་བརྒྱག་གི་ཡིན།

རྣམ་པ་འགོད་པ། རྩོད་པ་ནི་ཕྱོགས་སྔ་ཕྱོགས་ཕྱི་ཕྱོགས་གཉིས་པོའི་བར་གྱི་གྲུས་ཞབས་ལྡན་པའི་ཐོག་ནས་རང་ལུགས་འཛིན་པ་དང་དེ་ལ་བཀལ་ལན་བྱེད་པའི་རིགས་ལམ་གྱི་རྩོད་པ་ཞིག་རེད། ཕྱི་རྒོལ་གྱིས་སྔ་རྒོལ་གྱི་བཤད་པ་ལ་སེམས་མཐུན་ཡོད་མེད་གང་ལྟར་ཡང་སྔ་རྒོལ་གྱིས་ཚད་མའི་རིགས་ལམ་སྤྱད་དེ་དོན་དག་གོ་དཀའ་ས་ཞིག་ལ་ཞིབ་དཔྱོད་བྱེད་ཀྱི་རེད། སྔ་རྒོལ་གྱིས་ལུང་

རིགས་གཉིས་ཀྱི་ཐོག་ནས་ཕྱི་རྒོལ་གྱི་འདོད་པ་འགལ་འདུ་དང་ནོར་འཁྲུལ་ཅན་དུ་སྒྲུབ་ཐབས་བྱེད། རྒྱུན་དུ་སྔ་རྒོལ་བཞེངས་ནས་ཡོད་དུས་ཕྱི་རྒོལ་མདུན་དུ་བཞུགས་ཀྱི་ཡོད།

དགེ་འདུན་དམངས་ཕེབས་པའི་དམ་བཅའ་ཆེན་མོའི་སྐབས་སུ་ཕྱི་རྒོལ་བཞུགས་ཤིང་། སྔ་རྒོལ་རྣམས་ཁོང་གཉིས་ཀྱི་མདུན་དུ་ཡར་བཞེངས། དགེ་འདུན་དམངས་ཟླ་གམ་བགྲད་པའི་དབྱིབས་གཟུགས་ལྟར་བཞུགས། །གལ་ཏེ་མཁན་རིན་པོ་ཆེ་དང་དགེ་འདུན་པ་བགྲེས་པ་རྣམས་ཕེབས་ཡོད་ན་དམ་བཅའ་བའི་རྒྱབ་ཏུ་བཞུགས་གདན་མཐོ་བའི་སྟེང་ལ་བཞུགས།

རིམ་པ་དངོས། སྔ་རྒོལ་གྱིས་ཧྲི་སྐད་དང་ཐལ་མོ་བརྡབས་ནས་རྟགས་གསལ་དབུ་འཛུགས།འདི་དག་རེ་རེ་ལ་ནང་དོན་ཡོད་དེ། ཧྲི་ནི་ཤེས་རབ་ཀྱི་ལྷ་འཇམ་དཔལ་དབྱངས་ཀྱི་ཐུགས་ཀྱི་ས་བོན་ཡིན་པ་དང་། ཧྲི་སྐད་བརྒྱག་ནས་ཁྱད་དུ་འཕགས་པའི་ཤེས་རབ་ཀྱི་ལྷར་ཤར་བའི་རྗེ་བཙུན་འཇམ་དཔལ་དབྱངས་ལ་ཐུགས་རྗེ་དང་གསོལ་བ་འདེབས་པ་རེད། ཐལ་མོ་ལ་ཡང་ཐུན་མིན་གྱི་ཁྱད་ཆོས་ཡོད་དེ། ཕྱག་གཡས་པས་ཕྱག་གཡོན་མའི་ཕྱག་ངོས་ཡར་བསྟན་པ་ལ་བརྡབས་ནས་གཡོན་མ་ཁ་མར་བསློགས་ནས་གཡོན་ངོས་ནས་ཡར་འཐེན་པར་བྱེད། རྣམ་འགྱུར་འདིས་གདན་སའི་རྩོད་པའི་དགོས་དོན་གཙོ་བོ་སྟེ་མ་རིག་པས་བསྐྱེད་པའི་སྡུག་བསྔལ་བའི་སེམས་ཅན་རྣམས་སྡུག་བསྔལ་ལས་སྒྲོལ་བར་མཚོན། ཕྱག་གཡོན་མས་ཤེས་རབ་དང་གཡས་པས་ཐབས་མཚོན་ཏེ། ཐབས་ཤེས་་ཤེས་གཉིས་པོ་ནི་སངས་རྒྱས་ཀྱི་གོ་འཕང་འཐོབ་པའི་ཆེད་དུ་མ་རིག་པའི་གཉེན་པོར་ཟུང་དུ་འཇུག་པ་ཡིན།

དེ་ནས་སྔ་རྒོལ་གྱིས་ཕྱག་གཉིས་ཀྱི་དབར་ཕྲེང་བ་འཕྱུར་ཞོར་ཚིག་གཅིག་གམ་ཚིགས་བཅད། ཡང་ན་ལུང་ཚིག་ཞིག་སྐྱོར་ནས་དྲི་བ་ཞིག་དྲིས་པ་ན་དེ་རྩོད་པའི་བརྗོད་གཞིར་གྱུར་པ་རེད། ཕྲེང་བ་ལ་ཕྲེང་རྡོག་༡༠༨ཡོད་པ་དང་། འགྲེལ་བཤད་གཅིག་ལྟར་ན་དེས་ཆོས་ཐམས་ཅད་བརྗོད་བྱའམ་སྡེ་ཚན་(འགྲེས་རྐང་)༡༠༨དུ་བསྡུས་པར་མཚོན་ཟེར། (ཤེར་ཕྱིན་གྱི་མདོ་སྡེའི་ནང་རྒྱས་བཤད་བྱས་ཡོད།) ནམ་རྒྱུན་རྩོད་པ་རྩོད་དུས་ཕྲེང་བ་ཕྱག་གཡོན་མར་དགྲི།

སྔ་རྒོལ་གྱིས་ཐོག་མར་ཚིག་ཅིག་བཙུགས་ནས་དེ་གསུམ་གསུངས་པ་རེད་ཅེས་པ་ལྟ་བུ་དང་། གཞུང་གང་ལས་ཡིན་པ་དང་། གཞུང་ཚན་གང་ལས་ཡིན་པ། ས་བཅད་གང་ཡིན་ཞེས་པ་ལྟ་བུ་དྲིས་ཏེ་ཕྱི་རྒོལ་གྱི་གོ་རྟོགས་དཔོག་པར་བྱེད་ཅིང་། ཕྱི་རྒོལ་གྱིས་ཀྱང་རང་གི་ཕྱོགས་བཟུང་ནས་ལན་འདེབས་གང་མྱུར་བྱེད་དགོས། ལན་མགྱོགས་པོར་མ་ཐེབས་ཚེ་སྔ་རྒོལ་ཚོས་ཁྱེར། ཁྱེར། ཁྱེར་ཟེར་ནས་བརྒོལ།

རྩོད་པ་བཙུགས་ཚར་ནས་སྔ་རྒོལ་གྱིས་གཞུང་གང་གི་སྐོར་ཡིན་པ་དང་། གཞུང་དོན་གང་ཡིན། དོགས་སློང་བཅས་བྱེད་ཅིང་། སྔ་རྒོལ་མང་ཆེ་བས་གཞུང་དོན་བཤད་པ་བྱས་རྗེས་རིགས་ལམ་ཐོག་ནས་འདྲི་རྩད་དང་འཕྲོས་དོན་དུ་འཁྲིད་པར་བྱེད། ཕྱི་རྒོལ་གྱིས་ལན་བཞི་པོ་གང་རུང་གི་ཐོག་ནས་རང་གི་ཁས་ལེན་གང་ཡིན་ལན་འདེབས་མདོར་བསྡུས་ཁ་གསལ་བརྒྱབ་དགོས། ལན་བཞི་པོ་ནི། འདོད། ཅིའི་ཕྱིར། རྟགས་མ་གྲུབ།ཁྱབ་པ་མ་བྱུང་བཅས་བཞི་ཡིན་ལ།དེས་ཕྱི་རྒོལ་ལ་ཁོང་གི་ཁས་ལེན་གང་ཞིག་འདོད་མི་འདོད་ཏན་ཏན་ཏིག་ཏིག་བྱེད་དུ་འཇུག་པ་རེད། སྔ་རྒོལ་གྱིས་ཕྱི་རྒོལ་གྱི་ཁས་ལེན་ལ་སྐྱོན་འཚོལ་རྒྱུ་དང་། མ་ཁྱབ་པ་ངོས་འཛིན་རྒྱུ། ཐལ་བ་འཕེན་རྒྱུ་བཅས་བྱས་ནས་ནང་པའི་བསམ་བློ་རྒྱ་ཆེན་པོའི་ནང་དུ་འཁྲིད་པར་བྱེད།

རྣམ་འགྱུར་དང་ཐ་སྙད་ནི་རྩོད་པའི་གར་སྟབས་དམིགས་བསལ་ཅན་དུ་གྱུར་ཡོད། སྔ་རྒོལ་གྱིས་རྟགས་གསལ་དབུ་འཛུགས་དུས་ཕྱག་གཉིས་མཉམ་དུ་རྡེབ་ཅིང་ཕྱི་རྒོལ་གྱི་ཕྱོགས་ལ་ལན་འདེབས་དགོས་པའི་བརྡ་སྟོན་པ་ཡིན་ཞིང་། ཁོང་གིས་ཕྱག་རྡེབ་པ་དང་ལྷན་དུ་ཞབས་གཡོན་པ་མར་ས་ལ་བརྡབ་པ་དེས་ངན་འགྲོའི་སྒོ་འགོག་པར་མཚོན་པ་ཡིན་ལ། དེ་དང་མཉམ་དུ་ཕྱག་གཡས་པས་གཡོན་མར་ཕྲེང་བ་ཡར་སྒྲིལ་བ་དང་། ཕྱག་གནམ་ལ་འགྱོག་པ་དེས་མ་རིག་པའི་མུན་པ་བསལ་ནས་ཤེས་རབ་ཀྱི་སྣང་བ་རྒྱས་པར་བྱས་ཏེ་འགྲོ་བ་རྣམས་སྡུག་བསྔལ་ལས་སྒྲོལ་བར་མཚོན་པ་ཡིན།

རྣམ་འགྱུར་གཞན་གྱི་མཚོན་དོན་ནི། སྔ་རྒོལ་གྱིས་ཕྱག་གཡས་པའི་རྒྱབ་གཡོན་མའི་ནང་དུ་ཤུགས་ཆེར་རྡེབ་པ་དེ་ལ་ཚ་ཞེས་བརྗོད་ཅིང་། དེས་སྔ་རྒོལ་གྱིས་ཕྱི་རྒོལ་གྱི་ཁས་ལེན་སྔ་ཕྱི་འགལ་བ་དེ་སུན་དབྱུང་བ་མཚོན་ཞིང་། སྔ་རྒོལ་

གྱིས་ཕྱི་རྐོལ་ལ་ཁས་ལེན་དེ་འདོར་དགོས་པར་བརྗོད་ལ། གལ་ཏེ་ཕྱི་རྐོལ་གྱིས་སྔར་གྱི་ཁས་ལེན་དེ་མུ་མཐུད་ནས་བཟུང་ན། ད་དུང་ཡང་རྩོད་པ་བྱེད་ཅིང་གལ་ཏེ་ཕྱི་རྐོལ་གྱིས་ཁས་ལེན་སྔོན་མ་དོར་ནས་གསར་པ་བཟུང་བ་ཡིན་ན། ཕྱི་རྐོལ་དེས་ཁས་ལེན་དེ་ལ་དམིགས་བསལ་ལན་འདེབས་གསར་པ་བྱེད་དགོས་ཤིང་། འགྲོ་ལུགས་འདི་ལྟར་སྐོར་བ་ཐེངས་འགའ་ཤས་བྱེད་པ་དེས་ནོར་བ་དག་ལ་ཐབས་ལམ་དེ་དག་བརྒྱུད་ནས་ནོར་བཅོས་བྱེད་ཆོག་པ་ཡིན། རྣམ་འགྱུར་གཞན་ཞིག་ནི། སྔ་རྐོལ་གྱིས་ཕྱག་གཡས་པར་ཕྲེང་བ་བཟུང་ནས་ཕྱི་རྐོལ་གྱི་མགོ་ལ་སྐོར་བ་ལན་གསུམ་བྱེད་པ་འདི་ལ་འཁོར་གསུམ་ཞེས་བྱ་ཞིང་། དེ་ནས་སྔ་རྐོལ་གྱིས་ཕྱི་རྐོལ་ལ་ལན་འདེབས་ཇི་ལྟར་ནོར་བ་ཡིན་པའི་རྒྱུ་མཚན་ཡང་དག་པ་བརྗོད་དགོས།

གཞི་གང་གི་ཐོག་ཏུ་བརྩད་ན་ཡང་སྔ་རྐོལ་ཕྱི་རྐོལ་གང་རུང་ཞིག་གིས་ནོར་བ་ཁས་ལེན་བྱས་པ་ན་རྩོད་པའི་མཇུག་བསྡུ་བ་ཡིན་ཏེ། གལ་སྲིད་ཕྱི་རྐོལ་གྱིས་ལན་བཏབ་པ་དེས་སྔ་རྐོལ་གྱིས་རྟགས་གསལ་གཏོང་མི་ཐུབ་པར་བཟློས་པ་ན་སྔ་རྐོལ་གྱིས་ལག་པ་མགོ་ལ་བཞག་ནས་འགྲོ་ས་མེད་པའི་རྣམ་པ་བསྟན་པ་ན་རྩོད་མཚམས་འཇོག་ཅིང་། དེ་ནས་རྩོད་པ་གསར་པ་ཞིག་གི་མགོ་འཛུགས་པའམ་ཡང་ན་རྩོད་སྒྲུངས་གཞན་ལ་ཞུགས་པ་སོགས་ཡོད། རྩོད་གྲྭ་མ་གྲོལ་བར་དུ་འདི་ལྟར་བྱེད་པ་ཡིན།

ཉམས་མྱོང་།

སློབ་རྒྱུན་འདིའི་ནང་དུ། རྩོད་པ་ནི་དམིགས་ཡུལ་མིན་པར་ཐབས་ལམ་ཞིག་ཡིན། རྩོད་པའི་ལག་ལེན་དེ་ནང་པའི་དགོངས་དོན་ཏེ། ནང་དོན་རིག་པའི་འཕེལ་རྒྱས་ནི་ལམ་ལུགས་ལྡན་པའི་སློབ་སྦྱོང་དང་། དཔྱད་ཞིབ། གོ་རྟོགས་གོང་འཕེལ་བཅས་ལས་འགོ་འཛུགས་ཐུབ་པ་དང་། དེ་དག་སྒོམ་སྒྲུབ་དང་སྦྲེལ་ནས་རང་ཉིད་འགྱུར་བ་གཏོང་བའི་བརྒྱུད་རིམ་མདུན་སྐྱོད་བྱེད་པ་ཞེས་པ་དེའི་སྙིང་དུ་གནས་ཡོད། རྣམ་དཔྱོད་ཀྱི་དགོས་མཁོ་དང་། སྒུལ་ཤུགས་ཅན་གྱི་ཐབས་རྩལ། རིགས་ལམ་བཅས་ཀྱིས་རྩོད་པ་ནི་མིག་མང་ལྟ་བུའི་ཐབས་རྩལ་གྱི་རྩེད་རིགས་དང་ཡང་མཚུངས་པ་ཡིན།

རྩོད་པ་འདིས་སློབ་སྦྱོང་ལ་སྐུལ་མ་བྱེད་ཅིང་། སློབ་མས་རང་གིས་གང་ཤེས་པ་དེ་གཞན་ལ་སྟོན་མི་ནུས་པའི་ངོ་ཚ་སྤྲོང་བ་ལ་རྩོད་པའི་རིགས་ལམ་བེད་སྤྱོད་གཏོང་དགོས་པ་ལས། རྩ་བ་བློ་འཛིན་ཐུབ་པ་ཙམ་གྱིས་མི་འདང་བ་ཡིན། དེ་ལྟ་བུའི་རྩོད་པ་བྱེད་པ་ལ། དུས་ཆོད་དམ་འཛིན་དང་། ངོ་དམ་ནན་པོ། དེ་བཞིན་དགོས་ངེས་ཀྱི་བརྗོད་གཞི་གནད་ལ་ཁེལ་བ་དང་། གང་ལ་རྩོད་དང་ཇི་ལྟར་རྩོད་པ་སོགས་གྲ་འགྲིག་པོ་དགོས། དེ་ལྟར་བྱས་ན་རང་གིས་མ་ཤེས་པ་གསར་དུ་ཤེས་པ་དང་། བསམ་ཚུལ་དང་ལྟ་བ་མི་འདྲ་བ་ཕུན་སུམ་ཚོགས་པ་འབྱུང་ཐུབ།

བརྟན་པར་དག་གིས་ཁ་གསལ་པོའི་ངང་སྟོན་པ་བཞིན། རྩོད་པ་འདི་ནི་སྐུལ་མ་བྱེད་པའི་ནུས་ཤུགས་ལྡན་པའི་བྱ་འགུལ་ཞིག་རེད་ལ། འདིས་སེམས་ལ་ཚོར་བ་སྣ་ཚོགས་ཤིག་འདྲེན་པར་བྱེད། དཔེར་ན། བློ་དར། ཐེ་ཚོམ། བློ་སྤོབས། འཛེམས་དངངས་ལ་སོགས་པ་མང་པོ་ཡོང་། །རྩོད་པ་འདི་ལས་ཉམས་ལེན་དང་། སློབ་སྦྱོང་གང་ཅིའི་ཐད་བློ་སྟོབས་འཕེལ་ཞིང་། ཆུ་ཚོད་མང་པོའི་རིང་སློབ་མ་རྣམས་ཀྱི་རང་གི་རྣམ་དཔྱོད་དག་ཕན་ཚུན་བརྗེ་རེས་བྱས་པ་བརྒྱུད་ནས་ཕན་ཚུན་གྱི་བཀའ་དྲིན་དྲན་པའི་ཐོག་ནས་བསྔགས་བརྗོད་བྱེད་ཅིང་འདི་ལས་ཕན་ཚུན་ལ་རང་གི་དགེ་བའི་བཤེས་གཉེན་ལྟ་བུའི་འདུ་ཤེས་སྐྱུན་ཐུབ་པ་ཡིན།

དེར་བརྟེན། རྩོད་པ་འགོ་འཛུགས་པ་ནི་ཤེས་རིག་གི་རྩེད་མོ་ཞིག་དང་འདྲ་ན་ཡང་། འདི་ལ་བརྟེན་ནས་རྣམ་དཔྱོད་དང་གོ་རྟོགས་འཕེལ་ཞིང་། བརྗོད་གཞི་གཏིང་ཟབ་པོ་དག་རྟོག་ཞིབ་བྱེད་པའི་རིག་རྩལ་གྱི་ནུས་སྟོབས་སྐྱུན་ཐུབ་པས། ཕྱག་ལེན་དེ་ནི་ཆོས་ཀྱི་མདུན་བསྐྱོད་སློབ་སྦྱོང་དང་། ཞིབ་དཔྱོད། གོ་རྟོགས་དང་བཅས་པ་སྒོམ་ཉམས་ལེན་དང་སྦྲགས་ཏེ། རང་ཉིད་སྒྲུར་བཙོས་ཀྱི་རིམ་པ་ལམ་སྐྱོང་ཡོང་བ་བྱེད་དགོས་པའི་ནང་པའི་བཤད་སྲོལ་དང་མཐུན་པ་ཡིན།

རྩོད་པ་ཡག་པོ་ཞིག་བྱུང་མིན་ནི་ཕྱོགས་གཉིས་ཀྱི་ངོས་ནས་བསམ་བློ་གསར་པ་ཞིག་བྱུང་སྟེ་བཟང་ཕྱོགས་ཀྱི་འགྱུར་བ་ཞིག་གཏོང་ཐུབ་མིན་ལ་རག་ལས་ཡོད། རྩོད་པའི་སྐབས་སུ་སློབ་ཕྲུག་ཚོས་ཉམས་མྱོང་ཆེས་གཏིང་ཟབ་པོ་ཞིག་འབྱུང་བ་ནི་དོན་དམ་པར་རང་གི་སེམས་ལ་འགྱུར་བ་ཞིག་འབྱུང་བ་དེ་

རེད། སྐལ་ལྡན་རྒྱ་མཚོས་བཤད་པ་ལྟར་ན། ང་དཀར་ཟས་པ་ཞིག་ཆགས་པ་འདི་ནི་བྱང་ཆུབ་ཀྱི་སེམས་དང་སྙིང་རྗེའི་སྒོར་རྩོད་པ་བརྒྱབ་པ་དེས་ངའི་སེམས་ལ་འགྱུར་བ་བཏང་སོང་ཟེར། བསྟན་འཛིན་རྒྱལ་མཚན་གྱིས་བཤད་ན། ཀུན་སློང་དང་ཚུལ་ཁྲིམས་ལ་རྩོད་པ་བྱས་པ་དེས་ངའི་སྤྱོད་ལམ་བསྒྱུར་བྱུང་ཟེར།

རྩོད་པ་བྱས་པའི་གྲུབ་འབྲས་ནི་གལ་ཏེ་ སྡེ་ཚོགས་ཀྱིས་དཔེ་ཀློག་གནང་ནས་མཐོང་རྒྱ་ཆེན་པོའི་སྒོ་ནས་ཕེབས་ཡོད་ཚེ་ཕྱི་ཚོགས་ཀྱིས་ལན་གང་བཏབ་རུང་ཕྱོགས་མང་པོ་ནས་ཡར་མར་འཁྱིད་ཐུབ་ཅིང་། རྒྱུ་མཚན་དང་རིགས་པ་ཅི་ཞིག་ཡིན་མིན་ཐག་གཅོད་ཐུབ་པས་ཕྱོགས་གཉིས་ཀར་གོ་རྟོགས་གསར་པ་འབྱུང་ཐུབ།

སྔོན་ཚུལ།

རྩོད་པ་བྱེད་པའི་ལམ་ལུགས་དེ་ཐོར་སངས་རྒྱས་ཞལ་བཞུགས་པའི་སྐབས་དང་དེའི་གོང་དུ་ཡོད་པ་ཞིག་དང་། དེ་ཡང་སྟོན་པ་མངོན་པར་རྫོགས་པར་སངས་རྒྱས་པའི་ཚུལ་མཛད་པའི་གོང་དུ་ཕྱི་རོལ་པ་དང་ལྷན་དུ་རྩོད་པ་གནང་སྐྱོང་བ་དང་། དེ་ནས་ཚད་མ་པ་ཕྱོགས་གླང་གིས་ལམ་ལུགས་དང་ལྡན་པའི་ཐོག་ནས་དར་སྤེལ་མཛད་ཅིང་། དེའི་རྗེས་དཔལ་ཆོས་ཀྱི་གྲགས་པས་ཐོར་ཀྱི་ལམ་སྲོལ་དེ་ཕྱོགས་ཡོངས་ནས་འཛིན་སྐྱོང་གནང་བ་མ་ཟད། ལམ་ལུགས་འདི་ནི་ཚད་མའམ་ལེགས་སྦྱར་སྐད་དུ་པྲ་མ་ཎ་ཞེས་པ་འཚོལ་བའི་ཐབས་དང་། ལྟ་བ་གཏན་ལ་འབེབ་བྱེད་ཀྱི་ཐབས་ཤིག་ཏུ་སྤྱད་པ་ཡིན་ཞིང་། བོད་དུ་རྔོག་ལོ་ཙྪ་བ་བློ་ལྡན་ཤེས་རབ་(༡༠༥༩-༡༡༠༩)དང་རྒྱ་གར་གྱི་མཁས་གྲུབ་དུ་མའི་བརྒྱུད་ནས་དར་ཞིང་། བོད་རང་དུ་ཆ་པ་ཆོས་སེང་(༡༡༠༩-༦༩)སོགས་ཀྱིས་ཚད་མའི་འཆད་ཉན་ལ་རྣམ་པ་མི་འདྲ་བའི་ཐོག་ནས་གོང་འཕེལ་བཏང་གནང་མཛད་ལ། ཚད་མ་རིག་པ་སྦྱོང་བ་ནི་དྲི་བ་དང་བརྟག་དཔྱད་ཀྱི་ལམ་ནས་རྟོགས་པ་དང་ཤེས་རབ་རྒྱུད་ལ་སྐྱེ་བར་བྱེད་པའི་ཐབས་ལ་བརྟེན་པ་ཞིག་ཡིན།

རྩོད་པའི་སྐབས་ཞིག་ལ་ངས་གནས་ཚུལ་ཆ་ཚང་བ་ཞིག་མ་ཤེས་པར་ཁ་ཚོན་གཅོད་མི་ཉུང་བར་སྟོན་པའི་མ་དམིགས་པའི་རྟགས་ཡང་དག་གི་དོན་གོ་ཐབས་བྱས་པ་ཡིན། དེ་ཡང་མདོ་ལས། ང་དང་ང་འདྲ་བས་གང་གི་ཚོད་བཟུང་གི། གང་ཟག་གིས་གང་ཟག་ལ་ཚོད་བཟུང་བར་མི་བྱ་སྟེ། ཉམས་པར་འགྱུར་ཏ་རེ། ཞེས་གསུང་ཡོད།

ཚད་མ་རིག་པའི་གཞུང་ལུགས་སྦྱང་བར་རྟགས་རིགས་སྦྱང་བ་ནི་རྩོད་པའི་གཞི་རྩ་ཡིན་པས། རྟགས་རིགས་ཀྱི་གཞུང་ལ་སྦྱངས་པ་དང་རྩོད་པའི་གཞི་རྩའི་བརྗོད་བྱ་ལ་རྩོད་པའི་སྐབས་སུ། ང་རང་ལ་ཤུགས་རྐྱེན་ཆེས་ཆེར་ཐེབས་ཏེ། རྩོད་པའི་སྦྱང་འབྲས་ལ་སྤྲོ་བ་འཕེལ་བར་གྱུར། འོན་ཀྱང་། ངས་རྩོད་པ་དེ་གཞུང་ལུགས་སྦྱང་བའི་སྐབས་ཁོ་ན་མ་ཡིན་པར། མི་དང་མི་ཡི་བར་གྱི་འབྲེལ་འདྲིས་ཀྱི་སྐབས་སུའང་བཀོལ་སྤྱོད་བྱེད་བཞིན་ཡོད། དེ་ཡང་མི་དང་མི་ཡི་བར་གྱི་འབྲེལ་འདྲིས་བྱེད་སྐབས། ངས་རང་གི་སྦྱང་འབྲས་ལ་བརྟེན་ནས་གཞན་གྱི་དྲི་བར་གོ་བ་ལེན་ཐུབ་པ་དང་། ལན་འདེབས་ཚུལ་ལ་གོ་བ་ལེན་ཐུབ་པས། ངས་གཞན་གྱི་ལྟ་བ་ལ་ཡོང་བ་ལྟར་ཁས་ལེན་མི་བྱེད་པར། གཞན་གྱི་རྒྱུ་མཚན་ལ་དཔྱད་པ་བྱེད་ཐུབ་པར་གྱུར།

- ཐུབ་བསྟན་མཁས་བཙུན།

ཇི་སྐད་དུ། རྗེ་ཙོང་ཁ་པས།

ཡོན་ཏན་ཀུན་གྱི་གཞིར་གྱུར་དྲིན་ཅན་རྗེ།།
ཚུལ་བཞིན་བསྟེན་པ་ལམ་གྱི་རྩ་བ་རུ།།
ལེགས་པར་མཐོང་ནས་འབད་པ་དུ་མ་ཡིས།།
གུས་པ་ཆེན་པོས་བསྟེན་པར་བྱིན་གྱིས་རློབས།།

ཞེས་གསུངས་པ་ལྟར། བོད་ཀྱི་དགོན་སྡེ་ཁག་གི་དགེ་རྒན་དང་སློབ་མའི་འབྲེལ་བ་ནི་ཕ་བུ་ལྟ་བུ་ཞིག་ཡིན་ཏེ། དགེ་རྒན་གྱིས་སློབ་མ་རྣམས་ལ་ལུས་སེམས་གཉིས་ཀྱི་ཐད་ནས་སེམས་ཁུར་ཆེན་པོ་བླངས་ཏེ་བརྩེ་བས་སྐྱོང་གི་ཡོད་པས་སོ། ཁོང་ཚོའི་ལམ་སྟོན་ནི་སློབ་ཚན་ཁྲིད་པ་ལས་བརྒལ་ཏེ་ཡ་རབས་བཟང་སྤྱོད་ལྡན་པའི་མི་ཚད་ལྡན་ཞིག་བསྐྲུན་རྒྱུ་དེ་ཡང་ཚུད་ཡོད། དགེ་རྒན་རྣམ་པས་ལོ་དྲུག་བདུན་ཙམ་ནས་དགོན་པར་ཞུགས་པའི་རང་གི་དགེ་ཕྲུག་ཆེ་མང་ཆེ་བ་སློབ་གཉེར་གྱི་ལས་ཀ་ཁོ་ན་ལས་བརྒལ་ཏེ་གྱོན་གོས་འཁྲུ་བ་དང་། ཆོས་བུ་རྒྱུག་པ། ནད་གཡོག་དང་ཉིན་རེའི་འཚོ་བའི་མཐུན་རྐྱེན་སྦྱོར་བ་སོགས་ཀྱི་ཆ་ནས་འགན་ཁུར་ཆ་ཚང་ལེན་གྱི་ཡོད།

ང་རང་ལོ་ན་ཕྲ་བའི་སྐབས། དགེ་རྒན་གྱིས་ང་དང་གྲྭ་ཆུང་གཞན་པ་རྣམས་ཟླ་ལྟར་ཐེངས་གཉིས་རེར་ཉེ་འགྲམ་གྱི་གཙང་པོའི་འགྲམ་དུ་གོས་བཀྲུ་བར་ཁྲིད་གནང་གིས་རེད། ཁོང་གིས་ཐུགས་རྒྱུད་འཇམ་པོས་ང་ཚོའི་གོས་རྣམས་ལག་པས་བཀྲུས་ཤིང་། ང་ཚོས་ཆུ་རྐྱལ་བྱས་རྗེས་ཁོང་གིས་ང་ཚོ་རེ་རེ་བཞིན་ལུས་པོ་དཀྲུ་རོགས་བྱེད་ཀྱིས་རེད།

དགེ་རྒན་རྣམས་དེ་ལྟར་ལོ་ན་གས་པ་ན་སློབ་མ་རྣམས་ཀྱིས་དགེ་རྒན་ལ་ཟ་མ་གཡོ་བ་དང་ཉིན་རྒྱུན་གྱི་འཚོ་བའི་ཁྲོད་དུ་རོགས་རམ་བྱེད་པའི་འགན་འཁུར་དགོས་པ་རེད། དགེ་རྒན་དང་སློབ་མའི་བར་གྱི་འབྲེལ་བ་ནི་ཤིན་ཏུ་ཟབ་ཅིང་། གུས་བཀུར་དང་དད་འདུན་གྱིས་རྩ་བ་བརྟན་པོར་བཙུགས་ཡོད། དགེ་རྒན་ལ་ནད་ཚབས་ཆེན་གྱིས་མནར་བའི་སྐབས་སུ། སློབ་མ་རྣམས་ཀྱིས་ཁོང་གི་མལ་ཆས་དང་། གྱོན་གོས། སྣེར་གྱི་དངོས་པོ་སོགས་གཙང་སྦྲ་བྱེད་པ་དང་། ངལ་བ་མེད་པར་ཞབས་ཞུ་བྱེད་པ་བརྒྱུད་དྲིན་གཟོ་བར་བྱས་ཏེ། དེ་ལྟར་ན་དགེ་སློབ་ཀྱི་འབྲེལ་བ་དེ་ཡོངས་སུ་རྫོགས་པར་བྱེད།

- བྱམས་པ་རྒྱལ་མཚན།

ནང་པའི་དཔྱད་ཐབས་ཀྱི་ལམ་སྲོལ་དང་དེང་རབས་ཚན་རིག

རི་ཆརྜ་ རྣ་གེར

ནང་པའི་སློམ་སྦྱུབ་ཀྱི་སྲོལ་རྒྱུན་དང་དེང་རབས་ཚན་རིག་གཉིས་ཀས་དངོས་སྐྱོང་གི་རྒྱུ་མཚན་དང་། རིགས་པ། དཔང་པོའི་གལ་གནད་ངོས་འཛིན་དང་བགོ་བཤའ་བྱེད་པའི་ཐོག་ནས་བདེན་དོན་ལ་ཞིབ་འཇུག་བྱེད་ཀྱི་ཡོད། འོན་ཀྱང་ནང་པའི་གསུང་རབ་ཀྱང་པར་ཡིད་ཆེས་བྱེད་པ་དང་ཐབས་ལམ་གཉིས་དབར་འགལ་ཟླ་ཞིག་ཡོད། ཡིན་ནའང་ནང་པ་དང་ཚན་རིག་གི་ལྷ་གྲུབ་དང་ཐབས་ལམ་གཉིས་ཀར་ཐུན་མོང་གི་ཁྱད་ཆོས་ཤིག་ཡོད་པ་ནི་དངོས་སྐྱོང་གི་ཟིན་ཐོ་ལ་གཙོགས་ཆེན་བྱེད་པ་དེ་ཡིན། དེའི་རྐྱེན་གྱིས་སྲོལ་རྒྱུན་འདི་གཉིས་ཕན་ཚུན་ཤུགས་རྐྱེན་སློད་རེས་ཀྱི་ཐོག་ནས་འཕེལ་རྒྱས་འགྲོ་ཐུབ་ཀྱི་ཡོད།

“གོང་ས་སྐྱབས་མགོན་བཅུ་བཞི་པ་མཆོག་གིས་ནུབ་ཕྱོགས་ཀྱི་ཚན་རིག་གི་བསམ་བློ་དང་བོད་བརྒྱུད་ནང་བསྟན་གྱི་ཉམས་ལེན་གཉིས་མཉམ་དུ་གོང་འཕེལ་གཏོང་རྒྱུར་ཐུགས་སྣང་དང་ཁས་ལེན་གནང་བ་དེས་ཚོགས་པ་འགའ་ཤས་ཀྱིས་བོད་བརྒྱུད་ནང་བསྟན་གྱི་དགེ་འདུན་པ་རྣམས་ལ་སློབ་གསོ་དང་སྦྱོང་བརྡར་སྤྲོད་སྐབས་ཚན་རིག་གི་སློབ་ཚན་སྟོན་མ་བྱེད་པར་སྐྱུལ་མ་བྱུང་ཡོད། དཔེར་ན། ཨ་རིའི་ཨེ་ཊ་ལན་ཊའི་ཨེ་མོ་རི་གཙུག་ལག་སློབ་གཉེར་ཁང་གིས་རྟོ་ཕྱོགས་རྒྱ་གར་དུ་ཡོད་པའི་སེ་ར་སྨད། སེ་ར་བྱེས། འབྲས་སྤུངས། དགའ་ལྡན་བཅས་ཀྱི་དགོན་སྡེ་ཁག་གི་ཆེད་དུ་དམིགས་ནས་བཟོས་པའི་རོ་ཛྷ་ཊ་ཨེ་ལྨོལ་ཨེ་མོ་རི་བོད་ཀྱི་ཚན་རིག་ལས་རིམ་(ETSI)ཞེས་པའི་ཚན་རིག་གི་སློབ་ཚན་ཡོངས་རྫོགས་དེ་ཡིན།

ང་ཕྱི་ལོ་༢༠༡༨ ལོའི་དབྱར་ཁར་ཨེ་མོ་རི་དང་བོད་ཀྱི་ཚན་རིག་ལས་རིམ་(ETSI)གྱི་ཚོགས་མིའི་ཁོངས་སུ་རྒྱ་གར་ས་གནས་ རྡེལ་གོབ་ཏུ་དགེ་འདུན་པ་འགའ་ལ་དབང་རྩའི་ཚན་རིག་ཟབ་སྦྱོང་སྤྲད་སར་ཡོང་བ་ཡིན། ཉིན་དང་པོར་སྐྱིལ་མོ་དཀྱུང་དུ་བཞུགས་ནས་སྨྱུ་གུ་བཟུང་སྟེ་རྣ་བའི་དབང་པོ་ང་ལ་གཏད་དེ་ཡོད་ཚད་གྲ་སྒྲིག་དང་ཉན་བཞིན་པའི་དགེ་འདུན་པ་དྲུག་བཅུ་

རེ་ལྷ་ཡོད་སའི་འཛིན་ཁང་ཞིག་ཏུ་གཏམ་བཤད་བྱས། སློ་བུར་དུ་ངས་བཤད་པའི་སྐད་ཆ་རེ་རེ་བཞིན་སྦྱར་ཚན་རིག་ལ་སྦྱོང་བརྡར་གནང་སྦྱོང་མཁན་གྲྭ་བ་ཞིག་གིས་བོད་སྐད་དུ་བསྒྱུར་སོང་། སྐད་སྒྱུར་སློབ་གཉེར་བ་དེ་རྣམས་ལ་བསྟན་འཛིན་རྒྱ་མཚོ་ཚན་རིག་སློབ་ཡོན་བརྒྱུད་ཨེཊ་ལེན་ཊ་ལ་ཡོད་པའི་ཨེ་མོ་རིའི་མཐོ་སློབ་ཏུ་ཉེ་བའི་གཙུག་ལག་རབ་འབྱམས་པའི་སློབ་མ་རྣམས་དང་ལྷན་དུ་སློབ་ཚན་ལེན་པ་དང་། ཨེ་མོ་རི་དང་བོད་ཀྱི་ཚན་རིག་ལས་རིམ་གྱི་ཚོགས་མི་དགེ་རྒན་ཆེན་མོ་རྣམས་ནས་དབྱིན་ཇི་དང་། ཚན་རིག། ཨང་རྩིས་སོགས་ཀྱི་ཟུར་ཁྲིད་གོ་སྐབས་བྱུང་སྦྱོང་ཡོད་པ་ཡིན་འདུག

ངའི་གཏམ་བཤད་སྐད་སྒྱུར་ཚར་ནས་འཛིན་གྲྭའི་ནང་དུ་ཡར་ལངས་ནས་སློབ་ཁྲིད་བྱེད་པར་གྲ་སྒྲིག་བྱས་ཏེ་སློབ་ཁྲིད་བྱེད་པར་འགོ་ཚུགས་སྐབས་ཁོ་ཚོས་ལག་པ་ཡར་བཀྱགས་ཏེ་དྲི་བ་བཏང་སོང་། དེ་ནི་དགེ་འདུན་པ་ཆོས་རྒྱུན་དུ་བློ་འཛིན་དང་ཡང་ནས་ཡང་དུ་བསྐྱར་ཞིབ་བྱས་ཏེ་དྲི་བ་དང་རྩོད་པའི་བགྲོ་གླེང་བྱེད་པའི་སློབ་སྦྱོང་བྱེད་སྟངས་དེའི་དབང་གིས་བྱུང་བ་ཞིག་རེད་འདུག །ནང་པའི་དགོན་པའི་རྩོད་པའི་བགྲོ་གླེང་དེ་ནི་བོད་བརྒྱུད་ནང་བསྟན་དུ་ད་ཅང་གལ་གནད་ཆེན་པོ་ཞིག་དང་དུས་རབས་བརྒྱད་པའི་ནང་རྒྱ་གར་ནས་བོད་དུ་དར་བར་གྲགས།

ངས་ཡང་བསྐྱར་མཚམས་བཞག་སྟེ་ཚན་རིག་གི་ལམ་ནས་བགྲོ་གླེང་བྱེད་དགོས་པའི་གྲོས་འཆར་བཏོན། སྐར་མ་གཅིག་གི་ནང་དུ་དགེ་འདུན་པ་དེ་དག་ལན་འདེབས་མཁན་དང་རྟགས་གསལ་གཏོང་མཁན་ཏེ་ཚོ་ཁག་གཉིས་སུ་བགོས་སོང་། རྟགས་གསལ་གཏོང་མཁན་ཡང་ཇེ་མང་ནས་ཇེ་མང་དུ་ཕྱིན་སོང་། སྐབས་དེར་ངས་ལག་པའི་འགུལ་སྐྱོད་དང་ལུས་ཀྱི་ཉམས་འགྱུར། ཀྲོད་བྲོ་དང་འབྲེལ་བའི་བགྲོ་གླེང་དེར་ངོ་སྣང་བྱུང་། ཁོ་ཚོས་ཁས་ལེན་དེ་དམ་པོར་འཛིན་པ་དང་། གཞན་རྣམས་ཀྱིས་དེ་ལ་ནོར་སྐྱོན་གཏོང་རྒྱུ་དེ་རེད། ཐ་ཀོལ་དང་ཕྱི་ཀོལ་གཉིས་ཀྱིས་བར་མ་མཐུད་ནས་རྩོད་པའི་བགྲོ་གླེང་བྱས་པས་ཁུ་སིམ་པོ་ཆགས་པའི་དུས་ཤིག་མི་འདུག །ཐུབ་ཕྱོགས་པའི་བགྲོ་གླེང་བྱེད་སྟངས་དང་མི་འདྲ་བར་བོད་པའི་དགོན་སྡེ་ཁག་གི་བགྲོ་གླེང་བྱེད་སྟངས་ནི་མུ་མཐུད་ནས་དྲི་བ་གཏོང་རྒྱུར་ངོ་སྣང་བྱས་ཏེ་མཐའ་སྡོམ་ཞིག་ཀྲེད་རྒྱུ་དེ་ཡིན་ཞིང་། དེ་ནི་ཐོབ་

ཤོར་གྱི་སྐད་ཆ་མིན་པར་རྒྱུ་མཚན་ཡང་དག་ལ་བརྟེན་ནས་ཕན་ཚུན་དངོས་ཡོད་རྟོགས་པར་རོགས་བྱེད་རྒྱུ་དེ་རེད།

ཁོ་ཚོའི་ཤེས་ཡོན་ལ་ངས་ཤུགས་རྐྱེན་ཅི་ཞིག་སྤྲད་ཡོད་པ་དང་། དགེ་འདུན་པ་ཚོས་ང་ལ་ཤུགས་རྐྱེན་ཅི་ཞིག་སྤྲད་ཡོད་དམ། དེ་ནི་དུས་ཚོད་ཀྱིས་བཤད་ཡོང་བ་ཞིག་རེད། རྒྱུ་མཚན་ནི་ང་ཚོ་ཚང་མར་དུས་ཚོད་དང་བསྟུན་ནས་འཕོ་འགྱུར་ཧ་ཅང་ཆེན་པོ་འགྲོ་རྒྱུའི་གོ་སྐབས་ཡོད་པར་ང་ལ་ཡིད་ཆེས་ཡོད།

ང་རང་འཛིན་གྲོགས་ཚོ་དང་ལྷན་དུ་བྱང་ཆུབ་ཀྱི་སེམས་ཏེ། སེམས་ཅན་ཐམས་ཅད་སངས་རྒྱས་ཀྱི་གོ་འཕང་ལ་འགོད་པར་དམིགས་པའི་བྱང་ཆུབ་ཀྱི་སེམས་སྐྱེད་བྱེད་ཀྱི་རྩོད་པ་ལན་མང་བྱས་པ་དེས་ང་ལ་ཤུགས་རྐྱེན་ཟབ་མོ་བཞག་བྱུང་། རྩོད་གླེང་དེ་དག་གི་སྐབས་སུ། ང་ཚོས་ནང་པ་སངས་རྒྱས་པའི་གཞུང་ནས་གསུངས་པའི་ཐབས་ལམ་ཞིག་སྟེ། གཞན་གྱི་སྡུག་བསྔལ་དང་ན་ཟུག་རང་སྟེང་དུ་ལེན་ནས། དེའི་ཚེ་གཞན་ལ་ཞི་བདེ་དང་དགེ་བའི་སེམས་སྤེལ་ཏེ་གཏོང་ལེན་གྱི་སྒོམ་བེད་སྤྱོད་བྱེད་ཀྱི་ཡོད།

ཐབས་ལམ་འདིས་སྙིང་རྗེ་དང་། བྱམས་པ་བསྐྱེད་ཅིང་། དེ་ནི་བྱང་ཆུབ་ཀྱི་སྟེ། སེམས་ཅན་རྣམས་སྡུག་བསྔལ་ལས་གྲོལ་བར་འདོད་པའི་རྣམ་པ་ཅན་གྱི་སེམས་ཤིག་ཡིན། ཐབས་ལམ་འདི་དག་ལ་དཔྱད་པ་དང་ཉམས་ལེན་བྱས་པ་བརྒྱུད་ང་རང་དུད་འགྲོ་རྩིས་པའི་གཞན་སེམས་ཅན་ཚང་མར་དམིགས་པའི་བྱམས་པ་དང་སྙིང་རྗེ་སྐྱེས་ཤིང་། དམར་ཟས་སྤངས་ཏེ་དུད་འགྲོ་སེམས་ཅན་ལ་འཚེ་བ་མི་བྱེད་པའི་དམ་བཅའ་བཞག་པའི་བློ་སྤོབས་སྐྱེས་བྱུང་། མ་ཟད་རྩོད་པ་བྱས་པ་ལས་ངས་དཔྱད་ཞིབ་བྱེད་སྟངས་རྟོགས་བྱུང་། ཁྱེད་རང་གིས་རིགས་ལམ་འགྲོ་སྟངས་ཤེས་དུས། ལྟ་གྲུབ་རིག་པ་དང་། ཚན་རིག ཆོས་ལུགས་བཅས་གང་ཡིན་ཡང་། ཡོང་བའི་དད་པ་ལ་བརྟེན་མི་དགོས་པར་གཏིང་ཟབ་པོ་དང་བློ་གཟུ་བོའི་སྒོ་ནས་འཇུག་ཐུབ། ངས་རྩོད་པའི་ཉམས་མྱོང་དེ་ཉིན་རེའི་དཀའ་ངལ་སེལ་ཐབས་དང་། རྒྱུ་མཚན་དང་གཏན་ཚིགས་བཀོལ་ནས་བདེན་དོན་འཚོལ་ཐབས་སུ་བཀོལ་གྱི་ཡོད། མ་ཟད་དཀའ་རྙོག་གང་ཞིག་ལ་རྒྱུ་རྐྱེན་མང་པོ་ཡོད་པར་བསམ་གཞིག་བྱས་ནས་ཕྱོགས་ཡོངས་ནས་རྟོགས་ཐབས་བྱེད་ཀྱིས་ཡོད།

- སྐལ་ལྡན་རྒྱ་མཚོ།

སློབ་གྲྭ་ནས་གསར་དུ་ཐོན་རྗེས་རང་ལོ་བཅོ་བརྒྱད་ཐོག་ཐོག་མར་ཟླ་རམ་ས་ལར་ཡོད་པའི་མཚན་ཉིད་ལམ་སློབ་གཉེར་ཁང་དུ་ཆོས་ཞུགས་བྱས། དེར་ངོས་རང་ནང་ཆོས་སློབ་གཉེར་གྱི་ རྨང་གཞི་གཙོ་བོ་ཡིན་པའི་རིགས་ལམ་ངོ་སྤྲོད་བྱས་བྱུང་། ཕལ་ཆེར་ང་ཚོ་རིགས་ལམ་སྦྱོང་བརྡར་བྱེད་པར་ཞུགས་པ་ནས་ཟླ་བ་དྲུག་ཙམ་ལས་མ་ཕྱིན་ཡང་། ངས་རང་གི་ལངས་ཕྱོགས་དེ་གདེང་ཚོད་ཆེན་པོས་ཨུ་ཚུགས་ཀྱིས་རྒྱུན་འཁྱོངས་བྱེད་ཅིང་། འཛིན་གྲོགས་གཞན་དག་གིས་ངའི་ལངས་ཕྱོགས་ལ་དགག་རྒྱག་བྱེད་ཀྱིན་རེད། རང་ཉིད་ཀྱི་གླེན་རྟགས་དེ་ངོ་ཟིན་པར་ཉིན་འགའ་བསམ་གཞིག་བྱེད་དགོས་བྱུང་། ད་ཆ་ངའི་ནོར་འཁྲུལ་དེ་དག་མཐོང་ཐུབ་འོན་ཀྱང་སྔོན་ཆད་ངའི་བཅོས་མའི་ཡིད་ཆེས་དང་གདེང་སྟོབས་ཀྱིས་ང་རང་བཞད་འདུག །ཉམས་མྱོང་འདིས་ང་ཚོའི་རྒྱུད་ཀྱི་ལོག་རྟོག་འགའ་ཞིག་ནི་ང་ཚོའི་བསམ་ཡུལ་ལས་འདས་པའི་གཏིང་ཟབ་པོ་ཡོད་པ་ར་སྤྲོད་བྱས་བྱུང་། གནས་ལུགས་འདིས་ངའི་སློབ་སྦྱོང་དང་མི་ཚེའི་ནང་དུ་བརྗོད་གཞི་གསར་པ་ཁག་ལ་བསམ་བློ་གུ་ཡངས་ཀྱི་སྒོ་ནས་འཇུག་པར་ཕན་ཐོགས་བྱུང་།

བོད་བརྒྱུད་ནང་བསྟན་གྱི་རྩོད་པའི་ལམ་ལུགས་ཀྱིས་དཀའ་ངལ་རྒྱུས་ལོན་དང་། དོན་དང་ལྡན་པའི་ཐབས་ལམ་འཚོལ་བར་མཐུན་རྐྱེན་བསྐྲུན་གྱི་ཡོད། རྩོད་པའི་རྣམ་གཞག་གིས་ཁྱེད་ལ་ལྟ་གྲུབ་ཀྱི་དཔྱད་པ་གཏོང་བའི་ལག་ཆ་སྤྲོད་པ་དང་། དཀའ་ངལ་ཞིག་ལ་དཔྱད་པ་བྱེད་སྐབས་དོན་དངོས་ཀྱི་གནས་སྟངས་དང་མཐུན་པའི་ལྟ་སྟངས་གསར་པ་སྤྲོད་པ་མ་ཟད། རྣམ་རྟོག་གི་ཁྱེར་པོ་རྣམས་ཕུད་པར་རོགས་བྱེད།

བཀའ་བསྟན་ལས་གསུང་པ་ལྟར། རིགས་ལམ་གྱི་རྣམ་གཞག་འདི་རང་གི་སེམས་ཚོར་དང་། བསམ་བློའི་འཕྲེར་སོ། ལྟ་སྟངས། གོམས་གཤིས། བྱ་སྤྱོད་བཅས་ལ་དཔྱད་པ་བྱེད་པ་བརྒྱུད། བདེ་སྐྱིད་དང་དཔལ་འབྱོར་གྱི་བརྗོད་གཞིའི་ཐོག་བེད་སྤྱོད་བྱས་ན། དེ་བས་ཀྱང་དོན་སྙིང་ལྡན་པ་ཞིག་ཆགས་ཀྱི་ཡོད།

རྩོད་པ་ནི་ཤེས་རབ་ཕུན་སུམ་ཚོགས་པ་སྟེ། དེ་ཡང་ཤེས་རབ་སྦྱུར་བ། ཤེས་རབ་རྣོ་བ། ཤེས་རབ་ཟབ་པ། ཤེས་རབ་གསལ་བ་སོགས་གནས་སྐབས་གང་འདྲ་ཞིག་ཡིན་རུང་ཐེ་ཚོམ་མེད་པར་སྦྱུར་པོར་གཏོང་ལེན་བྱེད་ཐུབ་པ་བཅས་ཀྱི་ཁྱད་ཆོས་ལྡན་པའི་ཤེས་རབ་སྐྱེད་པར་བྱེད་པའི་ལག་ཆ་ཡ་མཚན་ཅན་ཞིག་ཡིན།

- དགེ་བཤེས་དགྲ་འདུལ་རྣམ་རྒྱལ།

ཐལ་མོ་རྡེབ་འཛོག – ཚན་རིག་དང་མཐུན་པའི་བགྲོ་གླེང་གི་མན་ངག

པོལ། གླེར་སི་ཡ།

གལ་ཏེ་ཁྱེད་རང་སྔོད་དུས་སུ་རྒྱ་གར་ལྷོ་ཕྱོགས་དགོན་པའི་ཉེ་འགྲམ་དུ་བསྐྱོད་ཚེ། ཐག་རིང་པོ་ནས་རྩོད་པའི་སྒྲ་ནི་སོབ་སོབ་ཞིག་གྲགས་འོང་། ཉུར་སྨྲིག་གི་ན་བཟའ་གྱོན་པའི་དགེ་འདུན་པ་བརྒྱ་སྟོང་དེ་དག་གི་གམ་དུ་ཕྱིན་ན་ཁུ་སིམ་པའི་མཚན་མོའི་ཁོར་ཡུག་དེ་རིམ་གྱིས་ཡལ་འགྲོ། ཐོས་པའི་སྒྲ་དེ་དག་ནི་རྒྱུན་ལྡན་གྱི་གླེང་མོལ་ཞིག་མིན། ལོ་ན་ཆུང་བའི་དགེ་འདུན་པ་ཚོ་ཆ་ཆ་བྱས་ནས་རྩོད་ཟླ་སྒྲིག་ཅིང་། དེ་ལས་ཅུང་ལོ་ན་རྒན་པའི་དགེ་འདུན་པ་རྣམས་ཚོ་ཚོ་བྱས་ནས་དམ་བཅའ་འཚོག་ཡོད། ཡར་བཞེངས་ཡོད་པའི་དགེ་འདུན་པ་དེ་ཚོས་དྲག་ཤུགས་ཆེན་པོས་མར་སྡོད་མཁན་གྱི་དམ་བཅའ་བ་དེ་དག་ལ་དྲི་བ་འགོད། རྩང་གཞིའི་དྲི་བའི་དཔེ་མཚོན་ཞིག་བཞག་ན། ཤིང་སྡོང་འདི་རྟག་པ་ཡིན་པར་ཐལ་ཞེས་འདྲི་སྲིད། དེ་ལ་དམ་བཅའ་བས་འདོད་ཅེས་ལན་བཏབ་ན། རྟགས་གསལ་གཏོང་མཁན་གྱིས་རྩི་ཤིང་གི་འཚོ་བའི་འཁོར་རྒྱུན་སྐོར་གྱི་དྲི་བ་ཁག་འདྲི་རྒྱུ་རེད། གལ་ཏེ་དམ་བཅའ་བས་ཅིའི་ཕྱིར་ཅེས་ལན་བཏབ་ན། རྟགས་གསལ་གཏོང་མཁན་གྱིས་དེ་ལ་དམ་བཅའ་བའི་ཁས་ལེན་དང་འགལ་བའི་དཔེ་མཚོན་ཤིང་སྡོང་བྱེ་བྲག་པ་དེ་འདྲའི་དྲན་ཤེས་སམ་ལོ་རྒྱུས་ཀྱི་ཁུངས་ལྟ་བུ་བེད་སྤྱོད་བྱེད་སྲིད།

ཁྱེད་རང་གིས་བགྲོ་གླེང་གི་སྐབས་སུ་བོད་སྐད་མི་ཤེས་ནའང་། མང་མོས་དང་ཉུང་མོས་ཀྱི་བསམ་ཚུལ་འཕར་འགྲིབ་དེ་གསལ་པོར་མཐོང་ཐུབ། ཕན་ཚུན་ལས་ལྷག་པ་ཡིན་པའི་རྣམ་འགྱུར་མང་པོ་མཐོང་རྒྱུ་ཡོད་ལ། བཞད་གད་ཀྱང་ཡང་ཡང་ཐོས་རྒྱུ་ཡོད། དེ་ནི་སྤྱིར་བཏང་གི་མི་ཚོགས་ཀྱི་གྲོས་མོལ་དེ་འདྲ་ཞིག་དང་འདྲ་པོ་ཡོད། འོན་ཀྱང་ཁྱད་ཆོས་གཅིག་གསལ་པོར་མངོན་གྱི་ཡོད། དེ་ནི་ཐལ་མོ་དྲག་པོ་རྡེབ་པ་དེ་རེད། རྩོད་པ་རྩོད་མཁན་གྱིས་དྲི་བའི་ཚིག་རྐང་མཐའ་མ་དང་མཉམ་དུ་ལག་པ་གཡས་པས་གཡོན་པའི་སྟེང་དུ་"ཐག་"ཅེས་པའི་སྒྲ་དང་བཅས་ཐལ་མོ་བརྡབས་ཏེ། དམ་བཅའ་བའི་གདོང་དང་ཏ་ཅང་ཉེ་བར་འཛིགས་སྣང་སློང་བའི་རྣམ་འགྱུར་སྟོན་གྱི་ཡོད། ཐལ་མོ་བརྡབས་རྗེས་

ལག་པ་གཡོན་པ་དེ་ཆེད་མངགས་ཀྱིས་ཕྱོགས་མར་བསྟན་ཏེ་དམའ་སར་འཇོག་གི་ཡོད། ཐལ་མོའི་སྒྲ་བྲག་ཅ་ཡལ་བར་འགྱུར་བའི་བར་དུ་ཚང་མས་སྒྲུག་པའི་སྐབས་སུ་དུས་ཡུན་ཐུང་ངུའི་རིང་ཁུ་སིམ་མེར་གནས་རྗེས། མར་བཞུགས་མཁན་གྱི་དགེ་འདུན་པ་དེས་ཞི་འཇམ་དང་ནས་ལན་འདེབས་གནང་གི་ཡོད།

ངག་ཐོག་གི་རྩོད་པ་དེ་སྒྱུ་རྩལ་གྱི་རྣམ་པས་མཚམས་འཇོག་བྱེད་པ་དེས་དགོས་པ་མང་པོ་ཞིག་སྒྲུབ་ཀྱི་འདུག། དགེ་འདུན་པ་རྣམས་ཞོགས་པ་སྔ་པོར་ལངས་ཀྱི་ཡོད་ལ། དགོན་པའི་སློབ་གཉེར་གྱི་དུས་ཚོད་ཁག་གི་ཐོག་ཏུ། ཉིན་རེའི་ལས་འགན་མང་པོ་ཞིག་ཀྱང་ཡོད། ཉིན་གང་པོར་སྒོམ་རྒྱག་པ་དང་། གླུ་གཞས་ལེན་པ། འདོན་པ་འདོན་པ། ཁ་ཏོན་འདོན་པ། ཐབ་ཚང་གི་ལས་ཀ་བྱེད་པ། དགོན་པའི་ཁོར་ཡུག་གཙང་མ་བཟོ་བ་བཅས་ཀྱི་རྗེས་སུ། ཧང་སངས་དགོས་པའི་ཐལ་སྒྲ་དེས་ཚང་མས་དོ་སྣང་གནང་རྒྱུར་ཕན་ཐོགས་བྱེད་ཀྱི་འདུག

འོན་ཀྱང་ཐལ་མོ་བརྡབས་རྗེས་ཀྱི་ལག་པའི་གནས་སྟངས་དེའང་གལ་ཆེན་པོ་ཡིན་ཏེ། རྩོད་མཁན་གྱི་ལག་པ་གཡོན་པ་དེ་དཔལ་པོའི་ངང་ནས་དམའ་རུ་དང་ཟུར་དུ་འགྲོ་གི་ཡོད། དེ་ནི་རྩོད་པ་རྩོད་མཁན་གྱིས་དམ་བཅའ་བ་ལ། རང་ཉིད་ཀྱི་འདོད་ཚུལ་ལ་གནོད་སྐྱེལ་བའི་སེམས་ཚོར་ངན་པ་རྣམས་མནན་ནས་སེམས་ཀྱི་བརྟན་ཚུགས་རྒྱུན་སྐྱོང་བྱེད་དགོས་པའི་དྲན་སྐུལ་ཞིག་ཡིན། རྩོད་པ་དེ་དག་ནི་ཁོང་ཁྲོ་དང་། ཕྲག་དོག འཁྱིང་བག ངོ་ཚ། འཇིགས་སྣང་བཅས་ཕྱི་རུ་མངོན་པའི་རྣམ་འགྱུར་དེ་དག་འདུལ་བར་བྱེད་པའི་ཐབས་ལམ་ཡག་པོ་ཞིག་ཡིན། ནུབ་ཕྱོགས་ཀྱི་སྨན་པའི་སྦྱོང་བརྡར་ཐོབ་པའི་ཚན་རིག་པ་ཞིག་ཡིན་པའི་ཆ་ནས། སེམས་འཚབ་དང་མང་ཚོགས་ཀྱི་དཀྱིལ་དུ་ངོ་ཚ་བ་དང་འབྲེལ་བའི་སེམས་ཚོར་ངན་པ་སྐྱོང་བ་དེ་ནི་(དགའ་སྣང་སྐྱེ་བ་ཞིག་མིན་ནའང་)དྲན་པའི་རོགས་རམ་ཡག་པོ་ཞིག་ཡིན་པ་ངས་ཤེས་ཀྱི་ཡོད། དམ་བཅའ་བ་དེ་ཚོའི་ལུས་པོའི་འགྱུར་ལྡོག་ལ་བརྟག་དཔྱད་བྱེད་སྐབས། ཁྲག་ཤེད་མཐོ་བ་དང་། དབུགས་འབྱིན་རྟབ་མགྱོགས་དྲགས་པ། སྙིང་གི་འཕར་ལྡིང་(སྐར་མ་རེར་ཐེངས་༡༨༠ ཙམ་)བཅས་ཐོ་འགོད་བྱུང་ཡོད། སེམས་ཚོར་འདི་དག་སྐྱོང་བའི་སྐབས་སུ་ཕྱི་ཡི་རྣམ་འགྱུར་ཉུང་ཤས་ལས་མི་མངོན་པའི་སྦྱོང་བརྡར་བྱེད་པ་དེས་ཉོན་མོངས་པའི་རིགས་འཇོམས་པ་བྱེད་པ་ལ་ཕན་གྱི་ཡོད།

སྐབས་རེ་དམ་བཅའ་བས་དམ་བཅའི་སྐབས་སུ་རྒྱུན་ལྡན་གནད་འགག་ཅན་གྱི་ལུང་དེ་འདྲ་ནོར་ནས་བརྗོད་ན། དགེ་འདུན་པ་འགའ་ཤས་རྩོད་པ་རྩོད་པོ་དང་མཉམ་དུ་ལངས་ནས། དམ་བཅའ་བའི་ལངས་ཕྱོགས་དེ་ནུས་མེད་བཟོ་བ་བྱེད་པ་ལ་བློ་འཛིན་བྱས་པའི་ལུང་དེ་དག་ཤུགས་ཆེན་པོས་སྐྱོར་བཞིན་འདུག །དགེ་འདུན་པ་རེ་རེས་རང་རང་གི་ཆོས་གོས་དམ་པོར་བསྡམས་རྗེས། ལག་པ་གཡས་པ་ක྄ ལྷུང་འཁོར་གྱི་རྣམ་པ་ལྟ་བུས་ཤུགས་ཆེན་པོར་བསྐོར་ནས་ལག་པ་གཡོན་པའི་སྟེང་དུ་བརྡབས་ཏེ་སློབ་ཚན་དེར་ནན་ཏན་བྱེད་ཀྱི་འདུག། ཡང་ན། གལ་ཏེ་དམ་བཅའ་བས་རང་གི་ལངས་ཕྱོགས་དེ་ཡིད་ཆེས་འཕེར་བ་ཞིག་བཤད་ཐུབ་ན། དགེ་འདུན་པ་གཞན་པ་རྣམས་ཁོང་གི་འཁྲིས་སུ་ཁུ་སིམ་མེར་སྡོད་འགོ་འཛུགས་ཀྱི་ཡོད། སྐབས་གཞན་དུ་རྟགས་གསལ་གཏོང་མཁན་གྱིས་རང་གི་རིགས་པའི་རྒྱུན་ཟུ་མཐུད་དེ་གཏོང་མི་ཐུབ་པའང་ཡོང་གི་ཡོད། དུས་ཚོད་མང་ཆེ་བར་དགོན་པའི་མཁར་རྫ་ཆེན་པོ་དེ་རྡུང་གི་ཡོད་ལ། དེའི་དུས་རྩོད་པ་མཚམས་བཞག་སྟེ་དགོང་མོའི་ཞལ་འདོན་ཡར་ཚོགས་བྱེད་པའི་བརྡ་ཞིག་ཡིན། ཡང་ཡང་རྩོད་པ་དེ་དག་བོད་བརྒྱུད་ནང་བསྟན་གྱི་ལྟ་གྲུབ་གཙོ་བོ་དཔེར་ན་སྟོང་ཉིད་(ལེགས་སྦྱར་སྐད་དུ་ཤུ་ཉྪ་ཏ་ཞེས་པ་)ལྟ་བུར་གཞོལ་གྱི་ཡོད། དགོས་དོན་གཙོ་བོ་ནི་ལྟ་གྲུབ་བྱེ་བྲག་པ་ཞིག་གི་གོ་རྟོགས་གཏིང་ཟབ་ཏུ་གཏོང་རྒྱུ་དང་། ངེས་ཤེས་ཀྱི་གོ་རྟོགས་དེ་དག་སྒོམ་སྒྲུབ་ཀྱི་དོན་དུ་སྤྱོད་རྒྱུ་ཡིན། རྩོད་མཁན་གྱིས་ལྟ་གྲུབ་གཙོ་བོ་དེ་དག་ཆ་འཛོམ་མེད་པར་བཟོ་སྲིད་པའི་ལྦོག་དཔེ་འཚོལ་ཞིབ་བྱེད་སྐབས། རང་གི་དཔྱད་ཞིབ་ཀྱི་རིགས་པའི་རྣོ་ངར་སྤེལ་གྱི་ཡོད། དེ་བཞིན་དུ་གལ་ཏེ་དམ་བཅའ་བས་ལྟ་གྲུབ་དེ་ཡག་པོ་རྟོགས་མེད་ན། ཁོང་གི་ལངས་ཕྱོགས་ཀྱི་རྨང་གཞི་བརྟག་སྟེ། བརྗོད་གཞི་གཙོ་བོ་དེ་དག་བསྐྱར་དུ་བསམ་གཞིགས་བྱེད་དགོས་པ་ཆགས་ཀྱི་ཡོད། དཔྱད་སྒོམ་ཞེས་པའི་ཞིབ་འཇུག་གི་ཐབས་ལམ་འདི་ནི་མ་རིག་པ་དང་ཉོན་མོངས་པའི་སེམས་ཚོར་ལས་རྣམ་པར་རྒྱལ་བར་ཤིན་ཏུ་གལ་ཆེན་པོ་ཡིན།

གྲྭ་པ་རྣམས་ཀྱིས་ཡང་དག་པའི་དངོས་པོའི་གནས་ལུགས་མ་ཤེས་པར་བྱང་ཆུབ་ཐོབ་པ་ནི་མི་སྲིད་པར་ཡིད་ཆེས་བྱེད་ཀྱི་ཡོད། དེས་ན་དངོས་པོ་ཞིག་གི་སྣང་ཚུལ་དང་དངོས་པོ་དེའི་གནས་ལུགས་དབར་གྱི་ཁྱད་པར་རྟོགས་

པར་གཙོགས་ཆེན་པོ་བྱེད་པ་དེ་ནི་སྙིང་པོ་ཞིག་ཡིན། ཤིང་སྡོང་དང་། གང་ཟག་ཚོགས་པ། བསམ་བློ་ཚུན་ཆད་ཀྱི་དངོས་པོ་ཐམས་ཅད་ལ་འཛིན་པའི་ལོག་རྟོག་དང་སེམས་ཚོར་ངན་པ་རྣམས་རྩ་མེད་དུ་ངེས་པར་དུ་གཏོང་དགོས་པ་ཞིག་ཡིན། སྣང་ཚུལ་ཁོ་ནར་དམིགས་ནས་གཏིང་ཟབ་པའི་དངོས་ཡོད་གནས་ལུགས་ཡོད་པ་ངོས་མ་ཟིན་ན་སྡུག་བསྔལ་ཆེན་པོའི་རྒྱུ་རུ་འགྱུར་སྲིད། སྟོང་པ་རྒྱལ་ཁ་ཐོབ་རྒྱུ་དེ་དམིགས་ཡུལ་མིན། སྟོང་པ་ནི་བྱང་ཆུབ་ཐོབ་པར་མེད་དུ་མི་རུང་བའི་ཤེས་ཡོན་འཐོབ་ཐབས་སུ་ཕན་ནུས་ལྡན་པའི་ལག་ཆ་ཞིག་ཡིན། མཚོན་དོན་གྱི་ཐོག་ནས་ཞུས་ན། ཐལ་མོ་རྗེབ་འཛོག་གི་ནང་དུ་བྱ་སྤྱོད་ཀྱི་ཕྱི་ཚུལ་དང་གནས་ཚུལ་གཉིས་ཀ་འཆར་གྱི་ཡོད།

གལ་ཏེ་ང་ཚོར་དེ་འདྲའི་སྟོང་པའི་སྲོལ་རྒྱུན་གྱི་སྦྱོང་བརྡར་ཐོབ་ཡོད་ན། ང་ཚོའི་མཁས་པའི་བགྲོ་གླེང་ཚོགས་འདུ་དང་ཚན་རིག་གི་སྒྲིག་འཛུགས་ཁག་ཏུ་འབྲེལ་བ་བྱེད་སྟངས་ཇི་འདྲ་ཞིག་ཏུ་འགྱུར་མིན་བསམ་བློ་མ་བཏང་རང་བཏང་རེད། ང་ཚོས་ཐེངས་ག་ཚོད་ལ་མིང་མེད་པའི་ཞིབ་འཇུག་པ་ཞིག་གི་བསམ་ཚུལ་ལ་བརྟེན་ནས་ཡིད་ཐང་ཆད་པའི་རྣམ་འགྱུར་ཇི་ཙམ་བསྟན་ཡོད་དམ། ང་ཚོའི་ཆེད་ལས་ཁག་ཏུ་ཚན་རིག་གི་སྟོད་རྙོག་ག་ཚོད་ཡོད་དམ། ཕལ་ཆེར་ང་ཚོས་ལག་པ་མར་ཕྱོགས་སུ་བརྐྱངས་ནས་ཁོད་སྙོམས་སུ་གནས་པས་མཚོན་པའི་རང་བྱུང་ངལ་གསོའི་གལ་གནད་སྣང་མེད་དུ་བཏང་སྟེ། ཐལ་སྦྲ་ཁོ་ནར་དམིགས་པ་གཏད་དྲགས་པས་ཡིན་སྲིད།

ངའི་སྤུན་མཆེད་དགེ་བཤེས་བློ་བཟང་རྡོ་རྗེ་ལགས་ནི་ངའི་མི་ཚེའི་ནང་ཧ་ཅང་གལ་ཆེན་ཞིག་ཆགས་ཡོད། ང་ལོ་བཅུ་ལ་སོན་པའི་སྐབས་སུ་ད་དུང་ཡང་གང་ཅིའི་ཐད་ནས་ཧ་ཅང་ཆུང་ཆུང་དང་སྤྱོད་པ་རྩིང་པོ་ཡོད་ནའང་། ངས་ཁོང་གིས་ལྷ་གྲུབ་སློབ་གཉེར་གནང་ས་སྦེལ་ཀོབ་བཀྲ་ཤིས་ལྷུན་པོའི་དགོན་དུ་ང་ཁོང་དང་མཉམ་དུ་ཁྲིད་ནས་འགྲོ་རོགས་ཞེས་རེ་བ་ཞུས་པ་ཡིན།

ཁོང་གིས་ང་ལ་ནང་ཆོས་ངོ་སྤྲོད་གནང་བ་དང་། ཐ་ན་གོས་བརྗེ་སྤྱོད་སྟངས་སོགས་བྱ་བ་ཚེ་ཕྲ་ཀུན་རང་རྐྱ་འཕེར་ཐུབ་པའི་བར་དུ་བསླབས་བྱུང་། ཁོང་གིས་ང་ལ་ཕ་མ་གཉིས་ལས་ལྷག་པའི་བཀའ་སློབ་གནང་བྱུང་། ང་ལོ་བཅུ་མ་ཟིན་བར་དུ་ཕ་མ་གཉིས་དང་མཉམ་དུ་བསྡད་པ་དང་། དེ་ནས་ལོ་ཉེར་གཉིས་རིང་ཁོང་དང་མཉམ་དུ་བསྡད་པ་ཡིན།

ང་རང་ལོ་ན་ཆུང་ཆུང་ཡིན་དུས་སྤུན་མཆེད་ཀྱིས་རྩོད་པ་རྒྱག་ས་ལྷ་སྒྲོང་ཡོད་པ་དྲན་གྱིས་འདུག རྩོད་པ་བྱས་རྗེས། ངས་ཁོ་ལ་དྲི་བ་འདོན་གྱི་ཡོད། དེར་བརྟེན་ངས་གསུང་རབ་དང་དེའི་འགྲེལ་བ་རྣམས་ཀློག་པ་དང་བློ་རུ་འཛིན་པ། དེ་དག་ལ་དུས་ཚོད་བཏང་ནས་འགྲེལ་བཤད་དང་དོན་རྟོགས་བྱེད་རྒྱུ་གལ་ཆེན་པོ་ཡིན་པ་ཤེས་བྱུང་། སྤུན་མཆེད་ཀྱིད་རྩོད་པ་རྒྱག་སྟངས་ལ་བལྟས་ནས། ང་རང་ལའང་རྩོད་པ་རྒྱག་འདོད་དང་རང་ཉིད་ཀྱི་ལྷ་གྲུབ་རྣམས་གཏན་ལ་འབེབ་སྟེ་ཁུངས་སྐྱེལ་ཐུབ་པའི་བློ་སྤོབས་སྟེར་བྱུང་།

- རིག་འཛིན་ནོར་བུ།

དགོན་པའི་རྩོད་རིག་ནི་དགེ་འདུན་པ་ཚོར་མཚོན་ན་མེད་དུ་མི་རུང་བ་ཞིག་ཡིན་འདུག ཤེས་བྱ་ལ་འབད་བརྩོན་བྱེད་མཁན་སུ་འདྲ་ཞིག་ཡིན་ཡང་ཕན་ཐོགས་ཆེན་པོ་ཡོད། དེ་ནི་བདེན་རྫུན་འབྱེད་པ་དང་རང་གི་རྣམ་དཔྱོད་འབྱེད་པའི་ལྡེ་མིག་ལྟ་བུ་ཞིག་རེད་ཅེས་བརྗོད་ཆོག

ང་རང་སྔོན་ཆད་མི་རྟག་པ་ཕྲ་མོའི་སྐོར་ལ་རྩོད་པ་བྱེད་སྐབས། ཚད་མ་རྣམ་འགྲེལ་ལས། རང་ཉིད་རྒྱུ་དང་རྐྱེན་ལ་བརྟེན་ནས་གྲུབ་པ་ཡིན་ན། མི་རྟག་པ་ཡིན་དགོས་ཤིང་། འགྱུར་བའི་རང་བཞིན་ཅན་ཞིག་ཡིན་དགོས་པར་གསུངས། དཔེར་ན། ལོ་བརྒྱད་ཅུ་ལོན་པའི་མི་ཞིག་ལ་བལྟས་པ་ཡིན་ན། སྐྱེས་པ་ནས་བཟུང་སྟེ་རང་དབང་མེད་པར་སྐད་ཅིག་སྐད་ཅིག་ལ་འགྱུར་བ་རྒྱུན་མ་ཆད།

འགྱུར་བ་ནི་ཡུན་དུ་གནས་པ་ཞིག་སྟེ། མཚམས་རེར་ཡར་རྒྱས་འགྲོ་བ་དང་མཚམས་རེར་ཉམས་རྒུད་འགྲོ་བཞིན་ཡོད། འགྱུར་བ་ནི་གཡོལ་ཐབས་མེད་པ་ཞིག་ཡིན་པ་རྟོགས་པ་དེས་ང་རང་འཛིག་རྟེན་ལ་བལྟ་སྟངས་གསར་པ་ཞིག་སྐྱེད་པ་དང་། དེས་དཀའ་ངལ་ལ་གདོང་ལེན་བྱེད་སྐབས་སེམས་མི་ཞུམ་པར་ཕན་ཐོགས་བྱུང་།

ངས་ལོ་ངོ་བཅུ་ལྷག་རིང་ནང་ཆོས་ཀྱི་ཚད་མ་རིག་པ་སློབ་སྦྱོང་བྱས་ཤིང་། དེའི་ནང་ནས་ངོ་མཚར་ཆེ་ཤོས་སུ་བརྩི་བའི་ལྟ་གྲུབ་གཅིག་ནི། དབུ་མའི་གཞུང་ནས་བཤད་པའི་རྟེན་འབྲེལ་གྱི་ལྟ་གྲུབ་དེ་ཡིན་ལ། རྟེན་འབྲེལ་གྱི་ལྟ་གྲུབ་འདིས་ཆོས་ཐམས་ཅད་ཕན་ཚུན་བརྟེན་ཅིང་འབྲེལ་ཡོད་པ་དང་། དེར་བརྟེན་ང་ཚོའི་བདེ་སྐྱིད་དང་། ང་ཚོའི་སྡུག་ཚོགས། ང་ཚོའི་ཁོར་ཡུག་བཅས་ཚང་མ་གཞན་ལ་རག་ལས་ཡོད་པར་བསྟན་གྱི་ཡོད།

- བློ་བཟང་དོན་གྲུབ།

སྲིན་བུ་སེམས་ལྡན་ཡིན་ནམ།
ཅིའི་ཕྱིར་དེར་དོ་སྣང་བྱེད་དགོས།

འབུམ་རམས་པ་ཨླར་རི་ཨེ་སེན།

འདས་པའི་ལོ་ངོ་བཅུ་ཕྲག་གཅིག་ལྷག་ཙམ་རིང་ངས་བོད་ཀྱི་གྲྭ་བཙུན་ཚོར་སྐྱེ་དངོས་ཚན་རིག་སློབ་ཁྲིད་བྱས་པ་ཡིན། བོད་ཀྱི་གྲྭ་བཙུན་ཚོ་དང་མ་འབྲད་གོང་ནས་ལོ་ཉི་ཤུའི་རིང་ཚན་རིག་སློབ་ཁྲིད་དང་ཚན་རིག་གི་བརྟག་དཔྱད་བྱས་མྱོང་ན་ཡང་། ཁོང་ཚོར་སློབ་ཁྲིད་བྱས་པའི་ཉམས་མྱོང་དེས་ངའི་སློབ་ཁྲིད་བྱེད་པའི་ཐབས་ལམ་དེར་མཐའ་གཅིག་ཏུ་འགྱུར་བ་ཆེན་པོ་ཞིག་བཏང་བྱུང་། དང་ཐོག་ངའི་བསམ་པར་ཚན་རིག་སློབ་ཁྲིད་ཡང་དག་པར་བྱེད་པར་ཆ་རྐྱེན་གང་ཚང་དགོས་པ་ཐམས་ཅད་ཤེས་ཀྱི་ཡོད་སྙམ་གྱི་ཡོད། རྗེས་སུ་ངའི་བསམ་བློ་དེར་འགྱུར་ལྡོག་བྱུང་བའི་རྒྱུ་རྐྱེན་གཙོ་བོ་ནི་བོད་ཀྱི་དགོན་སྡེའི་ནང་གི་རིགས་ལམ་གྱི་རྩོད་པ་དང་དེས་བོད་ཀྱི་གདན་སའི་སློབ་གཉེར་གྱི་གལ་ཆེའི་རང་བཞིན་མཚོན་པ་དེ་མཐོང་བས་ཡིན།

ང་རང་ཆེད་བཅར་ཚན་རིག་པའི་ངོ་བོར་རྒྱ་གར་དུ་འགྲོར་བའི་ལོ་དང་པོའི་ནང་གི་ཉིན་ཞིག་ལ་དབྱིན་སྐད་ཡག་པོ་ཤེས་མཁན་ཞུང་ཤས་ཤིག་ཡོད་པའི་ཁོངས་ཀྱི་དོན་གྲུབ་དང་ལྷན་དུ་ཧྭ་རམ་ས་ལའི་སྣང་གི་ཤིང་ནགས་ཀྱི་ལམ་ནས་མར་གོམ་བགྲོད་བྱེད་བཞིན་ཡོད། སྐབས་དེར་དགེ་འདུན་པ་ཚོས་ཐར་སྒྲུངས་ཟིན་པའི་ཁོར་ཡུག་དང་སྐྱེ་ལྡན་རྣམས་ཀྱིས་ཕན་ཚུན་ཤུགས་རྐྱེན་སྤྲོད་པའི་རྣམ་གཞག་དེར་ཚོད་ལྟའི་ཆེད་ངས་དགེ་འདུན་པའི་སྡེ་ཚན་གཅིག་ས་མཐོ་སར་ཁྲིད་པ་ཡིན།

དོན་གྲུབ་དང་ངེད་གཉིས་གཙོ་བོ་སེལ་པོལ་ལྷ་བུའི་ཕྲུན་མོང་གི་དོ་དབྱིངས་ཡོད་སའི་རིགས་ལས་འཁྲོས་ཏེ་དམིགས་བསལ་འབྲེལ་བ་བྱུང་བ་ཞིག་ཡིན། ཕྱིས་སུ་དགེ་འདུན་པ་མང་པོས་རྩེད་མོ་དེར་དགའ་མོས་བྱེད་ཀྱི་ཡོད་པ་ཤེས་བྱུང་། ངས་ཁོང་ལ་དགེ་འདུན་པ་ཚོས་སྒྲུབ་དགོས་པའི་བྱ་བཞག་མང་པོ་ཡོད་པ་དེ་དག་ཕར་བཞག་སྟེ་ཅིའི་ཕྱིར་འདིར་ཚན་རིག་སྦྱོང་བཞིན་ཡོད་ཅེས་

དྲིས་པ་ཡིན། དང་ཐོག་ཁོང་གིས་དེའི་ལན་དུ། གང་ཡིན་ཟེར་ན། སྤྱི་ནོར་ ༧གོང་ས་སྐྱབས་མགོན་ཆེན་པོས་ཚན་རིག་སྦྱངས་ན་དགེ་མཚན་ཡོད་པ་གསུངས་ཡོད། ཅེས་དང་། དེ་ནས་མུ་མཐུད་ཁོང་གིས། ངས་རང་ཉིད་ཀྱི་ནང་པའི་ཆོས་ཀྱི་གོ་རྟོགས་ཇེ་བཟང་དུ་གཏོང་བའི་ཆེད་དེང་རབས་ཀྱི་ཚན་རིག་སློབ་སྦྱོང་བྱེད་ཀྱི་ཡོད། ཅེས་གསུངས་སོང་། ཁོང་གིས་གསུངས་པའི་བཀའ་མོལ་དེར་ང་རང་ངོ་མཚར་སྐྱེས་བྱུང་། ངས་འཛིའུ་དང་ཡི་ཤུའི་འཛིག་རྟེན་གྱི་མི་སུ་གང་གིས་ཀྱང་སོ་སོའི་ཆོས་ལུགས་ལ་སྨོས་ཏེ་དེ་ལྟ་བུའི་བཀའ་མོལ་གསུང་རྒྱུ་ནི་བསམ་ཚོད་དཀའ་བ་ཞིག་རེད།

དོན་གྲུབ་ཀྱིས་དེ་ལྟར་བཤད་པ་དེ་ཁོ་པ་རང་ཉིད་ཀྱིས་སློབ་སྦྱོང་བྱེད་བཞིན་པའི་དཔལ་ན་ལེནྡྲའི་བཞེད་གཞུང་གཙོ་བོ་ཞིག་དང་འབྲེལ་ནས་བཤད་པ་ངས་རྗེས་སུ་ཤེས་རྟོགས་བྱུང་། ན་ལེནྡྲའི་ཆོས་བརྒྱུད་ནི་ཐོག་མར་རྒྱ་གར་ནས་དུས་རབས་ཁ་ཤས་གོང་ནས་དར་བ་ཞིག་ཡིན་ན་ཡང་། ད་ལྟའི་དུས་སུ་བོད་རིགས་གཅིག་པུས་རྒྱུན་འཛིན་དང་ཉམས་ལེན་བྱེད་བཞིན་ཡོད། གཏན་ཚིགས་ཀྱི་སྒྲུབ་བྱེད་ནི། དེང་རབས་ཀྱི་རིག་གསར་ཚན་རིག་སློབ་སྦྱོང་བྱས་པས་དོན་གྲུབ་ཀྱི་ནང་པའི་ཆོས་ལ་འགལ་རྐྱེན་དུ་འགྲོ་རྒྱུ་ལྟ་ཞོག་དེས་ནང་ཆོས་ཀྱི་སྤུས་ཚད་བཟང་དུ་གཏོང་བར་ཕན་ཐོགས་ཡོད་དེ། ཇི་སྲིད་གཞན་གྱི་འདོད་ཚུལ་མ་ཤེས་པ་དེ་སྲིད་དུ་རང་ལུགས་ཀྱི་བདག་དང་ཤེས་བྱའི་རྣམ་གཞག་རྣམས་ཤེས་མི་ཐུབ་པའི་ཕྱིར།

གནས་སྐབས་དེས་ང་ལ་བདེན་པའི་འོད་སྣང་མཐོང་བར་རམ་འདེགས་བྱས། ཐུབ་ཕྱོགས་པའི་ཤེས་ཡོན་སྤྱི་དང་ལྷག་པར་ཚན་རིག་གི་སློབ་སྦྱོང་ནང་། ངས་དེ་ཤེས་ལ་ཁྱེད་ཀྱིས་མི་ཤེས། དེར་བརྟེན་ངས་གང་ཤེས་པ་དེའི་ཕྱོགས་སུ་ཁྱེད་ཀྱི་ཁ་ཕྱོགས་བསྒྱུར་བའི་སྐད་ང་འདིར་སླེབས་ཡོད།ཅེས་པ་ལྟ་བུའི་ཕྱོགས་ལྷུང་དང་།ཐུར་མ་བརྗོད་པའམ་མ་ཤེས་པའི་གནད་དེར་བདེན་པའི་འོད་སྣང་འཕྲོ་བ་དེ་ངས་མཐོང་ཐུབ་པ་བྱུང་། དེའི་དགོངས་དོན་གཙོ་བོ་དེ་ཉིད་བོད་ཀྱི་དགོན་སྡེའི་ནང་གི་རིགས་ལམ་གྱི་རྩོད་པས་གསལ་པོར་མངོན་པར་བྱེད་ཀྱི་ཡོད་ལ། རྒྱུན་ལྡན་གྱི་ཉམས་ལེན་ནང་དུའང་འཛིན་གྱི་ཡོད་ཅིང་།སློབ་གཉེར་བ་ནང་ཁུལ་འབྲེལ་ལམ་ཟབ་ཏུ་གཏོང་གི་ཡོད། རྩོད་པ་ཐམས་ཅད་རིམ་པ་དང་ལྡན་པ་

ཞིག་ཡིན་ན་ཡང་། རང་གི་ངང་གིས་ཡོང་གི་ཡོད་ལ།ཤེས་བྱ་གསར་པ་དང་སྲོལ་རྒྱུན་གྱི་ཤེས་བྱ་གཉིས་མཐུན་པ་དང་མི་མཐུན་པའི་ཆ་རྣམས་ཤེས་རྟོགས་ཡོང་བར་ཤེས་བྱ་གསར་པ་དང་རྙིང་པ་མཚུངས་བསྡུར་བྱ་རྒྱུའི་གོ་སྐབས་ཡོད། རྩོད་ལེན་རིམ་བརྗེ་ཡིས་གོམ་པ་རྒྱབ་ཤིག་རྒྱག་པ་སོགས་ཀྱི་ཕར་སྤྲོད་ཚུར་ལེན་གྱི་གར་སྟབས་ཀྱི་རྣམ་པའི་སྒོ་ནས་ཕན་ཚུན་གྱི་འདོད་ཚུལ་ལ་གདོང་ལེན་བྱེད་པ་སྟེ། སུ་མཐུད་ནས་ཡིན་ད། ང་ཡར་རྒྱས་ཐོངས་དང་།ངས་ནོར་བར་སྐྱབས་དང་། མ་རེད། ཁྱེད་རང་ནོར་འདུག།དུས་ཚོད་རྫོགས་སོང་།ཞེས་པ་ལྟ་བུའོ། །ད་རྩོད་རྩོད་བྱས་ནས་བསམ་གཞིག་བྱོས།

སློབ་ཁྲིད་ཚད་ལྡན་ཡོང་རྒྱུ་དེ་མཐར་ཐུག་གི་དཀའ་གནད་ཅིག་ཡིན།མི་གཤིས་དམིགས་བསལ་བ་དང་།ཕོ་མོ།ཤེས་ཡོན་གྱི་རྒྱབ་ལྗོངས་འདྲ་མིན།ཉམས་མྱོང་འདྲ་མིན་བཅས་ཡོད་པའི་མིས་ཁེངས་པའི་ཁང་མིག་ཅིག་གི་ནང་ཅི་འདྲ་བྱས་ནས་འཛུལ་ཞུགས་དགོས་སམ།དེར་སླེབས་རྗེས་ཐབས་ལམ་འདྲ་མིན་ལ་བརྟེན་ནས་སློབ་སྦྱོང་བྱེད་པའི་མི་རྣམས་ཀྱི་ཆེད་ཤེས་བྱ་གསར་པ་དང་ཕོ་ཆོས་ཕལ་ཆེར་ཤེས་ཟིན་པའམ་མ་ཤེས་པའི་ཤེས་བྱའི་རིགས་མཉམ་བསྲེས་བྱེད་དགོས་སམ།ཡ་མཚན་པ་ཞིག་ལ།རྒྱ་གར་དུ་ཡོད་པའི་ནང་པའི་དགོན་སྡེའི་ནང་གི་ངའི་འཛིན་གྲྭ་ལས་ཀྱང་ཨེ་མོ་རི་མཐོ་སློབ་ཏུ་ངའི་སློབ་ཁྲིད་བྱ་སའི་འཛིན་གྲྭའི་ནང་སྒྲ་མང་རང་བཞིན་ཤུགས་ཆེ་བ་ཡོད།འོན་ཀྱང་དེ་ལྟ་བུའི་ཕོར་ཡུག་གཏན་ནས་མི་གཅིག་པའི་སར་ཕྱིན་ཏེ་སློབ་ཁྲིད་བྱས་པ་དེས་ངས་སློབ་ཁྲིད་ཡང་དག་པར་བྱེད་པའི་གནད་མཐིལ་ཕྱིན་པར་ཤེས་ཐུབ་པ་བྱུང་།

དགེ་འདུན་པ་ཚོར་སྲིན་བུ་དང་རིགས་རྩལ་གྱི་སྐོར་སློབ་ཁྲིད་ཇི་ལྟར་བྱེད་དགོས་སམ། འདི་དག་གི་བཀོད་པ་སུ་ཞིག་གིས་ཀྱང་མཐོང་དཀའ་བ་དང་བློ་ངོར་འཆར་དཀའ་བ་ཡིན། མ་ཟད་སངས་རྒྱས་ཀྱི་གོ་འཕང་ལ་དམིགས་པའི་ལྟ་གྲུབ་འཛིན་པའི་དགེ་འདུན་པ་ཚོའི་ཉིན་རེའི་བྱེད་སྒོ་དང་ཧ་ཅང་རྒྱང་ཐག་རིང་བ་ཡིན།།སྲིན་བུ་རྣམས་སེམས་ལྡན་ཡིན་ནམ་ཞེས་པའི་དྲི་བའི་ངོ་གདོང་ལས་བརྩམས་ཏེ་ང་ཚོས་སློབ་སྦྱོང་བྱས་པ་ཡིན། སྲིན་བུ་རྣམས་ལ་བདེ་སྡུག་ཚོར་བ་དང་ཡུལ་ཤེས་པ་སོགས་ཡོད་མེད་ཐད་ཁྱེད་ལ་ཁྱད་པར་དེ་ཙམ་མེད་མོད། དགེ་འདུན་པར་མཚོན་ན། ཀུན་སློང་ཡོད་མེད་ལ་མ་ལྟོས་པར་སྲིན་བུ་གསོད་

རྟུང་ངམ་མི་རྟུང་ཞེས་པའི་དྲི་བ་དེ་གནད་འགག་ཅན་གྱི་དྲི་བ་ཡིན།

དགོན་པའི་ནང་ང་ཚོའི་སློབ་ཁྲིད་གཅིག་གི་སྐབས་དགེ་འདུན་པ་ཆོས་སྐྱོའི་ལུང་ཐག་དང་། ཧ་མཆོགདེ་བཞིན་གནས་འདྲ་མིན་ནས་སྲིན་བུ་བླངས་ཏེ་སྲིན་བུ་སྐྱིད་སྲིང་བྱས། ཕོང་ཆོས་སྲིན་བུར་སེམས་ཡོད་མེད་ཐད་ཚོད་ལྟའི་ཆེད་བརྟག་དཔྱད་རིམ་པ་འཆར་འགོད་བྱས། ང་ཆོས་དམིགས་བསལ་ཐབས་ལམ་ཞིག་བཀོལ་སྤྱོད་བྱས། ཐབས་ལམ་དེ་ལ་བརྟེན་ནས་ཆེ་ཤེལ་ནང་མཐོང་ཐུབ་པའི་སྲིན་བུའི་སྐྱེ་འཕེལ་གྱི་ནང་དགེ་འདུན་པ་ཆོས་བྱེ་མ་ག་རའི་ཆུའམ། སྐྱུར་རྫས་ཅན་གྱི་ཆུ་བླུགས་པ་དང་དུས་མཚུངས་ཡུང་ངོས་སུ་དེའི་གཟུགས་བརྙན་ཤར་བར་བྱས། རྫས་རིགས་དེ་དག་བླུགས་པའི་རྗེས་སྲིན་བུ་དེ་དག་གློ་བུར་དུ་ཕྱོགས་གཅིག་ཏུའམ་གཞན་དུ་གར་འཕྲབ་པ་ལྟ་བུས་འགུལ་བསྐྱོད་བྱས། ལོ་ངོ་བརྒྱ་ཕྲག་ཁ་ཤས་གོང་ཕྲ་མཐོང་ཆེ་ཤེལ་བཀོལ་སྤྱོད་བྱེད་མཁན་ཐོག་མ་ལེའུ་ཝེན་ཧོག་དང་། སིཔལནཛ་ནི། པསེ་ཏེར་གསུམ་གྱིས་ཕྲ་དངོས་ཐོག་མར་མཐོང་སྐབས་མྱོང་ཚོར་ཇི་ལྟར་བྱུང་བ་ལྟར་དགེ་འདུན་པ་ཆོས་སྲིན་བུས་བརྡ་ལེན་སྤྲོད་ཚུལ་བལྟས་སྐབས་ཀྱི་མྱོང་ཚོར་སྨྲ་མའི་སྣང་བ་ལྟ་བུ་ངོ་མཚར་ཅན་ཏན་ཏན་བྱུང་ཡོད། ཏ་ལམ་འགྲོ་བ་མིའི་བྱུང་རབས་ལོ་རྒྱུས་ཚང་མའི་ནང་སྲོག་ལྡན་གྱི་གྲངས་འབོར་ཆེན་པོ་ཞིག་མ་མཐོང་བ་དང་མ་ཤེས་པ་ལུས་པ་དེར་བློ་ངོར་འཆར་ཐབས་བྱས་ནས་བསམ་བཞིག་ཕྱོས་དང་། དགེ་འདུན་པ་དང་བཙུན་མ་ཆོས་སྲིན་བུ་ཆུང་ངུ་དེ་དག་གི་བཀོད་པ་ཡ་མཚན་པ་དག་མཐོང་སྐབས་འཕར་ལྡིང་དང་པན་ཚུན་གླེང་མོལ་སོགས་བྱས།

བང་འགྲོས་བྱེད་པའི་སྲིན་བུ་དེ་དག་ལ་གྲྭ་བཙུན་རྣམས་དང་ལྷན་ཏུ་བལྟ་བ་དང་། སློབ་མ་ཆོས་དགའ་སྣང་དང་འཚེར་སྣང་བྱས་པ་དག་ཆོར་བས་ང་ལ་སྲིན་བུ་མཐོང་ཚུལ་མི་འདྲ་བ་ཞིག་བྱུང་། ང་ཚོ་རིག་གཞུང་གང་དུ་གཏོགས་པའི་རིག་གཞུང་དེས་ང་ཆོས་ཕྱིའི་ཡུལ་མཐོང་སྣང་ལ་ཁྱད་པར་བཟོ་གི་ཡོད་པ་ངས་ངོས་འཛིན་ཐུབ་པ་བྱུང་། ནུབ་ཕྱོགས་པ་རྣམས་ཀྱིས་ནད་གཞི་དང་འབྲེལ་བའི་སྲིན་བུའི་རིགས་གསར་རྙེད་བྱུང་བ་དང་དེ་ནས་ལོ་ངོ་བརྒྱ་ཕྲག་ཁ་ཤས་རིང་སྲིན་བུ་ཐམས་ཅད་གསོད་ཐབས་བྱས་ལ། བོད་ཀྱི་དགེ་འདུན་པས་སྲིན་བུ་གསར་རྙེད་བྱུང་སྟེ་སྲིན་བུ་དེ་དག་སེམས་ལྡན་དུ་བལྟ་བས་དེ་དག་

གསོད་རྒྱུའི་ཚབ་ཏུ་སྲིན་བུ་དེ་དག་གིས་ཚུར་མི་གནོད་པའི་ཆེད་ཁོ་ཚོས་སོ་སོའི་ཁོར་ཡུག་བཙོས་སྒྱུར་གཏོང་རྒྱུའི་ཐབས་ལམ་འཚོལ་བར་བྱས། གལ་ཏེ་དེ་མ་བྱུང་ཚེ་ད་གཟོད་འགྲོ་བ་མིའི་ལོ་རྒྱུས་དེ་འགྱུར་བ་མི་འདྲ་བ་ག་འདྲ་ཞིག་ཕྱིན་ཡོད་དམ་སྙམ་དུ་ཚོར་སྣང་སྐྱེ་གི་འདུག །རྗེས་སུ་ཤེས་རྟོགས་བྱུང་བ་ཞིག་ལ། ང་ཚོ་ནུབ་ཕྱོགས་པ་ཚོས་ཐུར་མ་ཤེས་པའི་གནད་དོན་གཅིག་སྟེ་ནད་འབུ་འགོག་བྱེད་ཀྱི་སྨན་གྱིས་སྲིན་བུ་སྡུག་པའི་རིགས་གསོད་པ་དང་དུས་མཚུངས་སྲིན་བུ་བཟང་པོའི་རིགས་ཀྱི་ཉེ་རིགས་དང་གལ་ཆེ་བའི་སྐྱེ་ལྡན་ཕན་ཐོག་ཅན་གྲངས་འབོར་ཆེན་པོ་ཞིག་གསོད་བཞིན་ཡོད། ད་ལྟའི་ཆར་ང་ཚོས་སྲིན་བུ་བཟང་པོའི་རིགས་དེ་དག་སྐྱེ་ལྡན་ཡིན་པ་གཞི་ནས་ཤེས་ཡོད། ང་ཚོའི་གཟུགས་པོའི་ནང་གི་སྐྱེ་དངོས་ཕྲ་རབ་དེ་དག་ནི་ལུས་སྟོབས་རྒྱས་པ་དང་། ནད་འགོག་མ་ལག་ཟས་འཇུ་བ། དེ་བཞིན་སེམས་ཁམས་བཅས་ཡར་རྒྱས་གཏོང་བར་ཆ་རྐྱེན་གཙོ་བོ་ཆགས་ཀྱི་ཡོད། དེ་ལྟ་བུའི་ཤེས་བྱའི་འོད་སྣང་མཐོང་བར་ཏོག་ཙམ་ཕྱི་དྲགས་ཡོད། སྙིང་གི་ནད་དང་། གཅིན་སྙིའི་ནད། རང་འགུལ་ནད་འགོག་རང་བཞིན་གྱི་ནད། སེམས་ངལ་གྱི་ནད་ལ་སོགས་པའི་དུས་རབས་ཉེར་གཅིག་པའི་ནུབ་ཕྱོགས་པ་རྣམས་ཀྱིས་མྱོང་བཞིན་པའི་གཙོང་ནད་དང་ཚབས་ཆེའི་ནད་རིགས་དེ་དག་སྐྱེ་ལྡན་ཕྲ་རགས་དེ་དག་དང་འབྲེལ་བ་ཡོད། ད་ལྟ་གཞི་ནས་ཚན་རིག་པ་ཁ་ཤས་ཀྱིས་ནང་པའི་ལངས་ཕྱོགས་བཟུང་ནས་སྲིན་བུ་སྡུག་པའི་རིགས་རྣམས་འཛོམས་པའི་ཆེད་སྲིན་བུ་བཟང་བ་རྣམས་བེད་སྤྱོད་གཏོང་བཞིན་ཡོད། དེ་མ་གཏོགས་གནས་སྟངས་དེ་ལས་གཞན་དུ་འགྱུར་སྲིད་པ་ཡིན།

དགེ་འདུན་པ་ཚོ་དང་ལྷན་དུ་དུས་ཡུན་བདུན་ཕྲག་གཅིག་གི་རིང་གཏམ་གླེང་དང་། རྟོག་ཞིབ་བྱས་ཤིང་། ཕྲ་ཕུང་གི་ཆ་ཤས་དང་། རིགས་རྫས་ཀྱི་བྱ་བ་བྱེད་ཚུལ།རིགས་རྫས་ཀྱི་གྲུབ་ཆ་དང་རིགས་རྫས་མངོན་རྣམ་ཅན་དང་། འདི་ཚོ་ཚང་མས་ཐུན་མོང་དུ་བྱ་བ་བྱེད་ཚུལ་དང་། དེ་བཞིན་སྲིན་བུ་སེམས་ལྡན་ཡིན་ནམ་ཞེས་པའི་དྲི་བར་ལན་འདེབས་བྱ་ཐབས་སོགས་བྱས། དེ་ནས་རྟོག་ཞིབ་མཐའ་མ་དེ་རིགས་ལམ་གྱི་རྩོད་པའི་ཐོག་ཡིན། ང་ཚོས་འཛིན་གྲྭ་དུམ་བུ་ཕྱེད་དུ་བགོས་ཏེ་སྡེ་ཚན་དང་པོས་སྲིན་བུ་སེམས་ལྡན་རེད་ཅེས་པའི་ཐད་ཕྱོགས་བཟུང་བ་དང་། སྡེ་ཚན་གཞན་དེས་ལོག་ཕྱོགས་བཟུང་། ཁོང་ཚོས་དེའི་

ཐད་ཕན་ཚུན་རྩོད་པ་ཤུགས་དྲག་བརྒྱབ། ང་ཚོའི་ཤེས་བྱ་གསར་པ་འདི་དང་བརྟག་དཔྱད་ཀྱི་རིམ་པ་དེ་དག་ང་ཚོས་ཤེས་པའི་ནང་པའི་ལྟ་གྲུབ་དང་ཇི་ཙམ་མཚམས་མིན་དང་། ནང་པའི་ལྟ་གྲུབ་དེ་ཕར་ཇི་ཙམ་མཚམས་མིན། ནང་པའི་ཆོས་འདི་ནོར་བ་ཡིན་ནམ། ཡང་ན་ཚན་རིག་ནོར་བ་ཡིན་ནམ། ཡང་ན་གཉིས་ཀ་འགྲིག་པ་ཡིན་ནམ། སེམས་ལྡན་གྱི་ཕྲ་འབུ་རྣམས་ལ་ཅི་ཞིག་ཡོད། སེམས་ལྡན་ཞེས་པ་དེ་གང་ཡིན་ཞེས་པའི་ཉམས་ཞིབ་ཀྱི་དྲི་བ་དེ་དག་བཀོད། ང་ཚོའི་འཛིན་ཁང་ཡོངས་ལ་རྩོད་པའི་མེ་ཤུགས་ཆེས་ཆེར་འབར་ཞིང་། ཤིན་ཏུ་སྤྲུར་ལ། ནུས་ཤུགས་ཤིན་ཏུ་དྲག་པའི་ཁར་ཡིད་དབང་འཕྲོག་པའི་རྣམ་པ་དང་ཡང་ལྡན་པས།སྐབས་དེའི་སྐད་སྒྱུར་བས་ཀྱང་གནས་ཚུལ་ཅི་ཞིག་བྱུང་མིན་ཐད་ང་ལ་སྐད་སྒྱུར་བྱེད་མ་ཐུབ་པ་བྱུང་། དེ་ནས་ངས། ད་འགྲིག་སོང་། མཚམས་འཇོག་བྱེད་པའི་དུས་ལ་སླེབས་སོང་ཞེས་ཞུས།

ངས་དེ་ལྟར་ཁ་ཕྱོགས་བསྒྱུར་བ་དང་དགེ་འདུན་པ་དང་བཙུན་མ་རྣམས་རང་འཇགས་ཞི་ཞིང་དུལ་བ་དང་སྐད་ཤུགས་ཆུང་ངུས་གད་མོ་ཤོར་བའི་དགེ་འདུན་པ་དང་བཙུན་མར་གྱུར། དེ་ནས་ང་ཚོ་ལྷན་འཛོམས་ཀྱི་བདུན་ཕྲག་གཅིག་རྫོགས། ངས་ཁོང་ཚོར། བྱས་ན། ཁྱེད་ཚོའི་ནང་ག་ཚོད་ཅིག་གིས་སྲིན་བུ་སེམས་ལྡན་རེད་སྙམ་གྱི་འདུག་གམ་ཞེས་དྲིས། ཕྱེད་ཀས་རེད་ཅེས་དང་ཕྱེད་ཀས་མ་རེད་ཅེས་འོས་འཕངས། རྩོད་པ་དེ་མཐུག་མ་རྫོགས་པ་གསལ་པོ་ཡིན།། །།

ང་རང་ལོ་ན་བརྒྱད་ཀྱི་སྐྱེང་དགོན་པར་ཞུགས་པ་ཡིན། དེའི་སྔོན་དུ་ང་རང་ནང་དང་ཐག་ཧ་ཅང་རིང་བའི་གཏན་སྡོད་སློབ་གྲྭ་ཞིག་ཏུ་ལོ་ངོ་གསུམ་རིང་སློབ་སྦྱོང་བྱས། ང་རང་གཏན་སྡོད་སློབ་གྲྭར་འགྲིམ་སྐབས་ང་གཅིག་པུར་ལུས་ཤིང་། ངས་རང་ཉིད་ཀྱི་རྣམ་དཔྱོད་འཚར་ལོངས་ལ་གནོད་པའི་དཀའ་ངལ་མང་པོ་ཞིག་བརྒྱུད་སོང་།

ང་རང་མི་ཡག་པོ་ཞིག་ཆགས་པར་ལམ་སྟོན་གནང་མཁན་བྱམས་སེམས་དང་བརྩེ་བ་ཅན་གྱི་དགེ་རྒན་ཞིག་ཡོད་པ་དེ་ང་རང་ཧ་ཅང་གི་བསོད་ནམས་ཆེན་པོ་ཡིན། ཁོང་གིས་བྱམས་སྐྱོང་མེད་ན་ང་རང་འདི་འདྲའི་བསམ་བློ་སྨིན་པའི་མི་ཞིག་ཆགས་ཡོད་རྒྱུ་མ་རེད་བསམ་གྱི་འདུག། ང་རང་དགེ་རྒན་གྱི་ལམ་སྟོན་འོག་ཏུ་གནས་པའི་དུས་སྐབས་རྣམས་རྟག་ཏུ་ཕྱིར་དྲན་དང་། རྟག་ཏུ་ཁོང་གི་བཀའ་དྲིན་ཆོར་ཀྱི་ཡོད།

ངས་མི་ཚེའི་ནང་དུ་འཕྲད་པའི་དཀའ་ངལ་རྣམས་བཟློག་པའི་ཕྱིར་དུ་གསུང་རབ་དག་བཀོལ་སྤྱོད་བྱེད་ཀྱི་ཡོད། གང་ཡིན་ཟེར་ན། དེ་དག་གི་ནང་དུ་རྒྱུ་མཚན་ལྡན་པའི་རིགས་ལམ་བརྒྱུད་དེ་ཉོན་མོངས་རྣམས་ལ་གདོང་ལེན་བྱེད་ཐབས་སྟོན་པས་ཡིན། ལྟ་གྲུབ་དང་རིགས་ལམ་སློབ་གཉེར་བྱེད་པ་དེས་ཉོན་མོངས་མགོ་གནོན་པ་དང་། དེ་དག་གིས་སེམས་ལ་དབང་སྒྱུར་བར་ཕན་ཐོགས་ཡོད།

\- ངག་དབང་ནོར་བུ།

ང་ལོ་བཅོ་ལྔ་ཡིན་སྐབས་ནང་པའི་ལྟ་གྲུབ་ཀྱི་རིགས་ལམ་སློབ་སྦྱོང་བྱེད་འགོ་བཙུགས་པ་ཡིན། རིགས་ལམ་སྦྱོང་བརྡར་བྱས་པས་ངའི་བསམ་བློའི་རྒྱ་བསྐྱེད་ཅིང་། བློ་སྒོ་ཕྱེས་པ་མ་ཟད། རང་གི་ཡིད་ཆེས་རྣམས་ལོང་བ་བཞིན་དང་ལེན་བྱེད་མི་ཉན་པའི་བློ་སྐྱེད་ཐོབ་བྱུང་ལ། རིགས་ལམ་བརྒྱུད་ནས་རང་གི་མཐོང་ཚུལ་རྣམས་ལ་དཔྱད་ཞིབ་བྱེད་དགོས་པའི་སེམས་ཤུགས་ཡང་སྐྱེས་བྱུང་།

རིགས་ལམ་ལ་སྨྲ་ཁ་མང་པོ་ཞིག་ཡོད་ནའང་། ང་རང་ལ་ཆེས་ཤུགས་རྐྱེན་ཆེ་བ་ནི་སྦྱོང་སྟོབས་ཀྱི་རྟགས་ལ་བརྟེན་ནས་བསྒྲུབ་བྱ་རྟོགས་པར་བྱེད་པའི་རྟགས་ཡང་དག་དེ་ཡིན། དཔེ་མཚོན་ཞིག་ཞུས་ན། དུ་བ་མཐོང་བ་ལས་མེ་ཡོད་པ་དཔོག་པ་དེ་ལྟ་བུ། རྗེས་དཔག་འདི་ནི་སྔར་མེ་ལས་དུ་བ་འབྱུང་བ་སྦྱོང་བས་གྲུབ་པ་ལ་བརྟེན་ནས་བྱུང་བ་རེད། འདིས་ཉམས་སྦྱོང་གི་གལ་ཆེན་རང་བཞིན་སྟོན་གྱི་ཡོད། འདི་ནི་ནང་པའི་ལྟ་གྲུབ་ཀྱི་ལྟེ་བ་ཡིན་ལ། ངོས་ཀྱི་མི་ཚེར་ཡུན་གནས་ཀྱི་བག་ཆགས་ཤིག་ཀྱང་ཡིན།

- དགེ་བཤེས་བསྟན་འཛིན་སྟོབས་ལྡན།

Challenger Defender: The Great Tradition of Buddhist Monastic Debate
By Nancy A. Scherl

Translations by Sera Jey Translation Department, Sera Jey Monastery, District Mysore, (K.S). Lead Translators: Thupten Tharchin and Lobsang "Paljor" Dorjee; Supporting Translators: Tsondue Samphel, Senior Translator and Interpreter, Emory-Tibet Science Initiative, Emory University, Atlanta; Kalden Gyatso, Sera Jey Translation Department, Sera Jey Monastery, District Mysore, (K.S).

First published by
MW Editions
www.mweditions.com
info@mweditions.com

Creative Direction: Takaaki Matsumoto, Matsumoto Incorporated, New York
Design: Robin Brunelle, Matsumoto Incorporated, New York
Editor: Amy Wilkins, Matsumoto Incorporated, New York

Printed and bound by Pristone, Singapore
ISBN: 979-8-9877845-6-3
Library of Congress Control Number: 2025902745

Distribution
D.A.P. / Distributed Art Publishers, Inc.
75 Broad Street, Suite 630
New York, NY 10004
www.artbook.com
orders@dapinc.com